FROM JERUSALEM
TO BEVERLY HILLS
Memoir of a Palestinian Jew

EITAN GONEN

authorHOUSE®

AuthorHouse™
1663 Liberty Drive
Bloomington, IN 47403
www.authorhouse.com
Phone: 1-800-839-8640

First published by AuthorHouse 11/17/2010

ISBN: 978-1-4520-9294-2 (sc)
ISBN: 978-1-4520-9295-9 (e)
ISBN: 978-1-4520-9293-5 (dj)

Library of Congress Control Number: 2010915620

Printed in the United States of America

This book is printed on acid-free paper.

Certain stock imagery © Thinkstock.

To Dina
For fifty years of love and friendship.

To Hadar and Jeff,
Ron and Ashley
For the people they turned out to be.

To Ben, Geffen and Tom
For inspiring me to write this book.

AUTHOR'S NOTES AND ACKNOWLEDGEMENTS

Shortly after I started to write this book I met with my childhood friend Meir Zinger (Doctor Yaron now). Reminiscing, I found that his recollection of his home, where his family had taken me in for food and shelter as a ten year old refugee, did not match my memory of the place. We differed on such a basic detail as whether their apartment had one or two bedrooms; eventually he remembered that my recollection was correct.

Visiting my sister Shifra, during her last days on earth, in a hospital in Tel Aviv, we reminisced and joked till her last breath. Her memories of some stories and details of our childhood did not match mine.

Realizing that people's memories of the same places, people or events may differ considerably, freed me to write this book. The stories in this memoir are all true, based on my memory.

My thanks to teacher/editor Amy Friedman of UCLA for her edit, enthusiasm and encouragement. Kudos to my word processor Leslie Moffett of Sherman Oaks; inexplicably, she could read my handwriting. Many thanks to my online writing teacher Kyle Minor of Gotham Writing Classes who showed me how to take the first step. Thanks to my friend, author Kurt Kamm for introducing writing teacher Jake Grapes who gave me his Image/Moment tip. Barbara Thornburg and Connie Von Briesen contributed excellent corrections and reviews.

Lastly, thanks to my wife Dina who helped me disappear for a few hours at a time to write my stories, and then was my first and gentle critic.

CHAPTER ONE

"Eitan!"

I heard my mother calling from the balcony of our apartment on the fourth walkup floor.

"Don't forget to get off at Chancellor Street."

I waved from the bus stop in front of our apartment building on Prophet Samuel Street; she could not hear me from down there. Our place was on the outskirts of the new city of Jerusalem, a building with no street address number, just a name - the landlord's name - "Cadoori House."

As the bus pulled up, I noticed a flyer someone had pasted on its side: **"Fight Hitler, Join the Jewish Brigade!"** I read in big block letters. I tried to read the smaller letters to see how exactly I could join. It seemed exciting; I could go to Europe.

"Hey boy, are you coming in?" the bus driver shouted, not willing to wait.

"Yes," I said and climbed the three steep steps. Inside I handed the driver three mills minted with the words "PALESTINE (EI)". The EI stood for Eretz Israel – Land of Israel. He looked at the coins, then at my face.

"How old are you boy?" he asked.

"I'll be five on Passover."

"Are you sure?"

"Yes."

I knew the regular bus fare was 5 mills, but children under five and invalids paid just 3 mills – equivalent to one American cent. Passover was still weeks away, and so was my fifth birthday, but I could see the bus driver was skeptical

"What year were you born?"

Surprised he couldn't calculate that, I answered "1938."

The driver, a member of a cooperative "Hamekasher" (The Connector), wanted to be sure I wasn't conning my way onto his bus. I had been riding the No. 2 bus for about a year and a half. At first I traveled with my sister,

1

Shifra, four years older than me, but one morning when I turned four, my mother said, "Here's your bus money. Don't forget to get off at the Chancellor Street bus stop." That's where my daycare/kindergarten was, and since then I'd been on my own.

"Hey driver," a man called from the back of the bus, "let's move on or the boy will be six before we get to work."

Still suspicious, he handed me the ticket and stuffed the coins I gave him into the multi cylinder coin holder. I walked to the back to find a seat as the bus chugged forward.

We drove along Prophet Samuel Street. On the right were ancient stone houses, on the left mostly open fields leading to Mount Scopus. On its ridge I could see Hadassah Hospital and the Augusta Victoria Monastery. Just before reaching the Old City, the route turned into Beit Israel, the older neighborhoods of the "new" city where the houses built at the end of the 19th century were small and crowded together. All of Jerusalem outside the Old City walls was considered the New City, even those parts like Beit Israel that were centuries old.

The bus drove on through Meah Shearim, 100 Gates, where the orthodox Jews lived. At one of the many stops, a man climbed onto the bus and sat next to me. He took out a pack of Universal cigarettes and lit one. The sign above the bus windows said clearly, "No Smoking and No Spitting in the Bus," in three languages -- Hebrew, English and Arabic, though I could read only the Hebrew. As the man smoked, I was sure a policeman, or at least the driver, would arrest him, but nothing happened.

The bus was crowded. A woman, her fat belly touching me, stood next to my seat. Her head was covered with the religious shawl, and she had what seemed to me the largest breasts in the world. For a moment I contemplated giving her my seat, but if I stood, my head would bump into her breasts, so I stayed where I was.

The woman sitting to my other side wore a black dress and sandals. She was skinny and talked to herself, her lips moving with no sound, the way people did during the quiet prayers at the synagogue. She held small paper notes arranged in a brick, like a pack of cards. Hand-written lines covered the note, and I bent closer to try to read the words.

"Do you want to have one, my child?" she asked in Hebrew, with an English accent.

At that time I read everything I passed - store signs, food packaging, advertisements and street signs. "Okay," I said.

She peeled off one of the notes and handed it to me.

"Keep your connection to the One," she said, "our Savior."

The bus turned onto Geula Street, and as we neared my destination, I grew more alert. When we turned onto Chancellor Street, the driver pushed the gas pedal, and the engine roared with a frightening growl as it climbed one of the steepest slopes in Jerusalem.

The lady with the large breasts bent down and peered at my note. "What is it?" she asked.

"I don't know," I said, turning to the skinny woman.

"Kesher La' Echad," she said, "Connection to the One."

The fat lady straightened her eyes wide. *"Oy, gevald!"* she cried in Yiddish, "a woman missionary!"

In spite of the crowd, passengers moved, creating a space around me. They stared at me and pointed at the skinny lady in black.

"She gave the little boy a *traif* Christian paper!" the fat lady shouted.

Through the window I saw the traffic policeman standing in the intersection of King George and Jaffa Streets, the center of Jerusalem, beyond my stop. The driver looked at the wide mirror above his seat, trying to make sense of the commotion. "What is it?" he asked.

Everyone began to speak, offering conflicting reports, and at last the driver stopped the bus, pulled up the hand break and stood.

"Get her off the bus," the fat lady shouted. Others shouted too, and I began to worry they would take the skinny woman to jail because of me. Perhaps they would take me too, if only for questioning. But I had to go to kindergarten.

"She did nothing wrong," I said, but over the noise, the driver could not hear me. People next to me began to smile. Behind me a man shouted, "The boy says she's done nothing wrong!"

The driver opened the door and two policemen climbed onto the bus and made their way through the crowd to my seat. "What did she give you boy?" the red-faced cop asked in English; the other translated into Hebrew.

I showed him the little note.

He looked at it, then at the skinny woman and rolled his eyes.

"It's nothing, I know her; she's the Kesher La'Echad lady. She hands out these notes all the time. It's something about her God."

Jerusalem attracted believers in the messiah from the world over. Some even believed they were the messiah. The skinny woman's lips kept moving in prayer, oblivious to all that was happening around us. The cops and some

3

other people hurried off the bus, and so did I. I started my walk all the way back up steep Chancellor Street to my Strauss Kindergarten.

In Jerusalem of 1943 civilian traffic was sparse, mainly trucks and busses. Only the rich or high government officials had cars of their own or were driven around. There were, however, dozens of British Army and Police vehicles. I crossed the steep street, running because I was nearly late, and out of breath I entered my kindergarten building through the big metal gate.

Just like every day for the past year, Rivka, the principal, was waiting at the door, her face severe. "Good morning, Eitan Makogon," she said.

"Good morning, Teacher," I said, astonished to discover she knew my first name. She always called kids by their last names—"Makogon, no running here; Levy, no shouting; Schwartz, stop fighting Makogon!" And more surprisingly this day she did not ask to see my fingernails or my handkerchief for cleanliness.

Rivka had been the principal teacher ever since I started going to the "Strauss" day care. It was run by a non-profit charity organization, named after Nathan Strauss, the American philanthropist. It was a beautiful stone building with a clean interior. The school day started at 8 a.m, and at noon we had lunch. After that, at 1 p.m., we helped move all the seats, tables and toys to clear an area so each of us could place his little mattress on the floor, right next to each other, and nap for one hour.

Usually I had trouble falling asleep during the nap hour, so most days I simply pretended. Teacher Rivka walked around like the sergeant in a military barracks and made sure the silence was not interrupted by anyone moving, let alone talking, but on this day I began to tell the boy next to me, who was also awake, about my morning bus ride.

"Who is speaking?" Teacher Rivka shouted.

I was sure her shout could wake the whole of Jerusalem. "Makogon, was that you?" she asked. "Come here!"

I closed my eyes and pretended to be asleep, but she marched to my sleeping area, bent down and pinched the skin on my neck, just below the chin.

"Stand," she said and I did, although I felt as if she were lifting me as she pulled.

"Don't you understand there should be no-talking-during-the-nap-hour?" She kept pinching and jerking me from side to side as she pronounced each word.

I cried quietly.

From that day on I kept my eyes shut during nap hour, whether or not I was asleep, and whether or not she was around. I also learned to dislike authority.

A few weeks passed, and one day she called me again. "Eitan Makogon, come to my office." I expected her to scold me again, but this time she handed me a folded piece of paper and said, "Give this to your mother. Put it in your pocket and don't lose it!" and she helped me put it in my pocket. I walked outside and waited for the bus home.

The same No. 2 bus stopped in front of the "Strauss" kindergarten, now on its way back to my neighborhood. I climbed in and handed my three coins to the driver who handed me the ticket with no questions. People were packed into the bus.

"Boy," the driver instructed me, "stand right here and hold onto the back of my seat."

We started to roll down Chancellor Street, the brakes shrieking. At the bottom of the slope we turned right onto Geula, a relief because this street was level and the ride was easier. I wanted to take the note out of my pocket to read it, but the bus was so tightly packed, I could not move to reach my pocket and besides, I worried that if the note fell on the floor it might get lost beneath passengers' feet or disappear into the greasy holes in the floor.

The bus was moving cautiously as we neared the end of Geula Street and turned onto Meah Shearim where the street narrowed to twelve feet wide. On the left side peering out of the windows of the old stone apartment buildings I could see the orthodox Jewish children wearing yarmulkes on their shaved heads, their only hair the *payes*, or earlocks. Walking the narrow sidewalks were orthodox women in long dresses, their heads covered with specially arranged shawls, most pregnant and holding a baby in their arms, some with one or two toddlers walking behind them. Men wearing black robes over their clothes, sporting furry *shtrimel* hats and *payes* walked ahead of them, their curled earlocks moving up and down like loose mattress springs.

The street was so narrow, I never understood how two busses could pass, but each day it happened. Sometimes the driver drove onto the sidewalk, and I always kept my hands inside the bus for fear they might be cut off by the passing bus. But I watched attentively to see that our bus did not roll over someone coming out of one of the many small shops. When we drove past the famous Angel Bakery, the smell of freshly baked bread made me hungry.

"Meah Shearim, Angel Bakery!" the driver announced, and the bus stopped. The man next to me was pushed forward by the passengers behind him; in turn he pressed on me.

"It will be ok in a minute boy, God willing," the man said.

Quite a few passengers were exiting, mainly men in Capotes, black robes, long beards and black fur rimmed *shtrimel* hats. As the bus emptied, the air inside became more breathable; only a few passengers remained standing. Some seats became available, but I knew the man next to me would not take a seat; these religious men were prohibited, by their rules, from sitting beside a female stranger. I sat next to a woman at the window and finally was able to safely pull the note out of my pocket. I was curious and afraid; I suspected the teacher was telling my mother once again about some mischief of mine.

Slowly unfolding it, I saw it was short:

> *Mrs. Hedva Makogon,*
> *This is to inform you that your son, Eitan Makogon, was*
> *found to be mature enough. Therefore, the Pedagogic Committee*
> *decided this will be his last year in our kindergarten. Please*
> *enroll him in first grade at a school for next year.*
> > *Rivka,*
> *April, 1943   Principal of the Nathan Strauss Kindergarten*

I do not remember the rest of the bus ride. I do remember being confused, elated, and scared, but happy. From now on, I thought, I would go to school every day with Shifra. I knew school brought with it some problems because Shifra often had arguments with my mother about what to wear in the morning. And my brother, Yudke, who was in high school, made my mother angry when he had not done his homework or brought home grades that made her unhappy. But mainly I was looking forward to giving the note to my mother and to being loved and praised.

I got off the bus, crossed Prophet Samuel Street and walked up the stairs to our fourth floor apartment. My mother was waiting for me.

"I have a tomato and garlic sandwich that you like," she said.

I could smell it. My mother expressed her love with the food she prepared. She was an excellent cook and made great meals with inexpensive ingredients. "*Ima,*" I said, "teacher Rivka gave me a note for you."

Her happy face turned pale. Notes from school never brought good news.

I was waiting for her to smile again, but for a long minute she read it silently.

"What am I going to do now?" she asked. "How am I going to find a school for you? I am always left holding the bag. He's never here. I have to raise three children all by myself and solve all the problems while he's taking it easy somewhere…" She ranted and wept and talked to herself and to an invisible friend only she could see. From past experience I knew this conversation with her invisible friend was going to last for some time, so I grabbed my sandwich and ran down to play in the street.

The "he" my mother was referring to in her rant was my father, Yoseph.

CHAPTER TWO

From across the street she heard a terrible cry, the sound of a pig being slaughtered from across the way, but there were neither pigs nor a slaughterhouse nearby. Her daughters were setting the table. She walked to the closed front window and pressed her forehead against the glass, trying to see as far as she could up and down both sides of the street.

There was nothing unusual. Dark clouds lay low, and in the distance she could hear the roar of a thunderstorm. The trees across the street hid the neighbor's home, the branches bent under the weight of snow. The glass fogged from her breath, and the fear in her stomach overcame her desire to return to the kitchen. She quickly opened the window, and cold air rushed in. She pulled the wooden shutters closed and locked them and the window.

A moment later she heard heavy footsteps in the snow, moving closer, and a man's voice. "The name on the door is Makogon."

She did not move from her place behind the locked door. In the dining area on the far side of the house her daughters were talking and laughing. She wanted to shush them, but she made no move. The smell of the "Haman's Ears," those wonderful cakes, now made her nauseous.

"It's not a Jewish name is it, Grisha?" the man outside asked.

She held her breath and heard her distant daughters still playfully noisy.

"Ivan, what's that name again?" another man asked.

"Makogon."

"No, it's Ukrainian," he said in heavy voice, Russian with a Ukrainian accent.

"Should we go next door then, Grisha?"

"Dah, let's move and find some Jids over there."

Trembling, she listened as the footsteps moved away until she could no longer hear them. She ran to the dining area, grabbed her three daughters and sat them on the sofa. From far off she heard the sounds of slaughter, and

8

she waited quietly for her husband, Abraham, to return with the boys from the synagogue. The table was set with the special meal she had prepared, ready to celebrate the Purim holiday. At noon on the Sabbath, February 15th, 1919, 16-year-old Yoseph, along with his father and brothers, heard the news about the pogrom while they were in the Synagogue. They hurriedly finished their prayers and rushed home where they found Yoseph's mother and sisters frightened but unharmed. They rushed outside to check on the neighbors and discovered the carnage. In the wooden home only 100 feet up the street they found their neighbor and her two daughters on the floor, their throats cut, their hands severed.

* * *

In 1919, following the Russian Revolution, the Communist Red militias arrived in the Ukraine, traveling south to enforce Moscow's rule. The local White militias and the Cossacks, under the leadership of Governor Symon Petlura, put up a fight. For a while they succeeded in pushing back the Reds. That February week, after winning a battle, the White Militias and the horseback-riding Cossacks returned to the garrison in Proskurove, the city not far from Yoseph's home. There they had a wild celebration that lasted throughout the entire night.

The next morning, Purim day, the Whites and the Cossacks went on a rampage, killing any Jews they could find. Of the 22,000 people in Proskurove, 7500 were Jews. Early that afternoon the Ukrainian killers rounded up their horses and wagons and left town, leaving behind 1500 dead Jewish men, women and children.

This pogrom initiated doubts about the future for Jews in Russia. After that day, Yoseph Makogon could not stop thinking about leaving. Seven years later, during the last months of 1926, when he faced the possibility of being drafted into the Soviet Army, his motivation grew, and so on a dreary, snowy day during one of the bad winters of Russia, my father, Yoseph Makogon, at the age of 23, made a fateful decision to leave Proskurove.

My father left behind his parents, eleven brothers and sisters, and a community that had existed for hundreds of years in this godforsaken Diaspora. He headed for the station to catch the train that would take him on his first leg of this life-changing journey. Yoseph was young, but he was mature enough to understand that his Russia, his motherland, would not improve for either him or for other Jews. He knew enough not to believe the daily newspapers that insisted Stalin would improve life for all Russians. His heart ached as he debated whether or not to tell the sister to whom he was closest, but he finally decided he would tell no one. Yoseph knew the danger involved in any move in the new Communist Soviet Union under Stalin.

He purposely carried only a small bag, and he walked slowly, as if he were merely out for an aimless walk, out for fresh air. He walked to see the river for the last time, and as the day turned to a cold evening and snow hardened on the ground, Yoseph entered the Proskurove train station and approached the ticket window. The ticket clerk was chatting with a uniformed armed guard; both were drinking vodka from large tea glasses. He waited for the clerk and the soldier to stop laughing long enough to acknowledge him. Finally the clerk looked up.

"Dah?"

"Odessa," Yoseph said.

"Why are you going there?" the guard asked, the stench of Vodka on his breath.

"To visit friends."

"Are you coming back?" the guard asked.

"Of course."

"You better buy a round trip ticket then."

"Sure," Yoseph said and paid for the ticket.

As he waited for the train, he read the paper and looked nervously around. The guard at the ticket window continued to drink noisily which must have been a relief to him; if anyone discovered his real plans, he would spend years in jail. The station was swarming with soldiers, some with bags that indicated they would be boarding the train to Odessa. At last the train lurched into sight, and a few minutes later was on its way, traveling through the dark night, making twelve stops in towns and villages before finally reaching Odessa in the early morning hours.

Alone in Odessa, Yoseph roamed the streets, trying to identify someone who might be Jewish. No one would want to admit to a stranger that he was Jewish, but Yoseph stopped a few people to ask. Finally in desperation he stopped a young woman who did not look the least bit Jewish; to his great relief it was she who introduced him to Jewish friends who took him to a private apartment that served as the office of a Zionist organization called *Hechalutz* (*The Pioneer*).

Yoseph spent a few stressful weeks in Odessa while *Hechalutz* arranged for legal papers he would need and for his boat passage to Istanbul and then on from there to Palestine. When at last the day of his departure arrived, my father boarded the boat with its passengers and cargo, and along with a group of pioneers, he began his journey to Zion.

Many days passed and one morning my father woke to a commotion on deck. Everyone was excited, and when he asked what was going on, someone told him they had arrived. "We're in Jaffa, in *Eretz Israel*." He looked into the distance. The shore of Palestine was still a mile or more away, and it was raining hard. Still, the deck was crowded. Not one of the passengers wanted to miss this moment, the moment their forefathers had dreamed about for millenniums.

"*Baruch Atah Adonai...*" a rabbi started crying in the middle of his prayer.

Everyone joined in. "Blessed be God for sustaining us and bringing us to this moment in time, and enabling us to return to the holy land, the Land of Israel – *Eretz Israel*."

People wept - exhausted from the long, rough trip, happy they had made it, sad remembering families left behind, families they might never again see. They faced an unknown life in a new country, and though this was exhilarating, they also felt the awesome weight of what it meant to be pioneers returning to their ancient land from which their forefathers had been exiled for 2000 years. In the distance, above the Mediterranean, they could see the ancient city of Jaffa, its houses seeming to grow out of each other. As the boat moved closer and anchored a few hundred yards from shore, a small fishing boat approached, followed by two more. Passengers carrying bags began to unload into the smaller boats, and as my father climbed into one of those boats, he was astonished to discover not one of the crew spoke any Russian, Hebrew or Yiddish. Rather they spoke in a strange, loud language he guessed was Arabic.

"Yalla, Yalla," the crew called as their passengers boarded. The men wore long robes and were either barefoot or sockless. They had thick mustaches. The boat, loaded to capacity, bobbed over the waves before they finally motored into a small harbor dense with fishing boats. As they climbed onto the land, Arab seamen helped them with their bags.

After a long wait, my father at last entered the passport control room where a uniformed man sat behind a small desk. In his hand he held a weapon – a long swat with which he attacked buzzing flies, the size of which my father had never seen before.

"Your certificate," the officer said.

My father was tense but happy at long last, to face British immigration. Though he couldn't understand the language, he figured the officer wanted to see his 'Sertificut'- the coveted document he had secured in Odessa, papers that permitted him to enter Palestine.

Before long another officer led him out of the passport control office, and my father took his first steps into Palestine. The street behind the port swarmed with people—merchants and their small pushcarts shouting praise for their fruits, vegetables, candies, hats and *caffiahs*. In the midst of the commotion he saw some of his fellow passengers crowding the young man from the *Hechalutz* who was there to receive newcomers. After a while the leader gathered everyone and led them onto a horse-driven flatbed wagon that would carry them to their temporary shelter.

They arrived at a sea of sand dunes at the end of town, near the beach. There my father saw tents erected on the sand. Everyone was told to find a vacant bed in one of those tents, and my father entered a tent with six folding beds, of which only one was occupied. A man sitting on the folding bed greeted him in Russian. "Welcome," he said, holding out his hand to shake my father's. The floor of the tent was made of sand. "I am Yashka Lituchy."

"Thanks. I am Yoseph Makogon."

"Take the bed next to me so we can talk," Yashka said.

On that day at the end of 1926, these two pioneers who came from the same area of the Ukraine, Russia, became friends.

* * *

After the White Militias and Cossacks brutally murdered 1500 Jews during the Proskurove pogrom, they left town, using some of the money and valuables they had stolen from the dead to buy food and vodka. They rode their horses and wagons a few miles away to the next small town, Felshtin. There they camped for the night, and two days after the Proskurove pogrom, on the morning of February 17, 1919, the Cossacks attacked again, this time Felshtin, a town of 4,000 people, about 1900 of which were Jews. To maximize the element of surprise, they slaughtered their victims with swords and knives, so while they were killing whole families, others heard no noise alerting them. The killing went on for four hours. When the murderers rode away that afternoon, their savagery left behind the dead bodies of 600 Jewish men, women and children.

In the early afternoon, a 13-year-old girl named Frieda Kristal picked up her brother, 9- year-old Moshe Kristal, and walked home from school. In the midst of all the commotion and shouting, the two children discovered that their home was on fire, their parents nowhere to be found. Someone they recognized as the synagogue worker rounded up some of the displaced children and took them to his home. That was the day my mother, Frieda Kristal, and her brother along with 200 other Jewish kids of

Felshtin became orphans. The children were placed in a hastily organized orphanage where they stayed for the next few months.

News of the massacres of Proskurove and Felshtin reached the United States where, in New York, people began a fundraising effort for the survivors. This resulted in the opening of an orphanage in the Ukraine town of Lvov (also known as Lemburg), midway between Proskurove and Felshtin. In 1920 the Felshtin orphans, including Frieda and Moshe, went to Lvov where they lived and studied for the next several years. During those years American Jews made efforts to take some of the orphans into their homes and to serve as foster parents, so as the years passed, dozens of orphans went to America.

For many years Frieda Kristal's dream was to go to America. She heard stories of the luxuries, modern conveniences and great future that country held, and she shared those stories with anyone who would listen. "In America the iron gets hot without coal," she would gush. "You just plug it into a wall." But the years passed, and Frieda did not go to America. In 1924, after six years in the orphanage, America closed its doors to immigrants, allowing in only a trickle.

When Frieda turned 20, in the winter of 1926, she gave up on her American dream. The *Hechalutz* Zionist organization had begun to increase its activities in Lvov, and a group of orphans decided they would go to Palestine - *Eretz Israel* – Zion. Frieda decided she could wait no longer, and she explained to her then teenage brother, Moshe, that she believed she would never make it to America and this was their only hope.

Moshe had not yet given up on the dream, but Frieda had made up her mind she was going to Palestine.

"What about me?" Moshe cried, "you are leaving me alone."

She told him she would go ahead, and once she was settled, if he had not yet gone to America, she would make arrangements for him to join her. Moshe wept, but Frieda decided he was a spoiled boy and ignored his tears. She felt unfairly burdened by having had to care for him her whole life. Still she promised as soon as she was settled in Eretz Israel she would send for him.

In January 1927, a small group of young people left the Lvov Jewish orphanage and set sail to Palestine. Frieda and her fellow passengers arrived during the first week of February at a temporary shelter in Tel Aviv. Friendships had formed on the boat—like the one Frieda forged with Sonia Freifeld whose brother, Shlomo, had gone to Palestine two years earlier. Those bonds made up for the families they had left behind or those they had lost.

In the streets and cafes of Tel Aviv, the newcomers met other newcomers, and it was in one of those cafes that a friend introduced Frieda to a handsome young man. He was tall with clear blue eyes, and his name was Yoseph Makogon. When she told him her name was Frieda Kristal, his first suggestion was that she change her name to a Hebrew name now that she lived in *Eretz Israel*.

"But my name means 'happy,'" Frieda said. "I want to keep it."

"There are words in Hebrew for happy," Yoseph said, offering a slew of synonyms: *Simcha, Gilla, Ditza, Hedva*.

She thanked him and told him she hoped she would see him again. When he asked how he would find her, she smiled.

"Ask for Hedva Kristal," she said.

* * *

On November 2, 1927, the *Yishuv* (Jewry of Palestine) celebrated the tenth anniversary of the Balfour Declaration, a declaration made by Lord Balfour, the British Secretary of the Foreign Office that included the promise to create in Palestine a home for the Jewish people. Later this promise would be made part of the League of Nations charter that created the British Mandate for Palestine and would become the legal foundation for the Jews' claim of the right to immigrate to Palestine.

It was on that anniversary that my brother Yudke was born to Hedva and Yoseph Makogon. Five days after Yudke was born, my father walked to the Tel Aviv Jewish Hospital to visit my mother to see if he could bring her and the baby home. On the way he picked up a newspaper in which a story caught his eye. It was the story of Petlura, the Ukrainian who was dubbed by Jews and the press The Angel of Death. The story, also published in *Time Magazine* of November 7, 1927, recounted history of the pogroms and how in 1919 Petlura and his "Gaydamacs" Cossacks lost their struggle with the Bolsheviks. Petlura fled to Poland, and later to Paris. On May 25, 1926, a Ukrainian watchmaker, Sholom Schwartzbard, a Jew who had become a French citizen, confronted Petlura on the famous Boulevard San Michel in Paris.

In a French court of law, where Schwartzbard now stood trial for premeditated murder, he told the story of what had happened during that confrontation.

"Here is my chance, I thought. 'Are you Petlura?' I asked him. He didn't

answer, simply lifting his cane. I knew it was him. I shot him five times. I shot him like a soldier..."

"A policeman came up..."

"When the policeman told me Petlura was dead I could not hide my joy. I leaped forward and hugged him."

"Then you admit premeditation?" asked the judge.

"Yes, yes!" replied Schwartzbard enthusiastically.

In the courtroom and outside, 400 Jews and reporters gathered, some actively participating in the trial, voicing their approval or opposition to the many witnesses.

The most heart wrenching witness was a nurse, Chaya Greenberg, 29 years old, with a soft, low voice who told about the 'Petluras' - that's what his men were called in the streets - and the blood bathed home of her grandparents; she added:

"I shall never forget the snow sleds, stained red with blood, filled with the hacked bodies on their way to a common pit. They brought the wounded to the hospital - armless and legless men, mutilated babies and young women whose screams became faint as their wounds overcame them."

In the first week of November 1927, after a deliberation of 35 minutes, the jury returned and acquitted Sholom Schwartzbard who was set free. The court heard someone shout "Vive la France!" and 400 voices echoed "Vive la France!"

* * *

My father had a respectable job as the secretary of the Tel Aviv School of Business and Trade, and my mother worked as the "household assistant," as she later told me with pride. She spun the fact that she had worked as a cleaning lady for Chaim Nachman Bialik, the undeclared Poet Laureate of the Jews in Israel and around the world, into a position of importance. She enjoyed serving the Tel Aviv Literati who assembled in Bialik's home. Later, equipped with his commendation, she got a job as the nanny for the twin boys of Eliezer Steinman, another famous writer of novels and essays whose boys eventually became the famous writers Nathan Shaham and David Shaham. Both men authored many books and plays; Nathan Shaham wrote over 30 books and 10 stage plays, all of which were translated into many languages (the last one published in 2001, *Rosendorf's Shadow*). My mother was always proud to have been his nanny.

In 1929 the economic depression that started in America extended across the globe, and in Palestine where conditions had been rough before

15

the Depression, life grew considerably more difficult. My father lost his job that year, and his young family was devastated. On the advice of a friend, they packed up and moved from Tel Aviv to Jerusalem where the British Mandate Authority, the government of Palestine, had its offices.

In our family my father was considered the learned one since he had finished high school and was teaching Russian and Hebrew in Soviet Russia before emigrating to Palestine. He had hoped to get a job with the government that would utilize his learning and intelligence, but once in Jerusalem, he realized this might take some time. Needing to feed his family and to pay rent, he temporarily took a construction job. The pay was better than a clerk's pay, and in spite of the pain caused by the calluses and the insecurity of being a day laborer with no assurance of finding work the next day, he was happy. He loved being a pioneer, building a new country.

In contrast, my mother began to have doubts about her decision to forego her possible passage to the United States. They had moved into a ground floor single room apartment with a small kitchen, and they had to use an outhouse in the backyard that served four other families all of whom had come from Tehran a few years earlier. In her mid-20s, my mother was glad for the friendship of the Persians, for it was they who taught her tricks of child rearing and Persian cooking using the least expensive ingredients. In general they taught her how to raise a family in poverty in Palestine, and she would be forever grateful. "The Persians were nice. They saved us," she always said.

When my sister, Shifra, was born in 1934, the extended family no longer fit in a single room, so my parents rented a one-bedroom apartment. They could afford only a fourth-floor walkup on the outskirts of the city, open fields separating it from the Arab villages. The new apartment had a small entry hall which also served as the dining room, a tiny bedroom, a salon 11 by 14 feet, a small kitchen and an indoor bathroom. In all the family of four lived in 564 square feet. By then Yudke was 7, and he and Shifra slept in the bedroom while my parents slept on a pullout bed in the living room. Still, they were happier in this new apartment, especially my mother who felt they were climbing the social ladder.

A few years later, on the eve of Passover, April 1938, my father brought my mother back home from Hadassah Hospital on Mount Scopus with me in her arms. They added a crib to the bedroom that I began to share with my 10-year-old brother and four-year-old sister.

3 years old with my family.

CHAPTER THREE

Little in our family ever was pre-planned; generally life just happened. And so, when I brought home the note from kindergarten letting my mother know I would need to attend school next year, for several months no one did anything. In September, the school year started, Yudke and Shifra began their studies, and one morning, a week into the school year, my mother dressed up in the only "costume" (suit) she owned, painted her lips with heavy red lipstick and told me we were off to register me for school.

We walked across town for over an hour until we reached *Beit Hinuch*, the elementary school where Shifra was in 4th grade. She had a monthly student pass so she rode the bus, but bus fare for me and my mother would amount to the extravagant fare of 3 Grush (3 cents), so we walked. We climbed narrow Bezalel Ashkenazi Street, walked through the Bucharim Market to Geula, crossed Chancelor, Strauss, King George and BenYehuda Streets.

We had no appointment; in those days only doctors and high officials had phones so we could not have called ahead. When we arrived, we had to wait an hour before the principal could see us.

In those days I was a skinny little boy with what some said was a disproportionately large head, but I knew this was only because of my thick, curly hair. "Sit up straight up," my mother instructed me as we waited. She wanted me to present more of a presence, to seem more mature than I was.

Finally a small gray haired man walked up to us, and my mother explained that we had come to register. She reminded him that Yudke had graduated from this school and that Shifra was currently attending.

He looked me over for a long while and finally asked, "How old is he?"

"5-1/2, but he is very developed," she said.

"When was he born?"

"April 9, 1938."

"So he is only 5 years and 5 months old," he said severely. I was sure he was angry that my mother had attempted to cheat my age by one month.

The principal studied me as if he were checking a puppy he thought he might buy. I thought I saw a faint smile, and my hopes shot up until he said again, "He's so young."

"You know my daughter Shifra," she said, "he is like her."

I felt warmth all over. Shifra was the smartest in our family, and my mother's saying that I was like her made me feel glad.

The principal thought for a long time but finally said, "He's too young. We cannot admit him to first grade. Besides, it will be bad for him."

My mother pleaded, explaining that she had to work and that the kindergarten would no longer keep me; she shared the note with him and told him she and my father were union members, early pioneers, here in *Eretz Israel* since 1927. "We deserve your help," she said.

But her arguments were useless, and we left the office for our long trip back home. Now it was noon and much hotter, and at home I felt exhausted and rejected.

My mother felt the same way. For a long time she complained—that everything fell on her, that she had to raise three children with no help, that she had made a foolish decision and should have waited to go to America. She complained about my father—that he didn't make enough money or help out enough. This was her regular tirade, one that she seemed to share with an invisible friend. Intermittently she would burst into tears. By then I knew that the rant would last at least an hour, and although I felt sad, I walked away.

The next morning, Mother dressed me in clean clothes, and we set out again, this time to a different school, *Alliance Francaise*. It was slightly closer to our home, but I wanted to attend *Beit Hinuch* because that's where my brother and sister had gone. "What kind of school is it?" I asked as we walked.

"It's a French school."

"But I don't know French," I said.

She told me they would teach me to read and write French. "It's an easy language," she said, "and you'll learn in no time because you're smart."

When she said that I felt excited about the idea of learning a language no one else in the family could understand; my heart soared as we walked into the building. It had been established by a French organization, and though the daily language used was Hebrew, most of the classes, even math, were conducted in French. Back then I knew just three French words: *Un, deux, trois,* because these were the words we used in the game of "stone- paper- scissors."

Alliance School was a formal place, and we met not with the principal but with a secretary who was short and nice but had the same message for us. I was too young; I would have to wait until I was six. Then they would be happy to accept me, and they might even consider a reduction in tuition.

When my mother realized there would be tuition involved, she gave up arguing. Still, she mentioned the fact that our family were among the early pioneers, and she talked about my father's unemployment. The answer was still the same, and as we began our walk back home, I cried quietly. That's when my mother decided this required a stop at the Café Volga on King George Street, a famous café in Jerusalem.

I had heard about the place many times, about how crazy it was to pay a whole grush for a cup of tea when at home we could drink 100 cups for less. Still, Café Volga had a window open to the street where we could buy ice cream, soda water and Gazoz, soda with syrup, and although we could not afford to sit at a table, Mother got me a heaping cone of mixed chocolate and vanilla ice cream, and I made this last almost halfway home. I began to enjoy this school registration process.

Still, our family was under pressure because of the school situation. Everyone was offering advice. Neighbors suggested my mother enroll me in a good Anglican Christian school that provided boarding; they would take me off her hands. A few days after hearing this suggestion, we walked up past my old kindergarten on Chancellor Street and then down the hill, turned left and entered the Anglican Christian School on Neviim Street. It was an old building made from enormous stones, with ceilings more than 20 feet high and stone floors partially covered with Oriental rugs. The big cavern-like hall was cool and totally quiet, and when I talked to my mother I could hear my words echoing.

"What is this man on the wall?" I asked.

"It's a statue," my mother said.

"Is it Moses?"

"No, it's some other man," she said.

"But why is his head down? And why are his arms stretched to the sides?"

"Because he suffered," she said.

"Is that blood dripping from his hands?"

"Leave it alone," she whispered. "Don't look at it."

"Why not?"

"We are not supposed to look at it."

A small group of men dressed in long brown dresses with belts of golden rope twisted round their bellies walked past us. Those belts were so long the tails dangled all the way to their sandals. After a while a woman approached us. She looked like a nurse because of her attire, but she invited us to her office, and again my mother explained that she needed a school for me, that she was raising three children on her own, that we were pioneers.

The woman explained in Hebrew spoken with a British accent that the decision would be made by a committee. If I was accepted, the school would provide me with all my needs, including food and uniforms.

My mother's eyes lit up at this.

"We will also provide your son with books and all he will need for school and prayers," she said, and with those words the color drained from my mother's face.

She told the woman she would have to discuss this with her husband when he returned from his job. I knew I would not register in this school. My mother invoked my father only when she was embarrassed about her own decision, but I knew this ploy. I had watched her employ it when we shopped together. She would look at everything, touching each skirt and scarf and dress, but she rarely bought anything for herself; when the salesman's pressure mounted, she invoked my father's name, allowing us to exit without buying.

As we began walking home, I asked for ice cream, but my mother was crying this time, and that day we walked straight home. Because I was home all day, my mother took me everywhere she went. No matter who we met, she began to talk about our predicament, and again everyone had a suggestion, including the guy who owned the food store downstairs, Menashe. He told her about religious schools in Meah Shearim, an orthodox *chader*. He explained they would take in any Jewish boy.

"But he will have to shave his head, wear a *yarmulke* and grow his *payes*," Menashe said.

My mother caressed my long curls while I cried.

Schools in Jerusalem had been in session for three weeks when one morning Mother dressed me up again, put on her lipstick, and we walked 45 minutes until we saw the school sign *Tachkimoni* ("make me smarter.") We stopped at the metal gate. A few steps led down from street level to what looked like a giant school yard full of children, most of them older than me. The boys wore hats of different shapes, but mostly dark berets. Only a few wore *yarmulkes* and even fewer wore the typical *Eretz Israel* "Covah Tembel" (Dumb hat), the cone shaped hat, a favorite of the left.

Children were running around, and when we entered the gate, a man walked out of the building carrying a bronze metal bell which he raised and started to shake. As the bell rang, the commotion stopped, and like a swarm of ants, the kids organized themselves into a stream that flowed into the building. Soon the yard was empty.

We climbed the wide steps into the building, my mother huffing and puffing, "Oy Gotinue," she asked God for his help.

The principal, Mr. Ilan, sat at a large, beautiful desk and listened to my mother's dissertation about her problems, her rights as an early pioneer, and about how developed I was—well beyond my years. Mr. Ilan was a tall, pleasant man. When we sat down he took off his hat and I saw he wore a *yarmulke* underneath. With all these hats, I gathered this was a religious school, but unlike the other principals, Mr. Ilan listened patiently to my mother, from time to time interjecting, "Yes, I understand." Finally he told us to wait and he left the room.

We sat, my mother stroking my head, whispering, "I am sorry we did not bring your hat."

Mr. Ilan returned holding a stack of cardboard cards and announced, "I will give him this little test and we shall see." He turned to me. "Ready?" he asked.

This was the first time in any of the schools we had visited that anyone had talked directly to me. He placed the first picture on the desk, face up. Each card had a picture of a person working at something. "What is this man's profession?" he asked.

"Doctor," I said.

"And this one," he asked, placing another picture card on the table.

"Farmer."

"And this?"

"Nurse, teacher, mechanic…" I called as he placed one card after another on the desk.

"Very good," he said. He showed me a picture of a man taking a loaf of bread out of an oven.

"*Rodeh*," I said. This was a Hebrew word describing specifically what the man in the picture was doing—my word was more accurate than *baker* would have been, and this pleased Mr. Ilan. For the first time he smiled.

"You are right, Mrs. Makogon, your son is well developed. I will admit him."

My mother wiped her eyes with her handkerchief and thanked him profusely, and she prodded me to thank him again.

I saw Mr. Ilan studying my mother's clothes and my bare head, and I knew that he knew this meant we were "free," not religious. He had a few more questions.

"You do keep Kosher and say the prayers at home right?" he asked.

"Of course," my mother said.

This was my first school lesson. Sometimes it was okay to lie to the teacher.

We started on our way. This area of town, Mekor Baruch, was a long walk from home, but it was a quiet, solid Jewish neighborhood. My mother told me I would walk to school alone. "It's safe," she said as we climbed a slightly sloped street, at the end of which we turned right onto Geula, a major street that stretched all the way from the Schneller Camp on the west to Meah Shearim to the east, ending not far from the wall of the Old City.

When we came to the corner of Geula, we could see the camp surrounded by a ten-foot wall topped by concertina--a roll of stretched barbed wire.

The Schneller Camp was built by the Germans who came to the Holy Land when it was still part of the Turkish Empire. Eventually, when the British took over, they made it into one of the most important military camps in the Middle East. It had an enormous entry gate with giant pillars on either side; armed British soldiers were always present. It was scary looking, and even my mother, who held my hand, felt uneasy, though she tried to alleviate my fears by explaining these guards were British soldiers.

"I know," I said.

"Your father works with them. They're much better than the British Police."

I said nothing.

"We're helping them fight Hitler."

I remained quiet.

"They take good care of little kids," she continued.

"I know," I said.

We often saw British convoys driving down our street, and when we did, I joined the older kids in waving to the troops and shouting, "Gimmie Chwinga, Gimmie Chwinga." Sometimes the soldiers took boxes out of their pockets, opened them up and tossed us packages of gum; we fought each other to collect these from the road. You needed to be aggressive and lucky to end up with any of the white candy-covered mint chewing gum, but whenever I managed to get one to chew, the whole world looked better.

"And down the street there is a branch of Volga Ice Cream, so we'll get some," my mother added, to my great delight.

CHAPTER FOUR

By the end of the first week of first grade, the excitement of starting school had faded. That's when I realized that the book we used to learn to read was the same one I had at home, the book Shifra had used four years earlier and that I already had read many times on my own. I spent my four hours in class every day bored and soon discovered there was no point in doing homework. When teacher Sarah called on me to read out loud, the only problem I had was locating the page the class was reading because I had drifted off.

Second grade reinforced my notion that homework was unnecessary, but school did become a little more difficult. Tests were not a problem; sometimes the teacher would call on us to read what we had written at home, so I spent most of that year hiding behind the boy who sat in front of me in order not to catch the teacher's eye.

From time to time some of the parents visited school to talk to the teacher about their child's progress, but we lived far from school, my father worked away from home, and the whole family knew I could read, write and do the basic arithmetic, so no one bothered to check on my schooling. As a result, no one at home had any idea that I never completed my homework.

Besides, there were other things going on in the house at the time. My mother, I had noticed, was plump, her belly significant, but I had heard her talk about trying to eat less. So I was surprised when one day she went to Hadassah for a few days and returned home with a little baby, Varda. Just like that, without any warning, we were four kids in one little bedroom. From that day on, my parents paid even less attention to my schooling than they had.

In the fall of 1945, when I started third grade, I knew everything was going to be different. On the first day of the school year I was standing in line with all the other kids in the paved school yard. Mr. Ilan stood in front of us for morning "roll call." This was a ritual that began when students entered third grade; we were arranged in pairs, forming a column for each class grade, six columns for third to eighth grade.

The chanting started: *"Adon Olam asher Bara..."* more than 200 students and teachers chanting the Morning Prayer to a familiar tune. "Ruler of the world which He created before any other creatures..." it continued with the words of adulation of His goodness and greatness and graciousness. The short prayer was followed with a short speech by Mr. Ilan who hoped God would guide us to a good and productive school year.

Unlike first and second grade, I now attended a classroom in the main building. Like most buildings in Jerusalem, it was built from the local limestone and consisted of two stories. Because it stood on a small hill and the school yard was slightly sunken and down below, to my 7-year-old eyes, it looked like a gigantic structure and aroused my great respect. Our third grade classroom was on the first floor, yet we still had to climb the ten steps from the schoolyard to the wide first floor corridor. I again chose one of the back seats in the classroom and placed my bag on the desk that seated two. On that desk I found the books I would need for the year.

A male teacher came in, and we all stood until he signaled us to sit. He was a big, wide man; if not for his *yarmulke* I would have thought he was one of the "Free" folks. He wore his hair cut short, and a neatly pressed dark suit with a brown tie. He was clean shaven, and his aftershave cologne gave off a whiff of flowers. I thought he wore the *yarmulke* just to get this job, so I was glad he did not have a religious demeanor. I thought I was going to like this guy.

"My name is Teacher Greenberg," he said, "and I'll be teaching you Mishna."

He had a deep, commanding voice.

"Do any of you know what Mishna is?" he roared.

I had heard of it but I knew nothing about it, so I kept my hands folded. A moment of silence passed, and two boys raised their hands. "You," Greenberg said, pointing at one of them.

"It's a prayer book," the boy said.

"What's your name?"

"David."

"Don't you have a full name?"

"Yes."

"What is it?"

"David Gabbai," the boy said, his quivering voice barely audible.

"Stand up, Gabbai," Mr. Greenberg said, and he walked between the columns of desks while 40 kids sat silent and unmoving. He remained quiet for a long minute; the only sound came from adjacent classroom where a teacher was talking.

"In my class, Gabbai," he gazed piercingly at each of us in turn, "in my class, if you want to say something, first you get permission, then you stand, and only then do you tell us your words of wisdom." His voice was so deep and loud the walls seemed to vibrate.

"You understand, Gabbai?"

David Gabbai's face was as white as the wall, his eyes gleaming with accumulated tears he would not allow to escape. "Yes," he said as one tear made it out and rolled down his cheek.

"Yes, Teacher, Gabbai!" Greenberg's voice echoed as if bellowing from a megaphone.

"Yes, Teacher," Gabbai said.

"And when you finally speak up it better not be any nonsense or stupidity like what you have just said, Gabbai. Sit down!"

David's body was convulsing. I looked at him and at this roaring giant, but I did not dare meet anyone's eyes.

"The Mishna is the book of Jewish law," the giant said, "open your books."

Relieved the incident had ended, I opened the book to the page we were told. This book, in fact, covered only a small portion of ancient Jewish law. Part of the language used was Aramaic, an ancient language, and the other was Hebrew, the two intertwined in sentences.

Reading the first case we began to learn about who was entitled to keep an item claimed by two people when each of those people claimed to have found it.

The lesson went like this:

"Two have found a *Talis*. This one says it's all mine and that one says it's all mine…"

From there the Mishna went on to describe the various possible ways to approach this problem—what questions to ask and what decision should be made in a variety of circumstances. I paid close attention until, at long last, the bell rang and class was over.

By the end of the day I felt afraid, not so much of Greenberg but because I realized that I had fallen behind. This was the first time we were studying something in class that I did not already know, and I wasn't sure how I would approach the coming year.

At home everyone wanted to know how the first day in the third grade had been. "Good," I told them, "no problem." I naturally assumed my mother, brother and sister understood nothing about Mishna, for if they knew about it, I would have heard about it from them before that day. I knew I would have to discuss this with my father when he came home for the weekend; he was the family member who knew about books and prayers and the Bible.

Friday afternoon was the most important time of the week, the time I loved most. Despite being free—non-religious—when I came home from school early on Friday afternoon my mother was already well on her way toward preparing for the *Shabbat*. The first thing she did each week was clean the house, and unlike her daily efforts, this was a major job. By the time I came home the house was shiny and smelled fresh. I would find my mother putting the last ingredients in pots that slowly cooked on the stove. The dough would be ready to be rolled flat on the cutting board and spread with apples, chocolate, apricots or cinnamon—whatever she had chosen for that weekend. Not having an oven, I would help carry the porcelain-covered steel baking sheet with two or three long rolls of cloth-covered cake dough down the stairs from the fourth floor, around our building that stood at the foothill, and up to the open field behind it, walking to the Buchari neighborhood and the Zion Bakery. Zion, the Buchari baker, who looked like he ate a lot of cakes, was always sweaty but cheerful, and he always welcomed us.

"Shalom, Hedva, what kind of cake is it today?"

I never knew if he asked because he had to know how to bake it or if he was merely curious. My mother would tell him what was folded in the dough that day, and each time he would say the same thing. "He's cute, but why is he so thin? Give him something to eat."

My mother always answered the same way. "He's a sickly boy. He has the English malady—soft bones you know."

From the Zion Bakery, we would walk to the Buchari market where we could do any number of things, from fixing a primus cooking device to buying food and vegetables to getting a cheap haircut. This neighborhood had been built in the early 1900s by the Jews who made *aliya* from Bukhara. Most of the families were religious, and large, and most were excellent merchants, distinguished by their colorful clothes and multicolor head covers sewn with gold stitches. The main street of Buchari Market traversed a hill and so, unlike so many Jerusalem streets, was relatively level, but the land to one side rose higher, and the other was below street level. The entryway to many of the "hole in the wall" shops offered steps we had to climb up to stores on the south side and down on the north.

Our Friday schedule was always the same. After leaving Zion Bakery, we went to buy 1/4 kilo of roasted sunflower seeds. I couldn't wait to enter this store with its fantastic variety of goods. On one corner next to the sunflower seeds were peanuts, almonds, walnuts, and pistachios, all freshly roasted and salted. Wooing me from the other side were open sacks of dried fruit – black plums, apricots, apples, figs, and dates, and dried fruit pressed into paper- thin rolls, we called "leather," hung from the ceiling.

The cacophony of colors and fragrances drove me nuts. I lusted for the sweets and cookies, but most of all I wanted the roasted pistachio nuts. Once a friend had let me taste a couple imported from Persia and Turkey, but they were too expensive for our family, so we always left the store with only a bag of sunflower seeds. My mother said they were healthier than pistachios.

Our last stop was the vegetable cart parked at the edge of the market.

"Marchava Giveret Hedva," the proprietor welcomed my mother in a mixture of Arabic and Hebrew.

"How are you today, Muhammad?" my mother asked. She and this merchant were friendly. She liked to buy his vegetables on Friday afternoon because the looming *Shabbat* brought down the prices. He liked her because she helped him clear out what was left of his produce before *Shabbat* rolled in, and so he could go home early on his holy Friday.

"*Ima*, ask him about little Ahmad," I said. The last time we'd bought vegetables from Muhammad, I had played with his son while my mother negotiated her vegetable deals. Ahmad was my age and helped his father loading boxes of fruit on the cart and with some other chores. I loved to play with him for a few minutes on Fridays. He spoke Arabic, and I spoke Hebrew, but we had no problem communicating.

"Weno Ahmad?" my mother asked, happy to speak the few Arabic words she had learned.

"Ahmad fil beit," Muhammad said, telling her that his son had stayed home.

"Kadesh Hada?" she asked, pointing to some cucumbers. She chose a few, and he placed them on the plate on one side of the scale; on the other side he tossed a rusty iron piece with its bold cast numbers. He picked up the plate and dumped the cucumbers into my mother's bag.

"Kadesh el Bandora?" my mother asked in Arabic about the price of the tomatoes. I knew that when Muhammad told her the price, she would say they were too expensive; this was their ritual.

"Ktir, Ktir Hada," she said.

He directed her to another box with some older, softer, dying tomatoes and told her he would give her a break on these. She nodded, he weighed some and dumped these into her bag.

Following our market foray we returned to Zion the baker and picked up the cakes we had left there. A tense moment always occurred as my mother inspected the results. Sometimes the cakes were under baked and rarely, though it did happen, the cakes were burnt because Zion the baker had not paid close attention. Mostly I was intoxicated with the cinnamon smell, and the tension passed as we prepared to walk back home.

We walked the narrow street that led down from the Buchari neighborhood. On hot summer days, the paved asphalt felt soft under our feet but the pavement ended at an open field behind Beit Kadoory. There was a rear gate to our building. We could walk down a few steep steps and enter the entry hall from the back, though we rarely did because of the smell that came from the outhouse at the corner of the yard, the outhouse that served the ground floor apartment. Instead, we preferred to climb down a steep, rocky slope on the side of the building to reach Prophet Samuel Street and enter through the front door. Carrying our bags of vegetables and the flat baking tray of cake rolls made this climb a feat, but week after week we did it. Then we walked up to the fourth floor and there, at home, we waited for my father to come home for what was our one-day weekend, *Shabbat*.

My father had taken a construction job with the British military that took him away from home to the camps the British were building in Palestine and to other parts of the Middle East as well, sometimes as far away as Transjordan and Egypt. Because he usually came home for *Shabbat*, Fridays were always days of great longing, expectation and joy. Yudke, Shifra and I would watch Prophet Samuel Street stretching out below our fourth story apartment. Yudke and Shifra usually stood at the railing on the balcony of the living room, and I would stand on the bed beside the bedroom window. My father usually arrived in the late afternoon.

One week my father arrived home early, at 3 p.m., and his knock on the door caught us off guard. After that we were determined this would not happen again. We wanted to see the military truck approaching from the end of the street; when we did see it, we raced down the stairs to see who would greet him first. Yudke could climb down five or six steps at a time and always beat me, and Shifra was usually second with me trailing behind.

My father was always composed, dressed like a British official in a pressed shirt, shorts that reached above the knees, socks that came up just below the knees and left a strip of suntanned leg showing. He wore brown shoes. He was trim and slim, with a full head of straight combed hair parted on the left. He had blue eyes and tanned skin and projected dignity and composure uncommon in most construction workers.

"*Aba, Aba!*" I would shout when I reached him. He would lift me up in the air and right then and there give each of us goodies--gum or cookies or ham sandwiches he had bought at the NAFI – the British military store.

As World War II ended, the British restricted the immigration of Jewish survivors. Jewish as well as Arab terrorist activities intensified. Some weeks my father worked too far or it was too dangerous for him to travel back home for *Shabbat*, and he had no telephone or other means to let us know. And so it was that one Friday I waited at my window. The view was unobstructed for miles, all the way to the top of the mountains surrounding the city. Our street delineated the edge of Jewish Jerusalem, and from my vantage point I could see the vacant rocky fields that stretched out to the foot hills upon which the northern part of Jerusalem was built, separating it from the mountains beyond, Mount Scopus and Mount of Olives.

At the other side of the fields, on the slopes of Mount Scopus, I could see the Arab village of Sheikh Jarakh and the black road climbing through it in sharp turns, splitting at a fork, one side heading to Hadassah Hospital, the Jerusalem University and the Augusta Victoria Monastery, all prominent mountain top structures. Beyond these the Judea Mountains rolled all the way down to the Dead Sea. The other side of the fork in the road led to Ramallah and beyond to Jericho. To the left of Sheikh Jarakh stood a large square building with a long row of windows that housed the British Police Academy for Palestine.

Waiting at the window that Friday, the noises of busses, trucks and markets died down, I heard the bells of the many churches ringing, those sounds blending with the calling to prayer of the Muezzins. The Jews and their synagogues did not have a similar call for their people; I always thought perhaps because the Jews of the world did not want to call too much attention to themselves.

Standing watch at the window I heard my mother putting the last touches to the food in the kitchen. The heavy cooking was done, leaving only the slow process of the low heat cooking to continue in the tiny kitchen.

"*Ochi Chornia, Ochi Krasnia…*" she sang one of her favorite Russian love songs. Like us, she was happy in anticipation of my father's arrival home.

"Black eyes, beautiful eyes," she continued. She had a good voice and could carry a tune. "*Ya lubluyava* (I love you)" the song continued. Her singing felt good. It meant we were going to have a great *Shabbat*.

Still at my window, I watched the lights beginning to appear in the distant Arab houses of Sheikh Jarakh, and at the Police Academy. Soon the hour got late and it got dark outside. The church bells and the Muezzins grew quiet, and *Shabbat* entered before my father returned.

My mother stopped singing. Deciding we could wait no longer, she sat us at the table and grumbled. "I have to do everything by myself. I am alone all the time, raising four children without a man in the house. He does not care. What a mistake I made. I should have gone to America…"

My mother launched into her rant, talking to her invisible friend as if we were not there, and Yudka, Shifra and I would eat in silence. Baby Varda slept.

CHAPTER FIVE

Two eggs sunny side up with lots of bread was the breakfast my mother prepared. She had to cook it just right, not too well done, and when she served my brother and sister she had to place the plate in front of them at the same instant or one of them would claim neglect and discrimination.

In spite of our hectic mornings, and taking care of Varda, Mother always packed a lunch for me of two dark bread sandwiches with tomatoes and garlic wrapped in old newspaper sheets and placed it in my backpack. At school I would eat one after two hours of class, during our break, and the other at lunchtime.

My friend Meir Zinger and I ate the snack together, but he did not stay for lunch, so one day I asked him if he wanted half a sandwich for lunch.

He said, "No, I eat lunch in the cafeteria."

The existence of a cafeteria was news to me, and he showed me it was across the schoolyard, in a small building.

"Come with me and we'll eat lunch together."

"Do you have to pay?" I asked.

"No," he assured me.

So the next day I went with Meir to the cafeteria and ate lunch with him. I liked the warm split pea soup, mashed potatoes with gravy and the banana for desert. After that, I began to join Meir every day. One day as my mother was making my lunch I said, "*Ima*, they serve lunch in school."

"Yes I know," she said, "but it costs too much and we can't afford it. I can feed the whole family for the price they charge for just one lunch."

I was stunned when she said this. Meir had said he didn't pay, and I never had either, but now I knew this lunch wasn't free. Now I understood why not everyone joined us in the little building for that delicious soup, and why those who were there were the kids from the well-to-do families. Their parents, I realized, had pre-paid.

The next day when Meir invited me to join him again, I hesitated for a moment, but thinking of that delicious food, I said, "Sure," and once again I joined him.

This went on for two whole months.

I loved the cafeteria lunch, and not just because of the food. Even more than those delicious mashed potatoes and hot soup and fruit, I liked the camaraderie with the other boys of all ages; I liked spending time with the kids of the well-off families. I liked the ambiance in the room—the feeling I would discover many years later eating in marvelous restaurants that "whole food experience."

So for those two months I ate two sandwiches for my morning snack and at lunch time I enjoyed a hot meal. I didn't tell my mother, and she never noticed anything different about me. But one Friday evening when we went to Zion the Buchari, he looked me up and down and said, "He looks better, your boy. No evil eye, but he gained weight."

My mother studied me and said, "He's a good boy."

On the day before Hanukah I once again joined Meir for lunch. This time the menu was the same except when it was time for desert, instead of an orange or a banana, the cafeteria manager, an orthodox man with a black hat and an overgrown beard, stood at the front of the room and announced a surprise. "Today in addition to our orange, we'll have a *Ponchik* (a jelly filled doughnut)."

All 50 children shouted approval.

"I am going to call your name and you will come forward to get your *Ponchik*," he went on.

I realized I was in trouble. As soon as they discovered my name wasn't on the list, they would find out about my freeloading. My hands began to tremble as the man read down the alphabetical list. As he called each name, a boy stood and walked to the front of the room to get his *Ponchik*. I stared at those rich, delicious looking treats, but I knew I had to get out of there.

Meir must have noticed I was pale. "What's wrong?" he asked.

"I have to go," I whispered.

"Now?" he asked. "Wait for the *Ponchik*."

"I can't," I said.

I took advantage of the chaos of kids walking to the front and returning, leaning forward to see more closely, staring at the sweets, and in the melee I sneaked out.

I never returned. I decided I had dodged a bullet, and I never said a word to anyone.

* * *

Our third grade "educator," Mr. Uri, was a middle aged, small man, always dressed in a dark suit, tie and hat. He had a thick, black moustache and was one of the most good-natured and caring teachers I ever had. He taught us Bible and Hebrew, and although we all loved him, I did not like the subjects he taught.

In contrast, Mr. Greenberg was a young, rude and ruthless teacher who hated children. He taught Mishna and geography, and all the kids were terrified of him. One wrong move, one wrong answer, one gesture that irritated this giant, he was quick to react—picking students up by our ears and punishing us in front of the entire class. But Mishna and geography were two of my favorite subjects; whenever Mr. Greenberg called on me to explain this or that legal dilemma, I always had the right answer, so I was seldom punished.

One cloudy spring morning—beset by such heavy clouds hanging low on the mountains, it seemed almost like winter—I set out to walk to school. In my backpack I carried the usual number of books and notebooks. My mother had insisted I wear the leather coat handed down to me from Yudke. The coat was ancient, and the lining was torn; finding the correct hole that led to the sleeve always presented a problem. I had been walking for about 30 minutes, and I was halfway to school when I noticed a commotion on one of the corners of Geula Street.

As I came closer I saw a British policeman shouting at an Arab woman. Her dress of black, velvety material with colorful stitching reached all the way to the ground, and she wore a white shawl over her head that contrasted with her dark, dried out skin and big black eyes. She stood beside a wide basket full of red and yellow peaches from Jericho. The peaches, each one the size of a tennis ball, looked delicious, without a single blemish.

"*Ruch min hon!*" the policeman shouted in Arabic, gesturing her to go away. "*Ruch min hon!*" the policeman said again, but the woman refused to move.

I stopped and stood against a wall, watching the struggle begin. The policeman got madder and shouted more loudly, and he began to blow his whistle. He approached the basket, kicked it turning it over. The peaches rolled across the sidewalk and dropped into the road, dispersing like billiard balls on a table after the break shot.

The Arab woman began to cry and curse as she ran after the fruit. I watched as a bus drove past and smashed some of the peaches.

I took off my backpack and placed it on the sidewalk so I could help her collect the peaches. At first she cursed me and made threatening gestures, but as she understood I was helping, she stopped cursing. Once she had gathered all the fruit that wasn't ruined, she raised the basket and put it on her head, shifting it back and forth until it was perfectly balanced.

I returned to harness my bag on my shoulders and stared at the smashed peaches still lying in the roadway. I was thinking of picking one up but had just decided against it and was walking away when I heard: "*Ya wallad!*"

I looked back and saw the peach woman calling after me. "*Ta'al hon.*" She gestured me to come over. With her right hand she held onto the basket while with her left she reached around the rim, grabbed a peach and held it out in front of her. "*Shukran,*" she thanked.

I reached and took the peach, placed it in my bag and walked to school.

Later, in class Mr. Greenberg was elaborating about a legal dilemma while I daydreamed about the peach. The most wonderful fragrance rising out of my bag was driving my appetite, and I could not wait for the bell. At some point when Mr. Greenberg was farthest from me, I slowly lowered my head, grabbed the peach and took a bite.

"Makogon, stand up!" The giant's voice sounded as if he were calling through a megaphone. I froze and tried to invisibly chew. I could not even think about spitting out this wonderful, precious treat.

"Makogon, stand up I said!"

I stood.

"Come forward, I want the class to see you."

I moved slowly to the front of the class where he stood at his desk. As I walked, I finished chewing and swallowed the peach.

"Didn't I say on the first day of class that there will be no eating, no talking and no moving in my class?"

I said nothing.

"Didn't I?"

"Yes, Teacher," I said.

"Didn't I say you should answer 'yes, Teacher Greenberg'?"

"Yes, Teacher Greenberg."

He took a few steps toward the desk, opened a drawer and took out a two-foot wooden ruler. He grabbed my hand in his so that my fingers were protruding up from his but held together at the base. "Because you ate in class only five minutes before it ends, you are going to get only five of these."

He proceeded to slap the top of my fingers with the flat side of the ruler five times. He slapped hard, and I cried quietly.

The bell rang. My fingers hurt, and I was embarrassed. None of the kids said anything. They all ran out to the yard to play. Only David Gabbai came to me.

"I hate him," he said. "Let's walk home together."

All day I brooded, and that night I could barely sleep. The next day during lunch break I approached my friend, Meir Zinger to tell him of my plan to organize the class to go on strike against Mr. Greenberg's harsh treatment because I was certain he would go along with my plan. I told him I planned to skip school the next day.

"Are you crazy?" he said.

"Let's skip school together and show them."

"If you behave yourself, he won't hit you anymore," Meir said.

"Come, let's have a good time. We'll play," I argued.

But Meir would not budge. He was a good student. He always did his homework, and he came to school eager to learn.

Undeterred, I talked to David Gabai and convinced him to join me. The two of us talked to other kids, some of whom were excited. We decided to meet in the morning at the school gate.

The next morning, eight of my classmates were at the gate. For a while we waited for others to join us, but when the bell rang, we left the school, running to the neighboring wooded area next to the Schneller Camp. There, in the pine woods, we played all day and went home at the end of the day, determined to continue our strike.

On the second day, only five kids met at the gate. This was Friday, and again we raced into the woods, played and ate our lunch before going home for the weekend.

There was no school on Saturday, so on the third day, Sunday, we met again at the school gate, but this time it was only me and Gabbai. He looked desolate. "I'm quitting," he said, and he walked into the school. I was on my own, and for two more days I didn't go to school.

I was no quitter.

At home, no one knew about my strike. We lived on the outskirts of Jerusalem, far from the school, and there was no phone so no one could contact my parents.

By Wednesday, I started to have second thoughts. I had no idea how this would end. I was too afraid to continue skipping school, but I was also afraid to return. Still, that morning I gathered all my courage and showed up when the others were already at Morning Prayer.

The kids turned and looked at me as if I were a dead man walking. No one talked to me, they only stared. We walked to class, and as we walked I felt as if I had just given up my freedom to become, once again, a slave.

I was at my desk when Mr. Greenberg walked into the room. "Makogon," he said, "what are you doing here?"

I didn't say a word.

"Get out of my class; you are not a student here!"

I did not move.

"You are the stupidest student I ever had. You are the scum of Jerusalem. Get out!"

I picked up my bag and walked out to the yard where I stayed all day, bored. During class breaks, I played with other kids. In the last hour of the afternoon class, Mr. Ilan walked outside and saw me sitting in the yard. He took me with him to his office and called in teacher Uri to join him in having a talk with me.

"Why did you skip class?" Mr. Uri asked.

I did not answer.

"Eitan, you have to tell us or you will have to bring your mother to school."

"My mother can't come to school," I said.

"Why?"

"Because she has my baby sister."

"So tell us why you skipped class," Mr. Ilan said.

"Because he hit me," I said.

"Who hit you?"

"Teacher Greenberg."

Principal Ilan and Mr. Uri exchanged looks. They were quiet for a few seconds, and then Ilan said, "Wait outside."

I stood in the wide dark corridor and waited for what seemed like a long time for their verdict. At last Mr. Uri walked into the hall.

"Go home now, Eitan," he said. "Do all the homework you missed, get the assignments from your friends and show up for class in the morning."

"Yes, Teacher," I said, and I ran all the way home.

The next day in class the giant teacher ignored me. He would not call on me, and he refused even to look in my direction. For the rest of that school year, Mr. Greenberg ignored me, treating me as if I were invisible.

I did not mind it at all; I felt my strike had been a success.

* * *

At night, Prophet Samuel Street presented many risks. I feared the Arabs in the area. I feared the Jewish terrorists of Etzel who had recently begun to bomb and shoot at British officers. I feared the British soldiers and the menacing darkness.

This particular night, the sky was moonless, and I knew the small man walking with me would be of no help in any of my imagined scenarios, but I had no choice. I had to keep walking even though I did not want to. Mr. Uri made it his job to visit the home of each student in his class at least once during the school year.

A week before his visit he gave me a note to give my parents in which he informed about his planned visit. This would be the first contact the school had had with my parents in almost three years. I was good at Hebrew; my spelling was excellent and my reading comprehension good. But I hated the detailed stories of the Bible and did not memorize any of them, so I knew I was in trouble. At home, no one ever punished me, but the prospect of my parents learning about my skipping class and avoiding homework terrified me.

It was late afternoon when Mr. Uri walked up to our apartment. He was heavyset and the four flights of stairs wore him out, so he reached the apartment out of breath. My father was away at his job, but my mother set Mr. Uri at the round terrazzo table in the entry hall and served tea, bread and jam. Mr. Uri looked around. From his seat he could see our entire apartment. I saw him notice we had just one bedroom.

"So, Mrs. Makogon, where does Eitan sleep?" he asked.

My mother showed him the bed I shared with Yudke. Then she showed him Shifra's bed and the crib where Baby Varda slept.

"And where does Eitan do his homework?" Mr. Uri asked.

"Wherever he wants," my mother said, "but I will tell you, he does not have that much homework and he does it very fast."

He glanced at me, his eyes inquisitive. I felt my heart racing.

"I have to tell you, Mrs. Makogon," he began, "we do have quite a bit of homework for our students every day."

I'd known it was coming. My mother's eyes registered her complaint. I knew she was asking silently: Why are you doing this to me?

"Many days I have noticed Eitan does not do his homework," Mr. Uri said.

With baby Varda in her arms, my mother began to wipe perspiration from her forehead. She shot me an angry look, and from the doorway, Shifra cast the same look my way.

"He is very capable, Eitan, but he does not want to apply himself.

He doesn't make enough effort," Uri said. "I would like you to pay more attention so he can excel."

Now that he had blamed her, I felt terrible. My mother began to explain how difficult it was raising four children with her husband away from home most of the time.

"I understand, these are difficult times," Mr. Uri said between sips of tea to wash down the bread he had slathered with jam. "Just watch him and he will be okay," he said as he stood.

My mother wiped the tears from her eyes with the corner of her apron.

Realizing there would be no discussion of the strike, my heart did a leap of joy, and I stood to show Mr. Uri the way out. He turned and said, "Now show me where Gabbai lives."

Shmuel Hanavi, our street, actually delineated the edge of Jerusalem. There was only one area on the other side of the street where a few Jewish homes were built; it was a slightly protruding, peninsula-like enclave closer to the Arab area. This area, *Shimon Hatzadik* (righteous Simon), was where Gabbai lived. An unpaved, rocky dirt road led to it.

I walked with Mr. Uri in total darkness, and I felt as if I were moving into no man's land, wide open to the enemy. We walked quietly, the sound of our steps on the rocky road sounding loud to me in the silence broken only by the occasional distant dog bark from the Arab neighborhood. When we came close to Gabbai's home, I pointed out the silhouette of the house.

"Very well, Eitan," Mr. Uri said, "you can run back home now."

And run home I did.

* * *

The days grew longer and warmer. After winning the skirmish with the cruel giant Greenberg, surviving Teacher Uri's visit, avoiding being caught as a freeloader, learning that for a strike to be successful it must be better planned, I deeply welcomed the approaching light at the end of the tunnel. For the few remaining school days, I coasted happily, and on the last day, with 60 days of vacation ahead of us, the teachers gave us our reports to take home. Even the small note at the bottom of the report could not squelch my jubilation. It read: *Eitan graduated from 3rd grade and is eligible to enroll in 4th grade pending passing a test in the subject: Bible.*

CHAPTER SIX

Nir and I stopped playing on our balcony when the railing became too hot to touch. It was a hot morning--Hamseen, a day so hot just breathing required an effort. Each summer Jerusalem endured at least five Hamseen, and each one felt like torture.

Nir was the son of Shlomo Freifeld, my parents' friend from their earliest days in Palestine. My mother, Shlomo and his sister had been orphans in the Lvov orphanage and considered each other as family. The Freifelds were farmers and lived in a *Moshav*, a cooperative farm, on a coastal plane in the center of the country named *Emek Heffer*, Valley of Heffer. Nir was staying with us because he needed dry Jerusalem mountain air to cure his asthma.

We were walking into our apartment, when my mother asked, "Nika, did you take your asthma pills?"

"No, I have to take them after breakfast," Nir said.

"*Ima*," I asked, "when am I going to Nika's farm?" This was, perhaps, the tenth time in as many days I had asked this question.

In exchange for Nir's soaking up the Jerusalem air at our home, each summer I would stay at their home on the farm. I loved being in the fields and riding their horse. During the school year I frequently dreamed about being there, and whenever I woke and discovered I was in Jerusalem, I felt disappointed.

"Maybe next year when things get better," my mother said.

"What things?"

"When the country is quieter," she said.

"It's quiet now," I argued.

"You never know what this guy Begin and his Etzel terrorists are going to do next," she said. "The British are mad and nervous right now. So are the Arabs."

Although at the time I was not a student of politics and history, I knew life was difficult for everyone. Following the British victory in World War

II, in which the Yishuv in Palestine helped by sending 25,000 volunteers to fight along with the British Armies, the Jews of *Eretz-Israel* had expected the Brits to relax restrictions placed on immigration of their European brethren. Everyone expected the survivors of the Holocaust to be permitted to settle in this country most of all, but this was not to be.

A new Labor government, with Mr. Bevin, who had anti-Semitic tendencies, as its Foreign Office minister, closed the gates to Palestine for those Jews who remained in Europe. On rare occasions, the Jewish leadership reached an agreement to unite against the White Paper restrictions on immigration, settlement, and land ownership. The two major factions, Hagana, The Defense, and Etzel, an acronym for National Military Organization, coordinated actions against the British authority.

On July 22, 1946, Etzel forces had planted a bomb in the British government headquarters housed in a wing of the King David Hotel. Shortly before the explosion, the fighting underground organization telephoned in a notice to the government about their intent to bomb, advising the British to evacuate the hotel.

For years this warning would arouse controversy—some insisting it had never been given. Thurston Clark, an American author, in his book *"By Blood and Fire"* elaborates the story of the three separate warnings given on that day. More recent research has revealed that this warning was transmitted to London, that Sir John Shaw, the British administration secretary, received it, but that his response was: "I give orders here; I don't take orders from Jews."

Shortly after midnight, an explosion rocked Jerusalem from the farthest churches in Bethlehem to the sleepy mosques of Sheikh Jarakh. The hotel crumbled and took with it the lives of 28 Britons, 41 Arabs, 17 Jews and 5 others, in all 91 people died. In the weeks that followed, tension in the country was high.

My mother's response to that tension was her refusal to allow us to travel. Still, she asked Nir, "Nika, what do you want to do today?"

She never asked me this kind of open choice question, but Nir was our guest. "I want to go see the Wailing Wall," he told her.

My mother hesitated. Of all the places of interest in Jerusalem, this seemed the least safe choice at the moment. Such a visit would require a trip to the Old City, and that included a walk through the Arab quarters. "Wouldn't you rather see a movie?" she tried to dissuade him.

I thought a movie sounded fine. Nir wasn't religious, and I couldn't imagine why he wanted to see the Wall. Surely he'd agree to a movie.

But he shook his head no. I suggested that *Gulliver in the Land of the Dwarves* might be a much better idea. I'd heard it was a good movie.

"I can see it in Kfar Haim," Nir said. "On the Moshav we watch movies for free."

"Or maybe the zoo?" my mother tried. I hadn't even known we had a zoo.

"The Wailing Wall!" Nir insisted.

Nir was a few years older than I was, so I watched his every move. I watched him take out his pill box, open it and remove two chocolate-covered pills. He gulped these down with a glass of milk, and I envied him for those little chocolate morsels and for the attention my mother gave him.

Shifra agreed to babysit Varda, who was now two, and with sandwiches in her handbag, my mother, Nir and I set out for a day trip to visit the most sacred spot for the Jewish people, the place Jews had, throughout the ages, prayed about. The Wall was a place that every morning for two millennia Jews everywhere promised never to forget. It was the place that held the remains of the ancient shrine, the Western Wall.

As we walked to the bus, I was prepared for an awe-inspiring experience.

We boarded bus line 2, the only line that passed by our house. This time we passed my old day care and continued on into the heart of the city. We approached the intersection of Jaffa Street and King George Street where a circular raised curbed area was covered by a gazebo under which stood a traffic policeman. He wore a meticulously pressed uniform with glowing white sleeves and gloves. On his head he wore the imperial oval-shaped white hat. He was directing traffic with theatrical, yet firm gestures.

He gave the signal, and the bus turned left onto Jaffa Street. We passed the Jerusalem Egged bus station, the Zion Square with its movie house, the large stone statue of a roaring lion at the Generalli office and bank building, and the city Commercial Center, and finally arrived at the last stop not far from the wall of the Old City.

The area outside the wall looked like a central station with busses lined up on the wide paved asphalt. The site was colorful—much like Sheikh Jarakh that I had seen in the distance from our window with hundreds of people. Arab women in full length black dresses and men in white robes, their heads covered with black and white *kaffiyehs* held down by the *Aggal*, a black loop of thick rope, moved chaotically between the busses, and the merchants stood beside their carts and stands shouting praise for their merchandise.

The stone wall surrounding the Old City was thick. On top of one section I saw a group of policemen, their commander pointing in front of him. We walked through the gate and continued on to a ten foot wide street paved with cobble stones and lined with an endless number of "hole- in-the-wall" stores and restaurants. Everywhere Arab men in their *kaffiyehs* stood or sat—some on tiny chairs at tables outside their cafes. They drank tea from glasses, muddy coffee from the tiniest porcelain cups, and many smoked Nargilahs. I stopped to look at the burning tobacco and the water bubbling up through the Nargilah as the men puffed on the end of a hose. The men were unshaven, and the hardened looks in their dark eyes fascinated me.

"Come, Eitan." My mother grabbed my hand, "we have to be careful with them."

The narrow street sloped slightly downward with a step every 20 to 30 feet. All the structures were built of stone, and the street narrowed as we continued down. After a few turns into even smaller passages, we arrived at a narrow alley, and I saw my mother's face light up with pleasure at the sight of Jews dressed in black, many praying with their eyes closed, moving forwards and backwards, as if in a trance. Some of the praying men stood at the wall of the alley and were praying and banging their heads at the enormous wall which dwarfed them.

"Excuse me," my mother asked a woman with a mountainous belly, her head covered, "where is the Western Wall?"

The woman looked at her, then at us, and for a moment she opened her mouth but no words came out. At last she said, "This is it!"

"Where?" my mother asked, straining to see.

"Here!" the woman said, shifting the baby she held to another arm and pointing to the men in black banging their heads at the gigantic rectangular boulders.

"Oh, thank you," my mother said, taking our hands in hers.

We walked closer to the section of the wall where several more women congregated. My mother fumbled in her bag. I thought she was reaching for the sandwiches she had prepared for lunch, but she could not find what she was looking for.

A man in a black hat and black coat walked up to her. His gray beard, grown wild, danced as he asked, in Yiddish, *"Vilst a Shtikale papier?"* He held out a 2"x 2" note and a pencil, and my mother looked at it, delighted. She began to write while the man waited patiently. After she had written a few words, she handed him the pencil and thanked him. He pushed forward a tin donation box with a slot on top. Again she fumbled in her bag until she found what she was looking for, and I watched as she dropped a coin into the box; it made a hollow, dinging sound as it dropped.

Mother approached the wall, placed the note in one of the crevices between the boulders, leaned against it, placed her shawl-covered forehead on the wall, closed her eyes and cried. Nir and I stood on either side of her, waiting. The air was suffocating, but she stood with both her hands flat on the wall above her head and kept crying, taking her time, whispering at the wall.

Suddenly Nir coughed once, and again, and my mother turned to look at him, her eyes red and worried. "Do you have your pills?" she asked.

"No. I left them at your home," Nir said.

My mother abruptly grabbed our hands and turned, retracing our steps back the way we had come. As we hurriedly climbed the narrow Via Dolorosa, Nir coughed again and again, and midway up the street, not too far from the gate, he was coughing hard and laboring for air. When he began to choke, we stopped.

An old Arab man came out of a store carrying a glass of water and gestured to my mother to give it to Nir, but the water didn't help. By then he couldn't drink or breathe, and my mother panicked.

A woman in long Arab garb rushed out of the store, grabbed Nir and pulled him inside. We followed behind as the woman led him into a back room. The air inside was cool and soothing, and even I could breathe more easily. The woman lay Nir on a narrow bed.

I looked around. The curved ceiling and walls were unpainted, but two colorful rugs hung on one wall, and on a low wooden table beside the bed sat a plate with a partially peeled orange. I accidentally bumped into a glass nargilah on the floor, but luckily it didn't break.

The room had no windows and was dark and cool, and Nir began to feel relief. The woman left the room and soon returned with a wet towel smelling of mint. She placed it over his nose and mouth, and as he inhaled through that, his breathing grew steady, normal.

Her face pale, eyes red with tears, my mother thanked the woman in Arabic. "*Shukran, Shukran,*" she said, and she reached into her bag again, taking out some money to give to her.

"*Lah, Lah!*" the woman said, refusing.

My mother smiled, and the three of us left, walking out of the Old City through Jaffa Gate and trudging towards the "Hamekasher" line number 2 bus stop.

"Good people," my mother said to herself as we took our seats and began the long ride home.

* * *

The British, after defeating General Rommel's German armies in North Africa's El Alamain, and later, following their victory in 1945, moved their troops around the Middle East to place them as needed to fill in the pieces of the puzzle that constituted parts of the British Empire. This meant moving troops to Iraq, Transjordan, Egypt and Palestine, and many of the military convoys, including troop carriers, armored vehicles and tanks, moved through Jerusalem as they made their way towards their destinations. Quite a few used our street, Prophet Samuel, as their path toward the cities of Ramallah in Palestine, Amman in the Kingdom of Transjordan, and Baghdad in Iraq.

These convoys drove at a snail's pace, and so for hours at a time, they would occupy our street and our attention, and we neighborhood kids were delighted by the sight.

One Friday morning at dawn, two weeks before the end of summer vacation, just before Rosh Hashanah, the New Year holiday, a British convoy crawled in front of our house. When I walked down from the fourth floor, kids were there already, shouting, "Gimmie chwinga, gimmie chwinga" to the soldiers manning the tanks and vehicles.

The convoy continued for hours, and I watched as soldiers of many nationalities drove past. I recognized the British with their fair skin, red and sweaty, the Australians with their wide hats, brims folded up on one side; the tall Sudanese with black skin that shone in the summer sun, and the Indians who wore strange round cloth head covers.

We kept up with our --"gimmie chwinga," calls, but our success was limited.

As the hours passed, the crowd of kids grew, and the struggle for a position ready to catch any candy the soldiers might toss our way became more difficult. A few solid lines formed, one behind the other like in a busy bar, the older, stronger kids up front.

At noon the trucks and tanks were still coming, and the crowd on our sidewalk kept shouting. One soldier, sitting on top of the tank, looked our way, heard our shouts, smiled and climbed down through his hatch into the tank before he reappeared holding a big box of candies. He ripped it open and in one swoop showered the contents onto the sidewalk and roadway. In the loud roar and ensuing tumult, nearly every kid nabbed some candies, and just as the tumult died down, a two-year-old boy jumped into the street, going after a candy left untouched a few feet away from the curb.

"Don't go there!" someone shouted at the boy, but he slipped, and the gigantic tank kept moving until his body was hidden beneath its tracks.

The crowd fell silent as the horror took hold. The tank passed, revealing the boy's tiny, flattened body. The crowd of kids exploded—yelling, shouting, crying—and in seconds a crowd of wailing men and women took over. I stood staring in horror.

The shouts, the cries, and the tumult around me vanished, as if I were in a silent movie that ran only in my head. The scene that played out over and over was the image of that little boy falling under the tank, and then the reappearance of his bloodied body. The scene repeated in my head, but this time instead of the little boy, the flattened body was mine.

"Hey boy, go home," someone said, and the movie in my mind stopped.

I climbed the stairs to our apartment. Standing at my bedroom window, I kept watching the unmoving crowd downstairs and the convoy that kept moving for hours.

* * *

I did not like Sunday mornings because after spending *Shabbat* with us, my father left home early in the morning. I slept late and missed his departure, knowing he would be away for the entire week. In *Eretz Israel* Sunday morning was the first workday of the week , and the first school day, and this Sunday was among the worst. It was the last week of summer and in a few days I would go back to school to start fourth grade. This felt like a heavy load.

Yudka, 18, Shifra, 12, baby Varda, who was 2, and 8-year-old me sat around our circular terrazzo-topped table as my mother carried from the little kitchen in the back of the apartment two plates, each with one egg sunny side up, accompanied by tomato and onion salad. She carefully placed the plates in front of Yudke and Shifra, at the same time touching the table.

She followed this years' old ritual, keeping peace and quiet at our meals and avoiding their complaints by giving them precisely the same thing at the same time.

My plate followed, but I had lost my appetite.

"Eat your breakfast," my mother said.

"I can't," I said.

"Are you sick?"

"No."

"There is no end to my troubles," my mother sighed.

"Are you afraid of going to fourth grade?" Yudke asked.

"It's nothing! Fourth grade is easy," Shifra said.

I did not reply. She kept examining my face.

Then suddenly Shifra said, "Have you done your booklets?"

I said nothing, but she continued. "I know, *Ima*. He didn't do his booklets."

The booklets were our homework for the summer. With 30 pages each, stories or math problems and spaces to be filled with the answers, they were required.

"Poor boy," my mother said. "You two!" She turned to Yudke and Shifra. "Help him fill out the booklets. There is no way he can finish them by himself in the few days now."

My parents were always helpful.

"But we can't fill them in," Shifra argued. "The teacher will know it's not his handwriting."

"Let's show him what to write, and he'll do the actual writing," Yudke said. "I'll take the math, and you take the Hebrew," he said to my older sister.

The three of us walked into the bedroom and sat on the bed. I opened my bag, pulling out the two booklets. Immediately Shifra and Yudke got busy, writing the answers below the lines in light letters so that I could copy these into the right spaces and erase their penciled drafts.

We finished in two days, but my anxiety did not diminish.

They had all forgotten about the note in my school report requiring me to pass a test in Bible prior to admittance to fourth grade, but I hadn't forgotten.

I took out my Bible and set out to study for the test, but I said nothing to anyone about my dire situation or my plan.

The test was going to be on the Bible book we had studied in third grade--the first Prophet Samuel book. I remembered the stories about King Saul, David and Jonathan, but I did not know how to begin studying. So I simply started reading.

"*Now there was a man of Ramathaim of Mount Efraim, and his name was Elkanah, the son of Yehoram, the son of Elihu, the son of Tohu, the son of Zuph, an Efrathite.*"

I read this and skimmed the remaining 31 chapters of the first book of

Samuel, all of which looked just as confusing as that first sentence. I tried to imagine what would be asked of me in the coming test, tried to memorize the sequence of sons and fathers and places they lived. When I realized that 40 pages of stories in small print lay ahead and that in three days I could not possibly master these, I gave up and spent my time dreading the approaching first day of fourth grade.

8 years old with my family.

CHAPTER SEVEN

I knocked on the door of the apartment on the fourth floor across from ours. A woman was singing loudly in English. I waited a moment and knocked more aggressively. The woman, who I knew was Tsvi's mother, paused her song long enough to shout, "Who is it?" and went on singing the foreign love song.

"Eitan," I said.

She paused again. "Who is it?" Although she could not hear me while she sang, she continued to sing.

Knowing it was futile, I called through the closed door, "Eitan."

I heard her walking to the door, and as she did, the singing grew louder. She abruptly stopped as she opened the door and said, "Good morning, Eitan. Why don't you answer?"

"I answered," I said.

"You should talk louder, like a man."

She was certainly a woman, blond and plump, sporting a new hairdo, a short dress, and revealing a voluptuous bosom.

"Tsvika is eating breakfast in the kitchen," she said.

For a while now I had been a regular in their home. Tsvi was one year younger than I, two grades below me. His nose was always snotty, and he was unkempt, his eyeglasses with one lens blacked out to correct his cross-eyed vision. He wasn't the most pleasant boy, but he was a convenient playmate.

I walked into the long hallway. On the left were the bedrooms. The first one belonged to Tsvika, his mother, Berta and his father, Moshe Hilman. Berta's three brothers, ages 20 to 30, shared the second. The last room was a convertible living room used by Berta's elderly parents of Russian origin who had, a few years earlier, come from Argentina.

In the kitchen Tsvi and his father were eating. Moshe Hillman stood and greeted me, "Hey Eitan." He picked me up and laughing, tossed me in the air. I almost hit the ceiling before he caught me coming down. He was

35, an athletic soccer player and coach. "Take care of Tsvika and be careful," he said as he placed me on the floor.

I just looked at him.

"There's no telling what these Etzel terrorists will do next," he said. He was a member of the *Hagana*, the other underground Jewish defense force. "Go straight to school and the same when you come back home," he said. "You come straight home."

"Okay," I promised him.

As we walked out the door, Tsvika said, "Do you want to take the bus?"

"I don't have any money," I said.

"But I have," he said, and he dug into his pocket as we were walking downstairs; at the bottom he showed me five mills in his palm.

"That isn't enough."

"But I want to go in the bus," he nagged.

"Okay," I said, "give me the money. We'll take the bus, but you'll have to tell the driver you're three years old."

"But I'm seven," he said.

"Say you're three," I said, "only if you're asked."

When the bus came, we climbed on, and I handed the driver five mills. "What's with him?" the driver asked.

"My brother's only three, so he can ride for free. Besides, we have to take the bus to school because we're afraid of the terrorists. You never know what they're up to."

The driver laughed out loud, as did all the passengers who sat up front.

"All right, move in," the driver said.

We rode as far as the bus went down Geula Street before it turned onto Chancellor Street and headed to the center of town, about halfway to school. British military cars, soldiers and policemen swarmed Geula. This was 1946, and Jewish pressure from the underground was mounting, so the British had assembled a formidable force of 100,000 soldiers in Palestine. The idea was to intimidate the 500,000 Jews and to prevent European Holocaust survivors from entering the country.

To me it seemed as if the entire British army had gathered and would keep us safe and well-guarded as we walked to school, and because I was focused on our bus ride scam, the fear of terrorists and the soldiers, I was distracted from my main problem until we had almost reached the school.

Only then did I remember the Bible test. It dawned on me that I would probably have to spend another year in third grade because there was no way I could pass a test about the book of Samuel. I could remember none of his forefather's names from the first sentence of the first chapter, and none of the rest of the book.

As we neared the school, I saw that the Schneller Camp was surrounded with armored cars, so we had to take a small detour to enter the schoolyard, but that day, unlike most other days I'd attended school, there was no chaotic noise and excitement in the school yard; instead teachers were quietly directing everyone to their classrooms. The morning roll call assembly and the chanting of *Adon Olam* prayer had been canceled.

When I walked into my old classroom and saw the third grade kids, I knew I wouldn't return to this class, no matter what happened. These kids were far too young. I walked out of the room and quickly found the fourth grade room where I sat in the back.

When Mr. Uri came in, we all stood. "Sit," he said. "Welcome to fourth grade," and he waited patiently for 40 kids to sit and for the noise of our chairs scraping the floor to subside.

"As you have seen outside the school, there are some serious security problems today. We will, therefore, temporarily change the rules. This morning there will be no assembly in the yard. We'll all stay indoors."

"Even during the breaks?" a boy asked.

"Yes, all through the day," Mr. Uri said. He proceeded to explain the subjects we would study this year, and as I listened I thought about how much I liked Mr. Uri and how happy I was to see that he was going to remain our teacher for this year. Still, I knew I wouldn't pass the Bible Exam, so I couldn't entirely enjoy the moment.

Saul Levi raised his hand.

"Yes, Saul?" Teacher Uri said.

"When am I going to take the test in arithmetic so I can enter fourth grade?" Saul asked.

The moment Saul asked that question, my hopes, based on sheer fantasy, that our tests might somehow go away, evaporated. I silently decided I would escape into the wilderness of the Judean Mountains and spend my life there rather than endure one more year in third grade.

"Because of the situation, all the tests are cancelled," Mr. Uri said. "You will do some extra remedial work instead."

My eyes filled with tears of joy, and I struggled to keep them from leaking out. I did not want the other boys to notice my relief, but at that moment I admired Mr. Uri, appreciated the British soldiers, adored the terrorists and loved my country.

A few weeks into fourth grade, life in school returned to the old routine. We had to be in the yard 30 minutes before the 8:00 a.m. bell, so I had to leave home before 7 which was not too bad except when it rained or snowed.

I liked school except for the homework. From an early age I was interested in arithmetic and physics-- subjects that were interesting and came easily to me. I preferred these over those subjects that required any memorization as I never had a good long-term memory. In fourth grade at my mildly religious school, more and more our education focused on God and religion, and somewhere along the way, I became convinced that I'd been born an atheist. As far back as I can remember I had never bought the idea of a God, invisible, unprovable, yet all capable and all knowing. As much as I tried, I just could not convince myself of the existence of such a concept.

Even though my father was traditional, and I enjoyed going with him to *Beit Knesset* (temple) on the High Holidays, we never discussed abstract subjects. I didn't discuss these subjects with either my father or my mother. Our family operated in survival mode—discussing what to eat, how to dress, doing homework. My parents would ask where I had been, would tell me when to go to bed, but never did they venture into the philosophical. I never had the slightest doubt that I was an atheist, and in school I did not discuss my belief or disbelief in God. I did, however, have a couple of good friends who I believed were of the same mind.

I noticed that one of these friends, Uri Epstein, had been absent from the Morning Prayer. Before long I realized that David Gabbai was also often missing from prayers sessions.

One day as David and I were walking home together, I asked if he was religious.

"Sure I am," he said.

"But I don't see you in the Morning Prayer at school."

"I don't have to be there," he told me, "because I go *to Beit-Knesset* every morning."

I was shocked. Going on the High Holidays made sense, but every morning?

"So, what time do you have to wake up?" I asked.

"Six o'clock, sometimes earlier," he said. "The days before Yom Kippur we wake up at five in the morning to say *sleihot*."

I knew the Sephardic religious people rose early before Yom Kippur. When I was younger and their temple leader walked around at 4:30 a.m. to wake his fellow temple members, shouting, "Moshe, wake up for the creator's work!" or "Yoseph, wake up, it's time to ask forgiveness!" I too would be wakened, but I never imagined the young boys also had to attend temple so early in the morning.

"That's why I don't have to come to pray in school," David explained.

"How does Teacher Uri know you go to temple?" I asked.

"My father gave me a note for him," he said.

I waited eagerly for Friday when my father would return home. That day I waited until things settled down in the house and we had had our *Shabbat* meal. After dinner my father moved to the living room where he sat reading his newspaper, and there I approached him. "*Aba*," I began.

He held up his hand, signaling for me to wait. He was reading about the recent terror actions by the underground, and he did not want to be disturbed. But when he finished the article, he turned to me and asked, "What's on your mind?"

"I don't want to go to school so early every day," I said.

"But you have to be there before school starts."

"Yes, but a lot of kids are allowed to skip the Morning Prayer and come later to school."

"Who?" he asked.

"David Gabbai."

"Oh, I know the Gabbais," he said. "They pray in temple every morning."

"Uri Epstein doesn't go to temple," I said. "But his father gave him a note saying that he prays at home in the morning."

My father smiled. "Ah, but you don't pray," he said.

"I've started," I said. "Every morning after waking I close my eyes and say the prayer in silence."

His smile grew wider as he caressed my head. "I will think about it," he said.

That Sunday when I woke, my father was already gone, but there beside my bed was the note he had left, and I never again had to pray in school.

* * *

Each day during those first months of 1947 walking to school became more frightening. When I got close I could see the British soldiers fortifying Schneller Camp, and one day in March, I walked as usual to Tsvi's apartment, but his father Moshe was not his usual jovial self.

"Which way do you take to school?" he asked.

"We first go up to Bukharim Market," I said.

"And then?" he asked. I described our route as he repeatedly asked, "and then, and then?" prodding me for every detail.

"We take Geula Street up to Chancellor and continue up to Schneller and then we turn left to the school street in Mekor Baruch," I said.

"So you walk right next to the Schneller camp?" he asked.

"No, we cross the street and walk by Schneller on the other side of the street."

Hillman looked serious. We had noticed day by day the addition of barbed wires and new watch stations on top of the wall surrounding the camp. Just a week earlier we had seen the British soldiers looking down at us as we walked by, machine guns in front of them, supported on sandbags.

"Take a short cut today," Hillman said, and he described in detail the route we had to take, turning into an open field and cutting to another street that would take us to school.

This so-called "shortcut" was actually a longer route, and that day Tsvi and I were late. The teacher, however, accepted my excuse, and I sensed, even then, the tension in the air throughout the city. At 1 p.m., after school, I picked up Tsvi at his class, and we walked home. When we reached Geula Street we saw a long military convoy moving slowly down the street towards Meah Shearim. We kept walking on the south side of the street, unable to cross at our usual spot because the line of troop carriers, armored trucks and big tanks was unending. We walked as far as we could and waited at the edge of the sidewalk for a chance to cross. Feeling responsible for Tsvi and frightened by the vivid memory of that little boy's body under the convoy tank, I didn't dare race across.

We simply waited. Hours passed.

It began to grow late, and the street became darker with the looming shadows of the houses when suddenly a motorcycle with a side car cut in front of the truck in the convoy and stopped next to us. Velvel, the oldest of Tsvi's uncles, had come to pick us up; they had been looking for us for hours. We climbed into the sidecar, and when we reached home, everyone treated us as if we were long-lost war heroes.

The next evening, Friday, we learned that the *Irgun-Etzel* underground had attacked and demolished the British Officer's Club at King George Street in the center of Jerusalem. Seventeen officers were killed and 27 were injured, some of them senior intelligence officers. That day the British government declared martial law in parts of the country. In Jerusalem troops surrounded the north of the city, including our street, with a barbed wire fence, and they imposed a curfew. From that moment we were imprisoned in our homes—no movement permitted. Stores closed. School was canceled. Anyone breaking the curfew would be shot.

Overnight our street was empty, filled only with a tense silence. Shifra, Varda and I stayed home, and my mother cleaned and cooked all day. On Monday morning we woke to commotion disturbing the stillness. British soldiers were conducting house to house searches, the reason for the total curfew. They were convinced that some underground elements were hiding in the northern part of the city, the area that included our neighborhood.

Many young men in our neighborhood were known to be members of the *Hagana*, the main underground force, but some were members of the *Etzel*, and it was these the British were seeking since the *Etzel* took bolder, more aggressive terrorist actions against the British. Our next door neighbor, Ben Dov, the one who lived in the third apartment on our floor, belonged to *Etzel*, or, at least, was a sympathizer. He also rented a room to a man who wrote books and authored essays and pamphlets justifying *Etzel's* actions and outlining the organization's philosophy. My parents never talked to those men, not because of philosophical differences. Past quarrels over neighborly things had caused the rift, and I considered him the neighbor from hell since he also snubbed me.

When the soldiers entered our building, they searched every apartment, starting from the bottom floor. As I listened to them downstairs, I secretly hoped they would take away Ben Dov. I was glad my brother was away in the *Palmach* Special Forces in the Galilee, and that my father was at his job with the British Army.

At midday my mother answered the knock on the door with "Who is it?" as if she didn't know, and she motioned us children to go into the bedroom and stay there.

"Police!" the soldier on the other side of the door answered. He continued to talk, speaking in a thick British accent none of us could understand.

"All right," my mother said.

Motioning us to be quiet, she opened the door. Three blond, red-faced soldiers stood there in their battle fatigues, each one holding a Tommy gun. They moved into our small apartment, and one of them instructed the others where to look. They opened and closed doors, lay on their stomachs to look under beds. Suddenly one of them called something. From his tone it sounded to me as if he were saying something like, "Johnny, look what I found!"

We all moved closer to see what he had found in a cabinet in the living room. As we did, one of them shouted at us and pointed his weapon. "Oy, oy vey, no, no!" my mother shouted.

The soldier who looked like a good guy because his face was softer, tried to calm her and physically moved us to the bedroom. He sat us down as the other soldier pulled things out of the cabinet, reaching in and pulling out the metal base with radio tubes attached to it; these tubes were attached to a messy ball of electrical wiring.

The soldiers began to talk excitedly among themselves, as if they had found a treasure. They carefully moved aside the wires. The sergeant said to my mother, "What is that?"

"My boy. School. Nothing, nothing," she said.

Unhappy, the soldier pulled out his walkie talkie, called somewhere and began to talk at length while the other three pointed their Tommy guns at us. "Please, nothing, this nothing," my mother tried again, but the soldiers did not move.

"This my boy, my son, now not home, in kibbutz," she continued, trying in her best English to explain that this belonged to my brother Yudke who had left home a few months earlier to join the *Palmach*. He lived in a kibbutz in the Galilee and was training to become a member of the top Special Forces. I was proud of him. We all were. Before he left home, in his last year in school, he had tried to build a radio receiver or transmitter as part of a school assignment, but he never finished it and had left the mess in this cabinet.

I looked at my mother, then at Shifra and Varda who were pale and frightened. I began to wonder if we might all go to prison and be hanged by the British. I knew they had already hanged a few *Etzelnicks*.

Ten eternal minutes passed when at last an enforcement unit came noisily up the stairs. They pushed open the doors to the other two apartments on the fourth floor where they set up security positions. From across the hall, I heard Moshe Hillman talking in English with the commander. They both walked into our apartment.

My mother turned to Moshe. "Tell them it's nothing. Just Yudke's hobby," she said.

As Hillman spoke to the officer, I started to feel hope flooding my body.

"What is he saying?" my mother asked.

"Don't worry. I'll take care of it," Hillman said.

After they had talked a while, the soldiers took Yudke's contraption,

57

wrapped everything into a bundle and walked out, carrying the "evidence."

"Thank *Got* for Hillman," my mother said when they were gone. "Poor Yudke, always problems. Who knows where he is now."

Through the open door we saw Ben Dov's tenant being led out by two British soldiers.

"I am just a writer," he pleaded, "not a terrorist." I was sorry for him, sorry they had not arrested Ben Dov.

And the crisis passed.

After the soldiers had finished their searches, the eerie silence returned to the neighborhood. For days we simply sat on the floor, sometimes playing, but often, for hours, doing nothing. I was not allowed to visit Tsvi, and I was bored. On the afternoon of the third day I walked through the living room, opened the door and slowly walked out to the open balcony; I stayed out of sight of the street. The balcony had a see-through wrought iron railing, and I could see that no one was in the street, not even soldiers. Emboldened, I took two steps closer so I could see better and stood watching the absolute stillness. As far as I could see, no one was anywhere in the street.

I took another step forward, and suddenly I heard an explosion above my head and a scream.

"You boy, get the bloody fuck back inside or I'll shoot you!" The shout was so loud, my knees gave, and I fell to the cold terrazzo floor. Above, standing on the roof, was a soldier in his combat gear with the red beret; he was leaning against the roof parapet, his machine gun supported on the parapet and pointed at me. His face looked vicious. I could not take my eyes off the machine gun, nor could I stand. I crawled back into the living room where my mother picked me up from the floor and held me tight. Both of us wept.

As the curfew continued, the British were forced to lift it for an hour or two so that we could buy food and supplies. We bought the newspaper where I read one item I will never forget: "Immediately after martial law was proclaimed, two Jews were shot and killed in Jerusalem, one of them a four- year-old girl standing on the balcony of her home in Mea Shearim quarter."

During the brief breaks in the curfew, many gathered at the barbed wire on both sides of the fence, where separated families and friends met to talk to each other. Some British soldiers helped pass parcels from one side to another. Shifra was worried because she was in eighth grade, the last year of grammar school, and she feared she would not graduate in time.

The next time the curfew was lifted for two hours she and I walked to the barbed wire fence and stood for a while next to a British soldier who had been helpful to people asking to transfer parcels. Shifra talked him into lifting her across. She wanted to go live with a girl from school.

The soldier lifted her, and I waved goodbye.

A few days later at a curfew break, Mother, Varda and I walked to this same spot to see Shifra who stood on the other side holding a package for us that this same soldier helped to pass.

This friendly soldier was not alone; many of them had families back home, and many empathized with the plight of the innocent populace. The *Etzel* had targeted the Schneller, the fortified camp within the curfew safety zone; they took advantage of those soldiers who were friendly and managed to smuggle in parcels of explosives. On March 12, almost two weeks into the curfew, an explosion in the camp's old buildings killed one soldier and wounded eight. This action and other explosions in different locations in the country made a strong impression on both the local and world press. In London, Churchill, then an opposition MP, declared:

> "How long does the Secretary of State for the Colonies expect that this state of squalid warfare will go on, at a cost of 30 or 40 million pounds a year, keeping 100,000 Englishmen away with the military force?"

And another London newspaper, *The Sunday Express*, expressed similar frustrations, the frustration of Londoners at the inability of their government to suppress the Jews in Palestine, by printing a banner headline that screamed:

"GOVERN OR GET OUT!"

The sixteen-day martial law and its curfew was revoked on March 17, 1947. They removed the barbed wire fence that had interned us. Shifra came back home, my father came for the weekend, and Tsvi and I returned to school.

We were free again, but that great curfew reinforced my contempt for the British in particular and for authority in general.

CHAPTER EIGHT

"Ohy, Riboyne Shell Oylem..." the singer sang his heart out to the Creator. His voice was accompanied by the hissing sound of an old, overused vinyl record. My father sat on the sofa listening, his eyes closed. I sat next to him. The strong smell of the Sabbath meal warming in the kitchen engulfed us.

"How come you like this song so much?" I asked.

My father seldom talked unless talk was absolutely necessary. He was a listener, a good one. He would patiently listen to me whenever I wanted to tell him something. He listened to my mother's endless rants without interrupting. Most of all he liked to listen to music and the news.

"It reminds me of my home, in Russia," he told me.

In his entire life, my father bought only two luxury items for himself that my mother did not push him to buy. In the early days of their marriage, before I was born, he had purchased a gramophone, or "patifone" as we called it. I'm certain he bought it used, and with it came a few 78s made of Bakelite, the predecessor of plastic. The "His Master's Voice" gramophone worked on a spring we had to wind with a special handle before each "plate" was played.

"Is this singer from Russia?" I asked.

"No, he's from America. New York. His name is Yossalle Rosenblatt, an excellent cantor."

My father had a few classical music "plates" but what he most liked were Jewish cantors, some of whom were excellent opera singers; they sang the Jewish *"Pirkey Hasanut"* - Cantor's Pieces. He also often played Mario Lanza, and I spent many *Shabbat* hours helping turn the handle that wound the spring, changing records at his requests, once in a while changing the needle. I liked being my father's DJ.

Years later, one weekend after the end of World War II, he came home with a carton box. In it was a small radio, the size of a big shoe box. It was made of dark brown Bakelite. The top front corner of the radio was diagonally sloped, covered with a glass plate, and on this were printed the

60

names of such cities as London, Paris, Moscow, Jerusalem, easily seen when the glass plate was backlit. The radio had two round knobs on the side, one for "on" and volume, the other for tuning to the different stations. We were fascinated with this marvel--a "Sierra" model made by Philips.

Of course, we listened most to the "Voice of Jerusalem," but I often wanted to hear from faraway places, the royal tone of "You are listening to the BBC from London," or the glorious Soviet Anthem followed by "This is Moscow," or the more jovial tenor of the "Voice of America." When I heard those faraway and foreign sounds inside our little apartment, I felt chills. This was an incomparable improbability—voices coming to us from places that seemed to me as far away as Mars or Jupiter.

One day as my mother was ironing shirts in the living room and I was sitting with my ear close to the radio, turning the dial to tune in to one of those stations, I heard "This was the news from The Voice of America." I stopped turning and listened.

My mother looked at me. "One day, Eitan, you will go to America," she said. At the time, in this tiny apartment on the outskirts of Jerusalem, the notion seemed improbable, but that radio voice freed my mind to imagine the possibility. "Everyone is rich in America," she said.

* * *

As 1947 progressed, the sentiment of the *Yishuv* turned increasingly anti-British as a result of the treatment and attitude of the British authorities toward the Jewish population and their treatment of the illegal *Olim*, the Holocaust survivors streaming in by ships arranged by the *Hagana*. The British blockaded *Eretz Israel* and intercepted those ships, sending the passengers back to live in exile in camps. The brutal treatment of these defenseless survivors who were seeking refuge in *Eretz Israel* from the graveyards back in Europe, created a political and moral storm everywhere around the world.

The failure of martial law forced His Majesty's government to bring the question of the future of Palestine to debate at the United Nations. Those debates raged for months. Finally, on November 29, 1947, the proposal for ending the British Mandate and the Partition plan of Palestine between Jews and Arabs was brought to a vote by the UN General Assembly. This was the first time that the idea of a Jewish State, a home country for world Jewry, had a chance of being created. The discussion and the vote were to be transmitted on *Kol Yerushalayim*, our local radio station.

In anticipation of this momentous occasion, my father wiped the radio until it was free of even a speck of dust. The UN had assembled at

Lake Success, a small town outside New York City. The seven hour time difference meant we would hear the event in Palestine beginning in late evening and lasting into the night. Our family sat around the radio in the living room as a reporter translated the discussion, but a few minutes into the program, I fell asleep. It was only later, listening to the recording of this fateful vote, that I heard what happened, heard each country's name called and its representative voicing that nation's vote. It went on for a long time.

Argentina – Yes

Brazil - Yes

France - Yes

Greece - No

Guatemala – Yes

Down the line of all the member nations, with each representative taking his time and offering his answer in his own language.

U.S.A. – Yes.

Soviet Union – Yes.

Yemen - No

Yugoslavia - Abstain

When the last vote was in, the results were announced: 33 - yes, 12 - no, 10 - abstained, 1 - not present (Thailand).

And the resolution was adopted. The mood of the Jews in Jerusalem exploded instantaneously—bursts of happiness, relief and joyful celebration. I woke that morning to the sound of cars outside honking, and from everywhere throughout the city the sound of singing, shouting, honking. People climbed on any moving vehicle; masses climbed atop trucks and busses. Even the British armored cars were loaded with Jewish riders. That morning I thought all our problems had been solved, that this would be the end of troubles and the beginning of peace.

That day we did not go to school, but our family sat down for breakfast.

"Yoska, I don't understand why you are not going to work," my mother said to my father.

"This is a great day," he said. "We are going to celebrate and be happy like everybody out there."

"I don't understand what the big celebration is about." She continued preparing food.

"We are going to have our own land," he said.

"Jerusalem is not included," she said. "We're not in the Jewish section of the Partition Plan."

"But the U.N. will take care of us here," my father insisted. He was in a good mood, enjoying the two sunny-side-up eggs my mother had placed in front of him. He dunked his bread into the yolks.

"Do you think Yudke will come back home now?" my mother asked.

"Every country has an army," he said.

"The *Palmach* will be the army?"

"It will," he said.

"How long will Yudke have to stay there?"

"We will find all this out soon."

Then in silence, he ate until at last he said, "Today we need to celebrate, come, Hedva, sit and eat with us."

She sat, and together we enjoyed breakfast as the noise outside began to diminish. My mother, never thin, scooped up her tomato and onion salad with lots of fresh bread. "The Arabs are not celebrating," she said, her mouth full.

"They have many countries. We are getting our first and only one," my father said.

As my mother wiped her plate with another slab of black country bread, capturing every morsel of tomato juice and oil, she shook her head. "I don't know," she said. "All my life I've lived through wars."

We sat in silence, the only sound the sipping of hot tea and the faraway celebrations that lasted well into the next night.

Four days later, on Tuesday, December 2nd, we heard a barrage of gunshots. Looking out the window, I saw a bus winding its way up the road to the Hadassa Hospital on Mount Scopus. It was driving through Sheikh Jarakh with flames shooting out of the rear windows. The gunshots continued, and the bus continued to struggle up the steep hill. After passing the village, the bus stopped. Some people ran out, put out the fire and the bus moved on.

That was the morning all my notions of peace evaporated, and the War of Independence began. Our street, *Shmuel Hanavi* , became the front line of the war in Jerusalem.

CHAPTER NINE

At first there were many days of calm, with only occasional shootings in our part of the city. In the week after the first shootings we celebrated Hanukah with school vacation, candle lighting, latkes and doughnut eating. All of this happened in a sea of calm, so easygoing, we even played in the street.

The peacefulness ended as December 1947 came to a close, after we returned to school. The shootings intensified, especially at night, and on the evening of December 31, I was tinkering with our radio when I stumbled upon a spot on the dial that stopped me. I thought I heard briefly *Hatikvah*, the anthem of the Jews in *Eretz-Israel*; it played for a second, and stopped. Slowly and with precision I attempted to find the dial again; the stations on our short wave had a narrow width, but finally I tuned in more clearly and heard the opening solo trumpet "Pa-Pa-Pa-Pa, Papapapa-paaa--", that portion of the anthem associated with the words: *"Od lo avdah Tikvatenu..."* (Our hope is still alive). And then again: "Pa-Pa-Pa-Pa-Papapapa-paaa..." repeated for a while and interrupted by a voice in Hebrew. "This is the voice of Hagana from Jerusalem."

I was always excited when I caught those foreign broadcasts, but this time there was no limit to my excitement –this was the sound of the coming of independence, for surely an independent country would have its own radio station; I knew this from my radio experience. The announcer continued to read the news in a low, deep voice: "A number of shooting incidents were reported today..." and I listened, rapt, as he described the shootings in Jerusalem as well as in other parts of the country. He went on to talk about David Ben Gurion and other leaders, and the broadcast ended with some statistics: "Our losses in the month of December in Jerusalem are as follows:

Civilians - 17 dead and 78 wounded.

Soldiers - 29 dead and 47 wounded."

Twenty minutes into the broadcast, the announcer offered this closing:

"This is the Voice of *Hagana* from Jerusalem. We will broadcast again tomorrow at the same time, same station."

From that night on, I had a sacred ritual—listening to the evening news broadcast.

In mid-January 1948, we stopped going to school because shootings had become a daily occurrence. The Arabs in Sheikh Jarakh and other Arab areas in proximity to our street had brought in sharpshooters who accurately shot any person they could target in their magnified sights. Among us kids, it was common knowledge that even though the Arabs were not good fighters, they were excellent sharpshooters.

One morning my mother told me we would be taking my sister Varda to *Tipat Halav* (Drop of Milk), the free clinic. It had been a brutal winter, cold and wet, and for a while Varda had a cold and a high temperature. My mother decided she needed a doctor. I had gone with my mother and Varda to *Tipat Halav* many times since Varda's birth; it was about a half mile down the street in the direction of the old city.

"What about the sharpshooters?" I asked.

"It's quiet today," my mother said. "Most of the way we'll be hidden by the houses on the other side of the street. We'll run through the open areas."

I carried the stroller down the steps, and my mother followed with Varda. We assembled at the bottom of the stairwell beside the metal doors that faced the Arab side of the street. These were punctured with bullet holes. I opened the door a crack and saw some people walking in the street, so I opened it all the way, and we stepped into the open. My mother rolled the stroller, and I followed as fast as I could. After 100 yards, hidden by buildings, we slowed to walking pace and continued through the city, arriving safely at the clinic where the doctor examined Varda.

On the way back home we saw more people walking in the streets, and I recognized David Gabbai with his family. For the previous few days I'd been thinking a lot about David. His home was in the *Shimon Hatzadik* area, the enclave in immediate proximity to Arab homes. One of those houses had been invaded by Arabs and set on fire. David was wearing an enormous backpack, and his father carried on his back a folded bedspread tied at four corners and filled with stuff. His mother was carrying his sister.

As we passed, I said hello, and I noticed how sad David looked.

"Who is this, David?" his mother asked him.

"Eitan, from school," he answered.

My mother looked at David and smiled. She recognized him for although I had never visited his home, he had played at our house many times. "How are you, David?" she asked.

"Fine," he said, though he did not look that way to me.

My mother and his parents looked eager to move along, but I wanted to talk to David. "Where are you going?" I asked.

"To my grandpa's house," he said. "We're moving in with him."

"For good?"

"No, only until the shooting stops."

"Who's going to be in your house?"

"Nobody."

I was stunned to silence; so David and his family, my schoolmate and near neighbor, had become almost overnight refugees.

"Eitan! Come, we have to run," my mother called to me, and as I ran to catch up with her, I called to David, "Come over and play some time."

When we reached our building, my mother said, "I'll carry the stroller upstairs and you walk with Varda." I took my sister by the hand, and we slowly climbed to the fourth floor.

"*Ima*, David is a refugee now," I told my mother.

"Yes, that's true."

"Can we invite him here?"

"His grandfather is a rich merchant," she said.

I knew David's grandfather was Sephardic, and I also knew that many of the richest people in the city were. Their families had immigrated to Palestine long before the first waves of Eastern European Zionists had. But I didn't care about that. I just wanted to play with David.

"He has a villa up in the Bukharim area," my mother continued. "David will like it better up there."

In January *Shimon Hatzadik* was vacated, all 25 homes abandoned by their Jewish owners. Before the exodus, five homes were blown up, and the nighttime explosions woke me. The Arabs were making sleeping through the night difficult, but I was glad we lived on the fourth floor. I thought we were safe—or safer at least than David's family had been. After days of shooting, I began to get used to the continuous ra-ta-ta-ta.

For two months we stayed home all day, never venturing outside. Every day Tsvi Hilman came to our apartment. His apartment was bigger than ours, but too many adults lived there. Some days, Ileana Hirshfeld, the girl from the ground floor apartment, joined us to play.

Once I asked her how it was living on the ground floor.

"It's good," she said. "We don't have to climb all these stairs."

"But aren't you afraid of the Arabs?"

"My father locks the front door," she said.

"But how do you get out when they shoot?"

"We have a back door."

"You go out next to the stinking outhouse?" I asked, appalled at the thought. I didn't envy her. Living on the fourth floor gave me confidence; from our window I could watch the war raging, but I thought it could not touch me.

On those winter days, evening came early. Tsvi, Ileana and I were on our knees on top of the bed at my bedroom window watching the occasional flares of light from exploding mortars and glowing illuminated bullet rounds bursting from a distant machine gun.

That's when we heard the boom, or felt it. We fell back onto the bed as the night sky became ablaze with light. Then we rose slowly and looked outside. The Arabs had exploded another one of the abandoned houses in the vacated area not far from us.

My mother came to the door and said. "Kids, it's time to go home."

My pals left. Varda and Shifra were in the living room listening to the news on the radio, for the daily calls to young men to join the defense forces in Jerusalem. "I'm glad Yudke is in the Galilee and Yoska is working in the camps," my mother said—her mantra in those days. "But it's hard to be in the war by myself with three children."

That night I could not fall asleep. I kept thinking about my brave brother, and I imagined him fighting the Arabs. I thought about my father, trying to envision the day when he could come back home to take care of us. And I thought about Ileana and wondered how she could sleep on the ground floor with the shooting going on all around.

Ra-ta-ta-ta. Some bullets hit the stone-wall outside. I heard pang-pang noises, but finally I fell asleep, into a dream about rescuing Ileana when the Arabs broke into her apartment and killed her parents. An enormous explosion ended my dream. Something big had hit our building. Lying in the darkness, I was certain the other half of our building, the half where Tsvi lived, had been demolished.

For one moment all was quiet and then suddenly neighbors began to swarm the hallway, talking, calling out, yelling. Everyone thought the others' apartments had exploded. A mortar had hit the wall of Hillman's apartment, but the damage was to the exterior only.

Everyone returned to bed, though I doubt anyone slept peacefully that night.

Over the next several days, some of our neighbors moved out of the building without even a goodbye. We would wake in the morning to discover this neighbor or that one was no longer there. Abandoned apartments remained vacant. Before long our building seemed to have lost its life. Still, I did not want to move. Where would we go? And when my father and Yudke returned, how would they find us?

CHAPTER TEN

On Monday, February 23, my Uncle Moshe came to stay with us. He was the only uncle we had. Usually when he visited, he would pick me up to hug me and to joke and play. This time when I opened the door for him, I saw his head covered with a white gauze bandage reddened by blood, and there was no playfulness about him.

After my mother left Lvov to move to Palestine, her brother, Moshe, stayed behind in the orphanage. All of the orphans had to learn a trade, and since he wanted to go to America, he chose to be trained as a jeweler; he thought that would be a good profession in rich America. But in the late 1920s, America closed its gates, and in letters to my mother, Moshe asked, begged and demanded that his sister arrange for his certificate and passage money to Palestine. Finally in early 1931 he had arrived.

My mother told me that he had come dressed in a suit, tie and hat and eager to begin work as a jeweler. Instead he fell into the open arms of my economically challenged family, and after staying for a while with my parents, he realized that this was not his Palestine dream. He went out on his own. From the pictures in our drawers, I knew he had held many jobs; he had worked as a *Gaphir*, a Jewish policeman in the British police, as a construction laborer, and as a clerk. But from my mother's complaints and discussions with my father about one more "last loan" uncle Moshe wanted, I knew that mostly he had been unemployed.

He was a most glorious unemployed person, and he inspired me to think that unemployment was not so bad. He dressed in the best suits, wore a tie, combed the few hairs left on his head, and covered these with a distinguished hat; then would waltz into the Café Europa. Sometimes when we passed, we saw him there sitting with beautiful women, sipping the iced coffee that cost as much as a family's weekly meals--at least that was my mother's estimate.

His visits to our home were a great injection of energy. He called me *Julik*, clown in Yiddish, and he played with great energy, roughing me up.

After a while those visits became rare to the point that we did not know exactly where in Jerusalem he lived or what he did for a living. But now he was here, with a bandage on his injured head.

We all stared, and when I looked at his hands to see what he had brought for me, I saw only more wounds.

"Moshe, what happened?" my mother asked.

"Don't ask, give me something to drink," he said.

She went to the kitchen to make some tea, and Moshe sat on the sofa with a big sigh. Although he was short of breath, he pulled out a Matossian pack of cigarettes and lit one.

"Julik," he called me over. "Come sit here."

The smell of his cigarettes was familiar, but all his usual energy, jokes, and stories, the teaching about physics he learned in the orphanage--the experiment about the frog leg that moved when it was touched by electricity--all that was gone.

"Julik," he said, still with warmth. "They are going to kill us."

"Who?"

"The Arabs are going to kill us," he said.

My mother returned to the living room carrying in one hand a glass of dark tea with a spoon in it and in the other a small bowl of tiny sugar cubes. "Oy vey, what happened to you?" she asked again. "Drink your tea."

"I was in Ben Yehuda," he began, but my mother interrupted with her lamentations in Yiddish. "Oy vey tzu mir! You always knew how to find trouble."

I was in awe. My uncle had been wounded in the war.

"But the British did it," I said.

"They just help the Arabs," he said, and he unfolded a newspaper and told the story.

On February 22, shortly after 6 a.m., a British military convoy had stopped at a checkpoint at the entry to Jerusalem, a checkpoint manned by Hagana. The convoy was composed of three military trucks and an armored communications vehicle, and when they were stopped, the British policeman in the turret of the armored car shouted and intimidated the guard, "Hey you miserable bastard, let us through!" When they did, the convoy continued on down Ben-Yehuda Street to the Vilenchuck Building. It was early, and only a few passersby saw the drivers of the trucks jump into the armored car that sped away. A half-hour later, a great explosion was heard all over the center of Jerusalem, and four multi-level buildings crumbled, while four others were partially demolished.

Hundreds rushed to help in the rescue operation and in fighting the fires, but the British commanders who arrived were chased away. Forty-nine people died, 140 were injured. The Jewish intelligence report and a statement issued by the government's press agency stated that four British Police deserters had used the stolen truck to pull off this terrorist attack. The men's names were Ross, White, Stephenson and Taylor [*The Palestine Post*].

Members of Etzel and the Lehi underground group flooded the streets and began to shoot at British cars. In return shots were fired, and this went on for most of the day. According to newspaper reports, shooting resulted in ten dead British soldiers, three dead Jews, and seven more people injured, and now one more injured man was in our living room, my Uncle Moshe.

Uncle Moshe drank his tea slowly, taking long sighs between sips.

"How did you get out?" my mother asked.

"I don't know," he said, nursing a sugar cube between his teeth.

"What do you mean you don't know, how can it be?"

"I was asleep in my room on the third floor and the next thing I know, I am walking in the street with blood dripping from my head."

"*Oy vey*," she sighed again.

"I can't figure out how I got down. I fell from the third floor, but maybe my mattress saved me," he said.

For the next two days my mother nursed Uncle Moshe's wounds, dressed his head with some black ointment and new bandages, and at the end of those two days, he gave me a special hug and departed again. We felt he was going back out to the war.

* * *

Tension between the Jews and the British in Jerusalem had reached a crescendo and few dared go into the streets; they had become doubly dangerous as both Arab snipers and British soldiers were shooting at us. Bombing and mortar explosions also became more frequent. Unlike previous isolated incidents, these constituted a continuous war that raged in our neighborhood, and most of the day I would stand at the window watching it.

One Friday morning toward the end of February, we woke to the usual barrage of bullets and mortars when we noticed a commotion out in the hallway. When my mother opened the door we saw Moshe Hillman and his brother-in-law moving stuff out of their apartment and down the stairs. Tsvika's family was moving out.

What would happen to us? I thought.

All this time my big brother, Yudke, had been out fighting with the special forces in the Galilee, and my father continued to work for the British. Through those days and nights of shootings and explosions, I had drawn confidence from the presence of our neighbors with the certainty that when we needed help we would be able to rely on Moshe Hillman who had connections both with the British authority by virtue of his job in the Palestine Electric Power Company and with the *Hagana*; he had been a coach and a member.

But now they, like so many other neighbors, were moving out, and the thought of my mother, Shifra, Varda and me staying behind all alone filled me with dread.

Berta Hillman saw the expression of horror on my mother's face. "Don't worry, Hedva," she tried to comfort her, "the *Hagana* fighters are moving to our apartment. They need it for the clear view of the area and to keep a watch on the Arabs at Sheikh Jarakh. They will protect you."

In truth, though, the presence of a *Haganah* station next door drew even more Arab attention and fire.

Three weeks after they moved in, the commander knocked on our door and told us he had arranged for us to move to a more secure location. Temporarily we would stay in a school located a little "inland," in a more populated area. He instructed us to take only some clothing since this would be a temporary move. He assured us we would be back soon and drove us as refugees to the Amal Trade school in the Bukharim neighborhood. We packed our things into a few bags, and he dropped us there and drove away.

CHAPTER ELEVEN

The man at the door of the Amal Technical School watched as we struggled carrying our load consisting of my school bag, neatly pressed clothes tied with a rope, crossing both ways and tied at the ends to create a handle, and a big bed cover filled with clothing, underwear and linens, tied at its four corners. He offered no help; he just stood there waiting and looking worried.

When we reached the door he opened it and instructed us to follow him.

"I don't know if I have space for all of you," he said as we followed him down the wide hallway with its high ceiling, void of life. Our footsteps created the only noise and echoed in that huge, empty space. On both sides of the hall were classrooms, doors open, no one there.

"You can't find space for us?" my mother asked.

"Not for all of you, but maybe," he said.

"Look at all this space," she pointed at the empty rooms around us.

"You can't stay in this space. I will show you what I have for you," he said.

We kept walking, all the way to the end of the hall where I could hear shooting in the distance. The school was on David Street, in a residential area, less than half a mile from our home but much higher up the hill. I thought we were far enough away from the Arabs, and I began to feel a little safer.

"You can leave your bags here," he said as he pulled a bundle of keys from his pocket and tried to open the last door in the hall. None of the keys worked, so he told us to wait as he climbed down a stairwell built onto the downhill side of the building. This end of the structure consisted of two stories, and the caretaker lived down below.

When the man returned, he unlocked the door and showed us into one small room. My mother stepped tentatively in and looked around, searching for a possible door to an additional room, but there was none.

"This is it?" she asked with a look of contempt.

"This is it."

"What about all those empty classrooms?"

"We need them."

"But school is out."

"Yes. You can be there during the day, but at night we use them for training the *Haganah* soldiers."

"*Oy vey*," my mother lamented.

"I arranged a bed and a Primus for cooking. I did what I could," he said. "I will try to help." For a long moment he looked at us, and he turned around and left.

I walked into the room. It was a storage room, small and rectangular with no windows. The only bed occupied two-thirds of the space, leaving a small area at the other end with one shelf on the wall with the Primus for cooking. When I opened the door it barely missed hitting the side of the bed. An electric bulb hung on a long wire from the high concrete ceiling. The walls and ceiling were both made of unfinished concrete.

"I am not staying here," Shifra said. "I'm going to stay with Carmela." She picked up her bag, and we watched as she walked away. Carmela's house was where she had stayed after she jumped the barbed wire.

My mother made up the bed and stored most of our stuff under it while I took Varda's hand and wandered around the classrooms, drawing on the blackboards with chalk that had been left behind. The view from the end of the hall was similar to our view from home, but Mount Scopus, Sheikh Jarakh and the Police Academy were farther away.

Varda and I stayed out of the room all day, waiting until bedtime to return. I didn't want to think about how we all would sleep on that single bed. But my mother had arranged things so that she and Varda lay one way, and I slept in the other direction, my feet in their faces, theirs in mine. Since I was exhausted, and for once heard no bullets flying or mortars exploding nearby, I slept deeply.

On the second week in our new home, I started to venture out to play in the street. One morning, I was playing with a few of the local kids when I heard someone call my name.

"Hey, Eitan, what are you doing here?" It was Meir Zinger, my friend from Tachkimoni School.

"I live here now," I said.

"Where?" He looked in the direction I pointed but naturally saw no home. I explained that I lived in the Amal School, that we had had to leave our home.

"So now you are refugees," he said.

"I guess so," I answered, though until then I hadn't exactly thought of us that way.

"Why don't you come to my home, and we'll play?" he said. He pointed down the same street, towards the east.

I left the game and walked with him to see where he lived. Although we had been good friends in school, the three months since I'd seen him had created a distance between us, and the fact that he had not experienced the war as I had, added to that sense. His home was far from the frontier, only a block from our temporary room at the school on David Street.

We entered through a metal gate into a wide courtyard surrounded by apartments. An old woman was standing at the stone water well in the center of the yard, pulling up with a rope a pail full of water. I followed Meir towards the end of the yard that rose from the front, which stood at ground level, to a second level in the back. Inside I saw the bedrooms in front, and we walked past these, down a step into the living room and the kitchen in the back, with a lovely view downhill. Meir showed me the large room, clean and with a big window, he shared with his brother.

My stomach tightened, not so much with envy, but the sight of Meir's home highlighted my own dire living conditions. When he showed me the book he was reading about Greek mythology, I realized how much time our family spent merely surviving.

I was amazed to see how normal his life had remained, and for the next couple of weeks, Meir and I spent a lot of time together, much of it in his house. His parents both worked full time as nurses in a hospital, and we were alone except when his older brother bothered us.

One day Meir asked, "Do you want to see a secret factory? You can't tell anyone." Of course I agreed.

We walked to the rocky open fields in the east, the area called *Tel Arza*, where Meir showed me a temporary structure in which welders were attaching steel armor to the cabins of trucks. We all knew about these armored trucks that took part in the convoys that brought supplies to our city.

From the beginning of the war, the Arabs had realized that only one road connected Jerusalem to the rest of the Jewish areas of the country, and they aimed to take over this road and cut off the city, cutting off the supply line. The Yishuv authority had organized convoys of trucks to carry men and weapons to defend Jerusalem. David Ben Gurion, the leader of the Yishuv in Palestine, believed that keeping Jerusalem from falling into Arab hands was essential to survival of Jews in *Eretz Israel*. He personally allocated resources to keep supplying the 100,000 Jews in the city, but the trucks were continuously being attacked, so they had to be equipped with armor. That's what I was seeing in this makeshift factory in *Tel Arza*. Meir and I watched all day, moving closer and closer, fascinated by the fireworks generated by the welding, and warmed by the feeling of Jewish might and hope.

At the end of the day, as we walked back towards his house, I asked Meir, "Do you want me to show you a secret place?" When he said yes, I took him to the Amal School and showed him one of the classrooms where a mix of young and middle aged men were learning how to use, take apart and put back together the submachine gun called the Sten.

"That's great," Meir whispered.

"Yeah," I said.

"Hey Eitan, where do you sleep?" he asked.

Until then I had shown no one the storage room we lived in. "Over there," I pointed reluctantly to our place.

"Show me," he said.

We walked into the room where my mother was frying something in the pan and Varda sat on the bed.

"*Ima*, this is Meir Zinger," I said.

"*Shalom*, Meir," she said.

He did not answer; he was still looking at the room. "That's it?" he asked.

"That's it," I said.

"And your sister?"

I hadn't wanted to show anyone where I lived because I knew I would have to answer questions, so I tried to dodge this one. "What about her?" I asked. I knew why he was asking, but I was seeking any delay I could find.

"Where is *her* bed?"

"Same one," I said.

He gazed at my mother who continued to cook on the Primus at the end of the bed. He said nothing more, until at last he said, "I have to go home now," and I showed him out.

Shootings, explosions, no school, dislocation and family separation left its profound impact on each of us, and my three-year-old sister, Varda, was no exception. She had begun to wet our communal bed. My mother placed a piece of rubberized sheet to protect the mattress, but some mornings when I woke my pajamas were wet and smelly, and one night Varda had diarrhea, which we discovered only in the morning. I was drenched.

My mother led us to the school bathroom which we usually used, and she placed each of us in a sink and washed us. It was the beginning of spring, but I'll never forget how brutally cold the water felt that morning.

I had been spending as much time away from our room as possible, often at Meir's house. That Saturday when I arrived at his home, he asked me why I hadn't visited the day before.

"I didn't feel well," I told him.

"What was wrong?" he asked.

I didn't want to tell him about Varda, but he was a good friend, and I had to unload. When I told him the story, he laughed so hard and so loudly, I immediately regretted telling him.

"What is it?" Meir's mother called from the kitchen.

"Say it's nothing," I begged him. "Please, don't tell her."

"Don't worry so much," he said. He walked to the kitchen, still laughing, to tell his mother about Varda's problem. They both returned, and although he was laughing, his mother's face looked serious. "Eitan, how would you like to live with us for a while?" Mrs. Zinger asked.

"Okay," I said, leaping at the opportunity.

"But, do you think your mother wouldn't mind?" she asked. "Maybe it's best if we go together to ask her."

I quickly agreed.

* * *

After my mother thanked Mrs. Zinger, I gathered some of my clothes and moved to live with Meir and his family, though right from the start, I encountered a terrible problem.

Meir's mother told us to take a bath, and as we were undressing, she came in. I stopped undressing, but Meir had already climbed into the tub.

"Eitan," she said, "come on, get in."

"He's shy," Meir said. "He doesn't want you to see him naked."

"Come on, Eitan," She said, "I see naked kids and grown men in the hospital every day. I'm a nurse." I undressed and climbed into the tub. Immediately I relaxed. I hadn't had a warm bath for three months.

It felt like heaven.

By the end of March, the road to Jerusalem had been conquered by Arab forces. Supply convoys could not break through, and food became more and more scarce. Even before this, the Arabs had blasted the water pumping stations that pumped drinking water up the mountain into Jerusalem's system. For years the supply of water to Jerusalem had been intermittent and had suffered from technical problems. As a result, every home was equipped with a reserve water tank to bridge the supply gaps, but by the end of March, even that was gone. Now water was available only from ancient wells, part of a cistern system spread around the city; some genius in charge had foreseen the possibility of shortage and had filled the underground system just before the war.

"Eitan," Meir said one day, "when are we going to eat one more of those cakes your mother makes?"

My mother was a good cook. She liked to eat well and had good taste, but her greatest virtue was that she could create amazing fare from the simplest and cheapest ingredients. She made fried cakes from weeds, something she had learned years earlier from Persian friends. "She'll make more," I said, "but we need to collect more of 'Bread of Birds' leaves."

There were plenty of rocky open fields in the neighborhood, and this weed, that the Arabs called *Hoobeizah*, grew everywhere. It had a tiny, quarter inch fruit in its center that the birds (and kids) liked, hence its name. Every morning Meir and I rushed to cut and collect these round leaves to give to my mother. She would use the little margarine she could find to fry our *Hoobeziah* cakes, and these we shared with the Zinger family. They were especially delicious given the dwindling supplies of other food.

In April, after some fierce battles, a convoy finally made its way to Jerusalem. One morning walking out of Meir's house, a young man standing at the back of the Super White truck loaded with cartons and parked across the street at a storage facility called to us. "Boys, come here a minute. We need your help."

All that day Meir and I helped to unload boxes of dry pasta, and as payment the young man gave us two boxes each. That was my first paying job, and I was thrilled. Not only had I helped with the war effort, I was able to bring home food we ate for the next few days.

On Friday, April 9th 1948, I woke up at Meir's house to find his mother in a cheerful mood. It was a beautiful spring morning, the start of the weekend, and cheered by her mood, I decided I would visit my mother and Varda at the Amal school.

When I arrived, Varda jumped on me and my mother gave me a big hug and said, "I missed you. I'm so glad you came."

"Me too," I said.

You're a big boy now," she said, looking me up and down.

"I know."

"How do you feel on this special day?" she asked.

"What's special?" I asked.

"You are ten years old today," she said.

I had forgotten it was my birthday since it was not yet Passover. That year had an extra *Adar* month as the Hebrew calendar had every fourth year; it's called a Pregnant Year in Hebrew; Passover would be later in April.

But our family never celebrated birthdays; in fact we seldom had celebrations of any kind. We never gave birthday gifts. A birthday was just a matter of fact, a date we mentioned, sometime, and for most of that relatively quiet day, I entertained my sister. Because there were few shootings or bomb blasts, I took her for a walk outside, but as we were returning to the Amal School, we heard cars honking and people shouting at the end of the street.

Seconds later three pickup trucks with young men standing and singing the *Etzel* anthem and raising their fists drove past us.

El, El, Israel
Two banks to River Jordan
This one's ours,
And that - as well

They sang, and I noticed in one truck a few Arab men in their *Kaffiyehs* tied to the side railing. Seconds later the noisy trucks disappeared.

Outside the school entry a group of *Haganah* guys stood in a huddle, deep in argument. Later that evening we learned that the guys on the trucks were returning from a battle at the Arab village of Dir Yasseen, located at the western edge of the city. That evening, in Meir's home, his parents were gloomy. Because they worked in the hospital each day, they were good sources of information about the war, so I listened closely to their conversation.

"I can't believe the Jews would do that," Meir's mother said.

"We don't know exactly what happened," his father said.

"Yes we do. I saw all these women in the emergency room," she said.

"This is war. They're killing us," he said.

"But we are Jews. We are not them," she said.

"It was a bad battle. They got caught in the middle," he said.

"But, so many women and children?"

"Twenty eight of our young guys died."

"I still can't believe it," she sighed.

The story of what happened in Dir Yasseen created an earthquake in the psyche of both Jews and Arabs, not only in Jerusalem, but in Palestine and around the world. For years rumors about what had actually happened swirled; few knew the details. Slowly, over the years, the truth emerged—or at least a version of the truth.

The Arab inhabitants of Dir Yasseen, a village at the western edge of Jerusalem, had decided to stay out of the war. In January 1948, they entered an agreement with the Jewish commanders of *Haganah*, agreeing to refrain from attacks, to keep any Arab forces out of the village and to exchange intelligence. For many months the Dir Yasseen villagers adhered to most of these conditions.

As the war continued and spring came to the land, the *Etzel* and *Lehy* organizations became less relevant; their military activity in Jerusalem diminished. That fateful night, April 8/9, their commanders decided to make a splash by attacking the non-combatant Arab village. One unit came with a pickup truck on which a loudspeaker was installed; the intention was to warn the villagers to avoid resistance and to surrender peacefully. Unfortunately at the entrance to the village, the truck hit an open ditch, and the loudspeaker equipment was destroyed. The villagers never heard a warning.

When they attacked, they encountered unexpectedly strong resistance, and most of the attacking commanders were killed in the first wave of the battle. Many units were untrained, and chaos ensued. A few hours later, after taking heavy casualties, the *Etzel* and *Lehy* fighters went on a rampage, shooting indiscriminately into homes, demolishing other homes with dynamite, killing their inhabitants, many of whom were women and children. That night and day 254 Arabs were killed.

As word of what happened spread, most Jerusalemites felt waves of contempt, shame and disgust at the killing of innocents, and at once the desecration of the humanity and honor of the Jewish fighter. Meir's parents were no exceptions; the mood in the house was even more somber than usual.

The next week, my mother and I walked out of the school carrying a couple of empty bags each. We were going back to our home on Prophet Samuel Street to get more clothes, underwear and other miscellany. My mother had wanted these things for a long time, but fierce fighting had prevented it. Now the day was relatively quiet, and most of all she wanted Varda's stroller.

The Buhkarim market was deserted except for two or three store owners cleaning or fixing their doors with heavier locks. We walked down the street leading to *Beit Cadoori*, our old apartment building. The descending street ended into an open field behind the building, and our old neighborhood was quiet. We saw no people or cars, nothing moved.

The frightening silence disturbed my mother.

"We will now run through the field," she said, "and we'll enter from the back gate."

"Okay," I agreed.

We ran. My mother, although heavy, ran fast, and when we reached the middle of the field, we heard a blast, followed by the ratcheting noise of machineguns and the whoosh of flying bullets. Instinctively we fell to the ground, lying on our stomachs, our faces touching the dirt. We were breathing hard, and my mother whispered, "Come closer to me."

I moved closer, and she tried to cover me with her body, but she managed to cover only my left side. Bullets were flying past, and they were close. I thought I heard the drumming of a machine gun from our own building. Not far from us I saw bullets hitting the ground.

We had nowhere to hide, and I thought we were going to die right there. I wanted to tell my mother we should crawl, but I could not bring myself to speak.

After ten eternal minutes there was a lull.

"Let's run now," my mother said.

When we reached the back gate, the barrage of shots, louder and faster, began again, but now we realized our big mistake. The bullets that were coming through the front entry of the building exited through the back, spraying the small backyard. My mother, holding my hand tightly, pulled me to the side and pushed both of us into the outhouse. She closed the dilapidated wooden door as if it could provide any protection. We could hear the pinging of bullets hitting walls and metal doors. I breathed a long sigh of relief. The latrine smelled worse than anything I ever smelled, but at least I felt safe.

There was a lull in fighting noise, but my mother held me. She did not want to leave, and for an hour we stood there, as the shooting started and stopped again and again. I began to think we would die suffocated, by the stench.

Finally, when it had been quiet for a while, we walked out, dashed through the entry hall, and climbed the stairs. The metal-framed windows in the stairwell between floors were mostly shattered.

Once we reached the fourth floor, my mother began to work the lock when the door across the hall suddenly opened, and a man asked, "What are you doing here?"

"We live here," my mother said.

"What?" he asked in disbelief, his hand reaching for his gun tucked under his belt.

"This is our apartment," my mother said.

Ra, ta, ta, ta… We heard the machine guns overhead, sounding like small blasts in the hallway.

When he noticed we ducked as the shooting began, he said, "It's okay, it's only the Spandau machine gun on the roof."

"Ours?" my mother asked.

"Yes, we have a post on the roof," he said. "Who are you?"

My mother introduced us, and he admonished us. "I thought you were looters," he said. "You shouldn't be here." When she tried to explain that we had only come to get our things, I could see from his expression that he did not believe her.

"Who was your neighbor?" He pointed to the door he had exited.

"The Hillmans. Do you know Moshe Hillman?"

"Sure I know Moshe," he said. "I work with him at the Electric Power Company. He was just here." I saw him relax a little, but he went on to explain there was a problem. The Arabs had just ambushed a convoy on the way to the Hadassah Hospital. Moshe had gone to ask the British to help; that was the battle we had heard.

"You must call me before you leave," he cautioned us. "You may have to leave in the dark." He turned to go back into Hillman's apartment.

"And who are you?" my mother asked.

"Tubiansky," he said, "Misha Tubiansky."

We said goodbye and entered our apartment, and as my mother began to gather things, I stood at the window, watching the action on the road at Sheikh Jarakh.

After she rounded up everything she wanted, my mother crossed the hall to tell Tubiansky we were ready to leave. He and the others explained that we would have to wait, that they would let us know when it was a good time.

We walked back into the apartment and stood at the window watching the road to Sheikh Jarakh where the convoy of trucks, busses and ambulances were not moving. They were too far away to see anything clearly, but I did see some armored cars coming and going.

Intermittently the machine gun above us rattled out a deafening ra-ta-ta-ta…, and we

saw *Kaffiyehed* Arabs converging in the vicinity of the convoy, shooting weapons of all kinds.

Three hours later, some vehicles caught fire, and the shooting subsided. By mid-afternoon it was quiet, and a young soldier knocked on our door to let us know we could leave. He walked with us all the way to the Bukharim market where he left us to continue on our way back to the school, now our home.

Varda was happy to see us, for the old school caretaker's wife had been babysitting her, and she began at once to complain that she had promised just an hour and now she had had to spend all day. My mother was exhausted, too tired to argue. When I returned to Meir's, I found his parents glued to the radio, listening to the trumpeting sound of *Hatikva*.

"This is the voice of *Haganah* from Jerusalem," the broadcast started. "Today, April 13, 1948, a convoy, including two ambulances, two busses and three trucks carrying supplies, nurses and doctors to Hadassah Hospital on Mount Scopus was ambushed at the Arab stronghold of Sheikh Jarakh…"

The newscast went on to explain that The British authority who had promised to protect the convoy, stood by and took no action, allowing the murderers a free hand. Of the 112 passengers, 78 were killed and 24 wounded, and among the dead was the head of the hospital, the world-renowned Dr. Yassky.

"May their memories be blessed," the announcer finished, lauding the heroic actions of our people.

For a few minutes after the report ended, Meir, his brother, parents and I, sat quietly. That was the first evening I began to think we might lose the war, and that we all might die.

"I'm sure the Brits let the Arabs kill our people as a revenge for Dir Yasseen," Meir's mother said at last.

My refuge at Zinger's home.

CHAPTER TWELVE

One month later, on May 14, 1948, in Tel Aviv, Ben Gurion declared the establishment of the new independent "State of Israel" with Jerusalem as its capital. Seven Arab countries declared war on Israel, each vying to attack Jerusalem and hoping to conquer it and control the Holy City. Among them they divided and selected sectors to attack. Jerusalem was attacked from the north by the Iraqis, then from the south by the Egyptians and from the east by the Legion Army of Transjordan.

Two days later, on May 16, we woke to the sound of blasts exploding nearby. For an hour heavy artillery shelled the neighborhood, and Meir's parents stayed home. A second barrage started at noon and lasted an hour. We huddled in the apartment, startled at the sound of each explosion and watched the window – expecting shrapnel to penetrate any moment. The ensuing quiet was even scarier since we had no idea when the next attack would begin.

Meir's mother said, "I think, Eitan, it's better now for you to be with your mother."

I wanted very much to be with my mother and sister to make sure they were all right, but I hated to give up the warmth and normalcy I felt in Meir's home. Still, I packed my bag and ran back to the school where Varda was crying and my mother was busy talking to a man in khaki. I assumed he was a *Haganah* official.

"How can you let us die in this storage room?" my mother was complaining.

"I understand the problem. It's the war," he said.

"But we're pioneers. We landed here in '27."

"There are a lot of refugees. It's a problem," he said.

"My husband is away because of the siege and my son fights in the Galilee."

"I understand," he said.

"Please help us find another arrangement," she begged.

"I will try, Hedva. I'll see what I can do."

"Where can I find you?"

"I'll be here tomorrow," he said. "*Shalom.*"

At night I rolled a blanket on the floor of one of the classrooms. I wouldn't sleep in the communal bed again. The shelling continued, though I still played outside with local kids. Now we were collecting shrapnel and playing games with them; the goal was to collect the most, those with the most unusual shapes. This fad lasted a few days, but as the shells continued to explode around us and shrapnel became more plentiful, its value vanished.

On May 19, the shelling grew closer and more frequent. The Arab Legion, Transjordan's army that was trained, led and supplied by the British military, placed a number of heavy cannons at Nabi Samuel, an Arab village strategically located on a mountain top. These long range "Twenty Five Pounder" cannons, named after the shell's weight, relentlessly pounded the northern parts of the city – our neighborhood. The night before, after *Etzel* units capitulated with little resistance, the Arab Legion had recaptured some areas previously held by our forces, including the Police Academy. They also re-occupied Sheikh Jarakh and captured portions of Prophet Samuel, before the *Haganah* pushed them back.

The war was following us, closer to the Bukharim area next to the Amal School, and my mother's survival instincts kicked in. She decided we had to move to a more secure area. That evening she again began to pester the man in khaki until at last he scribbled a few words on an official paper and gave it to her. That night, the Jordanian Legion made a big military push. After I rolled in my blanket onto the classroom floor and began to fall asleep, we heard people shouting in the street and we ran outside to look.

"They are going to slaughter us all," a guy shouted.

The street was filling up with people in pajamas rushing out of neighboring homes and apartments. A group of *Etzelnicks* who minutes earlier had been chased from their posts by the Jordanians were telling stories. "They're unstoppable," one man said, "a formidable force."

When we finally went back inside, I couldn't sleep.

Early the next morning we left our storage room. My mother locked it behind us and said, "We're going to a new place."

"Don't we take our stuff?" I asked.

"No. I'll come back for it," she said.

"Where is the place?" I asked.

"In the center of town."

"Close to where?" I insisted.

"I don't exactly know. Near Ben Yehuda Street."

This news delighted me. We had never lived in such a respected area. Ben Yehuda Street was where the wealthier Jerusalemites lived, or at least that's what I thought. My mother and I took turns pushing Varda's stroller, and as we walked we listened to the shelling far behind us. Streets were deserted, filled with potholes, and shrapnel was spread everywhere, like gravel.

I was hungry. We hadn't eaten much for the last few days, and now there was rationing, two slices of bread, dried egg powder and a piece of dried fish for each person per day.

Pushing the stroller up Chancellor Street slowed us to a crawl. Feeling weak, my mother and I pushed together until we reached the top. Downhill to the intersection of Jaffa and King George Streets was easy, but I was stunned to find the center of Jerusalem deserted. It was mid-morning when we turned from King George Street into Betsatel Street and arrived at a double metal gate. "This is the place," my mother said.

I looked up. The gate was the only opening in an eight foot high stone wall built straight up from the narrow asphalt sidewalk. The structure was old, with moss growing in the cracks and weeds wending up from the base of the wall where it met the sidewalk. The sign above the rusty gate said "The Betsalel Museum, Jerusalem."

"Are we going to live in a museum?" I asked.

"I think so," my mother said.

"But what if people visit?" I asked.

"Nonsense, who will visit with all the artillery shelling?" She was looking at the sign and back at the note.

"Hold the stroller," she said. Straightening up, she looked at her dress and knocked on the gate. No one answered, and after a while, she knocked again. A minute went by. She opened her purse, took out a key and knocked on the gate with the key. At last it opened, revealing an old man, his back bent and his gray hair in disarray. He clearly had not shaved for a while.

"I am Hedva Makogon," my mother said.

"*Vous?*" he asked in Yiddish.

She began to speak with him in Yiddish, but I could see the conversation was not going well. He cupped his hand behind his ear to focus it and asked repeatedly "*Vous zogst tee?*" What did you say? At last she handed him the note and pointed to the name on the bottom.

"*Noo goot, Kumt arein,*" he said, finally inviting us inside and locking the gate behind us.

Inside was a beautiful little garden, paved with stone walkways interwoven with a few small landscaped patches. There were raised planters and two structures, all built of stone.

We followed the old man into his home where he introduced us to his wife. I thought they must be at least 80 years old, they seemed so ancient.

They gave us a long room in which some pieces of art and some antiques were stored to one side, leaving a large open area in which two beds were placed. As I sat on the edge of the bed, exhausted, I missed my father and brother, and I wished Shifra knew where we were and would come to visit. But at least I finally had a bed to myself.

The siege of Jerusalem that had begun in January with the attacks on the convoy supply lines had, by April, become complete.

Dov Yoseph, a Canadian who had immigrated to Israel a few years earlier was appointed chief of administration and managed the rations to ensure there would be an equal distribution of the limited supplies of food to everyone. By May 20, our individual daily ration was reduced to 250 grams (8 ounces) of food per person, providing 900 calories a day, only 200 calories more than the daily ration in the Nazi concentration camp Bergen Belsen in World War II.

The next morning I went with my mother to look for food, our first foray into the new area. The streets were empty, and I was hungry, but I was enjoying this outing, for here and there we saw signs of life, especially near the food stores and the cafes and restaurants that somehow had managed to secure food for their customers.

We stopped at the store to get our rations both for us and the museum keeper and his wife. As we passed by Cafe Vienna, a young man called to us, "Hey Giveret, do you want some sardines?"

During the war compassion was scarce; most people lived each for himself, but that day, hungry as I was, I felt a wave of warmth coming from this young man. Sardines. My saliva instantly began to flow. "How much?" my mother asked.

"Two cigarettes for a can," he said.

"I don't smoke."

"You have three dollars lady?" he asked.

When she didn't answer, my heart contracted and my hopes collapsed. "Come Eitan," she said, "the rich can always have plenty of food." We walked away and after a while she added, "Even in the worst days of war."

When we reached King George Street we heard a familiar sound. The one good thing about 25-pound cannon shells about to explode is that they offer a warning, albeit short.

Whooooooo. The shriek of the shell in its final flight sounds like the down cycle of a fire engine siren, then silence for a couple of seconds and BOOM, the blast.

Hearing the shriek, I knew a shell was about to explode, but I didn't know where exactly. The stores lining Ben Yehuda Street were closed. A man ran across the deserted street into an open entry to a building, and we followed him.

The explosion up the street was followed shortly by another whooooooo, then silence, then the blast. The barrage of artillery shells and explosions continued.

I looked at the man hiding with us behind the flight of stairs and recognized him. How could he not recognize us? I wondered. He stared at us, then started a conversation, "Do you live around here?"

"No, we are refugees," my mother said, and suddenly she too recognized him. "Hey, you are Tubiansky!"

"Have we met?" he asked.

"Sure. You were at Hillman's apartment."

"Oh yes, yes I remember, the day of the Hadassah convoy."

"Do you live in this neighborhood?" my mother asked.

"No, my office is nearby. I am now in charge of the Air Force office."

"We have Air Force in Jerusalem?" My mother was surprised, and I could see she was suspicious. She thought he must be crazy, but I was encouraged. I thought now we would show them.

"Well, we have landing strips," he said.

"Have any airplanes landed here already?"

"Yes. Only Primus types so far," he said. I did not know what he was talking about. At the time all I knew was that a Primus was a cooking device though later I learned that the light airplanes were nicknamed Primus because the sound they made was similar to the sound of the cooker.

After thirty minutes, the barrage of shells stopped, and Tubiansky looked at me and said, "I have a son like you. I think we can go now." We followed him out of our hiding shelter to the street.

The street was now full of new potholes. Pieces of broken pavement and shrapnel were scattered everywhere. Some storefronts were shattered, and the smell of burnt dynamite filled the air. A dog limped along the sidewalk across the street searching for food. He was bleeding, leaving bloody paw prints from his wounded hind leg. His ribs protruded from his dirty skin.

"Can we take him home?" I asked my mother.

She looked at me as if I were out of my mind. "Eitan," she said, "we have no home. And no food."

Day and night heavy artillery shells fell over the city. The old couple asked us to move in with them because the old lady was frightened. They gave us the living room, and we moved our beds. To help his wife relax, the old man told her that some of the explosions she heard were from our cannons shelling the Arabs.

At night I could not fall asleep because after every blast, all day and all night, she would turn and ask, *"Dos is unzere oder yenems,"* wanting to know if the blast had been our shot or the Arabs, and in random order, the museum keeper would answer "ours" or "theirs," though nothing calmed her. Days went by, and all I could think about was how hungry I was.

One day my mother went out and returned with our rations which now consisted of two slices of bread and dried egg powder only. "I am going to make *Jarkoi* for everybody," she declared. "I bought a piece of lamb from one of the profiteers out there."

When she served us that evening, I looked at the lamb in the middle of a pool of brown gravy on my plate, watching it for a while without touching it in order to extend the pleasure. Varda said it stank, and indeed it was spoiled. But we all ate it, savoring every bit and using our half slice of bread to wipe our plates dry.

In the last days of May and the beginning of June, the Arab artillery fire intensified. We could not go out for food, and when we did go outside, the streets were deserted. Rumors began to circulate about the enormous casualty numbers and who had been killed. Death notices were posted on the electric power poles with pictures of the young soldiers, men and women, killed in action. One of them was the Chief City Administrator, Dov Yoseph's daughter.

On Saturday, June 5, the news included the announcement by Dov Yoseph that the rations would be cut yet again to 150 grams (5 ounces) of bread and some beans. On June 8, we got only two matzos. I walked outside to the garden behind the museum. A young relative of the museum caretakers had seeded some onions in a planter, and now they were sprouting, long and green. I cut and ate all the newly grown green onions. For the last month, I had been preoccupied with only two concerns -- food and surviving the shells.

A few minutes after 10 a.m. on Friday, June 11, 1948, the shelling stopped. An eerie silence replaced the constant bombardment, and my mother hesitantly cracked open the front gate. We saw some people in the street.

"It's a cease fire!" a woman shouted.

We walked outside and saw more people coming out of their shelters, beginning to fill the streets. No one looked happy. Everyone was simply searching for food and water.

That evening the news described the cease fire agreement. It would last for 30 days; so far, the announcers said, both sides were keeping to the agreement.

Still, I had no idea what this would mean for us. I don't think my mother knew either, though Shifra returned to stay with us, and she told us about her time away.

It turned out she had not stayed with her friend. When she had arrived there, that family would not host her; a neighbor, a Persian family whom Shifra had never met, took her in for the duration of the war. When the Cease Fire started, Shifra returned to the Amal School where she had last seen us, and it was there she learned that we were at the Betzalel Museum.

By Saturday rumors were flying all over the city, first, that a new road was open, a temporary road built in the last two weeks called the Burma Road, and second, that thousands of families were fleeing Jerusalem, leaving their apartments and most of their belongings behind. The siege had kept everybody from leaving, but by then many families had decided they had had enough. They left with no fanfare, few goodbyes, as quietly as possible to avoid possible government intervention and public criticism. In only a few days, approximately 30,000, or 30 percent of the population, left the city.

On Monday, two days into the truce, my father made it back home. He found us easily in the smaller, remaining population. Rent on the abandoned apartments was next to nothing; only a few refugee families like ours were looking for places to live. That is how my parents were able to rent an apartment in a good area, on Tsfania Street.

Three days into the truce we moved into the nicest apartment I had ever lived in with both my parents and both sisters. There were some advantages to war, I thought.

* * *

Late one night I woke to a commotion in the living room and saw my parents and Shifra running outside. There was Yudke, my hero brother, arriving in a big truck. He unloaded two sacks full of food, mainly fruit and vegetables, and all of us swarmed around him, exploding with pride for my khaki-clad brother with the submachine gun hanging from his shoulder.

Over tea and fruit, my mother tried to get him to tell us of his whereabouts and actions during the past 10 months; we hadn't heard a word from him in all that time.

My mother and father wept as they heard about the battles in the Galilee, especially a particularly vicious battle at a place named Malckia. Yudke had been wounded there and taken to a hospital for a lengthy stay.

For a couple of evenings, we all discussed the possibility of leaving Jerusalem and the prospect of moving to Tel Aviv. My mother did not need a lot of convincing. And on the news we listened to the summary of casualties since the beginning of the war:

Civilians - 204 dead, 1,018 wounded

Soldiers - 248 dead, 504 wounded

Of the total force in Jerusalem, 3,000 soldiers, approximately 25% were hurt.

On the last day of June 1948, we left our enjoyable new apartment to board a pickup truck. The driver helped us load a few belongings. My mother and Varda sat in the cabin next to the driver. Shifra and I sat on and among the packages in the bed of the truck. No one wore a seatbelt. The driver instructed us to hold on tight.

Rumor had it that the authorities would allow no more people to leave the city, but my father and Yudke were already back in Tel Aviv by then, and so we could claim family reunion rights. In addition, my mother dressed us in khaki and gave me clear instructions. "If someone stops us on the way, tell them you're a soldier."

I thought she was crazy and I shook with anxiety. How could a 10-year-old boy convince anyone he was a soldier?

As we departed the city, I felt sad and sorry to leave my home, my friends, the places I knew so well, but I also felt elated, filled with the wonderful feeling of freedom and unlimited future possibilities, the sense of escaping a jail in which the jailers were intent on killing us--by bombs, by thirst, by hunger, by breaking our spirit.

Here we were, showing them they would not succeed.

The pick-up truck was low, and Shifra and I leaned back against the packaged stuff, inhaling the fresh air. We watched the black road spooling out away from us as we drove down the mountain. We could not stop looking at the magnificent view of Jerusalem, built on a mountaintop, until slowly the stone city with its church and mosque towers disappeared and all we could see was the canyon with its pine forested hills rising on either side of us.

Still, even here we saw evidence of war, the damaged pumping station, which had once supplied water for all of Jerusalem, had been blasted. Everywhere around us we saw charred remains of trucks partially armored, part of the supply convoys that had not made it up to the city. This displayed vividly what had caused our thirst and hunger, our isolation.

At the end of the long downward sloping road we arrived at "Bab el Wad," the Arabic name for the "Gate of the Canyon." Numerous battles had been fought as both sides tried to keep it under their control, but it was now in Jewish hands. Soldiers of the new Israel Defense Force were directing the traffic, diverting it to the new Burma dirt road.

The Burma Road was the idea of an American General named David Marcus, nicknamed Mickey Stone, who volunteered to help the new country's army. Following numerous failed attempts to open the road to Jerusalem by battling the Arab Legion and trying to conquer Latrun, a strategic stronghold on the road, he had suggested building a new road circumventing that enemy stronghold. Ben Gurion gave him the job and the bulldozers, and within 10 days the road had opened.

It was a primitive dirt road with some very steep sections. Our pickup struggled to negotiate the rocky slope, but when we were unsuccessful, my euphoria began to evaporate, replaced by the thought that we might have to return. Soon the soldiers who needed to keep the narrow road open, arranged for a bulldozer, which pulled our pickup up the slope while we walked to the top of the hill.

We jumped back into the truck and rolled toward Tel Aviv.

"Where are we going to live?" I asked Shifra.

"I don't know," she said.

"Will we go back to school?"

"Sure."

"Will I have to repeat fifth grade?"

"I don't think so."

"Are *Aba* and Yudke going to live with us?"

"Maybe."

We were quiet for a while, my thoughts running between Jerusalem, my friends, our old neighbors and the unknown awaiting us in our new life in Tel Aviv.

"It will be better than Jerusalem," Shifra said, reading my mind.

Our refuge at the Bezalel Museum.

CHAPTER THIRTEEN

From my vantage point in the back of the truck rolling into Tel Aviv, I could tell at once that life as we knew it was going to change.

Driving along the store-lined Allenby Street, I stared at the large store windows bursting with merchandise. This place was a world away from the city I knew. These stores attracted people in droves—men, women and children filled the wide sidewalks that were paved not with the familiar tarred asphalt but with large pavers. I didn't see a single gown-wearing monk or a single Arab in a *Kaffiyeh*.

The truck turned on a downward sloping street, and I read the street sign as we drove past: King George Street, and then, one minute later, we turned onto Dizingoff Street. Before long we drove past the round Dizingoff square area with its fountain shooting water into the air. I was amazed by the trees that lined these wide streets and by the bright green hedges and beautifully landscaped lawns.

The truck stopped for people crossing the street. Some were half naked, wearing only swim suits. Some of the kids held black inner tubes, and others licked popsicles or ate corn on the cob. I looked into their faces and saw none of the angst or fear I'd become accustomed to seeing on the faces of Jerusalemites. I could hear the sound of the Mediterranean waves breaking on the nearby beach and could smell the salt aerosoling into the air.

My hopes that my father had found us a nice place to live—perhaps a villa by the sea or at least a big apartment in one of the high buildings with a view of the Mediterranean—rose as I inhaled that scent. We proceeded along wide Dizingoff Street, then turned right onto Nordau Boulevard and another immediate right onto Mandelstam Street. Each street had been named after a modern Zionist politician. Halfway down Mandelstam we stopped in front of a three story apartment building, and my mother, holding Varda, stepped out of the front cabin. "Wait here," she said.

Shifra and I stayed in the truck, and I watched my mother enter the front yard of the building I remembered from our last visit here, five years earlier. The trees and bushes surrounding the building had grown much taller and now reached all the way to the top of the building, shading the balconies. The sidewalk next to the building was laid with large square pavers, but the road was unpaved, and across the street was a vast open lot covered with sand. I so hoped we were going to get a place of our own.

After a little while my mother came out with my father and their friend, Yashka Lituchi. Shifra and I jumped out of the truck and ran to hug my father, competing for a place on his body to cling to. He looked even better than I had pictured him in my mind all during the war. He was tall with a full head of hair, parted on the left. He wore khaki shorts, brown shoes, and his khaki socks came to just below his knees, just the way I remembered him wearing them.

"Ok kids, lets unload our stuff from the truck," he said after we had exchanged hugs, and in that moment all the anxiety and longing I had felt for so long, vanished. I felt as if we had never been apart.

Yashka helped my father carry the heavier items, as we unloaded the truck, and as I walked into the small entry hall, Yashka said, "Come in, come in." I followed Shifra and Yashka through a narrow corridor to the first bedroom. It had a bed along one wall and was full with our bags and boxes. My father explained that we would be staying for a while with Yashka and his wife and daughter, but I was busily trying to figure where I would sleep. I walked down the hallway to the other, larger bedroom with its big bed with two nightstands. On one of them I saw, in a slanted frame, photographs of Yashka, his wife and daughter, all looking much younger. I walked on to the end of the corridor where there was a living room opening onto a porch that led to the backyard; the family had use of this backyard since the apartment was on the ground floor.

But that was all, and I couldn't figure out how we all would fit here.

"I hope we can find our own place soon," I heard my mother whisper to my father.

I walked out to the porch. On the left was a tiny kitchen, and the backyard was like a giant sandbox surrounded by a hedge. I hoped my mother's wish would come true.

In the evening, my parents moved the living room table to one side and opened the sofa into a bed, leaving no open space in the room. As my mother placed a folded bedspread on the floor beneath the table, she turned to me. "Eitan, you will sleep here, take off your shoes."

Still wearing my clothes, I lay down, and in my mind ran through the day's events. Soon I was asleep, but in my dream I was hiding from exploding shells, and I heard the sounds growing closer; I tried to run, but I couldn't, and then I woke up, thirsty, unable to figure out where I was.

After a few disoriented moments I saw the faint light that came through the patio door, and as quietly as I could, I walked out to the backyard and drank water from the hose I'd seen lying in a corner. The night was hot, the air still. An owl on a nearby tree called "whooo whooo." In the distance I could hear the comforting sound of waves breaking on the beach, and I tiptoed back to my makeshift bed and tried to sleep.

My father finally found a job with the new government, and my mother took care of Varda, who was almost four, while she looked for a place we could live. It was summer, and Shifra turned 14 and joined the youth movement, *Hashomer Hatsair*; the group provided her a new set of friends. Yudke, 21, was still a soldier in the *Palmach*, and I, except for the nights spent sleeping on the floor of Yashka's living room, spent my time in the backyard. Every morning I was left alone to play, and there in the sand, I built a miniature road system. As the days passed I added more and more features. In one corner I built a mountain of sand and dug a tunnel underneath. In another I dug a six-inch river and daily filled it with water from the hose so I could float the paper boats I made. After a while, the yard looked like a miniature country, and it filled me with pleasure. After all those years of restricted play and the months of rationing, playtime in the sand felt marvelous.

One day, while I was 'driving' a brick I used for a bus on one of the roads I had carved, my mother paid a visit to my paradise.

"What are you doing?" she asked.

I looked up at her standing on the patio. Behind her, the door to the outdoor kitchen was open, and I could see Yashka's wife cooking. The vapors from the soup rose and travelled along the roof of the patio above my mother's head. I thought my mother looked worse than she had during the siege of Jerusalem. She had gained weight and seemed more worried and in bad spirits.

"Nothing," I said. I looked back at my yard, admiring its mountains, rivers and highways.

"Yashka told me you ruined his back yard," she said. Her mouth was small, her lips tight.

"I'm just playing."

"Now we'll have to leave," she said.

I couldn't believe it. I dreaded being kicked out of paradise. I quickly said, "I'll put it all back the way it was."

"He said you wasted a lot of water."

I had hoped he wouldn't notice. "I'll fix it back just as it was."

"Aren't you ashamed? A 10-year-old boy playing like a baby, shame on you!"

My mother was seldom angry with me, even when I didn't do my homework or went out to play during the war. I couldn't believe what I was hearing now, and my heart sank.

Paradise had lasted only two weeks.

With each passing day in Tel Aviv, Yashka became more disgruntled, even after I stopped using the yard.

One night after dinner my mother said to him, "I saw a nice apartment today."

He looked at her, hopeful, saying nothing, waiting. "And?" he finally asked.

"It's too expensive," she said.

Yashka exchanged looks with his wife who lowered her eyes and sipped her tea. "Everything is expensive nowadays," he said. "You know you can stay here longer, but keep looking, soon your kids will go to school."

Yashka and his wife finished their tea and saying nothing more went to their bedroom.

We remained sitting. The room had bare walls, a sofa and a dining set. There were no plants, and the only flowers were those stitched into the center of the beige tablecloth. My mother studied the newspaper; she had been reading for hours, looking for an apartment.

"Yoseph," she said, "I heard they let people have the abandoned apartments."

My father took a sip of tea with his usual sucking noise, put down his cup and looked up. "Yes, but there aren't many available," he said. "A lot of Arab families stayed in their homes."

My mother put down the paper and rolled her eyes. "The paper said there are hundreds of abandoned homes in Jaffa," she pushed, as she so often did.

"I will ask about it tomorrow if you wish," he said.

"Wish or not, we can't stay with Yashka much longer."

"Okay, I will check it out," my father said.

"'If you wish' he says," my mother said, without looking at my father, "as if it's only my problem."

For a moment he looked at her. I could see he was trying to conjure another argument. After a few moments he said, "They give the homes to newcomers, the *olim* from Europe and holocaust survivors."

"We are also survivors," she said. "We survived the siege of Jerusalem, the Arab pogroms. We are pioneers, true Zionists turned refugees," she said. "We have more rights than they."

Sensing a fight brewing, my father sighed and finished the argument with, "I'll look into it," but I looked to my mother. I was counting on her to keep pressing.

"If you are persistent and firm, they will give you a house," she said.

Thankful the fight did not escalate, I arranged my bedspread on the floor and went to sleep.

Every day my mother looked for a place. In the evening she reported the results to Yashka and my father, and she continued to ask him about the status of our request for an abandoned apartment. At the end of that third week, my parents, sisters and I boarded a bus that drove us through the streets of Tel Aviv. At Jaffa Tel Aviv Street, the last stop, we got off. This was the border of the two cities: Jaffa, which was centuries old and Arab, and Tel Aviv, new and Jewish. On foot we walked into Jaffa, my mother holding the note with "State of Israel, Department of the Abandoned Properties" printed at the top along with our new address:

Ajami Street #34

Apartment #3

We had never been to Jaffa, but now we saw the ravages of war. Walls were partially demolished, many riddled with bullet holes. In a two-story building that was half destroyed, I saw that the thick walls were made of stone and mud. An apartment on the second floor had lost two of the walls; the floor was slanted with colorful, ornate Arab living room furniture still there. I wondered why the sofa had not slid from the slanted floor and why people had not stolen the furniture. Climbing up there looked too dangerous; there was shattered glass everywhere, and the whole scene reminded me of the devastation we'd suffered in Jerusalem.

I felt both angry at the Arabs and sorry for their kids. We walked along blocks of old narrow streets with no inhabitants but for stray cats, their shiny eyes following us as we walked. I had never seen cats that looked so threatening. No one said a word, and I felt a tightness in my stomach, the tension in our family growing by the moment.

"How are we going to find it?" Shifra asked.

I didn't mind walking farther. I hoped the place was not in this area.

"We will ask someone for directions," my father said.

The few people we saw did not speak Hebrew. My father spoke Arabic, Russian, and Yiddish but there seemed to be no one anywhere who could help us. Jaffa, just south of Tel Aviv, was also built along the Mediterranean shore, and I could hear the waves crashing on the beach. The air smelled smoky, mixed with the scent of fish and salt water.

"Let's turn right here," my mother said.

"How do you know where it is?" my father asked.

"It looks a little better over in that area," she said.

We turned right. The sound of the waves grew louder. I was hoping we would live near the beach. At least if we had to lose our Tel Aviv paradise, we'd have the sea.

My mother was right. The area looked better and more populated, with more children playing in the streets. Jaffa was a small town. In an hour we covered most of it on foot, and finally we found the address, an old building like the rest of them, three stories. Pieces of stucco were falling off, not from war damage, but from age.

The proximity to the beach expressed itself in rust--metal gates, hand rails, rickety electric boxes, I could see rust oozing through the concrete walls from the steel embedded inside. Arab kids played in the street. As we stopped to look at the building, they stopped playing and converged around us. My mother smiled nervously and tried her Arabic for chit chat. They did not respond.

We entered Ajami #34.

Apartment #1 occupied the whole first floor. My father knocked on the door and spoke in Arabic to the man who opened it. He sported a mustache and smelled of tobacco and coffee.

"Do you have the key to apartment #3?" my father asked.

"Yes, the owner left it with me," the man said.

"Where is the owner?"

"He fled to Lebanon," he said. "He feared the Jews." The man laughed and walked inside, returning with the key. "Me? I stayed here," he said. "I am not afraid of the Jews or anyone else."

He showed us up to the second floor, to apartment #3 and told us the owner's family had once lived there. The man unlocked the door, and we stepped inside, just far enough to let everyone in.

The floor was tiled with white, brown and blue tiles in beautiful patterns. It had a high ceiling and two tall windows in an extra thick wall. Some of the glass was cracked.

"You like?" the man asked in Arabic.

Yes, yes, I wanted to tell him as we stood in the living room. At one end I could see the kitchen, and we walked over to discover it was filled with well-used pots and pans stored on the bare wooden shelves. In some spots the light blue paint was peeling from the walls, and at the other end of the apartment were two large bedrooms. I didn't like the bathroom; it was dirty and had a broken toilet. But even that didn't diminish my enthusiasm. We were finally going to have a place of our own, and I might even have my own corner. "You like?" the guy with the mustache asked again.

"*Shwaye, shwaye,*" my father said. "Wait."

We walked into the hallway, and through an open door, I could smell the strong aroma of Arab cooking, lamb stew and burnt pita. I was hungry. The neighbors from apartment #2 across the way walked into the hall to see us, and in broken German told my father that they had just come from Bulgaria and were a little afraid in this Arab neighborhood.

Shifra started to cry.

"What's the matter?" my mother asked.

"I don't want to live here," Shifra said.

I couldn't believe she didn't like it, and I was certain her only objection was the fact that she didn't want to lose the new friends she had made in Tel Aviv.

"It's a much nicer apartment than we have ever lived in," my mother said.

"It's a bad place," Shifra cried. Varda started to cry too.

"Okay, let's go back now, and we'll think about it," my mother said.

My father took out a padlock he had brought with him and placed it on the front door. He talked some more with the Arab neighbor, and we walked back to the bus stop in silence.

Back home I discovered that my father was not enthused about the Jaffa apartment, but my mother pushed hard; she had learned that the rent would amount to pennies because the government wanted the area occupied. And so, for the next few days I waited for my parents to decide to take the place. I spent the time planning which corner would be mine and how it would look. I daydreamed about going to the beach, learning to swim and speaking better Arabic, playing with the local kids.

A few days later, my mother told me she was returning to Jaffa with a few items and to clean the place to prepare it for us to move in. I asked her to take me with her -- I planned to check out some of the kids, to see if they were worthy of friendship.

As we climbed the stairs to the second floor, we saw that the lock my father had placed on the door of apartment #3 was gone. My mother pushed open the door and a woman greeted us. Her husband and two kids joined her.

"Who are you?" mother asked.

"We live here," the woman said in Yiddish.

My heart sank. Now, I thought, we'd once again have to share an apartment.

"Who gave it to you?" my mother asked.

"We just came from Europe and the 'new immigrants' office sent us here."

My mother, her face sullen, told them it had been ours for the last few days, but she was going to let them be. I held back my tears.

"Come Eitan, let's go. We deserve better," she said.

We turned around and walked away. The woman called after us, telling us that she was sorry, and I heard the door slam shut behind us. We walked back through the war-torn area for the bus back to Yashka's home.

As time passed, now more than six weeks, life in Yashka's house became unbearable. My father went to work six days a week, but my mother spent the mornings getting the paper and reading the small ads, trying to avoid the hostility growing between our families. Every day she made a list and walked off to see the places to rent. Everything she found was beyond our means.

One evening, Yashka, who worked as an inspector for the city and nurtured many connections and sources of information, came with news. "I found a place for you," he said.

My father's face glowed with pleasure, but my mother asked, "What kind of place?" She sounded skeptical. How could he possibly have found something for us when she looked everywhere, every day.

"It's a small place, but a very good neighborhood very close by," Yashka said.

"How many rooms?" my mother asked.

"It's one big room, but it has a kitchen and a good bathroom," he said, "and it's inexpensive."

I thought anything would be better than staying with Yashka, and besides, this seemed the nicest way he could find to kick us out. And so it was that that weekend we moved to live temporarily at our new home at 55 Sokolov Street, another street named after another modern Zionist.

We moved our belongings on foot, each of us loaded with as much as we could carry. We took the short cut. The north of Tel Aviv was still sparsely built, and we walked through the open area, part of the sand dunes on which the city was built. With each step my foot sank into the sand, but finally, after a few exhausting round trips, we were in our new room.

I woke up at night to the noise of a door, slammed so hard that I mistook it for a shell's explosion in our room. It was followed by people talking.

"Naphtali, you bastard, where were you?" a woman shouted.

"None of your business," answered a man's voice.

"Where did you go tonight?" she asked.

"I was with good friends," he answered, in a heavy Yemenite accent.

"You smell like you drank a whole bottle of Arrack," she said, "you are wasting all our money," her voice grew louder.

"It's my money. I work hard for it, you whore," he said.

Then came what sounded to me like a slap in the face, shouting and an altercation as she shouted, "I'm going to bring the police on you!"

"Let me sleep, you bitch," he said.

Then it was quiet.

In the pitch dark, I said nothing. No one else in the family had been woken by the fight, or perhaps they'd all pretended to sleep.

It took a lot of thinking for me to fall back to sleep.

In the morning I got up early and so I could check out our new home and its vicinity. Practically all the buildings in the area were three to four story apartments or condos, built of concrete and finished with stucco. Our new home was different. It was a small, one story structure, built of lumber with a slanted tile roof. It was ancient, and in a prior life had served as a single home; at that time it was far outside the city, in the open and desolate sand dunes. Now it was a shack; everything built of wood was called a shack. But ours was a real one.

It had been built from planks of wood, made from recycled shipping crates. The walls were no more than 1/2" thick, and for water proofing they attached black tar paper on the outside; as a result, my new home was faded black on the outside, with a faded red roof. In many places the tar paper was worn off, revealing the water damaged wood of the walls.

My family was still asleep and the window shutters, unpainted recycled wooden boxes, were closed. I could still see a company insignia and the old shipping address on their planks. I ran back into the darkened room and touched my father's arm. "*Aba, Aba,* wake up!"

"What is it?" my father groaned, resisting the start to this new day.

"Look how thin the walls are," I said.

He raised his head from the pillow and reluctantly looked up. We could see a few uncovered cracks between the wood planks revealing the morning light shining through the wall.

"It's okay, Eitan. We'll fix it later."

"How?"

"We'll get some paper and cover it."

"But *Aba*, what about the bombs?" I had read in the papers that Tel Aviv was bombed sporadically during the war, with little consequence; still, in Jerusalem, these thin walls would have meant certain death.

"Bombs are different," my father said.

"How?"

"Before the Egyptian airplanes arrive, you'll hear a siren that allows enough time for us to run to the shelter across the street."

"Ah, I see," I said, the relief coursing through my body. Life was going to be different.

My mother, sleeping next to my father, woke but without rising, complained, "He is always thinking, thinking. Go out to play before your head explodes, Eitan."

I walked outside again. Remembering the events of the night, I realized we had neighbors in close quarters, so I began to explore. It turned out the shack had four apartments, each occupying a corner. From the kids I learned that one was occupied by a quiet elderly couple; the second, by a newly arrived Polish immigrant family with two kids; the third, by a family that had come a few years earlier from Yemen, and us in the northwest corner, facing the backyard, which was unlimited as it was exposed, no fence, to the sandy space beyond.

A few days after we had moved in, on a balmy night, I could not fall asleep. Tel Aviv summer had many nights where the temperature remained in the 80s through the night, with humidity close to 100 percent. I was sweating so heavily, my sheets were soaked, and I lay on those wet sheets with no cover, holding my hands over my ears to avoid the sound of the buzzing mosquitoes. At around midnight, the neighborhood siren went off, and my father grabbed Varda, and all of us, wearing only our underwear and pajamas, ran across the street to take shelter in the staircase space of a three-story apartment building. A brick wall had been erected in front of the entry to stop any bomb ricochets. Neighbors were already there.

"Who are you?" someone asked in the dark.

"We live in the shack," my mother said.

"This is a very small shelter, you know," a woman said in German accent.

We did not answer. In the dark we were unable to see who was who, and we listened to the monotonous humming sound of bomber airplanes flying, but not directly over us. I looked up, wondering if the roof could stop a direct hit from falling through. The faint sound of bombs exploding far away echoed in the shelter, and ten minutes later, the siren roared again with the all clear signal.

We walked back to our shack across the street, and as we did, I thought this was kid's play—this wasn't real war.

At our shack with my sister Varda

CHAPTER FOURTEEN

From the first day we moved into the shack, I had a crush on a cute little girl named Rivka K. She was also a refugee from Jerusalem, and that was probably what triggered my crush. Her eyes were green, and her dark hair, parted in braids, made it seem darker still.

I'd been prepared in advance, but I was still shocked on my first day of sixth grade to see girls in my co-ed school. When the teacher came in, I rose. Everyone else stayed seated. The students didn't even stand when they were called upon to speak but when the teacher called my name, I automatically stood.

"You can remain seated," he said, and for a moment I just stood there, unable to understand. The boy beside me pulled on my shirt, and I sat.

The next morning during roll call, the teacher again called my name, and I instinctively stood again. Everyone laughed. I blushed and sat down, determined to shake my habits. I realized I would have to adapt to the new freedom of my life in Tel Aviv, to a school with girls, and to plenty of food. I learned to do so quickly, though I could never bring myself to tell Rivka I wanted her to be my girlfriend.

I had always wanted to join the youth movement *Hashomer Hatsair* ("the Young Guard"). Yudke had belonged to that movement in Jerusalem, and my friend Meir Zinger had joined in fourth grade because of his brother's membership. This was the group Shifra had joined as soon as we moved to Tel Aviv. Finally one Saturday I walked into the Hashomer Hatsair's "nest." That is what they called their center. This one was the Tel Aviv "North Nest."

The nest was centrally located on a little street just behind Dizingoff Street. Previously a single home, it had a main hall which I entered, and I sat down with about 50 boys and girls my age, none of whom I knew. Paintings of beautiful, muscular workers were pasted on the walls, with large lettered slogans: "Workers of the world – UNITE!"

There we met three evenings a week to play, sing and learn new songs, and to talk about current events, political subjects or simply to engage in an intellectual conversation, each one slanted to indoctrinate us into pioneering socialist thought. There were plenty of youth movements in the new Israel, all politically oriented, most with party affiliations. Ours was the most intellectual and left leaning and found nothing wrong with anything either Russia or Stalin had done. At the same time it was a Zionist organization with a strong volunteering philosophy that for many years sent its high school graduates to establish *Kibbutzim* and to serve where the country most needed them. Naturally I was drawn to it since my brother and sister had belonged, and I also liked being treated as a person, not as a child.

These meetings at the "nest" were called "actions." My mother gave me money to buy a blue shirt with a white lace front that was part of the movement uniform, and before long I became friends with many of the kids- -Tony, Edna, Fat Reuvan and a thin one, Gideon, as well as many others. One day one of the girls asked, "Eitan, why do you always leave after the action?"

"You all go the other direction," I said.

"No, we go to the falafel stand. Come with us," she said.

"Still, it's the wrong way for me," I said.

"Come on, we just buy falafel and soda and have a good time for a while. Do you have to be home early?" she asked.

"No."

"So, come with us," she said.

I didn't tell her, but I had avoided these gatherings because I had no money. This time I promised I would join them next time. As usual, I left.

It was Saturday, and I arrived home after 8 p.m. to find the room dimly lit. My parents saved on electrical power, and Varda was asleep in her bed.

We had a nice table and chairs in the center of the room and four single steel beds with thin mattresses pressed against the bare walls. My appearance at home drew no reactions. My father was sitting on my parents' bed reading a book, his face grim. My mother was at the table holding a newspaper, talking to it, or to her invisible friend, about her bad luck--the usual rant--but this time she was using a napkin to wipe tears from her eyes.

Recently my father had begun to stay overtime at work, trying to make some extra liras to bring home. But my mother was suspicious, and when he wasn't around, she would mutter, "He thinks I'm a fool. He thinks I don't know about this woman, this whore of his." She had added a new tack to her repertoire of complaints.

That night I went to bed and covered my head with blankets so I could think about where I could find some money. I needed a weekly allowance so that I could join the others for falafels and sodas and to have a good time. I had already tried asking my mother, but her response was only, "What do you need falafel for? It's unhealthy, and we have plenty to eat at home for much less."

The important weekly meal at our home was served on Saturday, starting at 1 p.m. and lasting at least an hour and a half. The next Saturday I noticed the table at the center of the big shack was extended. I helped my father by holding one side while he pulled on the other, which opened the center, and together we pulled the extra table top piece from under a bed, wiped it clean, and placed in the center. We added two extra chairs.

Yashka and his wife joined us that day.

My mother had prepared a meal fit for a king, beginning with salad, followed by chicken soup and the main course of beef stew with mashed potatoes. We finished with fruit compote. Sweet wine by Rishon Le Zion Winery accompanied the meal, which made my parents, and especially Yashka, happy. As we ate, he told jokes in Yiddish until my mother was laughing and crying at the same time. Even my father laughed, though not that hard.

At the height of the joking, when my parents could not breathe well, Yaska said, "Eitan, look! Are you watching?"

He proceeded to take his teeth out of his mouth and placed them on the table. I was shocked. Everyone laughed harder, but I knew nothing about false teeth, had no idea he had them or that they could be removed like that. Yashka looked suddenly old and ugly, and in the midst of everyone's laughter I started to cry.

"Oy-vey, Eipam, don't cry," he said mispronouncing the words without his teeth.

"Leave him alone," my mother said.

"He is all right," my father said, walking to my side and stroking my head.

"What's wrong with him?" Yashka asked.

"Nothing. He's just sensitive," my mother said.

"You know what, Eitan?" Yashka put his teeth back in his mouth and said "I got two more houses to do; I need someone to help me. Come work for me."

Yashka had been moonlighting to earn extra income; he had been doing some landscape maintenance for apartment buildings in the area, and once or twice I had helped him. Now it was as if my prayers had been answered, and I stopped crying and accepted his proposition. From then on, on Tuesdays and Fridays after school, I helped Yashka clean and water yards, and I earned enough weekly cash for the Saturday night falafel.

It was August, 1948, and I was 10 years old, and the war continued, but the new consolidated armed forces had succeeded in stopping the Egyptian army in its march toward Tel Aviv, at Ashdod, 20 miles south. Tel Aviv was quiet. Jaffa had already surrendered. We'd survived one of the worst air raids when a lone Egyptian Spitfire plane dive bombed the central bus station, resulting in 42 dead and 65 wounded. Now the air raids were light and sporadic, occurring only every four or five days.

At the end of one of the youth movement "actions," the leader said, "There will be an important gathering next Friday. This is our national gathering. It will take place in the Hapoel Theater Hall."

We were all excited to hear this news.

"It will be later than our usual actions. We'll start at 8:30 and end at 10:30. Those of you who think your parents will let you go, raise your hand." A few kids raised their hands. Many were hesitant, unsure as to whether or not their parents would allow them to attend.

I confidently and proudly raised mine. By that time I could do what I wanted. My parents were preoccupied with their own hardships, and besides, they believed they could rely on me to stay out of trouble. *Hashomer Hatsair* was a feeder to establish more *Kibbutzim*, the collective settlements which manifested the purest Communism principles. Members of the kibbutz "gave according to their ability, and received according to their needs," and some of the best and bravest *Kibbutzim*, from Yechiam in the north to Nirim and Gvulot in the south, were established by our movement. In turn *The Kibbutzim* sent back to the city some of their best people to be leaders in the movement.

That Friday night at the Hapoel Center in Tel Aviv hundreds of the members as well as some of the important leadership gathered. We listened to lectures and to some musical entertainment, and at 10 p.m., an air raid siren sounded and the lights went off. For a few moments the crowd was confused, but when the emergency doors opened, we streamed onto the sidewalk. Some kids were crying. "How can I go home?" one kid cried out.

But I felt no fear.

We had been told to wait for the all-clear siren, and I was doing just that when I heard someone call, "Eitan!" I looked around in the dark but recognized no one.

"Eitan!" I heard again and I recognized the voice. To my complete surprise, my father grabbed and hugged me.

"How did you know where I was?" I asked.

"I asked around." He said. "Come, let's go home."

This, my father's sudden warmth, concern, attention and his efforts to locate me and come to find me during the raid brought tears to my eyes, though in the dark no one noticed.

And by the end of that summer, Israel's War of Independence ended.

I continued to attend the meetings in the North Nest of the youth movement. I enjoyed them, and I enjoyed especially the after action activity, hanging out on Dizingoff Street. I worked after school, making sure to save and keep about five cents, enough for the weekend. After a while I had a few friends, and some kids even knew my name.

One night my new friend Uri invited me to go for some falafel.

Some of the kids, clustered into small groups, were walking to Dizengoff Street where most of the stores closed for Sabbath, but cafes and restaurants remained open, and as we walked along, I realized we had passed our usual hang-out. I asked Uri where we were going.

"Tonight we decided to go to Café Nogah," Uri said.

I went along, but I knew Café Nogah was an expensive hangout, and that I did not have enough money. I ordered a soda but did not buy a falafel. Luckily no one noticed. I was sitting and watching the boys and girls talking and laughing when a girl looked at the clock and said, "Oh my God, it's 8 already. My mother is going to kill me. I'll have to run home."

Suddenly the whole group seemed eager to leave.

For a while I sat alone, not interested in returning so early to our shack. I could stay out as late as I wanted to. I sat and thought about why breaking through and feeling like one of them felt so difficult. I understood: They had more money than I did, but I had more time. They came from well-to-do families and had not suffered in the war. They had not endured the siege of Jerusalem. We were entirely different from each other.

After that night, I never returned to the North Nest.

CHAPTER FIFTEEN

The best thing about living in our shack was its location in the true "North Tel Aviv." It was at the edge of town, in an area developing quickly into the most desirable residential section. Some streets ran west to east, beginning at the beach and ending in orchards and open fields. Others ran south to north, starting at Jaffa or downtown and ending in some open fields that reached all the way to the river *Yarkon* (Green).

Since I no longer attended the actions, I was spending more time at the beach where I met new friends, interesting people who also seemed to have a lot of time on their hands. None of us bothered with homework, and some didn't bother going to school altogether. I was almost eleven, but some of these new friends were as old as 15 and more.

"Who is this big boy I saw you with?" my mother asked one day. I never brought anyone to the shack and was surprised she had seen me with someone. I raised my eyebrows, curious.

"I went to the store and saw you with some boys sitting on the sand in the open field." "Oh," I said. "That was Yoyne."

"Yoyne?" she asked.

"Yes. His name is Jonah but everyone calls him Yoyne."

"And who was the other one? He looked Sephardic," she said.

"He's Yeheskel Shami," I said.

"Shami? Is he Syrian?"

"No. His family came from Iraq."

Her eyes opened wide, and she compressed her lips. She looked unhappy.

"Why do you have to go with these street kids?" she asked. "Better do your homework. Why have you left the *Hashomer Hatsair*? They are much better company."

"I didn't like it there," I said.

"What's not to like? Look at Shifra. She belongs to the same nest, and she's happy there. Yudke went there. A lot of important people came out of this movement."

"I'll think about it," I said. I wanted this lecture to end.

"You know I have no problem with the Sephardics. I lived with them. I love the Persians. I even had good relations with some Arabs, but these street kids are not good for you. You'll get in trouble. Do you hear, Eitan?"

"Okay, okay. I won't get in trouble," I said, impatiently ending the conversation and once again going outside.

I loved to hang out with the kids my mother called "street kids." They had no family constraints, no worries, or so it seemed. And most of all I liked Yoyne.

He was fifteen years old, tall and heavy as an adult. He had a big head and a good face with blue eyes. If he had not been so big, he could have been handsome.

One morning I skipped school and went to the beach where Yoyne told me he was going to swim to Altalena. "Do you want to swim with me?" he asked.

Menachem Begin was the leader of the *Irgun*, the *Etzel*, and Begin objected to Ben Gurion, leader of the *Haganah* and the majority of Israel. Ben Gurion had demanded that all the armed groups be folded into the new official Israel Armed Forces while Begin hoped that his militia would survive independently under his leadership, even after Israel became a state.

Begin had secretly organized a shipment of men, weapons and ammunition from France on a cargo ship named Altalena. In June 1948, just a month after the declaration of independence, and a few days before our family arrived in Tel Aviv, the Altalena ended up on a Tel Aviv beach. Ben Gurion, head of the provisional government, ordered the ship stopped, and when Begin refused to give up their weapons, the heavy guns on the beach, under the command of a young officer named Itzhak Rabin, shelled the ship. It had caught fire, some of the people aboard were killed and its cargo was burned and exploded. The Altalena sank 500 yards from the bathing beach. There it remained, grounded and rusting.

"Why do you want to go there?" I asked Yoyne.

"I want to check it out," he said. "There's a lot of stuff left inside."

The white sand reflected the sun so vividly, grains gleamed in my eyes. The beach was deserted except for Yoyne, his two friends and me. The waves broke forcefully on the sand.

"Are you coming?" Yoyne asked.

To reach the rusting ship we would have to swim over 500 yards. I had never learned how to swim in a pool much less in the open sea.

"I'd rather not," I said.

"Okay, so you'll guard our stuff here," he said. "Don't leave."

I watched as Yoyne and the two boys swam into the waves. As they disappeared, I watched the Altalena, waiting to see them climbing aboard. Luckily I'd worn a hat. The sun was baking my body, though thankfully a breeze blew offshore, cooling me. I sat and waited on the deserted sandy beach for Yoyne to return, but as time passed, I saw no one.

Finally I heard a voice behind me. "Eitan." It was Yoyne.

"How did you get here?" I asked.

"We swam, but the currents carried us, and we landed near Gordon Street Beach and walked back here," he said. He wasn't breathing heavily, and he was already dry from the long walk. I could barely tell he had just swum a great distance.

"Come, Eitan," he said. "I want to show you something." I followed him along the sandy beach, heading north towards the spot where the River Yarkon opened to the sea.

"Not you, only Eitan," Yoyne said to the others who had begun to follow us. They stopped, their faces sad.

Yoyne commanded a lot of respect from all the kids. He had big scary hands and a big face, but he also had a good nature, often quiet, never shouting. Whenever a kid tried to disrespectfully challenge him, he put his big hand on his shoulder and gently pushed him aside, never hitting anyone.

"Look here, Eitan," Yoyne said when we were near the mouth of the river. He got to his knees, dug and cleared away some sand, revealing a wooden cover, which he lifted. He looked proud, as if he had unearthed a treasure. In the box I saw a few pipe-like, rusty rifle barrels and other mechanisms, all rusted, some with traces of burnt wood attached.

"This is what I've got so far from the Altalena," Yoyne said.

"What are you going to do with them?" I asked.

"I am selling them," he said.

"Selling to who?" I was stunned.

"To kids, and some adults," he said.

Who would buy burnt out, rusting gun barrels, I wondered. I thought Yoyne was making this up. Perhaps he was fantasizing.

"What do they do with it?" I asked.

"I don't know. Maybe for memories, or to use it," Yoyne said. He seemed to be unhappy with my questions, and he frowned and said, "Look, Eitan, don't tell anyone or…" He stopped, his sentence unfinished.

"Who do you think I am?" I said, pretending he had insulted me. "How much are they?"

Yoyne began to explain what each piece was and why one was worth more than another; "This, I sell for four lira ($8), those for six lira each and the long ones for eight lira each." I studied the contents. There were about fifteen pieces in the box, and the amounts he was quoting stunned me. Yashka paid me a dime for an entire afternoon's work. I wasn't sure, but I thought my father's monthly pay came to twenty-eight to thirty lira, no more. I was certain that a new bike cost twelve.

"So how much do you have here altogether?" I asked.

"I don't know," he said. "There's a guy who wants to buy all of it. I told him I'll think about it."

"How much are you going to ask?"

"I don't know," he said, "I want you to calculate it for me."

I knew Yoyne did not go to school, and now I realized he could not do the arithmetic and needed my help. I suddenly flashed back to my mother's worries about my association with street kids, and as I pondered this, Yoyne asked, "What are you thinking about?"

"Nothing. Only how to calculate," I lied.

We counted the pieces of each type. Every few seconds Yoyne looked around. A long way down the beach a couple sat hugging. He kept an eye on them, while I calculated.

"The total comes to 78 Lira," I said. He looked at me for a second, then at the couple in the distance, and without a word he fell to his knees, lowered the box and scooped sand over it until it was covered with a thick layer. This he ruffled so that it looked no different from any other spot on the beach.

A week later, I was walking down Dizingoff Street. As I passed Café Lipchitz at the corner of Basel Street, across from the police station, Yoyne called to me to join him. He was sitting at a table with a dark-skinned guy in his 20s.

"This is Eitan," Yoyne said. "He's the smartest little kid in the neighborhood."

The man barely looked up from his drink.

"This is for you, Eitan," Yoyne said, and he shoved four whole paper Liras into my pocket. I had just become rich, and I liked the way it felt.

My first winter in Tel Aviv was ferocious. The city was not as cold as Jerusalem, but it was wetter and windier, and we lived just blocks from the beach. The winds, blowing over the water, had no chance to slow before they reached our house, and rain fell slanted and forceful. Every day I looked up at the bare roof of our shack trying to understand why no rain leaked in.

Our shack stood on the last few feet of sand, at the end of the dune. Sokolov Street, in front of it, was not paved, and the dirt turned to mud with the first rain. Many brave truck drivers tried to drive this road in winter only to sink into the mud and require a tow truck to pull them out. There were no sidewalks. Walking to school through the mud and puddles, keeping dry was a challenge. I didn't skip school during those winter days.

One day I was sitting in class day dreaming when suddenly the secretary called me to the Principal's office.

I knocked on his door. When I opened it, I saw him facing me, holding a paper in his hand. My mother was sitting at his desk, her hair wet from the rain, her eyes wet with tears.

"I called your mother to come for a meeting to discuss your truancy," he said. "She says she didn't know you skipped school so much and she didn't sign those notes you've turned in."

He shoved a note in front of me. I remembered it. It said I missed school because I didn't feel well; it had my mother's signature. I had both written and signed it.

"Forgery is a serious matter," the principal said sternly. "It may lead to much worse in the future."

My mother cried, and as we rose to leave, so did I.

"There are a lot of bad street kids now," she told the principal.

When we were outside, she turned to me. "Why did you do this?"

I did not answer.

"If you told me you wanted so much to skip a day of school, I would have given you a note. You don't have to forge it," she said.

My mother's forgiving goodness made me cry even harder.

My father was always in the same mood, not too happy, not too sad. He usually was in a serious, contemplative state of mind. He was a reader, not a teller of stories. He was a listener, not a talker. I never heard him sing.

My mother was of the swinging mood type—with wide swings. She liked to sing, both old Russian songs and Hebrew songs of the pioneers, and especially those of the pioneer poetess Rachel. The one she liked best was about the Sea of Galilee, the water on which Jesus had supposedly walked. In Hebrew that Sea is called *Keeneret*, and this is what she often sang.

O' Keeneret of mine
O' Keeneret divine
Are you real?
Or just in my dream.

When my mother was in a good mood she would sing and talk to my father, telling him what she had heard that day. They would gossip together. But when her mood swung low, she talked to herself or to her invisible friend, and there was no singing.

Every evening as I walked home, I prayed to hear singing.

One evening I came home late. Varda was asleep already and Shifra was still out. My father was reading a book in Russian. My mother was reading the newspaper. "Yoska!" she said. That was my father's name when she was happy.

"Yoska, you will not believe it. Eitan, you too."

"What is it, Hedva?" my father asked.

"Wait a minute. I'll finish reading this article," she said.

We waited for a few moments, and suddenly she said, in Yiddish, "Ich cholesh avec!" She was going to faint.

We waited to hear why.

"They killed him. They killed Tubiansky. I can't believe it; they say he was a spy!"

She pulled me to her side, talking fast. "You remember, Eitan? This is the Haganah man we saw at our home on the day the Convoy to Hadassah Hospital was ambushed."

"Sure I remember. We saw him again the day we hid from the shelling, close to King George Street," I reminded her.

"Exactly. He was a handsome, good man," she said. "I cannot believe a man like that would be a spy."

She read the news article aloud from beginning to end, all in an astounded tone.

It turned out Meir (aka Misha) Tubiansky had held a high ranking position in the defense force in Jerusalem, commander of the Schneller Camp and later in charge of the three landing strips in Jerusalem and vicinity. In World War II he had joined the British Army and reached the rank of Major. As a civilian he had been an engineer for the Jerusalem Electric Power Company which was run by the British, with whom he had close contacts.

During the siege and shelling of Jerusalem, the high command noticed that there were suspiciously accurate hits on some important, sensitive targets in the city. Eventually they came to suspect that Tubiansky had given his British friends secret information, and three agents of the *Haganah* Secret Service interrogated him.

On the last day of June 1948, the day we left Jerusalem for Tel Aviv, Tubiansky was brought to an abandoned Arab farming village called Beit Geez for a field military court in which the same three agents, now serving as judges, found him guilty of treason. They summoned a firing squad. He was shot and buried in an unmarked grave. Now an attorney for his widow and eleven-year-old son were demanding an investigation.

As my mother read the story to us, I realized, I very much wanted to know the truth. I wanted justice to prevail.

That year my mother often read the paper aloud, and it was during these readings that I learned about news and events, for instance about the American General named David Marcus, aka Mickey Stone. Marcus had come as a volunteer to help with the war effort and was in charge of building the Burma Road, the alternate road that broke the Arab siege of Jerusalem. In the stories my mother read, I learned that one night the General got out of his tent to pee in an open field; as he returned, a guard asked him for a password in Hebrew. Marcus didn't speak Hebrew, and the guard who had been ordered to let no one pass without the password, shot him to death.

The entire new country mourned him.

From another story my mother read to us, I learned about the killing of Count Bernadott, a Swede sent by the UN to mediate peace between the Arabs and Israelis. He had been murdered in a barrage of firings by the Jewish underground splinter group, *Lehi*. Among the interesting details to me was the fact that at the time of his murder, a Jewish officer who served as his liaison and was seated beside him, survived the attack. This was none other than Moshe Hillman, our next door neighbor at Beit Cadoori on Prophet Samuel Street.

After the war ended, my Uncle Moshe Kristal served as a sergeant in a supply depot at Sarafend, one of the largest army camps. One evening before my twelfth birthday, he visited us at the shack and brought with him a used bike, a nondescript work bike, with damaged paint and patches of rusty pipe showing. A month later he brought a gift for Shifra, a beautiful, brand new, green, shiny sport bike by Philips. He told us a friend of his had found the bike in an abandoned Arab village. For years I used my bike, and later Shifra's, for work and pleasure.

Yudke had not lived with us in the shack, but on one of his visits, before he got out of the army, he hid a handgun in a drawer. It had a long barrel which made it heavy, even without the rounds, which we did not have. When no one was looking, I played with that German-made Mouser. In spite of being poor refugees, those news items, my father's job with the Defense Ministry and my brother's being a hero in the *Palmach* Special Forces, made me feel as if we were important participants in this war of independence, as if we were part of the establishment, taking part in the making of history. And those bikes my uncle brought us felt like richly deserved spoils of war.

CHAPTER SIXTEEN

"How is my *Julik* doing?" Uncle Moshe asked on one of his visits.

"He could do better," my mother said.

"Why, what's wrong?" he asked as he engulfed me in his arms and in the strong odor of cigarettes.

"I had a conference with the seventh grade teacher," she said. "He claimed Eitan does no homework whatsoever."

"No way," he chuckled. "Nothing?"

My mother squeezed her lips together, raised her hand to her side and let it fall, slapping the side of her thigh as she moved her head up and down and complained about her bad luck. "*Mine mazzel!*"

"So is he going to fail and stay in the seventh grade for one more year?" My uncle was concerned.

"Are you kidding me? Even with doing nothing he still is in the top of the class." I detected a note of pride in her lament.

"So what's the problem?" he asked.

"He could be much better," she said.

"Come here *Julik*," he said. "I love this *Julik*." He pulled out a dime and gave it to me.

My focus in seventh grade was on earning money, and I looked to spend my after-school time in a profitable way, looking for odd jobs. I remembered the time I calculated Yoyne's deal but recognized that as a special, non-recurring opportunity.

Around the corner from our shack was the Macabee Tennis Club with two courts. I watched the games through the fence. Middle age men dressed in white played, and I figured they were rich if they could afford the equipment, the attire and the time to play when normal people were at work. Some days two little kids fetched runaway balls for the players. Fascinated, I watched, and one day one of the men called, "Hey boy, you want to help us with the balls?"

After that I spent my afternoons on the courts collecting tennis balls for a dime an hour. Some days I even skipped school to make more money.

On Friday afternoons I delivered flowers on my bike from the flower shops to any address in Tel Aviv. I came to know the city, end to end, and I came to know people, too--the flower store owners who recognized my reliable service and the characters who received flowers. Among them were happy people, sad people, sick people, old and young, grumpy and nice and most importantly to me, cheapskates and those who tipped generously. I began to play a game with myself, trying to predict by the first response to my knock what type lived inside.

My bike became the source of my allowance since I still lived at home. But I also had a few expenses—new tires to replace flats, and occasionally I had to replace a chain. Before long I realized the flower shop was a better source of income for me than the tennis job, and in the fall of 1950, as I entered eighth grade, I decided to start my own flower business.

After the first rain, I went to the Yarkon, rented a small row boat and crossed to the other side where an open uninhabited field lay at the north side of the river. Everyone called this area "Trans Yarkon," with its sand dunes that extended from the Mediterranean shore. The only structures there were the electric power station called "Reading Station," and beside it a small airfield, formerly British, now serving the new Israeli Air Force.

Between the river and the edge of the Sde Dov airfield was a vast open area where tens of acres with thousands of wild flowers of all colors and shapes grew. When I first discovered that field, I knew I had found a treasure.

On Fridays I skipped school and with a friend rowed across to Trans Yarkon to cut flowers; we loaded them onto the boat and later onto our bikes. At the corner of Basel and Dizengoff Streets we set the flowers in buckets of water and sold them to passersby. We could never carry enough flowers to satisfy the demand; before the day folded into the Sabbath, we would run out.

That fall, with its high holidays, we had a fantastic business, and I contemplated dropping out of school. However, soon winter came, the holidays long gone, the Trans Yarkon turned into a muddy swamp, and we watched our business wither with the landscape.

By spring of 1951, just before my thirteenth birthday, the War of Independence had been over for some time. My family, however, was still deeply affected and much involved in the effects of the aftermath. Yudke was 23, looking for a job and a future. We still lived in the one room shack, but one of the neighbors had left, so we broke an opening in the thin wall and added their room to ours. Still we felt like refugees. My father's job with the Defense Department was as a secretary of a small office called "The Office for the Memorializing of the Fallen Soldier." This office was in charge of the military cemeteries, of relations with the grieving families and of memorial projects, so the war, naturally, was never far from his mind. At that time he was involved in the project *Yiscor*, a memorial book in which each fallen soldier would have a page, his biography and his picture. Over 5,000 soldiers had died in the war.

Ben Gurion, Prime Minister and Minister of Defense, set a deadline for publishing this book, and to meet the deadline, the office outsourced the editing and preparation for printing. To help to make ends meet, my father became one of the editors. His job was to gather biographies from the soldiers' friends and families, edit them and type each on one page. It was a time consuming, low-paying job, and one evening at dinner my mother was complaining about my father's late return home. Again, she was accusing him of neglect and infidelity.

"Eitan, do you want to help your father?" he asked.

Surprised, my mother stopped her rant in mid word.

"Sure," I said, puzzled, unable to imagine how I could help.

"Why don't you come to my office after school," he said.

"*Lose'em op,*" she said, "Leave him alone."

"To do what?" I asked.

"Well, you know I have to type all these stories for the *Yiscor* book," he said.

"I can't believe you," she said in Yiddish.

"Yes," I said.

"It takes a long time for me to read the page and type it on the typewriter because I never learned blind typing," he said, "If you'll read it out loud for me it will go much faster."

After that, every afternoon I rode my bike to the center of town. My father's office was in the *Beit Hadar* building near the central bus station and the Jaffa train station, from which the train left for Jerusalem.

When I arrived, the building was deserted of all government employees except for the cleaners and my father in his small office, typing with two fingers. I read slowly to match his typing speed, and I learned about the lives of many of our fallen soldiers—men and women, the young and the old—who had given their lives for the defense of their country.

I also blunted my mother's accusations of infidelity.

My thirteenth birthday fell on a Saturday of the third week of Passover vacation.

"Eitan, we'll have your Bar Mitzvah in temple, yes?" my father asked.

"No, I don't want it," I said.

"Why?" I did not want to tell him the real reason. I had looked at the Torah section –*Tazria*-- I would have to read on that Sabbath. It dealt with all the Jewish rules about sex. But I couldn't tell him that, so I said, "I'm an atheist." This also was true.

He did not say anything, but his eyes grew cold with sadness.

"I will have a party for my class," I said to try to cheer him.

On the last day of school before the Passover vacation began, I invited everyone to my party, but by the third week of vacation most of my classmates had forgotten about it, and only a handful arrived at our shack. They spent most of the time there just looking around, stunned to disbelief about our living conditions. One girl had organized a collection and they gave me a present – a statue of Beethoven.

Soon after Passover summer again invaded us, and the crush I had developed all those years before on Rivka Klatchco was still burning inside me. She had grown even more attractive, but she was more interested in my friend Yeheskel Shami than she was in me. He though, was interested in Pnina Cohen, a thin blond girl who had a nice face but was flat-chested. Alas, Pnina Cohen had a crush on me, and no matter how hard I tried to dissuade her from this crush, whenever I looked, she was there beside me, chatting.

Rachel Shragenheim was a tall, slender, beautiful girl who looked like she had stepped out of the frame of a James Dean movie. She had spent one extra year in sixth grade, one reason for her nicely overdeveloped attractiveness. And Rachel was interested in a number of us.

One clear, blue skied Saturday, I rode my bike to our regular class meeting spot on Nordau Boulevard at Dizingoff Street. That street was divided in the center with a wide landscaped section, hence the Boulevard of its name.

When I arrived, Rachel was already there, and after a while, when no one else showed up, she asked me what I wanted to do.

Before I could answer, she said, "Let's go to the Yarkon." We mounted our bikes, and I followed her. She wore short khaki shorts and a white T-shirt with the sleeves cut short, revealing her arms in full, including part of her shoulders. The shirt had a collar and a v-cut and in my white cotton shirt with its long sleeves folded up, I felt overdressed.

We left our bikes and walked down an embankment leading to a small wooden pier. On one side of that pier a line of people stood waiting to board a motor boat that would take them on a ride along the tiny river, all the way to its source called Seven Mills, three miles or so each way. On the other side of the pier anyone could rent a small row boat by the hour. I rented the smallest boat I could. It had two wooden seats. I took the rowing seat, and Rachel sat facing me. After we had rowed upstream for a while, Rachel grew bored and asked to change places. We both stood, trying to move to the opposite sides, but we rocked so badly, I thought we would capsize. It was common knowledge among us kids that if you fell into that contaminated river, you would get sick and pee blood. Rachel grabbed and hugged me, and there we froze until the boat stabilized. Then we sat in our new positions facing each other again.

When Rachel started to row, I realized immediately what a fantastic vantage point I had. Every time she moved the oars backwards, her body moved forward, revealing those beautiful breasts; Rachel hated bras. Her breasts were full, solid and springy and her movements made them jump around like two agile gazelles.

Rachel was happy and talkative for the whole hour, after which we returned the boat to the pier. Walking up the river bank to our bikes, Rachel put her hand around my shoulders and glued a kiss to my cheek. I felt her right gazelle touch me.

"Thanks, Eitan. I enjoyed it," she said. She kept her hand on my shoulders as we walked to our bikes. I was sorry we had left them so close to the river.

"What do you want to do now?" she asked.

For a fleeting moment I wanted to tell her the truth, but I lacked the courage.

"Let's go and see if more kids showed up at the Nordau Boulevard place," I said instead of telling her what I most wanted to do.

She looked at me, contemplating.

"No, I think I'll go home," she said, and she raised her hand for *shalom* and biked away.

The next week I saw her in school holding hands with Eli Machboob, a tall, strong, dark Yemenite who also had had the privilege of spending two years in one of the lower grades. I looked at them and felt both envy and relief; I could not have handled such a girl.

The last year of our primary school was coming quickly to its end. The principal informed us that of the ten students who had taken scholarship exams, three had earned a scholarship that would pay for their high school tuition. I was one of those three.

The scholarship, proof of my scholarly standing, also helped me to be accepted by the best high school in Tel Aviv, *Ironit Aleph* Highshool.

CHAPTER SEVENTEEN

One of the unique aspects of the Israel Workers' Union was that it owned most of the big corporations, one of which developed new housing projects. My parents, members and pioneers were eligible to buy a house, and they chose one in a new development in Holon, a small town south of Tel Aviv. In the summer of 1951, three years after we had moved from Jerusalem to Tel Aviv, we left our shack and moved to Holon.

My mother was elated. Finally, she thought, she had received something from the government as a reward for being a pioneer who came long before those newcomers she felt were less deserving.

It was midday when we arrived at 28 Halutz Street, at the first home our family had ever owned. It was 600 square feet with one bedroom - a duplex that cost $1000. The house was in a new area called Pioneers' Housing Area and looked as if it were built in the Sahara Desert. Every inch of the area was built on sand dunes, the only solid ground the asphalt streets and interior floors. Everything else was sand, and fine grains were everywhere.

I squinted at the house; it was difficult to see it in the bright sunshine reflecting off the white sand below.

"This one is ours," my father said.

"Yoska, how do you know?" my mother asked, "they all look the same."

She was right. The entire area was lined with concrete boxes with the same *shpritz* stucco finish and red tile roofs. The boxes were planted in the sand in straight lines and reminded me of the stones in a military cemetery.

My father pointed to the piece of white metal on the wall, painted with the number 28 in blue. We walked inside, opened all doors and windows to let in some fresh, hot air, and I squinted out at the wide expanse of white sand outside.

"We'll build a fence, Eitan. We'll bring some top soil and grow fruit trees and a wonderful garden," my father said.

I needed a lot of imagination to believe it.

But my father ordered the blocks, cement, steel bars and tools, and we spent our afternoons out there at work. For days we graded the sand and I wheel barrowed "Khamra" – topsoil, from a pile dumped at the edge of the street in front of our house. I was 14 and building strong muscles.

One Saturday afternoon as I was loading my wheelbarrow I heard someone call, "Hey boy, what's your name?"

When I looked up I saw a girl sitting on her bike, one foot on the ground, her fat bottom spilling over the sides of the little seat. She had a big smile.

"What can I do for you?" I asked. I took notice of her blue blouse, tied in front with white lace, the uniform of the *HashomerHatsair*.

"My name is Edna and I belong to the..."

"I know, I can see it," I cut her off.

"We're having a recruiting effort today. Would you join us?"

"I'm busy you can see," I said. Secretly I longed to be in the company of kids, but I couldn't let my father down.

"Come for a short time. We'll have a lot of fun in the nest," Edna insisted.

I dropped the hoe, climbed into the cargo seat of her bike, and we rode for ten minutes to join the Holon Nest of the youth movement.

I stayed for the next four years.

* * *

Three months passed, and we slowly settled in.

Most days, ten minutes after I woke, I was standing in line at the bus stop waiting among a familiar swarm of people—our neighbors on their way to work in Tel Aviv. I was going to the *Ironit Aleph* High School, and this day I was still full from eating all those Hanukah latkes and doughnuts the night before at the youth movement action.

From the central station in Tel Aviv, I walked to the center of town, glad to reach school on time. My new school was strict and accepted only serious students. We had to stand when called upon, and my teachers did not tolerate tardiness, nor were they willing to adjust to my system of "no homework necessary as long as you knew the material." The students were competitive—everyone striving to finish their homework in the most elaborate way.

In second hour we had an Arabic language class, and our teacher surprised us with a quiz. He distributed the questions--all in Arabic. I didn't understand some of them, and those I understood stumped me. I stared at the pages for a while realizing this was my moment of truth.

I decided I would have to leave school, and so, once the teacher began to review our papers, I stopped listening.

Instead I wrote a note and passed it to the one good friend I had made in school. He sat in the next row, and as I passed it, the teacher caught me and intercepted the note. I had written to tell my friend I was leaving, and beside that I had scribbled a common Arab profanity that involved the teacher's mother.

The teacher's face reddened and he looked at me. He said nothing.

After the bell rang, I gathered my stuff, walked out of *Ironit Aleph* and took the bus back to Holon. I felt as if I were escaping prison, and the next day I went to the office of the only high school in town, the school many of my new friends attended.

I told the principal there about my tuition scholarship and my first months in *Ironit Aleph*. I explained I could no longer *shlep* over there; I didn't have the time or the money for the bus.

"Just bring your papers and have your parents sign this," he said, handing me a form.

That evening, my mother lamented for a while but signed the form. "Don't tell your father," she said, "He has enough aggravation."

And so I began my education in the Holon High in mid-school year. I was surprised how much I had learned at *Ironit Aleph* in just three months; I was way ahead of my new class in most subjects, and I made a good impression on the teachers, especially in math and geometry. A few times when called upon I stood when I did not need to, and everyone laughed, but I soon dropped that habit.

Eleventh grade was supposed to be the easiest grade because all the emphasis was on twelfth when we would take the matriculation exams, the grades of which determined whether or not we would go to university. Because of its ease, it wasn't terribly exciting, and hoping to generate some excitement, I auditioned for the drama club for a biblical show they were doing. When I did not land the role of young King David, the star, I quit, despite the fact that the drama club attracted some of the best looking girls in our school.

I began to spend more and more time at the nest of the youth movement. Our battalion was near the top, with just one older group above us, and we were getting closer to fulfillment--that is, going to live and work in a Kibbutz for the rest of our life.

On the day I quit the drama club I went to the nest for the afternoon meeting and discovered we had a new leader, Israel Zamir.

Israel Zamir was a well-built, muscular if small man with thick curly blond hair on his head, chest and his hands. His noticeable nose and very blue eyes were prominent on his reddish face, and I noticed he spoke with an accent, not the one we *Sabras* (Israeli born) spoke. At the time, our country was a true melting pot and I was learning to detect people's origins by their accents in Hebrew; I also could do some good imitations.

Zamir laid out the program for the coming year and invited us to ask any questions, but hard as I tried, I could not determine what his accent was. Finally I asked where he was from.

"From *Kibbutz Beit Alpha*," he said.

Everyone laughed and he blushed red as a tomato.

I had not meant to embarrass him, so I quickly said, "The way you speak...that's not a Beit Alpha accent."

"I came as a kid from Poland," Zamir said.

The group got quiet, and his blush subsided. "Let me tell you a bit about myself so we could advance our friendship faster," he said, smiling at us, and smiling at the young woman who stood beside him.

"I am 24 years old and a member of Kibbutz Beit Alpha," he said, "and at the age of 3, my father abandoned me and my mother. A few years later we came to Israel. I served in the Army and fought in the south, in the Negev, during the war. In my Kibbutz, I work at the fisheries, but for now I have been sent to lead this Holon Nest."

I kept looking at the girl beside him. She had a beautiful face and long, straight brown hair. She was tall and slender, and I tried to guess her age, but could tell only that she was older than us and younger than our new leader, Israel Zamir.

"When did you come here?" Eitan Marcus asked Zamir.

"I was six," he said.

"And your father? Did he stay in Poland? Was he trapped in the holocaust?"

"No," Zamir said. "He went to the US. He lives in New York now. He writes books."

"Is he famous?" Michael Shvager asked. Michael was the intellectual of our group, what I thought of as "artsy."

"No. He writes mainly in Yiddish," Israel said, "but he has published a few books."

"I assume his name is not Zamir," Michael continued. Zamir was a Hebrew word, and like many others, he seemed to have changed his name to a Hebrew one.

"I changed my last name only a couple of years ago from Zinger to Zamir," he said. "but my father publishes under the name Itzhak Bashevis Zinger."

We had never heard of his father, but many years later when he became famous and received the Nobel Prize for literature, I remembered that day vividly; Israel later wrote a book called, *Visits with My Father*. But that day he dropped the subject and turned to introduce us to the young woman beside him. "This is the new *schlicha* who will be the leader of the younger battalion. Shulamit Gal. Shula comes from Kibbutz *'Ein Hamifrats*."

Shula waved hello to us, and I thought she looked beautiful, intelligent and mature.

As the year progressed, I spent more time at the movement nest than I did either in school or at home. We were a group of 15 to 16 year olds who had no homework to do or, in many cases, chose not to do our assignments. We would hang at the nest from afternoon late into the night discussing world affairs, politics and Marxist-Leninist ideology. Some of the subjects we talked about--Communist philosophies like "Dialectic Materialism"– sounded intellectual but remained beyond me, I think because our instructor never actually understood the ideas he rattled on about. Communist double talk, I thought, and I said so.

The tentacles of the Soviet Union were spreading worldwide and touching our group as well. We passionately argued about whether Stalin was right to kill all those Russian doctors (mostly Jewish) and whether the Rosenberg couple were real spies or falsely charged and hanged in America. In both cases, I opposed the establishment. I thought the poor Russian doctors were innocent and the American Rosenbergs guilty. My expressed beliefs created a heated friction between me and Israel Zamir.

He and Shula Gal lived in a house rented by the movement for them. This communal house served all the movement's out-of-towners and accordingly was called "the Commune" and was located in my development.

Frequently, at the end of our nightly political discussions, Israel Zamir, Shula Gal and I walked home together, and our discussions continued until we reached my home. Zamir was a staunch socialist and toed the party line while Shula began to move closer to my way of thinking. After a while, Israel had to stay later at the nest, and Shula and I walked home together. She was smart and eloquent, but not too argumentative. She would put forth her opinions in a soft-spoken way, often injecting good humor, and in time I became attracted to her and was sorry she was so much older than I. She was a grand old 19 to my almost 16.

One evening, when we reached my house and were about to say our goodnights, she said, "Hey Eitan, how about walking me to the Commune?"

We'd read reports in the paper about some Arab *Fedayeen* infiltrating Israel to commit terrorist acts, so I assumed she was frightened. "No problem," I said. "Are you afraid to walk alone?"

"Do I need to be afraid for us to walk together?" she asked with a nervous laugh. "I like your company."

After a few more steps I put my arm around her, and in that moment we became a couple. I liked her a great deal, but I also was proud. This relationship made me feel like a man, and although we decided not to reveal our relationship to the nest, we spent many late night hours together out on the sand dunes at the edge of town or in the Commune.

In short order everyone knew, and one evening when I came to the nest, my friend Eitan Marcus pulled me aside and said, "*Kol Hakavod*, Eitan. I heard you have a girlfriend." Yankalle, Ezra and Vidi joined us, slapping my shoulder and joking happily as if I had won the lottery. Michael Shvager was reserved. He liked to be, and in most cases he had been, first in everything—the best student, best musician, best basketball player and best writer among us. That night he could not hide his envy. Israel Zamir, Itzhak Bashevis Zinger's son, was furious and directed his anger both at me and at Shula. He warned me not to use the Commune for our dates. This had brought Shula and me closer; now we had the feeling of "us against him".

* * *

The War of Independence produced a new crop of writers. They wrote about the young Israelis, their struggle in turning Palestine into Israel. They wrote about their fighting, their relationships and their struggles. One of the more prolific and best known of these writers was Nathan Shacham. He was born in 1925, and in the late 1920s, my mother had worked as his nanny. In March, a month before my sixteenth birthday, we had our regular Saturday action in the nest where first we sang all our Russian songs, then our Israeli songs and followed this with a political discussion. When our discussion was finishing up, Israel Zamir said, "I have an announcement to make."

We all quieted down, and Israel told us he planned to celebrate Israel's sixth Independence Day in a big way, including a parade in town, and producing a play about the war in which we would be the actors. He wanted us to put it on in Armon, the main theater in town.

We gasped at the idea. This was an unheard of expense, but Israel had managed to secure a large budget from the movement's central committee.

"What is the play?" Michael Shvager asked.

"*Hem Yagiu Mahar* by Nathan Shacham," Zamir announced with pride and importance. "He's my friend and a member of my kibbutz."

Michael's eyes shone with excitement, but you did not have to be a bookworm like he was to know about this important play and its writer. The play had been previously produced at the Kameri National Theater starring Mr. Itzhak Shiloh, one of the leading actors in Israel. The press compared him to Paul Newman.

The name of the play in English is "They Will Arrive Tomorrow," and tells the story of a small army unit who sat on top of a hill they conquered a few days earlier from the enemy. After the battle they discover that the hill all around them is full of land mines, and because they do not know the locations, they cannot safely leave the place. The main characters are Jonah, the commander; Alex, the operations officer, and Rina, Alex's beautiful sister, a communications officer. The play also features a few soldiers and a few Arab war prisoners.

The play is about a small unit of Israeli soldiers, torn by practical and moral dilemmas, who want to escape this place alive. Jonah wants to send one or two of the captured enemy Arabs to walk down the hill, to establish a clear path for the rest of them. Alex objects to this plan on moral grounds because, obviously, the Arabs could be blown up by a landmine. As a subplot, Jonah wants Rina to love him, but she rejects his advances.

Over the next weeks and months, the play took center stage in our lives. School was just a place to show up some mornings so as not to be expelled. Zamir had even managed to arrange, with help of the playwright, to get Itzhak Shiloh to direct our production. For two weeks Shiloh joined our meetings as an observer. He wanted to choose the actors by observing us in real life.

After those two weeks, Israel Zamir announced the decisions.

"Eitan Makogon will play Jonah, the commander. Shula will play Rina, the communications girl. Eitan Marcus will play Alex, Rina's brother. Michael - Soldier 1. Yankelle - Soldier 2." He continued to announce the smaller parts and explained that Itzhak Shiloh had cast the play, and his decisions were final.

There was silence. No one moved, but I could feel my heart racing. Not only would I get to play the main character, but Shula was going to play my romantic desire.

For our first reading we were invited to the Tel Aviv apartment of Itzhak Shiloh which felt as exciting as if I were visiting Paul Newman.

In the beginning, rehearsals were twice weekly, but before long they expanded to three and four times. Shiloh was generally happy with my acting except when Jonah tries to grab Rina and kiss her. Both Shula and I felt awkward kissing in public, and we weren't convincing.

"I wish Eitan had more experience kissing," Shiloh said.

No one had told him we were a couple.

We appeared in front of more than 400 people in the biggest theater in town, and the show was a marvelous success.

The only problem was when it was finished, I felt a great letdown, and all the work we had put into this felt like a waste for one evening only.

Still, like everyone in the play, for a while I considered pursuing a career as an actor.

Instead, I got a job in the movies.

CHAPTER EIGHTEEN

Throughout my teen years I did few if any homework assignments and only crammed for exams. Still I did well. Some of my best friends didn't like the ease with which I succeeded; not only did they work harder, I had time to hang out with the other loafers and to take part-time jobs that provided me the income needed for hanging out in the evenings.

When I was in ninth grade I helped my father build the two-room addition to our house while also working in the office of the developer of our neighborhood. In tenth grade I worked as a laborer at construction sites, took a tree spraying job, and delivered *Al Hmishmar*, the socialist party daily. In summer, I worked as hired help in a kibbutz. And in the middle of my eleventh grade year, my classmate Haim Schneider approached me during a break with an offer.

Haim and I were not the best of friends. He had come with his family from Romania only a few years earlier and did not mix well with us *Sabras*. But he had a good sense of humor, and we laughed a lot together. "Okay, Haim, what is it?" I asked.

"Would you be interested in taking over my job?" he asked. He spoke with a Romanian accent I had imitated, but he also spoke German, Russian, and some Italian. He worked as a translator at the movie theater.

"You mean your job in the movies?" I asked, thinking this was one of his jokes, but he wasn't joking. He was doing poorly in school, and his parents insisted he quit his night job.

That's how I became the translator of the movies at the *Migdal* movie theater in Holon. At the time all movies shown in Israel were in foreign languages; there were no Hebrew films shown. Melting pot that our country was, agents were importing movies from all over the world, mostly in English but also in Russian, Italian, French, Arabic, Hindu, and more.

When I went to talk to the theater manager, he asked me if I spoke English.

"Sure. I grew up with the Brits in Jerusalem," I said.

"And Russian?" he asked.

"My parents are Russian," I said, and because he was too busy to continue the interview, he gave me the job.

Since the movies had no Hebrew subtitles, the theater screen had a sideline, one fifth the width of the screen, dedicated to the translation. The real translators wrote the dialog and monolog by hand in Hebrew on a transparent strip of celluloid that was projected onto the right side of the movie, like the margin on a writing pad. It was rolled slowly, by hand, in order to match the dialogue being spoken in the movie.

I was the guy in the machine room who rolled this strip.

The pay was good, and I got to see a lot of movies, and as a special benefit, I was able to get my friends into the theater for free. My scant knowledge of English allowed me to do reasonably good translations, but when I had to translate movies in other languages, the most I could do was pick up a word, a name or another clue, here and there and try to roll correctly. It worked in most cases, but not all. In one Russian war movie, I could pick up only the name of the Russian Navy boat and that of the Admiral, but I could not keep up with what was going on. And my errors drew angry protests from the crowd. The manager gave everyone a free pass for another evening, and by then I was more familiar with the movie.

My eleventh grade final report showed some decent grades, but on the bottom it said: "Eligible to start the twelfth grade, but not in our school."

I had already decided to drop out of school. I was going to be a *Kibbutznik* and work on tractors. Still, that report hurt, so I put it in my bag and told no one.

That summer Shula finished her assignment in our nest. She was 20 now, and her deferment from the army that had been arranged by her Kibbutz and the youth movement had expired. She left town to join the army, and when she wrote to me from boot camp, I answered the first time. After that I didn't reply; I collected her letters and tucked them away with that report. Around that time Israel Zamir was given permission from his Kibbutz to visit his estranged father in New York, Itzhak Bashevis Zinger.

Israel promised to write to us from America, but he never did.

I decided to join my friends working as volunteers in Kibbutz Zikim in the south, at the border with Gaza; after we had volunteered for a month, the Kibbutz hired us. Some of my 17-year-old friends worked nights as guards, but I was 16 still, and I worked in the fields, riding a combine, tying the bags of seeds as they filled. I worked two shifts, sixteen hours a day and made good money, but after two weeks I had to visit a doctor to treat the pain in my muscles. When I could no longer move my hand, I returned home.

Two weeks before the start of the school year, I told my parents I planned to drop out of high school and go to work full time. They were unhappy, but they also were accustomed to my independent streak and, not without a struggle, arguments and cajoling, they finally accepted my decision.

As my friends began twelfth grade, I took a job with a steel company, erecting steel structures for new factories in the industrial zones around Tel Aviv and Holon.

On Sunday, the first workday of my third week as a steel worker, the clock alarm went off at 5:30 a.m., and I groaned. I did not want to go to work, but I knew I would. I made my own sandwiches for lunch and rode my bike to the job site and like the previous two weeks, I readied myself to work with a group of men unloading steel beams from trucks and placing them in the location on site for welding onto the structure. My muscles were developing rapidly, but that morning I ached everywhere.

"We need manpower, not boy power," one co-worker said, only half jokingly.

"This is not a job for a *Vusvus*," another one said, making them all laugh. One of them said something in Moroccan, and they laughed harder. Those new immigrants from North Africa, their skin dark and tanned, their muscles bulging, enjoyed putting me, a fair skinned *Vusvos* (a derogatory name for an Ashkenazi, similar to "whitey") down.

At lunch they would tell their real or, perhaps, imaginary tales about their weekend sexual escapades with women, their wives, their girlfriends and the street "stewardesses" they hired.

The next day, when my alarm again went off at 5:30, I pushed the button and fell back to sleep; my mother didn't disturb me. "Sleep is more important for his health than school or work," she always said. A few hours later I woke, dressed and went to my former high school to see Mr. Elyashiv, the old principal. I ached—physically and mentally—to return to school, and when I saw all the boys and girls hanging around at break, I longed to be with them again.

"You read the note on your eleventh grade final report, didn't you?" the principal asked. He was a good natured, soft-spoken man who looked old and tired.

"Yes, but my grades are good," I said.

"Your behavior last year was unacceptable," he said.

"I know, but I am changed. I'll behave."

"It's easy to say. I know the real you, Eitan."

But I thought he didn't know the half of me. Of course I remembered the day I stole one of the few cars in town and drove without a license to school to show off. I remembered seeing him walking out of the school and offering him a ride home, which he refused. I wondered if he remembered. But I hurried on. "It's all because I planned to drop out last year, but now I really want to return and graduate."

"Look Eitan…," he was struggling. "Our decision is final, I can't take you back."

"What am I going to do?" I asked. I'm sure my desperation showed in my face, and I noticed his eyes filling with tears. His face revealed the empathy he felt, but he said, "You can go to another school."

"Tell me where," I said.

"Here is what I can do," he told me. "Choose any high school and I will help you get accepted there."

I could not believe his words. He wanted to help me, but he was determined not to accept me back to his school, the only high school in my town. Any other school I chose would be in Tel Aviv, and I did not want to go back to *Ironit Aleph*.

"If so, I would like to try *Tichon Hadash*," I said. "My sister Shifra graduated there."

"Good. I know Tony Halle, the principal. She'll help us," he said.

'Help *us*.' I was thrilled.

CHAPTER NINETEEN

At 9 a.m. the next morning, I met Mr. Elyashiv at the bus stop to travel with him to one of the best high schools in Tel Aviv, *Tichon Hadash* ("New High"). When we got on the bus, Elyashiv said matter of factly, "You'll have to pay. I brought no money, but I'll do my best to help you when we're there."

I paid for the bus tickets, but since there were no seats available, we stood next to each other and rode silently. For the first few minutes of the 45-minute ride, I kept thinking I ought to say something; I ran some subjects through my head. He was interested in politics, and I thought to tell him about the earthquake in Algeria that killed 1500, or perhaps discuss President Eisenhower cooling off relations with Israel. At last I thought to ask about his elderly father who was suffering from Alzheimer's Disease, but I had been quiet for so long, that felt awkward.

"I think what we should say…" he broke the silence but so startled me I interrupted with "What?"

He carried on. "I think we should tell Tony that you had 'broken family' problems."

I had expected him to help me get into the school, but I was surprised at his willingness to lie. I kept quiet. "Do you mind if we blame your family problems for your behavior in class?" he asked.

"What kind of problems?" I did not like the idea of tainting my family's reputation, especially because Shifra had graduated from that school and had been an excellent student.

"We'll just say family problems, nothing particular. Leave it to me," he said.

Tichon Hadash was in a new building on the road to Haifa, at the edge of Tel Aviv. In the school office we learned that Tony, the principal and Mr. Elyashiv's friend, was at home sick. He spoke briefly to the vice principal who made it clear they never accepted new students to 12th grade, and only Tony could make an exception.

I paid for our bus ride back to Holon, and Mr. Elyashiv and I sat beside one another in unspoken defeat.

Shifra, who was now a student at Hebrew University in Jerusalem, came home that weekend. For months she had tried to convince me not to quit high school and now, when I told her about my unfruitful visit to the *Tichon Hadash* she told me Tony liked her, but she was reluctant to ask for favors. "Protexia" was what she called it.

Four years earlier Tony had wanted Shifra, then in 12th grade, to give the first-day welcome speech to the new students of the 9th grade. Since school was still out on summer vacation, Tony had sent her assistant to our home, the shack in Tel Aviv, with a note for Shifra. The assistant returned to school and told Tony about our shack, and Tony scolded Shifra for never telling her about her living conditions; after that she valued Shifra's excellence even more.

Shifra and I decided to pay Tony a visit at her home in a nice middle class neighborhood, near Dizinghoff and Frishman streets. We knocked on the door, and inside we found her in bed, nursing her illness. She was a small woman, in her 50s or early 60s, and she spoke with a thick German accent. After she had asked me some questions about myself, she said, "I know Shifra very well. If you are only half as good as she is, you'll have no problem."

She would accept me on the condition that I pass a test in math and write an essay. Naturally I agreed, and I aced the math test but just barely passed the essay, the subject of which was "out of sight, out of heart." I spent too much time searching for ideas and finally wrote about the relations between the Jews of America and Israel. It was a thin essay.

All that year I rode the Philips Sport bike I had inherited from Shifra to Tel Aviv, about 10 miles each way, and at the end of the year, I graduated by successfully passing the national Matriculation Exam.

During that year, the leadership of our youth movement decided to merge our group ("Battalion") to the same age group in the Tel Aviv "Central Nest." We were destined to go to our own kibbutz, one that had been established right after the war of independence by ex-*Palmach* fighters who had actually fought over these same hills on their way to Jerusalem; they belonged to the Harel Brigade and had settled near the abandoned Arab village of Beit Geez. Now, five years since the war, most of these ex-*Palmachnics* had left the kibbutz for the more conventional, convenient life in the big city; only a few caretakers still lived in Harel. Our seed group of graduates from the Holon and Central Nests had been chosen to revive what was left of the kibbutz. When we learned we would have our own kibbutz, I felt goose bumps crawl up my arms. That feeling stayed with me for days. Everyone I met congratulated me with claps on the shoulder, as if I had won Olympic gold, and the news inspired a group of guys from another youth movement, *Hanoar Haoved* (the working youth), to join us. This group joined us also because our group was endowed with many beautiful girls.

I was dating one of those girls and so spent many evenings in Tel Aviv, returning home late at night. The last bus left Tel Aviv at midnight, and many evenings I made the bus only at the last minute. On the nights I missed the last bus, I had a choice—I could take a taxi for a lot of money or walk the 10 miles. One rainy night I ran to catch the midnight bus, I had almost reached it when it pulled out of the station. On the right side of the back of the bus hung a ladder that was used on longer trips to climb to the top to place luggage; that night I grabbed the ladder and rode home on the back of the bus.

The forward movement slightly shielded me from the pouring rain, but soon I was soaked. Passing drivers honked and signaled with high and low beams to the bus driver, but the bus kept going until the first stop in Holon. I thought about climbing down and walking inside, but I was so wet and exhausted, I decided to save the fare. I rode all the way home where I was.

On a summer night after graduation, I entered the last bus at midnight. It was one of the newest vehicles, imported from France and made by Chausonne. Passengers entered the back door, and while the bus drove on, passengers paid a cashier who sat in a glass booth in back. It had fewer seats, forcing most passengers to stand. That night I was standing, holding the handle that hung from the roof and letting my tired body sway side to side and back and forth. At the first stop, Shlomo Peeri entered the bus. He was one of the working youth who had just joined our group. Everyone called him Flochick. He paid the cashier and moved towards me.

"Had a good date?" he asked.

"Who said I had a date?"

"First of all, only guys who had a date ride the last bus at midnight, alone," he said. "Second of all, I know you have a girlfriend."

"You know everything," I said.

"Not really. Do you know when we're supposed go to the kibbutz?"

"In two weeks."

"Are you looking forward to it?" he asked.

"Not really," I said.

"Are you serious? I thought you were one of those who's dedicated to the cause."

"Maybe, but my girlfriend's staying in the city, and I don't have a Grush on me. I'm broke."

"So you're not going to the kibbutz?"

"I won't jump ship," I said, "but I want to make money before I go."

Flochick's eyes grew wide as he examined my face. He was small, maybe 5'5", but strongly built. He attended the best tech school in town where the students worked half days as mechanics, welders and in other trades. This had improved his body strength. "I know how we could make some good money," he said.

"Okay, spit it out," I said.

"But it's hard work. I don't know if it's suitable for a bookworm," he said.

His prejudice wasn't unusual for his group and mostly masked a feeling of inferiority they had when dealing with high school graduates. "So what is it?" I asked.

"It's in Sedom," he said, meaning the place known in the Bible as the other half of Gomorrah, the lowest land in the world, at the shores of the Dead Sea. When I said nothing, his smile slowly turned upside down, expressing his disappointment. "The pay is good," he said.

"How much?"

"A friend of mine made five dollars a day."

"Five dollars?" I repeated. He was not sure if I was saying that was good or bad.

"It's good. Room and food are free," he said. "And I hear it's not that hot over there."

The thought of having a hundred dollars before I went to the kibbutz, inspired me. In the kibbutz I would earn five dollars a month, but that wouldn't be enough. "Let's go tomorrow," I said.

Flochick looked at me, unsure as to whether or not I actually wanted to go.

"I'm serious," I said. I was. "Let's meet tomorrow at eight a.m."

The next morning we hitched a ride on a truck that took us as far south as Beer Sheba, an hour and a half away. Then, for two hours, we sat on our backpacks on the road leading to Sedom, but not a single car passed. We were in the "wild south" of Israel, on the road that led to Eilat, Israel's southernmost point. The area was nearly deserted.

At noon, a big truck loaded with steel parts and wooden crates stopped, and the driver called, "Hey kids, where you going?"

We jumped off our backpacks, and I shouted, "Sedom."

"What for?" he called back.

"To work," we shouted together, yelling over the rumbling engine. I looked with envy at the "Super White" truck. In the kibbutz I thought I would drive a truck.

"They gave you kids a job there?" he shouted, surprised.

"Yes," Flochick bellowed the lie before I could decide what to answer.

When the driver turned off the engine, it was quiet, and we could hear two passengers inside speaking in Moroccan. The driver, tanned and blond, looked and talked like a *Sabra*, like some of my brother's friends, like an ex-*Palmachnick*.

He instructed us to sit on top of the cargo and strung a rope to both sides of the truck and told us to hold on tight. We climbed to the top, and once again, the diesel engine came alive. Off we drove. Hot wind dried our sweaty faces, and I felt my lips cracking slowly. We took in the view from our seats more than ten feet above the road. The monochromatic beige of everything around us exacerbated the brightness and heat of the midday sun. There wasn't a spot of green for miles around.

Sedom was 1,378 feet below sea level, and the road from Beer Sheba was downhill, cutting into the mountainous surroundings. I looked at the mountain beside us, a study in geology with distinct layers of varying tones of beige revealing clues about the formation of this earth. As we trundled down the road toward the lower levels, the air became still dryer and warmer. Breathing felt as if I was sucking each breath from a hot open oven – part of the punishment for the people of Sodom and Gemorah.

"It's not that bad," Flochick called over the noise, his lips white with dryness. He felt responsible for our adventure, and he still thought of me as a softy like all those high school guys he knew.

"It's okay. Don't worry," I said.

"When we get there, you tell them you graduated from my trade school, the Max Fine school," he said.

I nodded okay but was not sure I could pull off this lie.

Suddenly we were blinded by a blistering reflection, the sunlight reflecting off the wide Dead Sea. From our vantage point on top of the truck, the Dead Sea looked like a shiny silver platter in the midst of a ring of dry mountains. It did look dead, like everything around it. And suddenly the paved road ended and turned to dirt. The truck bounced wildly, and despite its reduced speed, we held onto the rope for our lives. The fine white dust created by the wheels caught up to us from behind; now we were breathing dry hot air with white powder; I felt like I was breathing flour.

I looked at Flochick unsure whether to laugh or cry. He looked as if he'd been dusted with powder, a bun ready for baking. I held my hat to my face and breathed through it, eyes closed.

The truck stopped, the driver killed the engine, and the silence filled me with relief. We dusted off ourselves and our backpacks and climbed down. We were at a gate with a metal chain hung across it and a small wooden guard booth on one side. A sign was attached to the fence that read: "Dead Sea Potash Company," and under that in big letters, "Plant B." In smaller letters we read: "Scheduled to open December 1955."

December was four months hence.

The driver seemed familiar with the guard; they were talking and joking. He walked back to the truck, looked at us and laughed loudly. "Sorry guys," he said, "the dust is part of the show. Take a shower in the evening."

"Where should we go?" Flochick asked.

"I told the guard about you guys. He's calling the office. Wait here. Good luck." He climbed into the cabin and drove through the gate into the large fenced compound. The guard picked up the phone, a military "point to point" type. He quickly turned a small handle to ring the phone at the office, and after he had talked for a while, he hung up and walked toward us. "The girl in the office said they don't expect no new workers today."

"But we were told we could have a job," Flochick said.

I let him do the talking. No harm done, I thought. Even if we didn't get a job, we could float in the waters of the Dead Sea, hike the area, perhaps even climb Massada one more time. A year earlier we had hiked for a week with the youth movement and then climbed to Massada.

"Who told you?" the guard asked.

"The lady in the company office in Tel Aviv," Flochick lied.

"No, no, no, no," the guard laughed. "You had to be sent by the union, the *Histadroot*."

"But we came all this way," Flochick pleaded.

"You'll have to go back," he said. "But if you want, wait for the manager. He'll be here later."

We leaned our backpacks against the fence and sat on them, waiting for the manager. A 12-inch diameter thermometer hung on the guard's booth, and its big red pointer was stuck on 113 Fahrenheit (44 degrees centigrade). Every few minutes we moved, trying to stay in the small patch of shade made by the booth. As the shade moved with the movement of the sun, we stood and shuffled slowly as not to disturb the powdery topsoil.

One hundred feet from the gate was a small shack that served as an office. Beyond it we saw a few acres of giant metal contraptions with pipes, two to three feet in diameter, leading to bright stainless steel helixes and gigantic tanks, all standing idle. In the distance we could see a small duplicate, which I assumed was Plant A. The plant had been in production for years making potash; some of my childhood friends' fathers had worked here. They too left their families in the city for a week or two at a time, just as my father had for all those years.

I asked the guard for water and he pointed to a low hose bib beyond the gate.

"It's okay, you can go in," he said.

I turned on the tap, and the hot water ran out of the hose; I let it run for a while to let it cool. "You better drink this," the guard said. "It's not going to get any cooler."

A cloud of swirling dust approached and covered us, the guard, and the gate, but after the dust settled, we saw an open jeep with a tall driver wearing a wide brimmed hat. His skin was tan and dry, worn from the heat and sun of this cursed biblical place. He looked like a cowboy in one of the movies I'd seen. The jeep, a military type of WWII vintage, was covered with white dust, masking its original color. The guard, on his way to lower the chain to clear the entry, looked at us when we jumped to our feet. He raised his hand and pointed a finger side to side, signaling to us that this was not the manager we awaited.

"Who are these kids?" the Cowboy driver asked.

"City kids, came for a job," the guard said. "But they weren't sent by the union."

The driver idled the jeep, blocking the gate. He stood and his boots sank into the top soil. "What can you do?" he asked.

"I can do anything with metal," Flochick said. "I can even weld. I graduated from Max Fine trade school."

I stayed two steps behind him.

"And him?" The driver pointed at me.

"The same," Flochick said.

"I can use them," the driver told the guard.

"Hop onto the jeep," he said to us. "I'm the main private contractor here."

And so I had a job as the helper for an expert welder.

Within the first hour of work, he was frustrated with me. He sent me to get a pipe wrench. "Go get the *jabka*," he said, but I had no idea what a *jabka* was, so after looking a while I returned and told him I couldn't find it. He walked to the tool box and showed me a big pipe wrench. "It's right here in front of your eyes!"

When he asked me to retrieve the next tool, the same thing happened, and after the third time, he was angry. "That's it, I've had it!"

I was sure he would fire me, but instead he said, "I can't believe how little they teach these kids in trade schools nowadays. You know nothing!"

I waited to hear the word "fired."

"I have no choice. I'm going to teach you everything from the start."

After that day, his frustration turned to joy. He enjoyed teaching me about steel work, welding, and bolt tightening to exact torque levels, and we spent days slowly building the new potash plant. At midday the temperature reached extreme levels; when I touched a piece of steel without a glove I got burned and needed medical help.

In the late afternoon, all the workers climbed onto the back of a truck, gloves still on to avoid touching metal, and the driver drove us back to camp, a sea of one story wood structures. The big rooms had sixteen beds in two rows, with less than a foot between them. The big openings in the walls were windowless, covered only with screens, and 50 feet in the distance, we could see the Dead Sea and smell its salty vapors. Flochick and I were the only teenagers in camp. All the other workers were adults, Jewish immigrants from Arab countries, most with families living up north. Every night a man named Shabbat who came from Tunis, who slept two beds away from mine, stood naked and gestured at me saying he loved me while the other men roared with laughter.

"I'm going to cut it off," I said, and the others laughed harder. But I stayed awake, on guard, until I heard Shabbat snoring.

We worked seven days a week. We all were there to make a lot of money in a short time, so we worked every day for three weeks, then traveled up north for a weekend and came back for another three-week stint.

We stayed in Sedom without working on just one day—Yom Kippur 1955. It was scorching hot, so Flochick and I went to explore some shady areas in the mountain that rose west of our camp. We came to a big cave, the entry to which was round, about 20 feet in diameter, and tunneled 200 feet into the mountain, narrowing and growing darker towards the end.

As we entered the cave, we felt as if we had entered an air conditioned space and were astonished and puzzled by the cool, fresh-smelling air. As we explored, we found that the cave had an opening in its ceiling, like a flue, five feet in diameter and rising all the way to the top of the mountain, a few hundred feet up, in the spot where the biblical Gomorrah stood. This was where Lot's wife turned to a salt pillar, where the air was cool and flowed into the cave. There we stayed, spending our Yom Kippur in air conditioned luxury.

At the end of the day we went to the dining cafeteria to eat, and before we retired to our room, I stuck a large knife under my shirt. As he had every evening, before lights went out, the little weasel Shabbat showed everyone his dick and called across the room to me, "Shabbat loves you. When Eitan sleep, Shabbat come to fuck him."

The loud laughter of the twenty men stopped abruptly when I pulled the big kitchen knife from under my pillow. Flochick was stunned and did not move.

"When Shabbat sleeps," I said, holding up the knife, "Eitan is going to cut off Shabbat's dick."

There was a moment of silence. Shabbat's face drained of color. Someone said, "He's only kidding, he's just joking, Eitan."

"One more joke like this and Shabbat will be sorry," I said, slipping the knife back under my pillow. After that, Shabbat never said another word to me; after that, I expect he stayed awake and on guard, making sure I was asleep before he slept. And all the tough guys who worked with us began to show me greater respect.

As fall began to turn to winter, I counted my savings. I'd made 250 bucks, so I quit the job and went back north. I spent every evening in Tel Aviv, preparing to move to my new home, our Kibbutz Harel, God's Mountain.

CHAPTER TWENTY

The bus to Jerusalem climbed a hill up the main road. A car, coming down from the eternal city, passed in the opposite direction, and afterwards we were alone on the one lane road as we had been for most of the trip. Passengers looked out the windows at the majestic green hills and valleys. Before we'd reached the top, I pulled the bell to signal the driver to stop. Everyone looked around, curious about who wanted to disembark at this beautiful but semi-desolate area near Jordan's border, close to Latrun.

The bus stopped at a metal post with a sign that read: *Harel*.

I got off, and when the bus departed, I was left in complete silence. I mounted my backpack and crossed the main road towards the narrow one that led to the kibbutz. The pure, cool breeze, and the whisper of the trees in the wind only accentuated the quiet, and Mountain of God certainly seemed the appropriate name for my new home.

As I got closer I heard in the distance dogs barking and bells ringing muted as if on the radio with the volume turned low.

My friends, now members of the kibbutz, had arrived months earlier, and as I walked, I felt the excitement of entering a new way of life, one I had prepared for throughout my teenage years. I wondered about the trucks, tractors, combines and other machines I would work with; I couldn't wait.

As I got closer, I saw a small building; on the door was a small sign that said "Armory." From my work and visits in other *kibbutzim*, I knew this building stored the guns, semi-automatics and rifles for the guards. Exterior stairs led to the second floor where a sign shaped like an arrow pointed diagonally up and said: *Secretariat*. This, then, was the office of the kibbutz management.

I climbed the stairs, opened the door and walked into a large room with bare white walls. Three simple desks and a few chairs were scattered about. At the main desk sat Shula, a girl from Tel Aviv who had a nice face but, unlike my ex girlfriend, this Shula did not watch her weight--hence her nickname – Shula the Fat. It seemed to me that in the three months they had been here in Harel, she had doubled in size. A few other kids were sitting around. Danny smoked, puffing clouds of pleasant superior Virginia tobacco smoke into the room.

I was by now an expert on cigarettes since I had started smoking at 16 with my friend, Asher Hashiloni. I hid this fact from my group at the *Hashomer Hatsair* youth movement because the most strictly enforced of the ten commandments of the Young Guard prohibited it. The commandment said, "The Young Guard does not drink alcohol, does not smoke and keeps the purity of sex." I had broken all the commandments, but here I was standing at the epitome of the movement, in the kibbutz secretariat no less, and the room swirled with cigarette smoke. I had the feeling that life here was going to be different from what I had imagined.

"Hi guys, what are you all doing here in the middle of the day?" I asked.

They stopped talking and looked at me as if an alien had dropped in, one unfamiliar with the language and the rules.

"I thought it's all work here," I continued, trying to be funny.

No one smiled even the slightest smile. "We are working," Shula the Fat said. "We thought you were going to show up here a couple months ago."

"Everyone knew I went to work in Sedom," I said.

"I'm not everyone," she said, "I'm the secretary of the kibbutz, and you should have told me."

I had expected a warm welcome; after all it had been my decision to answer the call of national and social duty, to give up the wonderfully decadent urban life style, but instead I felt attacked by the Communist-emulating committee people who only weeks earlier had been peers.

I decided to cut this conversation short. "So, how come you smoke those expensive Virginias?" I asked Danny. My question actually contained two: Why do you smoke in public and how did you manage to get such expensive cigarettes?

"I was in Tel Aviv and someone gave me a pack," he said nervously blinking.

"In Tel Aviv?" I asked.

"Yes. I drive our Super White truck," he smiled.

"Wow," I said, "and I wanted so much to be the kibbutz truck driver."

"You should have come with all of us," Shula the Fat said. "You could have had a chance."

"It's okay. I'll work on tractors. I like to plow the fields."

"Well, Itsick is in charge of work assignments," she said. "You should see him this evening in the dining hall."

"Itsick the Weasel?" I asked. He was an ugly wallflower of a guy, and he was stupid.

"He's doing a very good job," she said, looking insulted.

I left and set off to look for my friends, Michael Schvager, Eitan Marcus, Yankale Schuster, Flochick and others. I found Flochick who had arrived two weeks earlier. We had grown close during our months in Sedom, and he was the first to offer any warmth at seeing me. We hugged, and he said, "It's good to see your face here finally. I thought you'd never show up."

"How do you get a room around here?" I asked.

"Just take a vacant one. There are plenty."

We went to look at some rooms, and I chose one next to his, one of six in one long structure.

I was back to living in a wooden shack.

In the evening I went for dinner in the dining hall and saw every one of my friends. Ten rectangular tables arranged in two columns with long benches seating eight to ten at each made me feel the kibbutz was bigger than I had thought. Through the double doors at the end of the hall, servers pushing shiny stainless carts loaded with food on plates from the kitchen, and I was amazed to see my friends, boys and girls, working as cooks and waiters now.

As I entered the dining hall, everyone turned to look, and many called me to their table. After I sat the server placed a plate with mashed potatoes and meatballs in gravy before me, but I noticed they were also serving a boiled meat plate which I preferred. I asked for that.

"This is only for the ulcer sufferers," the server said with some disdain at my lack of knowledge of kibbutz rules.

After dinner I found Itsick the Weasel standing in a corner beside a big board on the wall with notices tacked on it, and I stopped to ask him about my assignment. "I want to work on a tractor," I said.

"Right now I don't need a tractorist," he said. "I'll watch for an opening, but for a few days you'll work with the sheep."

That was how I became a reluctant shepherd.

On my first work day in Kibbutz Harel, and for the next few months, I woke at 5:30 and walked to the shepherd shed. The Deernicks, the guys who worked there, showed me the ropes. We would bring in a herd of sheep to feed, and while they were chowing down on their smelly feed, the shepherd would milk them. I was surprised at how he had taught me to approach. I knew from the movies how to milk a cow—from the side—but my instructor showed me, to my surprise, that sheep are milked from the back. So I sat on a stool behind the sheep, spread her legs, placed a shallow pail under her, and reached for the nipples to milk. I did so well with my first, my instructor left me on my own.

I had begun to milk a second sheep when, without warning, she began to poop and pee right into my hands. I walked to the spigot to wash, but as I did, my co-worker complained, "You'll never finish if you wash your hands every time they pee on you."

"You mean I'm to continue to milk with the shit on my hands?" I asked.

"Just wipe it off on the wool and continue," he said, "and by the way, usually the poop comes out in solid little balls."

He was right about most of the time. Still, I was disgusted. "What about the pee and crap that falls into the pail?"

"First of all it's only a little," he said, "and we strain the milk we make into cheese."

For years after that conversation, I couldn't eat sheep or goat cheese, and still whenever I do, I remember that conversation.

The milking was the fun part of my job. After they were milked, the herd was led out to graze in the fields so they would produce more milk. My job was to clean up, which took two more hours of gathering, pushing, piling and moving shit.

I loved the break that followed. I would return to my room until late afternoon and come back to work for the evening milking.

Everyone knew where I worked; there was no escaping the smell. I tried to shower in hot water with plenty of soap, rubbing my skin for a long, long time, but nothing helped. When I got to the dining room, I could see people's faces react. The less politically correct lifted their plates and moved away. A few friends didn't mind that much; they worked with the cows.

One of my co-workers in the sheep herd shack was a girl named Yaffa (Beauty), who looked like a sheep; she had a small face and a blond Afro, and besides being unattractive, she was stupid. On the days Yaffa shepherded the herd out for grazing, the evening milk yield was lower than usual, but she always defended herself by saying that a girl—she was 18—should not veer too far from the kibbutz. The other shepherds blamed her laziness; when Yaffa led the herd, they did not move around enough because she expended so little effort.

One day she decided to take the herd to an area thick with wild, fragrant pea vines. When she brought the herd back for the evening milking, most of the sheep were bigger than usual, their bellies blown up like balloons. Soon we heard an explosion. We turned and saw a sheep lying dead on the floor, its belly badly bloated. Panic took over.

I ran up the hill and had someone call the veterinarian who arrived only after ten more sheep had exploded. He used a long syringe to poke the bellies of the still-living sheep to release the gas inside, caused by all the peas they had eaten.

After that, I was chosen to replace Yaffa as shepherd, and this relieved me from the evening's milking session. In the morning I would milk, then walk out with the herd to lead them to graze on the hills surrounding the kibbutz.

Soon I discovered that shepherding was more art than science. When I walked the herd all day, they groused more but had spent too much energy, and milk production was only average. If I did not move enough, they consumed little, and milk production was poor. I began to take the herd to some untouched hills closer to the border with Jordan—(the Arabs had not yet claimed the Palestine name and were governed by the Kingdom of Jordan). When I did this, milk production increased significantly. Yaffa was furious with me, and so were the others. She claimed I was taking the heard to eat the fragrant peas again, but I pointed out that no sheep had exploded under my watch. "Pure milk, no gas," I said.

A few weeks later, I again asked Itsick the Weasel about my desire for the tractor assignment he had promised. He told me rumor had it that I brought in more milk than the other shepherds and I should stay at my job. Besides, he said, winter was coming and the work on tractors was much reduced. "Maybe in the spring," he said.

Flochick was put in charge of animal feed storage and supply for the sheep, cows and chickens, and in the evenings we commiserated—I about my dirty, smelly job and he about how tough and lonely his was. He was the only one in the feed storage, receiving big sacks one day each week and on the other days spreading them out for the consumers. "I'm alone with sacks of feed all day," he said.

"And I am alone with four legged sacks," I said. He laughed and felt better.

One day I visited Flochick in his storage place. He was miserable in the corrugated tin storage structure next to which stood an old concrete structure which he also used.

"Do you know what happened in there?" I asked him.

"Happened where?"

"In your little storage place, in this concrete structure here," I pointed.

"What?"

"This is where they killed Tubiansky," I said.

"Who's Tubiansky?" he asked.

I was stunned he didn't know about such an important part of our recent history.

"A guy I knew was killed here for spying," I said.

"You knew a guy who was a spy?" He was astonished.

"He wasn't. He was falsely accused." I told him the whole story.

"That's it!" he said.

"What?" I asked. "What's it?"

"That's it," he repeated. "Now I know."

"What?"

"Every day in the darkness of early evening I see his ghost," he said.

I laughed hard.

"You can laugh all you want," Flochick said, "and I didn't want to tell anyone what I saw. But I tell you, now I know it's him."

Over the next few months Flochick assembled books and old papers with articles about the Tubiansky case and became obsessed with the story. "Can you believe they brought six *Palmachnicks* of the Harel division to kill him here at my storage?" he told everyone he met, until the whole kibbutz knew the story.

Each night two members of the kibbutz stood guard, but when times were tense, the number increased. At the end of that year, 1955, tension at the border was rising, mostly at the southern border with Egypt. A number of Egyptian Jews were hanged to death after being convicted on spying charges, and in the wake of those convictions, attacks and counter attacks became more frequent. The border with Jordan was less problematic, but one earlier murderous attack was fresh in everyone's mind. A bus on its way to Eilat had been ambushed at 'Ma'ale Akrabim' - the most winding, steepest, mountainous section of the road that led to the southern tip of Israel. Terrorists, who infiltrated from Jordan, had opened fire and killed the driver first, then climbed into the bus and fired at everyone. "I saw my mother and everyone on the bus fall asleep, so I pretended to be asleep too," said one five-year-old girl who survived.

After that the number of guards at Harel increased to three, and for a few nights I was the third. In the early evening I checked out a rifle made in Czechoslovakia, loaded it with bullets, and began to roam the kibbutz.

We stayed awake all night, eating a meal at 3 or 4 a.m. We walked to the dining hall, the only kitchen in the kibbutz, to fry some eggs in butter and to eat the leftovers we found in the big fridge.

When my assignment as a guard ended, I invited the guards to come eat their night meal in my room. Yankale was surprised. "We should wake you?" he asked.

"Yes," I assured him, "and we'll eat together."

"Why would you want to do that?" he asked in disbelief.

I told him that sleeping through the night meant I only had a chance to enjoy falling asleep once, while if I woke in the middle of the night for a midnight meal, I could enjoy falling asleep twice. And after that, every night, the guards woke me and we ate generous portions of French fries with four sunny side up eggs. During those meals we discussed the news—at the time mostly revolving around the court case of Mr. Kastner, a Hungarian Jew from Budapest who had been accused of being a Nazi collaborator for having saved only 1700 Jews from Budapest. We told a few new jokes, and afterwards I fell back to sleep. Although the guards loved our nightly sessions, I began to get a reputation for being an oddball.

In spite of my desire to be a tractorist and the promises that I would be, I continued to be a shepherd. I did learn to enjoy the hours I spent alone on the hills of Judea, and some days I walked to the border area. One day I saw across the border, on the Arab side, a young shepherd herding a flock of goats, and I called "*Marhaba*," hello.

"*Marhabtain*," he answered--hello times two, in Arabic.

"*Shoo Esmak?*" I asked for his name.

"Ahmed," he shouted back.

"*Ana Eitan*," I told him mine.

From a distance of 200 yards, he stood and looked at me for a long time. I was 17 years old, and he looked to be about the same age, and that night I dreamed about Ahmed, the little boy I had played with at the Buchari market in Jerusalem when he came with his father to sell vegetables. After that I returned to the border area for days, hoping to see Ahmed again, wondering if this might be my old friend. But he didn't return.

On other days I took the flock to graze in the hills closer to the main road to Jerusalem. Traffic was sparse, but every ten minutes or so a bus, truck or a car passed by, and once in a while, a large luxury American car would pass with a quiet whisper that conveyed importance. The driver in front and the sun screen shielding the back seat confirmed the passenger was a V.I.P – a government official, a general or a millionaire. I would watch the whispering American cars and try to guess who was inside, and I made up my mind that one day I would own a car like that, a big, whispering Ford, or perhaps even a Buick.

As winter set in, the soil in our kibbutz turned to sticky, slushy mud. It showed up everywhere--in the dining hall, the kitchen, our rooms. In the evenings there was little to do, and many members coupled up and moved in together. The remaining singles would gather in my room to discuss life, philosophy, politics and kibbutz gossip. We smoked the cheap cigarettes provided--Degel or Silon that smelled like horse manure.

One evening Michael Shvager showed up and tried to elevate our discussion to a higher literary level.

"Hey Shvager," I said, "relax, have a cigarette."

He refused. He did not smoke.

"And don't call me Shvager," he complained.

"Okay. We'll call you Michael."

"Don't call me Michael."

We all laughed. He was the artsy type and wrote short stories emulating the style of the newly emerging famous writers like Nathan Shaham and Moshe Shamir.

"So what's your name for us?" I asked. "What should we call you?"

"Micha Shagrir!" he said. "That's my new name." When the laughing died down he added, "I'm going to be a writer."

After that evening, he often showed me his stories and essays, many of which dealt with the disillusionment with the communal way of life and disappointment in the kibbutz. He was an intellectual rebel, and I empathized with his stories.

In the beginning of April, my girlfriend, Talma, who stayed back in Tel Aviv to finish high school, sent me a postcard to let me know she planned to visit on Saturday, April 9, my eighteenth birthday. I informed my colleagues that I would be taking the day off, and Yaffa immediately objected. I ignored her.

That Thursday evening Itsick the Weasel called to inform me that I would not be given *Shabbat* off. I pointed out that he and the rest of the "jobnicks" in the secretariat office not only did no real work but they also preserved their time and energy to get laid every night. "I'm taking the Shabbat off whether you like it or not," I told him.

He responded, "You'll be sorry."

Talma and I spent a wonderful Saturday hiking out on the Judean hills, and when we returned to the dining hall for dinner, I saw on the notice board the Secretariat announcement. The following Thursday we would have a special meeting to discuss two subjects:

1. The men peeping through holes in the shower wall separating the men's and women's showers.

1. Eitan Makogon's work assignment violation.

On Tuesday morning, I gathered my stuff, placed it all on the bedspread sheet, folded the four corners and tied them together. As I was doing this, Flochick showed up in my room. "What are you doing?" he asked.

"I've had it," I said, "I'm leaving."

On one hand my departure was inevitable. I was an individualist, a nonconformist; when I left the city to join the kibbutz, I did so as a nonconformist act, but on the kibbutz I quickly saw how much control the small management group had over my life. Being an independent-minded maverick hadn't helped to make me popular with various committees, and that was a definite requirement for getting what you wanted in the kibbutz.

"Boy, how did you gather the courage?" Flochick asked.

He was right to ask; breaking the bond we had created throughout our teenage years took strength, and more, it took courage to realize that our dream had been an illusion. Picking up and leaving the people with whom I'd grown up, and with whom I had dreamed, took strength of character, but it was time for me to be on my own.

Flochick and I had shared another dream—both of us had dreamed about going to America one day to study engineering. Now he asked me if I was sure of what I was doing. "You'll go alone to the army," he said, and tears began to fall. I didn't know if his tears came because of his attachment to me or because he felt sorry for himself being unable to leave.

I put my packed belongings on my back and walked down the long road from the kibbutz to the bus stop on the main road. Flochick walked beside me.

As I climbed onto the bus, I turned and called to him, "See you in the army."

CHAPTER TWENTY-ONE

Even for an Israeli summer, that day in late August 1956 was unusually balmy, steamy hot. Fifty of us stood under the scorching sun, arranged in three lines. We wore the new khaki uniforms we had checked out two days earlier, black boots on our feet and khaki green berets, welcome protection from the sun. We waited beside our tents to meet our sergeant.

A stocky, muscular man dressed in an immaculately pressed khaki uniform appeared before us and in a deep Moroccan accent, introduced himself. "My name is Buzhaglo, and I am going to be your shtaff sharghent." He wore his shiny rank insignia on a leather strap on his right wrist, like a watch. "I know all of you *Vousvous* guys are intelligent high school graduates," he said.

He used a derogatory name new immigrants who had fled Arab countries used for us *Ashkenazim*, people of European lineage. European newcomers asked a lot "vous?" (*what* in Yiddish) because they did not understand their Sefardic brethren.

"But here," he continued, "I am God."

I wasn't sure if he was putting on his thick Moroccan accent cynically, mocking in a play to our racist expectations. The new recruits stood there puzzled, unsure how to react. Someone chuckled.

"Who wazh that?" Bozaglo asked. "Take two shtepsh forward."

He ordered the guy who had laughed to run around the group for the next half hour, until he almost fainted, and while he ran, Staff Sergeant Bozaglo talked.

"My mother wazh a whore, my shishter izh a whore and I am going to shcrew you," he said. No one dared laugh or say a word, and over the next few days, he pushed us—we ran long distances, marched in unison, cleaned our tents and the camp's toilets. For a few hours each day we took tests and had interviews to determine what army unit we would serve in and what our job for the next three years in the armed forces would be.

I told one interviewer that I wanted to be an officer, and I was sent to take more tests.

The tests for officer candidates were conducted in the field. For my first test I was assigned a task and a small eight-man unit. As unit commander, I was to get my men and equipment across a man-made river. In the crossing some of my men fell into the water, but our equipment crossed intact. I ended up with my feet wet, boots full of mud.

For the next few days I waited for results, aware that the army was demonstrating the universal clichéd behavior: "Hurry up and wait." During one of those days I met up with one of the new recruits, Amos Ettinger. I had known Amos for several years; we'd originally met on one of the many cross country hikes I had made with the youth movement. He was from Rehovot, a small southern town. "I thought you went to *Kibbutz Harel*," he said.

"I decided to leave," I said. "What's with you?"

"I'm going to be in entertainment," he said.

Puzzled, I asked what he did, and he explained that he wrote songs; the military had created an entertainment group for each of its divisions. Amos was the nucleus of the Central Command Entertainers.

"How did you get your assignment before joining the army?" I wondered aloud.

"I have connections," he said.

I'd known this, but the conversation reminded me that in Israel "protexia" was the way everyone made it, and Amos, I realized, must have had "protexia." Not only would he serve in this entertainment group, he had the task of auditioning others, and he included me and a musician friend of his, Arie Levanon, on the audition committee. As a result, for two days a bunch of new recruits auditioned in front of us. Most of the guys who auditioned had no talent; rather they were compelled by their desire to get away from fighting units, to land an easy job, to be a "Jobnick."

Then I received a letter.

Dear Eitan Makogon,

The results of your preliminary tests show you have the ability to be a pilot. I would like to personally call upon you to volunteer to be an Air Force pilot and be one of the most important defenders of our skies and country.

The letter was signed by General Dan Tulkovsky, Chief Commander of the Air Force.

At the bottom of the letter I read the slogan:

"THE BEST GO FLYING"

Both the slogan and the personal appeal of the commander's letter appealed to me. The Air Force exams took about two weeks, which I would spend on an Air Force base where, rumor had it, the girls were beautiful and the food excellent.

Naturally, I volunteered.

One hundred volunteers took the first few tests--aptitude, math, eye/hand coordination and attitude tests. Most were diehard fans of the Air Force, and most had hobbies that included building and flying toy airplanes. Most had dreamed for years about flying for the Air Force and had talked about flight theory and practice. I felt out of place among these fellows, convinced I had no chance competing against these experienced aviators. Some of my fellow volunteers described their plans to fly aerobatics, but I could only listen, trying to absorb some of what they were talking about, worried I might be asked about it in the coming tests.

At the end of our first day, 60 volunteers were dismissed. Most of yesterday's "expert aviators" who had talked like experienced and confident pilots were suddenly out of the game. The remaining 40, myself included, felt an ego-boost and were ready for the next set of tests.

The next day we were sent to an Air Force base called Tel Noff where we continued to take tests. There we saw pilots in the American P-51 Mustangs and British Mosquito fighter planes taking off and landing beside us. The sight was uplifting. Flying one of these planes, I thought, might be even more fun than driving a tractor. On top of that, the stories we heard about the beautiful girls and the good food turned out to be true.

After days of exams, we finally headed to the Flying Medical Committee where more than ten doctors examined us. We each moved from one room to another—subjected to eyesight tests, tests for depth perception, color blindness, heart problems, psychiatric issues, brain function and some mysterious exams requiring much poking and prodding. In the end, of the 100 volunteers who had begun the series of tests, only eight met the criteria required to go to the Flying Training School of the Israel Air Force.

I was thrilled to be one of those eight.

But first we had to join the other new draftees at Army boot camp. I arrived three weeks into my military service. On the first morning the sergeant inspected us, checking our shaving quality by pulling a playing card from his pocket and running its edge across our faces to listen for any scratching sounds.

I was 18, but I had never shaved and had barely any facial hair.

"Private, what's your name?" the sergeant asked harshly.

"Private Makogon, sir," I said.

"Private what?" he rolled his eyes.

"Makogon, sir."

People in the ranks chuckled at my strange name and at the sergeant's reaction. I knew he now would remember me, while my intention had been to blend in. He ran the edge of his card on my face. "Private Makogon, did you shave this morning?"

"No, sir."

"Why?"

"I have never shaved," I said.

Now the whole platoon laughed out loud.

"Well, Private, welcome to manhood," he said. "Start running around us until I stop you."

I ran around until my backpack ripped into my back and felt as if it had gained 100 pounds; I was sweating heavily and close to fainting when he finally stopped me.

"Think you'll shave tomorrow, Private Makogon?" he asked.

"Yes, Sir," I answered with a forced smile.

I heard the military message loud and clear, "do as you're told" even when, in my humble opinion, it wasn't necessary, and every day since then, I shaved.

Our 30-man platoon was a study in the diversified citizenry of the new state of Israel. Our motley collection of new recruits had varying destinations and myriad assignments. Some would go to intelligence, others to operate heavy equipment, to cook, to manage inventory, to the Air Force and more. There were newcomers from Romania, Iraq, Morocco, Tunis and even one guy who had volunteered all the way from Brazil.

The platoon sergeant had us hike, run long distances with and without equipment, and in the course of those two difficult months, we gained strength and cohesion.

For the finale of basic training, we went on a field exercise for three weeks, leaving the base and heading south to an area next to the Gaza Strip, on the Mediterranean coast. We landed in the sand dunes near a southern Kibbutz called *Zikim*, an area with which I was familiar from the summer I had spent working in that kibbutz. Our first task was to raise our tents and build the camp grounds. The training went on all day and night.

One day I said to the platoon sergeant, "Sir, I can show you a nice place to rest."

"What is it, Makogon?" he asked.

He was forever using my name; he found it unusual and easy to remember, for after all, my family was the only Makogon in the entire country, one Makogon in a forest of Cohens, Levis and Greenbergs. After the sergeant learned I was destined for the Flight Training School of the Air Force, he called on me numerous times a day--"Hey Makogon, the pilot, do this, do that, come here, go there."

"Let me surprise you and the platoon, Sir," I said.

"Ok pilot, take us there," he laughed.

For ten minutes I led the men, during which time both the sergeant and my platoon comrades complained and made jokes about me. Then, suddenly, we were in an abandoned fruit grove surrounded by guava, grapes, peaches, oranges, almonds, and figs. The orchard had been left by Arab farmers who fled during the war, and the grove remained untouched, hidden by surrounding wild growth.

"Hey Makogon, that's pretty good for a pilot." The others gathered around, and the sergeant said, "Platoon, three cheers for Makogon!"

Everyone cheered and slapped my back in appreciation, and the area became our platoon's secret resting place between exercises. We ate a lot of fruit. A few days later, some Arab Fadayeen infiltrated from Gaza, attacking citizens inside Israel in a town close to our temporary camp in the dunes. The order came down to dig a ditch around the camp for security. "Makogon, you'll be in charge of this operation," the sergeant said. "You'll be digging until everyone's head is below ground when they're standing up in the ditch."

Each of us had a hoe as part of our equipment, but digging a ditch around the camp with these little hoes was a monumental task. We began, but the longer we worked, the more the sand slid back in, filling the ditch. We worked day and night, and the guys grumbled. "Enough Makogon, let's go to sleep," someone said.

"Makogon, haven't you finished yet?" asked the sergeant.

So digging could continue, I sent people in shifts to take naps, but by morning we were still digging, and I saw no end in sight. The men were angry, the sergeant disappointed, and at 10 a.m. on the second day, I heard a voice I didn't recognize.

"Private Makogon! Raise your hand!"

It was the company staff sergeant. I was in the ditch, and his shoes were at my eye level, their shiny polish blinding me. I tried to guess what infraction I had committed but could come up with nothing.

I raised my hand.

"Okay, come up here," he ordered.

I climbed out of the ditch.

"Private Even Nir," he called.

A guy from the other platoon identified himself.

"Okay, you two are moving to Flying Training School. Here are your moving orders." He handed each of us a piece of paper.

"You mean right now?" Even Nir asked.

"Yes Private," he said. "Beat it!"

I could not hide my joy. In one moment the platoon and the sergeant were history. I gathered my belongings and left the area hearing the shouts behind me—shouts of derision and of congratulations.

Even Nir and I hitchhiked our way to Tel Nof. As we traveled, Nir told me he'd been raised in a kibbutz in the north, close to an Air Force base. For most of his life he had seen fighter airplanes taking off and landing, and from youth he had wanted to be a pilot. He knew a lot about planes, and though I was convinced my lack of knowledge doomed me to failure, I decided I would try my best.

At the entry gate of Tel Nof, the Military Policeman looked at our documents.

"Going to be pilots, eh?" he said. "Good luck, boys. You'll need it."

In the office of the Flight Training School, the Staff Sergeant told us we were the last of 100 cadets to arrive for course number 25, the 25th course for the young Air Force. The first course had been in 1948.

"Attention!" the sergeant shouted.

One hundred of us jumped to our feet as this handsome guy, not yet 30 years old, walked in; he wore the shiny stripes of a Colonel on his shoulder.

"Sit down," he said. "In the battle of England during World War II Churchill said, 'Never in history has so much been owed by so many to so few.'" He was talking about the fighter pilots of the British Air Force, and he went on. "You are going to be the 'few,' the heroes of the State of Israel. You are going to be the guardians of our skies and our country."

The sudden and startling transition from digging trenches in the dunes at boot camp to hearing these words from the commander sucked every drop of cynicism out of me. Now I was part of a group of cadets training for the most respected job in the military.

After the school commander left, the class commander, a Captain, explained the first four months of our program. As in boot camp, we would split our time between ground school and field exercises, but this training was more intelligent and demanding. We would be observed at all times and assessed based on our effort, behavior, character, and any infractions. He estimated that about one-third of us would not make it to the next stage--the flying lessons.

It had been a year since President Nasser of Egypt had blockaded the Tiran Straits, eliminating Israeli ships from reaching the southern port of Eilat. Now, mid-October 1956, tension in the Middle East was rising since Nasser had nationalized the Suez Canal that connected the Red Sea with the Mediterranean; he threatened to block Israeli and Western ships from using the Canal.

Ben Gurion and Moshe Dayan, the chief of the Israeli Armed Forces, were quoted daily in the papers, warning Nasser not to close the canal. The papers called the act *Casus Belli*, an event that justifies war.

Israel was preparing for war.

The flight school commander told our assembly that school would be dismissed until the war danger passed, and that we air cadets would receive emergency assignments.

Under emergency war rules, every able person in Israel could be drafted for the war efforts. Drivers who owned a vehicle were drafted with that vehicle, and for my first commanding job, I was assigned a taxi driver and his cab.

"The driver and taxi are under your command," the officer said. "Here's a list of 100 drivers and their home addresses. It's your responsibility to have them show up at this base, ASAP."

I had no idea how long such an assignment should take or what would happen if one or more of the drivers didn't show up, but by that time I had learned in the military not to ask too many questions. So I walked out of the office, list in hand, into a crowd of civilians who were standing around.

"Who is Abraham Yoseph?" I shouted to the crowd.

"That's me," said a heavy guy with a thick moustache. Abraham Yoseph looked to be about 40.

"You are now my driver," I told him. "We're going to work together for the next few days." I tried to project as much authority as an 18-year-old could.

Abraham Yoseph and I drove all over the center of Israel--Rehovot, Rishon, Holon, Tel Aviv and Ramat Gan--looking for the addresses on my list, knocking on doors and handing draft orders to civilian drivers. Abraham was very helpful, but at midday he said, "Eitan, I'm hungry."

I had not planned for this and had no food or money. We were in Tel Aviv, and for a moment I thought about going to my parents' house, but that would waste time.

I explained I had no money, but Abraham said, "You're my commander. You're supposed to take care of me."

"In the evening we'll go back to camp to get some food," I said.

But Abraham had an idea. "This is a taxi, after all," he said, smiling, and I could see he had been cooking up this plan for a while.

"So?" I said, pretending not to get it.

"We take some fares, and with the money we make, we buy food and petrol," he said.

What an excellent idea, but was it ok to make money this way in the middle of the war? On the other hand, it would save time. "Okay, but only if we agree to work late into the night."

"Agreed," he said.

The shortage of busses and taxis which had been created because so many had been drafted quickly provided us with eager, paying passengers and soon enough money for meals.

By midnight we had delivered the draft orders to 25 of the drivers on my list, and I realized to finish would take about a week. Driving back to the base would waste hours, so I directed Abraham to go to Dizingoff Street. He was happy, thinking about having fun, but I directed him to Sokolov Street, the quiet street where I had lived in our one bedroom shack. We parked, and I took the back seat of the seven passenger cab. There we slept.

At 6 a.m., someone needing a taxi knocked on the windows and woke us, and we continued to work 18-hour days.

Most of the drivers to whom we delivered the notices were expecting it and willingly siged on, though a few tried to get out of this draft. "I can't go," said one. "My daughter is sick."

"I only deliver the notice," I said, "I can't relieve you from the draft."

"But come in and see," he insisted. "My wife's in hospital!"

"I can't help you. Go to the base and talk to your commander," I said.

"But how can I?" he asked as his wife appeared and told him in Romanian to stop the bullshit.

After four grueling days and some pretty good restaurant meals,

Abraham and I divided equally the extra ten bucks left unspent and drove back to Tel Nof.

* * *

The rumor mill at flight school worked overtime, and one of the rumors I believed was that we were, somehow, being watched all the time. I thought the 18 hour days I had spent recruiting all those drivers would be well appreciated and would contribute to my success. Back at the base I made my way through the new draftees and their vehicles and entered the office.

"Hi, I'm Eitan Makogon. I'm back with Abraham Yoseph, the taxi driver," I told the officer who had a few days earlier assigned me the task.

"So?" he said.

"We finished the list," I said, but even as the words left my mouth I realized he didn't care, that no one was actually watching us or evaluating our performance one way or the other.

"Now go to hangar fifteen and work there," he instructed me.

"Yes sir," I said. For a few days we worked shifts preparing chains of 20 millimeter shells to be loaded on the P-51 Mustang fighter planes and loading bombs onto their wings. The busy base looked like a disorganized factory, with fighter planes taking off and landing after their missions at all hours. Attached to the Air Force base was a camp of paratroopers who were also training and jumping out of transports, DC3's, all day and night.

On October 29, 1956 war broke out.

Israel, France, and Britain coordinated operations, and in only a couple of days Israel had achieved its goals, placing the Sinai Peninsula in Israeli hands.

The World Powers, England and France, were not as successful. Their forces were bogged down with little progress. The US, led by President Eisenhower, had done all it could to reverse the results of the war—and pressed Israel to give up the occupation of parts of Egypt. In a few weeks, the Air Force returned to normal operations and we, the cadets of course #25, returned to restart pilot training, now as war veterans.

One evening a bunch of us went to a movie at the base theater, and as I was leaving, someone called my name. I turned around to see an older man who looked like a professor, in corduroy pants, a sweater with elbow patches, and graying hair. He looked familiar, but I could not place him. "Hi, Eitan, I see you don't recognize me," he said.

"I am sure I know you, but I can't …"

"We met at Ahia Hashiloni's house," he said without waiting for me to finish.

I had met him when I went with my friend Asher Hashiloni to visit his 30-year-old brother, an Air Force pilot.

"Did you spend the war here in Tel Nof?" I asked. I thought he might be one of the drafted reservists, many of whom wore civilian clothes.

"Yes," he said. "What did you think of the war?"

"Oh, we were just assisting. We're only peons," I said.

"I worked here throughout the war," he said, "and I actually saw you working pretty hard for a few days."

We continued walking on the road leading to the flight school, but after a while I began to feel suspicious. What was his job here? Why was he still here? Was he somehow involved with the flight school? I summarily dismissed my concerns. "Yeah, we all worked pretty hard."

"But what's your take on the war?" he said, returning to his question.

I was flattered that a professor wanted my opinion, but for a moment I was quiet. Finally I said, "Not much, frankly," and we continued on toward my barracks. "But if you twist my arm I'll tell you I learned a few things."

He smiled. "Such as?"

"That the war was one big chaotic mess. That even in war some people make money (Abraham and I had), some profit from the war itself, and that as the lowest guy on the totem pole you have no idea what's going on and that you should take care of yourself because no one else will."

"Interesting," he said. "Do you still want to be a pilot?"

"Sure!" I said. My suspicions would not go away, and I wondered if he might be spying on cadets during off-duty time. "What do you do here?" I asked.

"I'm a sociologist," he said. "The sociologist of the flight school."

I stopped walking and began to rewind my conversation tape in my mind, reviewing any possible disaster.

"Don't worry, Eitan," he said.

But I was worried.

"This is a private conversation," he said, "and besides, you're pretty high on my list."

Back in the barracks, still worried about my conversation with the sociologist, I twisted and turned for hours before I was able to fall asleep.

My second boot camp continued for the next few months. I spent half of each day learning math, physics, principles of flight, aircraft identification, meteorology, navigation principles. In the first math class, the teacher, a young female Lieutenant, called out our names. When she got to mine, she said, "Who is Eitan Makogon?"

I raised my hand.

"Do you have a sister named Shifra?" she asked.

"Yes," I said.

"I was with her in the math department of the Hebrew University in Jerusalem," she said. "Shifra is a genius." And I could see that she expected good things from me.

My strange last name, which in many cases helped get me into trouble, had finally proved to be helpful, thanks to my smart sister.

We spent the other half of the day in physical training, doing running exercises, hiking on roads and in the hilly countryside, learning survival skills for an emergency when we might have to abandon our plane and parachute into enemy territory. We learned to overcome an enemy guard with our bare hands and we took long navigation hikes at night, as well as participating in other confidence and muscle building exercises.

Along the way, people started to drop out. Some decided the training was too hard for them (one, Michael B, later became a member of the Knesset, Israel's parliament); others just could not keep up; some were dismissed as not fit to be fighter pilots. For the finale of the preparatory stage, we were divided into squads of five cadets each and driven in the dark of night to an unspecified point in the country.

The members of our group could not have been more different from each other. Haggai was the "smart kibbutznick," born and raised in a kibbutz in the north of Israel; Benny was "the happy Russian," who had immigrated to Israel when he was 10; Dov was the "rich kid' from the city of Haifa; Booker was the "religious guy," from Afula who spoke Hebrew with a Yiddish accent, and then there was me.

It was midnight when the command car stopped and we got out. The driver and the sergeant did not get out of the cabin, and as they drove off, the sergeant called, "I'll see you in Shivta in three days."

Shivta was an ancient city in ruins that had been a caravan stop for the old Nabatians on the incense route that passed through the desert in the south of Canaan, now the Negev Desert. The city had flourished from the fourth to the seventh centuries when the Christians settled there and built churches and other public buildings.

I donned my vest, mounted my backpack and unfolded my Uzi submachine gun. The night was clear and very cold. There was not a light anywhere. The stars were shining so brightly, I felt as if I could reach out and grab them. I looked up and easily found the North Star, so at least we knew which way was north.

"Ok guys, let's get going," Haggai said.

For the last month we had had many hours of survival training and had learned to navigate, identify edible from poisonous plants, and to use the equipment and supplies included in the survival vest we wore when flying a mission. The goal was to survive for a few days in enemy territory while making our way back to the homeland, unnoticed.

"I suggest we start walking right now," said the smart kibbutznick.

That suited me. I was eager to get going.

"Are you crazy?" said the rich kid. "Walk where?"

"I think we should head south," said Benny, the happy Russian.

At this point I realized something we had not thought about. In a real survival situation, when you abandoned your airplane, you would be on your own, alone, but that night in the desert there were five of us, with no hierarchy, no chain of command.

"We don't even know where we are," said Dov, the rich kid.

"He's correct," I said. "Let's first assess, or guess our position."

It took a minute for us to take out the maps of the southern half of Israel.

"We're certainly south of the base," Haggai said.

"How so?" Benny asked.

"Well, the sergeant said we need to be in Shivta in three days, that's how," Haggai said.

"I suggest we prepare to sleep right here," Dov said. "We're all tired, and it'll be easier in the morning."

"I agree." Booker, the religious guy, talked for the first time.

It became clear that we would need to make every decision by consensus, and the thought annoyed me; but it was the only way.

"I think we should push ahead," Haggai said. "What do you think, Eitan?"

I was looking for a compromise, hoping to avoid discussion. To buy time, I said, "Not sure. Maybe we should walk for only an hour so we can limit the damage if we head in a wrong direction. Then we can call it a night."

We walked for a long while--the kibbutznick adamantly wanting to continue, the rich kid just as firmly wanting to stop.

"Oh my God," Booker said.

"You and your God," Benny laughed.

We all looked at Booker to hear what had caused him to invoke God.

"I had a scary thought," he said. "We may have crossed the border."

He was right. The long border with Egypt was not fenced and was sparsely marked, and the possibility did exist. "There could be land mines at the border," Booker said.

No one said anything. I looked up at the sky and saw no stars; clouds had moved in from the west. I unloaded my backpack and took out the sleeping bag.

"I'm calling it a night," I said, and exhausted, I cleared a small path among the rocks, climbed into my bag and fell asleep.

At some point on that freezing night, I felt a light rain falling, but I was too tired and too lazy to worry about it. In the morning we woke to see the vast land around us, a desert reflecting grey skies above. Booker was standing, wearing all his religious accessories and praying. We had, we discovered, slept on the bed of a dry river that had filled with a couple of inches of water during the night. We were cold and wet.

I checked the items we had on us to see if there was any coffee or tea, but the only edibles we had in our emergency vest were a few crackers, a can of ten candies that were supposed to have sugar and protein and vitamins, each one good for a meal, and water purifying pills. I thought the best thing to do was to start walking so we could dry off.

For five hours we walked south but saw not a single living thing. A few times we saw tracks on the ground which we followed for a while, hoping these would lead us to someplace or to someone. Nothing and no one showed up.

In mid-afternoon we saw some people on the horizon and walked in that direction. We were cold and hungry, and as we got closer, we saw that these were Bedouin shepherds herding a flock. As soon as they saw us, two of the men fled, leaving a woman and the flock behind. We came closer and realized she was old and dirty and chewing some grass.

"*Marhava,*" I said hello in Arabic. My limited Arabic was better than anyone else's. "Where are we?" I asked.

"Here," she said. Her teeth were black, and she spat on the ground.

"What's the name of 'here'?" I asked.

She just looked at me, at all of us, five young fellows with weapons. She was reluctant to say anything, and when she did talk, with all this grass in her mouth and between her teeth, I could not make out her words.

"Let's take one of those little lambs and go," said the rich kid. She was herding about 130 newborn lambs, and the thought sounded good—one of them would make a nice dinner.

"No way," said Haggai, the kibbutznick.

"Why not?" I asked.

"This is their livelihood," he said. "Do you know how difficult it is for them to keep a flock alive in this desert?"

"One little lamb will make no difference," I said. "I was a shepherd, I know."

"I'm absolutely against it," Haggai said.

"Me too," Booker said. "I will not eat it. It's not kosher."

"You're in survival training," I said, "not at a humanitarian symposium or in a synagogue."

We could not reach a consensus on this matter, and I took out my water pouch which was close to empty and asked the old lady to give me some milk.

"*Atini haleeb*," I said.

She looked around, chose one of the sheep and milked her into my water pouch. I drank some. It was delicious, and I didn't want to leave. I had a nagging suspicion we had crossed the Egyptian border into the Sinai.

"*Min when anta?*" I asked her where she was from. She pointed to the west. "From there."

"What's the name of 'there'?" I asked.

"Abu Ageila," she said.

This confirmed it. These Bedouins were Egyptians, and it appeared we had crossed into Egyptian territory. We changed course to the southeast to return to the Israeli Negev Desert. Just before dark, as everyone complained about hunger, we all began to express regrets about not taking the lamb. The rich kid was fantasizing aloud about the lamb he would have cooked on the open fire, and the rest of us salivated at the thought. Suddenly in the dwindling light, I saw two quail walking on the ground fifty yards away. Instinctively I raised my Uzi , aimed and squeezed the trigger, firing ten rounds. The sound amplified in the quiet dessert, and my squad members fell to their bellies, their weapons ready.

"Okay guys, war's over," I said. "I think we have dinner."

I had hit only one of the quail, but we built a fire and grilled the bird on the rocks we arranged around it.

"It's not kosher," Booker said, "I can't eat it."

I told him what I had learned in third grade in my religious school in Jerusalem and it was this: "Matters of Survival trump the Sabbath," which in Judaism means: "When life is at stake, all religious rules are off." He was easily convinced, and so we all ate our portions, including chewing the bones. Dov told me I was "street stupid" because I had convinced Booker to share in the meal, but we all slept well around the dying fire.

The third day of our hike in the desert was particularly cold and wet. The top soil turned to mud and stuck to our boots, making them heavier, and our march was slow. But by evening we had arrived at Shivta, totally drenched and shivering.

We found an old grave dug into the hill like a cave at a slightly higher level, probably made for a prominent ancient family. We mustered our last drop of strength and moved the boulder that had covered the entrance for hundreds of years, and we discovered the grave was big enough for all five of us, and it was dry. It was also freezing cold.

"Eitan, let's sleep together," Benny the happy Russian said.

Everyone burst into nervous laughter. "What will your girlfriend say?" they asked. Benny explained that's what they did during the cold winters in Russia, and he and I slipped into the same sleeping bag. We slept through the night, hugging each other for warmth. In the morning we climbed out of the old grave to find the sun was out and the sergeant sitting in the command car on the road below us. He informed us he'd looked but had been unable to find us, and the drive back to base was quiet. We knew decision time had arrived--who would stay and who was going to be kicked out of flight school.

By the end of the week Dov and Booker were let go along with 30 other cadets, about a third of those who had started with us.

"So far so good," Benny the Russian said, slapping my back, "We managed to stay in."

"Yeah," I said. "We fooled them."

CHAPTER TWENTY-TWO

"Seatbelts?" my instructor asked. I was about to take my first flight in Air Force Flight School, and I was sitting on my parachute in the back seat of the two-seater bi-plane. My helmet was made of cloth with earphones built into it. The wide band of the microphone hugged my neck like a woman's choker. I put on my goggles.

"Tied," I said.

The instructor sat in front of me in the only other seat. His flight jacket was nicer than mine, newer, and he also wore a silk scarf that reminded me of the Red Baron from an old World War I movie.

"We're going to start the engine. Are you ready?" the instructor asked.

He was talking to me through the microphone. The front seat had a mirror, like one in a car, and each time he said something to me he glanced in the mirror to see my face. He smiled at the sight of my happy face.

"Ready," I said.

He looked around to make sure no one was in the propeller area, looked at the mechanic and shouted, "All clear!" His soft L and rolling R revealed his Romanian origins.

The wings, above and below, connected by sticks and wires, had skin made of cloth, painted light orange with big numerals in black. We sat in the open, with only a windshield in front of each of us. The instructor signaled his thumb up to the mechanic.

The plane was a "Stearman" built by Boeing before World War II, and I watched as the mechanic turned the flywheel with a handle. This plane had no electric starter, and the wheel made a whining sound that grew louder and louder until it sounded like a fire engine siren.

"Engaged!" the mechanic called, and the engine came alive.

Fire with white smoke that smelled like burnt oil spewed out of the engine and quickly dissipated. I felt the wind thrown back by the propeller, and the mechanic removed the blocks from the front wheels.

We taxied to the runway.

"Remember," my instructor said, "this flight is just for you to watch and enjoy."

He had already explained in the briefing that we should just experience and enjoy this flight because after this lesson it was going to be all hard work.

We rolled onto the runway, and he glanced at me in the mirror. "Here we go," he said. He moved the throttle forward, and the engine roared.

In spite of his instruction to just sit and watch, ever so softly I placed my hands on the throttle and stick. The night before, I had gone with my friend Benny to the Shekem for a drink. At the next table sat a group of cadets, and Rami was telling a story about flying gliders, bragging about his flying prowess. He said he was going to ask his instructor to let him fly the airplane on his first flight so he could impress him with his ability.

Eager for some real flying experience, I kept my hands on the controls to feel what my instructor was doing.

We accelerated down the runway, and he brought the nose down so the rear wheel rose off the ground. Soon we were in the air. I looked down and the runway seemed to be getting smaller and smaller as the wind whooshed past us. Inside the open cockpit felt calm. I tried to put my hand outside the cockpit, but wind forced it back inside, and my glove nearly flew off my hand.

"Look down," my instructor said over the intercom, "you can see the airfield."

It was a sprawling crisscross of runways, with hundreds of colored square fields surrounding it: brown fields recently plowed, green ones with growing crops and yellow ones already reaped. The ground met the sky at the horizon and formed a circle around us. As we climbed to a higher altitude, it became colder, and I tried to listen as the instructor pointed out places of interest on the ground. In my exhilaration I did not hear half of what he said. "How are you feeling?" he suddenly asked.

I wanted to say I was in heaven, but I thought I'd better not show too much excitement. Instead I said, "Great."

"Would you like to fly it a little?" he asked.

"Sure sir," I said.

I didn't know what was expected of me. At that time, we were obsessed with the suspicion that we were being tested at all times, and I didn't want to do something foolish.

"It's all yours," he said, and to prove it, he placed both his hands on the windshield.

I let the airplane continue flying straight, but after a moment I pulled on the stick, and the nose abruptly rose.

"Easy, Eitan," the instructor said, "treat it softly, gently; the way you handle a woman." More gently I eased the Stearman up and down, turned left and right. After a few minutes, the instructor said, "Ok, Eitan, I'll take it home now," and he took over the controls, lowering a wing to start a turn.

I felt as if only five minutes had passed, but my watch showed we had been flying for half an hour. He moved the throttle back, and we glided with the engine idling in the direction of the airfield. After circling the field we turned, came down and landed back on the runway. We taxied back to the line at the Primary Squadron, and the instructor stayed in his seat with the engine running while I got out to let in the next cadet.

Back at the cadet quarters, guys were noisy and excited as each of us told the others about his flight experience. When I walked in, I saw Rami standing with one foot on a long bench at the table, talking to a bunch of cadets. A white board hung on the wall behind them, showing the check lists in large letters. A few unfinished orange soda bottles were strewn across the table. Rami combed his light brown hair, the kind of hair I could tell had once been blond. He had blue eyes and looked, as he always did, as if he had just had a haircut. His flight coverall was clean and pressed, and he used his hand as a model to show every move of his flight, in detail.

"My instructor told me 'it's all yours'," Rami said, "so I took the controls and raised the nose way up." He showed his hand making a climb.

"That's it?" Benny asked in his Russian accent, "you just raised your nose?"

"Wait a minute," Rami said, "then I lowered the wing and turned until we were almost upside down."

The guys at the table were waiting for more stories, and I looked at him in disbelief. Benny took a draw off his cigarette, threw the butt on the concrete floor and stepped on it. "Bullshit," Benny said, "you're full of it, Rami."

I thought Benny was right, but Rami always had some guys around him drinking up his stories, and this time was no exception.

"That's the truth," Rami said, "my instructor even said he could see I had flying experience."

I walked away, my chest bursting with pride and happiness. I wanted to share my feelings about flying but not with my classmates. I wanted to share them with my family and friends from high school, from the youth movement, from the kibbutz.

Flying lessons continued, becoming more demanding as we progressed. My instructor was animated and shouted in the air, and I didn't understand half of what he shouted because of his thick Romanian accent, even more incomprehensible over the intercom.

A few lessons later we practiced take-offs and landings. Things were moving fast, and my instructor was continuously shouting instructions: "Look back," he said after takeoff. "You have to keep in line with the runway."

I looked back and inadvertently pulled on the stick.

"Your nose, your nose is too high!" he shouted. He didn't have different volumes for different levels of urgency. I pushed the nose down a little.

"Too low, watch your airspeed," he said, and then, "turn, turn, turn now!"

No matter what I did, he was a few seconds ahead of me. I kept the nose level with the horizon, checked the airspeed, made sure the wings were level and that we flew square with the runway. "Level off, level off," he said, "you need to keep 1000 feet." While trying to level off, I reached 1100 feet, so I lowered the nose and reduced power to lose the extra altitude and trimmed. I was happy with my quick correction.

"Turn now," he shouted, "turn downwind."

I turned left to fly along the runway, watched the heading, kept the altitude and corrected RPM. In my head I talked to him: "You see lieutenant, if you would only keep quiet and let me collect my thoughts, I could fly."

But he kept pushing. "Correct for the wind," he said. "Too late! Turn to Base Leg!"

I turned, reduced the engine to idle, lowered the nose and trimmed to maintain the gliding speed. "This is our last one," he said, "you're going to land it all by yourself now."

Finally I thought I would have a chance to show him what I could do.

But unable to keep quiet, a moment later he said, "Keep straight with the runway…You're too high, too low, flare, flare, and nose up, not so much!"

We touched down, slowed and turned off the runway to taxi back to the squadron. "My aircraft!" he said and took over. We taxied at high speed to the "line" of the parked planes, and I climbed out of the plane, took off my helmet with the earphones, untied my parachute and carried it on my back to the squadron. My flight coverall was soaking from perspiration, and I was sure this would be my last lesson, that they were about to let me go.

Back in the cadet quarters I saw two cadets emptying their lockers and packing their equipment. One of them was Rami. When I asked what was going on, they turned to me. When I saw their faces, I was sorry I'd asked.

"They terminated us," Rami said.

I felt punched in the stomach. We weren't friends, and his endless bragging had annoyed me for a long time, but now I felt sorry for him. All his life he had dreamed of becoming a pilot, and I tried to imagine how I would deal with the same news. But I didn't know what to say, and the only word I could think of came out of my mouth before I could stop it. "Why?"

"They said I don't have what it takes to be a pilot." Rami burst into tears and continued to stuff belongings into his kitbag, then pulled the string to close it. It looked like a boxer's punch bag, and Rami punched it twice with his fist.

"What are you going to do now?" I asked.

He lifted the bag onto his shoulder, one hand holding it, and walked away without a word. At the door he turned and looked at me and the room for a long moment. "I have no idea," he said. "Good luck, Eitan." He walked away.

That's it, I thought. If Rami had been sacked, surely I was next.

Later, in the debriefing session, my instructor was cool and calm and told me I had a fairly good flight and in two or three more lessons, I could solo.

I breathed a sigh of relief. At least, I thought, I was going to fly again.

That weekend we were permitted off base on a little off duty R&R, and I went to Holon to see my parents. I hadn't seen them for a month, but once there I slept most of the time. On *Shabbat* evening I met some friends in Tel Aviv and came home late, and on the way home I felt a pain shoot across my back. I thought I had pulled a muscle from sitting for a long evening at the café with the cold air of the beach.

In the morning I woke with excruciating back pain and a temperature of 104. My father called the "City Officer," the military offices in Tel Aviv, and an hour later a military ambulance showed up. They checked my temperature and listened to my chest and back with a stethoscope.

"Private," the medic said, "we have to take you to the hospital."

I was worried about not showing up at my squadron on time. I wanted to go back there first, and I told them as much.

"You'll go first to the hospital," he said. "The doctor will determine if you can go back to your squadron."

They loaded me into the ambulance and sped me to a military hospital in an old British camp once called Sarafend; now it had the Hebrew name of *Tsrifin*. There they moved me to a stretcher, gave me some medicine, and I fell asleep.

"How are you doing cadet?" I heard the soft voice of a woman. I wasn't sure if I was awake or dreaming. A tall blond nurse with a boyish haircut stood next to my bed. Her green eyes softened her concerned look. If I had not been in a hurry to return to fly, I would have wanted to date her.

"I have to go back to flight school," I said.

She took my hand and checked my pulse. I couldn't stop looking at her face.

"I know," she said, "but first we'll deal with your problem." She was dressed in a white nurse's top coat over her military khaki shirt and skirt and spoke with authority.

"What's my problem?" I asked. "And what's your name?"

She hesitated, trying to decide whether or not to tell me. I felt weak. "You have pneumonia," she said. "It's a tough one, but we'll discuss it later."

She may have told me her name, but I didn't hear it before I fell back to sleep. I dreamed I had come back to flight school but couldn't fly because I had lost my parachute and my instructor asked, "How can you be a pilot if you can't even keep your parachute?"

When I woke up the lights in the room were on and it was dark outside. I must have slept for hours. For the first time I saw the room was huge, with at least one hundred beds arranged in rows and occupied by young men. It had a concrete floor and an exposed wooden ceiling with old roof beams. The white steel beds showed aging and were peeling, but the sheets were clean and so was the room. An upside down forest of lights hung from electric wires on the beams.

A nurse I hadn't seen before, small and stocky, came to my bed. In a hoarse voice she said, "Lieutenant Nili left these for you to take when you woke up," and she handed me some pills in a cup.

"Who is Lieutenant Nili?" I asked.

"Stop kidding," she said. "She's your nurse who'll be back tomorrow."

I was surprised how happy this piece of news made me.

Over the next few days Lieutenant Nili took care of me. Whenever she came to give me the medicine, she lingered a while. My bed was high so she had to pull her skirt up a little to sit on the edge; I could see her thighs and I noticed a couple of guys staring at her.

"I'm glad to meet another pilot," she said one evening.

Did she really think I was a pilot? Should I tell her I wasn't one yet? And why had she said "another?" Surely I was going to disappoint her.

"I'm not a pilot," I said.

"I know," she said, "but you'll become one, I'm sure." Her face was serious. "I just hope you'll be careful," she added.

"What do you mean?" I asked.

Her eyes filled with tears as she told me about a guy from her school, two years older than she, who had been killed in a plane crash only two months after he became an Air Force pilot. "We were very close," she said. Her boyfriend, I assumed.

After she left, the guy three beds away smiled at me and gave me the thumbs up. "Have you noticed her thighs?" he shouted. "She's all right, the lieutenant!" The other men in my area voiced their approval.

I had not dated anyone for months, and with every passing day, I liked her more.

One evening as usual she pulled up her skirt and sat on the edge of my bed, but this time she pulled the bed spread over so that she was partially under the covers with me. My hand felt her smooth skin. "Let's go out for a movie tonight," I said.

"I can't," she said, "I'm on duty."

"So let's go out for a short walk."

"You're too weak." She smiled. "Come back when you're a strong pilot," she said, caressing my head. Then she stood and walked away.

One more reason to succeed in flight school, I thought.

Two weeks later, clear of pneumonia but still weak, I went home for a week to recuperate. Three weeks after I had left, I opened the door to my room in the barracks I shared. Five beds were arranged along the walls, covered with thin military blankets in random colors—grey, brown, olive green. Benny, the happy Russian, was lying on his bed reading the evening paper, the only one in the room. He moved the paper away, still reading one last line, then looked up to see who had entered. His eyes opened wide, his jaw dropped.

"Hey Eitan, where were you?" By now he and I were close friends, as close as air cadets allowed themselves to get. In this environment, people frequently washed out and friendships were terminated abruptly. Most friendships were, then, precarious, and fleeting. But I was still taken aback when I learned that Benny hadn't known where I was and hadn't inquired.

"In the hospital," I said, "pneumonia."

He continued to stare, but now a shallow smile formed on his face. He placed the unfolded paper on his bed, stood up and slapped my shoulder so hard, I almost lost my balance. "We thought you washed out."

My heart skipped a beat. Have they heard something? "Where are the guys?" I asked.

"David's in the shower, and the other two are out." He moved his hand across his neck in a throat cutting gesture.

"Wow, I didn't even have a chance to say goodbye," I said.

"Once they wash out, they disappear quickly."

"How's your flying?" I asked. "What do you do now?"

"Great, we're all flying solo now," he gave me a thumbs up. "Anyone who couldn't qualify for solo is out, finished." He said it as a matter of fact, neither happy nor sad about it, but I tensed as I realized how far behind I had fallen. I wasn't sure they would bother to accelerate my flying so I could catch up.

That evening in the mess hall the atmosphere was subdued. There was less kidding around, less laughter. The guys talked seriously about their recent lessons using words I did not know--lazy eights, chandelles and spins. I was devastated. In less than three weeks my classmates had matured, were flying solo and had what it took to survive selection.

"Hey Eitan," Haggai said, "are you going to catch up with us?"

"Not sure," I said, "I'll know more tomorrow."

The next day at the primary squadron, my instructor told me I had missed too much, but since I showed "some potential," they had decided to give me a chance to continue. However, I would have to join the following class - course number 26.

The news was a blow, and back in the dining hall, when I told the guys, they were quiet. No one showed much excitement about my predicament.

"It's not that bad, Eitan," Benny said, "you'll get your wings only four months after us."

"If we get them at all," Haggai said.

Everyone laughed nervously as they continued to eat. I felt as if I had been wounded and left behind on the battlefield, despite knowing my classmates could do nothing to help me.

In the morning I left the room I shared with my fellow cadets of Course 25 and moved in with my new mates, the cadets of Course 26. They asked a lot about my flying experience and treated me as their elder, which I enjoyed. But I braced myself for the long wait for my next flight.

* * *

Months passed. I was back at the cadets' quarters of the primary squadron, in my flight coveralls, at the table rehearsing the checklists from a spiral booklet made of cards.

"Cadet Makogon?"

A tall lieutenant stood at the door. He had curly hair and blue eyes. He looked as if he had not yet started to shave. The pilot wings on his chest hung in a loose, nonchalant way and the black ribbon on his arm indicated he was an instructor.

"That's me," I said and rose from the bench.

"I'm lieutenant Shadmi, your instructor. I saw you reading checklists. Are you ready?" His voice was soft and his eyes piercing. I hadn't flown for three months, and I wasn't sure he knew this. Should I tell him? Had he been sent to check up on me?

"Sure, I'm ready," I said.

"I know you've practiced takeoffs and landings," he said, "but to refresh you, I would like you to take me out, climb and level at 4000 feet and show me your turns and steep turns. You've done this before, right?"

It was still unclear as to whether this was a test or a lesson. "Yes, I have done all of these," I said.

"Ok, go check out the airplane," he said, "and wait for me."

Twenty minutes later we were on the taxi way as I maneuvered the plane to the spot near the runway where we did the check list. I reached the last item and asked, "Are you tied?"

"Tied," he answered. This was the first time I had heard his voice over the intercom.

A moment passed and I realized he wanted me to act, not wait for his instructions. I looked at the tower, saw the green light directed at us, and rolled onto the runway and took off.

We climbed up to the designated training area. I turned to avoid the scattered clouds. Lieutenant Shadmi said nothing. For a moment I thought he had fallen asleep. When I tried to level off at 4000 feet we ended up 100 feet too high, and without a word, Shadmi used his hand as a model airplane to show me to go down a bit. Later he used his hand to signal left turn, right turn, go up, go down. "Ok, Eitan," the intercom came alive, "let's go back home."

I turned toward the airfield, joined the pattern and brought the plane down to the final leg for landing. Just before touchdown I felt my instructor holding the controls with me. Once on the runway, he intervened to keep it straight.

"Take off again," he said.

We continued to practice takeoffs and landings. After the third landing, Shadmi took the controls, taxied off the runway and stopped. We sat there for a moment. It seemed like he was contemplating what to do next. Then, with sharp movements, he released his seat harness and climbed out of his cockpit. I thought he was going to check on something, but he turned around, his parachute dangling on his back, and tied the harness in his now-empty cockpit.

My heart started pumping faster. Was he going to let me fly solo? And could I? I had dreamed about this moment for days and nights.

Lieutenant Shadmi moved down the wing toward my seat, pulled down my throttle to idle the engine. "So you can hear me," he said. With his face two inches from mine, I saw the deep blue of his eyes staring at me. I expected him to brief me, offer last minute instructions for my solo flight, but all he said was, "Pick me up right here," and jumped off the wing onto the tarmac where he sat on his parachute at the edge of the taxiway.

I felt my heart booming in my chest. I wanted to shout, but I was afraid Shadmi would hear and think I was nuts, so I kept quiet.

I got the green light from the tower, moved onto the short runway 32, checked the harness again, the instruments. I smelled the burned fuel, or was it oil? I wondered if something was wrong. I noticed the wires connecting the wings begin to vibrate. Why hadn't I noticed this before? Was it normal? I looked straight ahead. The seat in front of me was empty.

It's time, I told myself.

I opened the throttle and roared ahead. I pushed the stick forward to get the tail wheel off the ground and ran straight until I was in the air. After take-off, I went through the checklist, and just before turning left, I uncorked my bottled exhilaration and shouted my lungs out.

Busy with tasks, I stopped hearing the thumping in my chest. Take-off was the easy part. Now I had to land by myself, with no one there to correct my errors.

Gliding with the engine idling, I turned, aligned with the runway, got a green light from the tower, flared and touched down. A gust of air caused the plane to swerve left, and I pushed my right leg all the way and pressed the brake. I heard the wheels squeak as the plane swerved all the way to the right. Realizing my over-correction, I corrected to the left, heard the lower wing touch the runway with a slight scratching sound, but it came back up and the plane ran straight and slowed.

I turned the plane around and taxied toward Lieutenant Shadmi. Cadets on the ground watching the planes take off and land were laughing, shouting and waving. I taxied off the runway and stopped where Shadmi was waiting. He climbed on the wing.

"That's okay, Eitan," he said with a smile, "you made it back."

We taxied back to the line. Shadmi got out and walked back to the squadron office. I got out and tied down the plane. Suddenly, three guys jumped out and poured buckets of cold water on me. When I looked up I saw my course mates around me clapping and laughing.

"You're a lucky dog," someone said.

"A wet one," I said. Wet and cold, I carried my parachute and walked back to the squadron quarters. I thought about how my life had changed. In six months I had transformed from a shepherd in the kibbutz to an Air Force cadet, flying solo.

At my quarters I changed to a dry uniform, got a bottle of orange soda and drank it, sitting alone. It was going to be a long haul.

I continued to fly with Captain Shadmi who talked little. He taught me, mainly by demonstrating, turns, steep turns, lazy eights, emergency exercises, stalls, spins, forced landings and even slow roll and other aerobatics. After each lesson I flew solo to practice what I had learned. In the last of these solo flights I flew up to 4000 feet and practiced everything. While still in the air, I looked below and saw the city of Ramle, a mixed Arab and Jewish town on the road from Tel Aviv to Jerusalem; I looked at the buildings that so contrasted with the old mud huts, and at the minarets dotting the city, like needles poking into the sky. As I started a turn to avoid leaving my practice area a little to the east, I saw the kibbutz I had left only a few months earlier. It looked so close, I felt a sudden urge to visit it from the air.

At high speed I descended to a lower level and flew along the road in the direction of Jerusalem. I had traveled this road many times—when I left Jerusalem after the war, when I lived in the kibbutz. As a shepherd I had watched the whispering cars passing by, and now, though I still had no driver's license, I was flying over those fancy cars, without permission, breaking orders.

I hesitated for a moment but then thought a short visit would be ok. I was eager to see some of my old friends--Eitan Marcus, Micha Shagrir, Yankale Shuster, Flochick or perhaps one of the shepherds I had worked with. I hoped they would be there to see me.

As I got closer I could see the kibbutz was green, covered with the vegetation of a mild winter. I saw the dining hall, the community showers on the slope, and almost at the top of the hill, my room in the long wooden structure. Down the hill was the sheep barn, its corrugated tin roof rusted. John Deere tractors, combines and other pieces of machinery were scattered around, left to rust. I was surprised at the neglect which depressed what little nostalgia I felt.

I circled the kibbutz at 300 feet and saw some people at the sheep barn but could not identify them. I descended to a lower level and circled again at 50 to 100 feet. More people came out of the structures to look up at me, and I saw someone waving but couldn't make out who it was. I wanted to stay longer, but I knew I shouldn't have been there at all, so I waved my wings for goodbye and turned to fly over the nearby fields, the ones where once I had taken flocks of sheep to graze. Flying close to the ground which disappeared under me at a speed I had not experienced before, I saw the flock with its shepherd and made a pass only a few feet above them. After I pulled up and turned slightly, I looked back down and realized that I had scared the herd which scattered all over the field. The shepherd angrily moved his fist in the air in a threatening gesture, and as I turned to leave I saw another flock a few hundred yards away, across the border. An Arab kid was walking with it and looking at me.

I pushed the throttle to full power, raised the nose above the horizon and trimmed the airplane to a steady climb, heading back to base. I checked the speed, 70 knots, oil temperature and pressure normal. I looked around and saw no other airplanes in the vicinity. Still I felt a knot in my stomach. I could not stop thinking about what I had just done. I could be sacked for such an infraction.

Only a month earlier, a cadet had been terminated because he flew above his home at low level and his neighbor called the Air Force to complain. If caught, I could even go to jail. The aircraft ID number was marked in giant numerals on the bottom of the wing. It would be easy to know who had been flying this airplane. The more I thought about it the more worried I got, sickened by the thought of how disappointed Lieutenant Shadmi was going to be. I was nauseated all the way back to the runway.

After landing, I pulled into position in the line of airplanes at the squadron, praying I wouldn't get caught. As I jumped down from the wing I saw my roommate, Effie.

"So, what now?" he asked. He was a thin guy, smart and cynical and competitive. He always asked provocative questions. He grinned. I feared he might already know something.

"What do you mean?" I asked. He had a wide smile. Wicked, I thought.

"This is your last flight, isn't it?" he said, keeping the smirk.

I felt the blood draining from my face. "My last one in this airplane," I said and walked away, refusing to continue this conversation. I walked back to the quadroon where Shadmi called me over. "I want to talk to you," he said, "go to the briefing room."

The knot in my belly tightened. I placed my parachute and gear in the locker and walked to the briefing room. Shadmi came in holding a folder, but someone called him and he placed the folder on the table and said, "I'll be right back."

When he walked out, I glanced at the file with my name on the cover.

Shadmi returned and sat across from me, looked at my file and for a long time sat silent.

"You were a member of kibbutz Harel, weren't you?" he asked.

OK, Eitan, I thought, you're going to tell the truth now. That's the least you can do to limit the damage and be fair with Shadmi who may be fair to you in return. But I knew this could be the end of this road for me. "Yes," I said, "I left Harel shortly before joining the Air Force."

"Have you seen it from the air yet?" he asked, "flown over it?"

The checklists book slipped from my sweating hand and fell on the floor. I bent down to pick it up and slowly straightened. "I always wanted to," I said, thinking hard about my next sentence. How would I tell him?

Effie entered the room. I stopped talking and turned to look at him, and so did Shadmi. When Effie understood he was interrupting, he said, "Sorry," and walked out.

"I'm a member of kibbutz Ma'abarot," Shadmi said.

"Yes, I know," I said. His kibbutz and mine belonged to the same political movement.

"I didn't know you were from Harel," he said looking at my file. "I would have flown you to see it."

I said nothing and wondered if he could hear my heart beating as loudly as it could. I wiped the sweat from my forehead with my flight suit sleeve.

"It's ok, Eitan," he said. "You'll have a chance to fly over Harel sometime." He spoke to me at length about my flying, stressing items I should work on to improve. He offered tips for the next stage and looked at me as if he expected me to say something or ask questions.

I wanted to tell him how much I appreciated his patience and lack of verbosity but I couldn't get the words out. Outside, a Harvard airplane was going "round again" and passed above us shattering the quiet with its roar.

Lieutenant Shadmi pointed up with a smile and said, "Your next airplane. Good Luck!"

I wanted to hug him, but I held back. "Thank you, Sir," I said. "I'm ready."

CHAPTER TWENTY-THREE

Thirty one cadets, only a third of those of us who had begun training, were sitting in the assembly room of the "Basic" squadron at the beginning of a new trimester, the Air Force called it a "Period." The squadron commander began with congratulations to all of us, and went on. "You're going to fly the AT-6 'Harvard which is more complex and much less forgiving than the simple Stearman you've flown so far."

On our shoulder straps, we now wore the wide white stripe indicating our more advanced standing in the flight school's hierarchy. We also all wore serious, attentive expressions; we had quickly matured, much more quickly than we might have expected to in a single year.

"I am going to introduce your instructors," the commander said. Seated next to him and facing us sat a group of flight instructors, all young fighters, some only two years older than I: Zorick, Avnery, Chankin, Salant, Alroi and others, he introduced them one by one.

Soon afterwards, we began flying the Harvard, and I realized quickly that this plane required closer attention and effort. It had a variable pitch propeller, retractable gear, flaps, a closed cockpit, and instead of sitting behind the instructor, on this aircraft I sat in front of him.

We lost a few more course cadets, and quickly reached flight solo stage. My instructor, Captain Salant, was teaching me maneuvers I knew but in this new plane they were harder. He and I had good chemistry on the ground during our briefing and debriefing. One day after a flight, I noticed he was sweating almost as much as I was. I could see he wanted me to succeed.

And so I did.

Basic flight training lasted four months. I passed the flight check once again and graduated to the advanced stage, the next "period." I couldn't wait.

That evening I told Benny, the happy Russian, I had passed Basic's final check. We had maintained a loose friendship despite my having dropped to a lower level class, and thus to lower status. "Eitan, let's have a drink now that you're moving up in life," he said.

"Please don't tell me you have another blind date for me," I said, as we sat down in the Shekem to drink our orange soda. Months earlier, on one off duty weekend, he and his girlfriend had invited me to meet them in Tel Aviv and had brought along a blind date for me. She was overweight, shortsighted, and boring.

"No, but I can easily arrange one," he said. "With my uniform I meet a lot of girls." The cadets in the advanced squadron had replaced their standard berets with officers' hats, the one with a visor; they also had the newest and coolest flight crew sunglasses and coats.

I described the different maneuvers and the forced landing I'd completed for my flight check; the flight checker had let me almost touch the ground of a plowed field before, at the last minute, he told me to "go round again."

"How's your flying, Benny?" I asked.

He told me I would love advanced flying, and when I asked him what he liked best, he said he excelled at and loved aerobatics.

"Is aerobatics the main thing?"

"No," he said, "but it's the main fun. You also need to be good in formation, navigation, instruments flight, and flying at night."

"You're a lucky dog," I said. "I envy you."

"You'll be there in only four months," he assured me. "But I won't lie to you. I can't wait to be an officer and get my wings."

Benny was going for his final check in general flight and aerobatics the next day, and if there was anyone I would have bet on to make it, it was Benny. He was smart, handsome, charismatic and passionate about flying. "Think you'll pass?" I asked.

He smiled widely, but his eyes did not. "I'm as good as anyone in my course," he said. "I'm going to be an excellent pilot."

I envied his confidence, and suddenly four more months looked like an eternity.

The next evening at Shekem I saw Benny sitting in his flying jacket and dark pilot glasses looking like a real Russian pilot. I quickly approached to ask him how the test had gone.

He looked away and said nothing. Slowly he removed his flying jacket and pointed at his shoulder straps. They were bare; the wide white stripes indicating he was an 'advanced' cadet were gone. He removed the cool dark glasses and I saw his eyes were rimmed with red.

"They kicked me out," he said.

My heart sank, and for a moment I felt nauseous. Without a word, we embraced. I couldn't imagine how the man I had been certain would succeed could have failed. After a few moments I asked what he planned to do.

"They offered to let me fly light airplanes."

"And?"

"No fighter – jet, no flying, I told them."

We had a couple of sodas and reminisced about the time we had shared a sleeping bag during our survival trek in the desert, and when we parted, he shook my hand. "Good luck, Eitan. At least one of us will be a pilot."

I slapped his back, raised my hand for goodbye, and choking back tears, I walked away thinking that if Benny was out, making the cut was going to be even harder than I had imagined. That night I tossed and turned—aerobatics, formation, navigation, instrument flight—suddenly the load seemed very heavy.

* * *

After vacation I sat with the remaining cadets of our class in the briefing room of the advanced squadron. There were 20 of us, each wearing our new hats, styled like the officer's hat but with a white stripe around it to indicate we were still cadets.

"Attention!" the cadet on duty called, and we stood.

The flight instructors walked into the room and sat before us. Behind them came the new squadron commander who stood behind a desk in front. As we sat, the room filled with noise from our chairs scraping the floor, but the tumult settled quickly, and our squadron commander spoke in a slightly high-pitched voice. "My name is Major Shyke Bee and I am your squadron commander."

He was small, 5'4" or 5'5" at most, thin, with deep eye sockets from which his black eyes seemed to bolt. His hair was thinning on top, and his uniform impeccably pressed, the creases sharp and in all the right places. Most pilots dressed less formally since flying was deemed more important and looking cool was more *de rigueur* than was looking pressed. The disciplined staff sergeants, however, favored impeccability. I noticed the major's insignia on his shoulder were shiny, the pilot wings on his chest perfectly placed. He looked like a midget British officer, or a German one.

"I am going to require of everyone the utmost dedication," he said, and as he raised his voice, I detected an accent, though I could not tell precisely what.

The room was silent.

"And don't tell me about how lenient my predecessor was," he continued.

"I require total discipline." His face reddened and became more animated as he continued, and his eyes seemed restless and even more pronounced.

"I lived in Poland during the Second World War and I know how important it is to defend our country." By now he was almost shouting. "I will require you to follow orders with no exception." His eyes moved rapidly from side to side. It seemed he wanted to say more but changed his mind. Then he saluted.

"Attention!" the duty cadet called.

We stood as the major walked out of the room. The instructors looked at each other, some of them smiled, and they followed him out of the room.

The 20 of us sat quietly for a while. Our new squadron commander was a complete contrast to our experience; up until then, Cadet-Commander relations had been friendly and informal. Now I knew I was in for something new.

* * *

Etti was not a beauty queen, but if the contest were held for the Tel Nof Air base girls only, she could have been a contestant. She was a pleasant girl from a kibbutz in the Jezrael Valley in the north, and she had fair skin, a slim body and lovely breasts. She was also terribly neat, and best of all, secretary to the flight school commander, Colonel Shaya Gazit. This last fact kept many a cadet away from her, but it didn't bother me.

One free evening she agreed to go out with me, and in the darkness of the back row of the base movie theater she became my girlfriend. I don't remember the movie, only that that was the beginning of many evenings with Etti. On weekends when most of the cadets went home, she and I stayed on the base, mostly in her room.

Meantime, our flying program grew into more complex areas and maneuvers, leaving us less and less free time. Aerobatics, instruments and navigation required studying and preparations on the ground, and though busy, I felt satisfied. We were becoming real pilots.

One afternoon I was at the squadron, on the cadets' side, preparing for a flight when I heard someone call my name. I looked up and saw the squadron commander standing by the door to his office in the adjacent building. "Makogon, come to my office," he said. He walked back inside.

It was the first time anyone had summoned me to that office, and I had no idea what it was about, but I wasn't worried. The invitation felt friendly. I walked to his office, saluted, and he motioned me to sit across from him at his desk which was covered with telephones and a shiny silver trophy in the corner. His chair had an extra cushion to make him appear taller, and he looked spic and span.

Suddenly I realized how dirty my flying overall was, and I smelled from unwashed sweat.

"I heard you were voted to be the head of the Cadets' Council," he said with what seemed like a wry smile. "That's an important position."

"Yes Sir."

"So you feel superior now, don't you?"

"Not really," I said.

"You think you're smarter?" he asked.

I said nothing, not knowing what he wanted me to say.

"You think that you are smart, ha?" he asked again. "I am asking you, ha?"

I quickly ran some possible answers through my mind. If I said yes, he'd think me arrogant, but if I said no, I might reveal a lack of confidence; he might think me a *shmatte*. Cold sweat ran down my face and beneath my arms. Finally I managed, "not particularly."

"You had it so easy. You played here while I was in Warsaw in WWII. We had no food, no shelter. I had to rummage in garbage cans to look for food. Every day I looked for potato peels, which, if I was lucky enough to find some, I ate raw. What do you think about that?"

What I actually thought was that he seemed crazy, not because he had suffered but because he was telling me all this out of context, with no reason. I wanted to tell him we had suffered too, that I'd been a refugee, hungry in Jerusalem under Arab siege. But I silently told myself to stay cool. "Sorry to hear about that Sir," I said.

"You guys think you're champions," he continued. "You think that because you were born here, because you're *Sabras*, you are superior people, am I right?"

I said nothing, but deep down I knew we *Sabras* did feel we were the new, improved generation. We would never go to slaughter without resistance like those "Diasporans" had, like those Holocaust survivors, or "soaps," as we called them.

His voice rose as he ranted on. By the end he shouted, "Get the hell out of my office."

I quickly returned to cadets' quarters, sat down and looked at the map. I wanted to study the route for my navigation flight, but I could not concentrate. Why always me, I wondered as I recalled every word. Was it my name? My face? My attitude?

That day I flew a terrible flight.

In the evening, when I told Etti what had happened with Major Bee, she looked at me and said, "Oh my God, I'm so sorry."

"For what?" I asked.

"I didn't tell you something I should have," she said.

She explained that a few weeks earlier Major Bee had asked her to go out with him. Her face was sullen, as she spoke, and for a long moment I was quiet as I pictured this balding, older officer—he was over 26—asking my girlfriend for a date.

"And you didn't tell me?"

"I feel terrible," she said.

"So, what did you tell him?"

"I tried to ignore it," she said, "but when he persisted, I told him I had a boyfriend. He wanted to know if it was an officer in the flight school, and finally I had to tell him it was you."

I wasn't upset with Etti, but I began to worry. Having a disturbed commander could not be helpful. I asked her to tell me if he'd said anything more, and she began to sob.

"He said I was stupid," she said through tears. "He said I could get any pilot, any officer, I could even get him to be my boyfriend, and instead I was dating a lowly cadet with a questionable future."

I was quiet, thinking. No matter how hard I tried, I always found trouble. I was here because General Dan Tulkovsky had invited me to volunteer, and I'd expected support, not this nonsense. I didn't know what to do, and I could think of no one to ask.

* * *

I loved this stage of my flight training, and I felt good about my performance in aerobatics. Not long after this debacle, we assembled one morning in the briefing room—all the cadets and instructors—when Major Bee strode in and began a new rant. He repeated his story about the potato peels from the garbage in Warsaw. Then he was quiet a while, seemingly deep in thought. I looked around and saw everyone's faces etched in disbelief.

Suddenly Major Bee said, "In my opinion, a flying cadet is seven degrees below the rank of a private, do you agree?"

No one moved. We did not understand where he was going with this idea. He looked around and repeated, "Seven degrees below private. Do you agree?"

There was a screaming silence.

"Who doesn't agree?" he asked.

No one moved. Like others, I tried to hide behind the cadet in front of me. If I could avoid any eye contact, I thought he would leave me alone.

"Makogon," he called, "do you agree a cadet is ranked seven degrees below a private?"

There I was, in trouble again. If I agreed, I would look stupid and cowardly. I felt everyone's eyes looking at me as he shouted again, "Do you agree?"

"No Sir," I said, "but I don't mean to say we are superior, and I don't think it's relevant. I barely know how to fly but I'm working to learn. I know very little about how to define military ranks."

His face was red and his eyes bulging with rage. With his perfect uniform and shiny insignia, he again reminded me of a German officer like those he had escaped in childhood. Why emulate them, I wondered silently. "Makogon, get out. You are washed out of this flight school!" he said even before I had finished my sentence.

No one in the silent room moved. I was stunned. Could he do this? Throw me out just like that? What about all my effort these last two years? What about all the flying hours the Air Force had invested in me? Why wouldn't one of my instructors say something?

"I said, get the hell out!" he shouted. "You're washed out!"

I looked up. He wore a wry, triumphant smile, an expression as if he had just called "Check Mate!" in a game of chess.

The others looked at the floor as I walked out of the room.

A few hours later Lieutenant Salant, my instructor, came to my room. "I'll try to see what I can do," he said. "For now you won't fly."

As days passed, sources told me there were discussions in the headquarters about my future, but no one could reach an agreement. The school commander thought I should continue to fly, and the subject moved up the chain of command.

A week later, Major Bee called me to his office. "I wanted you out," he said, "but the higher ups convinced me to give you a chance. I won't lie to you; they've forced me to give you another chance. For the next two weeks you'll be on probation." He looked at me with his now familiar bitter smile. "I'll be watching you!"

I continued to fly, trying my hardest to do everything right, but more importantly, to stay out of Major Bee's sight. Finally, at the end of two weeks, he called me to his office. "I've watched you and I saw that you tried hard." He was still wearing that smile.

"However, I have here a list of your infractions." He picked up a paper from his desk and read aloud the days, dates and infractions: One day I had walked out without my hat, another I had not shined my shoes properly. I had made no flying errors.

"In view of all that," he said, "I could throw you out of this flight school, but I have decided to let you stay," he said, looking intently at me. "Don't thank me yet. You'll drop out of this class and wait to continue with Course # 27."

I felt as if someone had punctured me and all the air inside was gone. More months of waiting? A new group of cadets? Impossible.

I decided to take a week's vacation at home, during which I was contemplating quitting. After all, I had come to the Air Force to try it, not because I'd always wanted to be a pilot. If I quit I would have to serve only a few more months to complete my military service and I could go for plan B which was to study Engineering in the States. My parents encouraged me to quit, and I thought seriously it was time to go.

I went to meet with my friend Asher Hashiloni. When I told him I was thinking of quitting, he was stunned. "You only have to wait a few months," he said.

"I like to fly," I said, "but I don't like the military."

Asher began to articulate all the arguments against quitting--not everyone has this chance, his brother loved flying and being an officer, and then he added one more thing. "But it has to remain between us," he said.

"What is it?" I asked.

"My brother's friend Nissan, the sociologist at the flight school, told me your file shows you have an excellent chance to be a good pilot and to advance rapidly."

"Bull," I said.

"It's true," Asher said. "He told me not to tell you."

I returned to the base and moved to a new room with the cadets of course number 27. By the time this group caught up with my level of flight lessons, only a dozen remained.

The cadet body of the flight school elected a Cadet Council whose function it was to help the cadets represent their interest in meetings with commanders. I was elected to the council and then further, as Cadet Leader. I thought they had selected me for my seniority, but I think they also wanted to spite Major Bee.

The Tel Noff air base had a large theater hall, and there, at the end of the "Period" we held a flight school gathering to celebrate. All the mechanics, cadets, flight instructors, squadron commanders and some guests--a few hundred people--attended. One of the guests was Brigadier General Eyzer Weitzman, the new chief of the Israeli Air Force. The school commander took the stage and summarized the activities and improvements of the last four months. He then called for the outgoing cadet leader and me to come to the stage to say a few words.

The outgoing cadet leader talked in detail about his committee's accomplishments under his leadership; his speech was long and disorganized. I noticed the crowd growing antsy as he went on, and I saw even Eyzer Weitzman in the first row wouldn't wait for the speech to end. When he finished, there was faint applause, and Colonel Gazit, the commander, called me to the mic.

I leaned in and said, "With much pride but not without worry, I accept my appointment," and I stepped away.

The hall burst into a loud applause, and afterwards Eyzer Weitzman came to me and shook my hand warmly. "Makogon," he said, "great speech!"

Our advanced flying training continued. I liked the freedom of the aerobatics that required our own individual planning and execution. In contrast, I also enjoyed the strict constraint of the close formation flights with two airplanes flying just two to three feet apart, number two following the leader. Later we flew in formations of three and four planes. For the first time I saw other cadets in flight up close. For almost two years, I had flown with instructors who debriefed me about what happened in the air, about what and how I should improve, but the instructors and checkers seldom were explicit as to my grade for a flight just completed. We had no idea as to how we stacked up in comparison to our fellow cadets or what our chances were for successfully completing training, and this added to the stress we felt. One Thursday afternoon after our instructors had left the squadron, we cadets realized we were alone.

By then only ten cadets remained in course 27.

"Let's go look at our files," someone said—that someone may even have been me, but I don't recall. In silent agreement, we walked to the instructor's room where they kept the files and each of us found the file with his name, pulled it out and began to read records of every flight we had ever flown with an instructor.

Not sure if I actually wanted to see what my instructors had written about me, I hesitated. Then, inhaling deeply, I opened the file and found a glued page with printed instructions for filling out the forms and a list of grades and their interpretations.

Below Average - Fail
Low Average - Fair
Average - Good
High Average - Very Good
Above Average - Excellent

My file was especially thick. Each flight lesson was described in more detail than I had expected, notes handwritten and each with a grade. The file also contained letters regarding my stay in the hospital and the transfers I had endured. Afraid of getting caught, I wanted to have a quick look and get out of there—this infraction could finish our careers. I turned to the most recent pages and felt cold sweat running down my back. My fingers trembled as I turned the pages until finally I saw a page with the most recent period summary evaluation. It had a list of flight subjects and my grade for each subject across from it:

> General Flight - Above Average
> Aerobatics - Above Average
> Instruments - High Average
> Formation - High Average
> Navigation - Average
> Airmanship - High Average

I thought my knees were going to give. I wanted to study it longer—I couldn't believe my eyes. All those months I'd been wracked with insecurity. I read my grades once more, closed the file, placed it back in the cabinet and ran out of the room. Heart pounding, I felt bursts of blood flowing to my head. Suddenly the fuzzy picture of my future became vividly clear, as if I had turned the camera lens and brought the near future into sharp focus.

I was going to be a pilot. Thoughts about studying to be an engineer evaporated, especially my plan to go to study in the U.S.A.

I did not volunteer to any of my fellow cadets what I had just seen, and I did not ask my mates what they discovered in their files, though later when Yuval asked me about my grades, I said, "Not so bad, okay." I did not ask him. I thought the less we discussed it, the better.

That evening Etti asked me why I was in such a good mood.

"I know now I am going to be a good pilot."

"How come you're so sure?" she asked.

"I just know," I said.

With my fellow cadets – the remains of course #27.

CHAPTER TWENTY-FOUR

We had arrived at Ramat David, the northern base of the Israeli Air Force situated in a beautiful area of the Jezrael Valley. Next to the base was a kibbutz of the same name and to the west was a farming village – *Moshav Nhalal*, known for producing many famous Israelis, the most famous of whom was the venerable Moshe Dayan, the one-eyed chief of the Army and Minister of Defense. We were here to get our last period of flight training. Upon finishing, we would get our pilots' wings and the rank of Second Lieutenant. At *Ramat David*, we learned to fly the Meteor, the first jet plane of the Israel Air Force as well as the British Royal Air Force.

The transition from the single engine, propeller driven Harvard trainer to the twin engine jet fighter was exciting and challenging. A group of veteran reserve fighter pilots arrived at the 117 squadron to train with us and we enjoyed the camaraderie. I enjoyed flying my first jet and the weeks passed quickly. One morning, during the preflight exterior check, I was crouching under the wing of the Meteor, checking the undercarriage, or wheel bay, when I heard a car come to a screeching halt nearby. Emerging from under the wing I was surprised to see one of my favorite Hollywood stars standing in front of me.

Danny Kay, the comic actor, stepped out of the sleek military olive green Plymouth accompanied by the commander-in-chief of the Air Force, Brigadier General Eyzer Weitzman. His driver remained in the car.

"Meet one of our young pilots," Eyzer said.

This was going to be one of our last flights, but I noticed Eyzer had described me as a "young pilot," not a "young cadet."

"Danny," he said, "it's nice to meet you." Danny Kay shook my hand. "What are you going to fly now?"

"Close formation," I said. "Four of us."

For a minute or two, a military photographer shot some pictures of the actor with me, and the plane, and they departed.

Later, after we had landed, we all went to lunch, and although we had no officer rank or wings, in this northern base we were treated like pilots, sharing a dining hall with the officers and pilots of the base.

Outside the dining hall I again saw the Plymouth and stopped to have a closer look. It reminded me of the cars I had seen passing by just two years earlier when I was a shepherd.

"Makogon, why are you staring at it so hard?" a voice asked.

It was Eyzer with his entourage, walking outside from their lunch with Danny Kay and the base commander.

"I am admiring your car, Sir," I said, stunned he had remembered my name. "Sir, please tell your driver to take good care of it."

He looked down at me, his blue eyes wide open, eyebrows raised. He clearly wasn't accustomed to a peon like me making a comment.

"Why?" he asked.

I had hoped he would. I offered my punch line. "Because one day he will have to drive me in it."

Eyzer and Danny Kay laughed loudly, and so did the accompanying reporter. I noticed the base commander's lips tighten--no laugh from him.

A week later we were briefed for a formation flight, our last. A photographer and a reporter from the military weekly magazine *Bamachane* were to fly with us and take pictures, and two weeks later the story was printed in the magazine with lots of pictures. I appeared in many of those photographs under the title, "First Steps in Jets." I called home, and when my mother answered and heard my voice, she asked why I was calling. "Is everything all right?" She was unaccustomed to hearing from me.

"Yes, yes, all is well," I said.

"So why are you calling?"

"I was calling to tell you to buy this week's *Bamachan* magazine," I said. "They have a story about me."

"Don't they give it to you free over there?" she asked.

"No, buy it," I said. "You'll enjoy the story and you'll see my pictures."

"How much is this magazine?" she asked.

When I told her it cost fifty cents, she agreed to buy a copy.

* * *

At long last, two and a half years after arriving at flight school, I was preparing for the wings ceremony. The Air Force made a big deal out of these graduations and some of the previous occasions had been attended by such luminaries as David Ben Gurion, the founding Prime Minister and Secretary of Defense. They had taken place on a runway and included an aerobatic show and low passing formations of the fighter planes.

February 25, 1959, the day of my graduation, was one of the gloomiest of Israeli winter days. The skies were steel gray, the rain did not stop falling. The poorly drained tarmac designated for the ceremony was full of puddles, and naturally the crowd who had braved the weather to come was small—mainly family and close friends. Because our Course #27 had only a handful of graduates receiving pilot wings that day—only four—the crowd was even smaller.

The weather caused the commanders to cancel the air show and move the ceremony to the theater hall of the Tel Nof air base. We were disappointed. Prime Minister Ben Gurion hadn't shown up, there were no low passes of jet formations, and no aerobatic teams displaying their craft. More than anything else, I felt sorry that my family had missed the grand show.

We stood on stage. The tall chief of the Air Force ran up the steps and called our names. Each of us already wore the rank of Second Lieutenant, brass depicting an olive branch. Colonel Shaya Gazit, commander of the flight school, walked to the mic, and the hall grew silent.

"Cadet of Excellence, Second Lieutenant Yuval Efrat," he called.

Yuval, a small, sturdy guy from kibbutz Givat Brener stepped forward and the Chief of the Air Force fixed the wings on his chest. I had known for a while that Yuval had been chosen number one in the class, and I had gotten over my envy. Besides, with my "disciplinary" record, they could not give me this honor.

"Second Lieutenant Nissim Ashkenazy," Gazit called.

Nissim was a redhead, a fact reflected in his character. He came to Israel as a boy from Bulgaria and was a no-nonsense but friendly guy. He stepped forward and got his wings.

"Second Lieutenant Haggai Ronen."

Haggai was from Kibbutz Afikim, one of the largest in the country. For a while he had been unable to get into flying school because of some problem with his eye sight, so he had become a company commander in the infantry. Eventually, with his persistence and perseverance he had been admitted. Eyzer attached his wings, and he stepped back.

"Second Lieutenant Eitan Makogon."

I stepped forward, and Eyzer Wietzman placed the wings on my chest. "I expect a lot from you," he said. I saluted and stepped back.

Eyzer gave a short speech.

I looked at the hall and saw my mother, father and brother Yudke wiping tears from their eyes.

I had finally become a jet pilot.

197

Bamachane Magazine depiction of my Preflight
check, and the following formation flight.

CHAPTER TWENTY-FIVE

Marcel Dassault was a Jewish entrepreneur who built an aircraft manufacturing company in France bearing his name. Charles de Gaulle, the legendary President of France, had a war going in Algeria, a North African country that had been part of the French Empire. The local Arab population was fighting for self-rule. Because Israel was experienced in fending off Arab attacks, and because he figured " the enemy of my enemy is my friend," De Gaulle decided that cooperation between the countries would be helpful in France's struggle. For a while, in the mid-1950s, France was the only country selling jets to Israel.

After I got my wings, I was sent with my group to fly the Uragan, the first French jet fighter. It was a single engine, single seat fighter, and although we had some ground school to learn all the technical data, the systems, emergency procedures and the flight characteristics and behavior of the aircraft, for the first take-off, we were on our own with no flight instructor.

On a sunny morning I climbed the ladder and got into the cockpit of the Uragan. A line mechanic climbed after me and helped me as I struggled to tie the harness, connect my helmet to the communications equipment and the mask to the oxygen hose. "I could be a pilot," he said.

I wanted to make sure I would touch the right switches and get ready to start my first flight in an unfamiliar jet and was in no mood to schmooze with my mechanic.

"I fly gliders. I won prizes," he continued. "You can ask about me. My name is Buky."

"Okay, Buky, leave me alone. Right now I have to concentrate."

I started the engine, and after Buky removed the ladder, I taxied to the take-off position at runway 27 in the southern air base, Hatzor.

"One six clear for takeoff," I heard over the radio.

I pushed the throttle to full power and took off. In the air I tried turns, low speeds, high speeds, and simulated landing, using the altitude of 10,000 feet as if the runway were there. After two tries I gave up; I had "crashed" below the altitude I was trying to maintain.

"One six, coming for landing," I radioed, trying to hide my excitement, using a low, measured voice.

"Roger One Six, Runway Two Seven. Call downwind," the tower controller said.

I noticed a layer of clouds over the Mediterranean and decided to use its flat top as if it were the ground; I tried to execute one more simulated landing on it. I idled and reduced speed, circled around, lowered flaps, gear down and entered a long final leg. At low speeds this Uragan was sluggish, and the controls were extremely heavy as there were no hydraulics or electrical help for the pilot. The stick was connected by cables and demanded a great deal of strength.

I tried to flare the Uragan above the cloud layer; again I could not keep it up and sank into a cloud. I realized if this had been the ground, I'd have crashed.

My breathing sped up.

I joined the pattern with a shallow buzz over the runway, pulled up to lower speed, lowered flaps. I switched the gear down and saw the three green lights indicating it was down and locked. I adjusted the final speed, kept in line with the runway and ended with a smooth landing.

I'd been instructed to try the brakes after touchdown, though I was not sure why. What could we do if we found there were no brakes? Call for the rescue trucks, I guessed. I tried to brake slightly, but as soon as I touched the pedal, I heard an explosion and the plane swung violently to the left. It was heading off the runway in the direction of the control tower. I tried to correct with the right brake in order to stay on the runway, and a few seconds later I heard a second explosion and my plane came to a screeching halt.

I shut down the jet engine, and when I opened the canopy, I heard the sirens of the rescue vehicles. The air smelled of burnt rubber and overheated brake pads, and seconds later the rescue trucks arrived. Fireman worked on killing the fire at the wheels to save the plane.

At the squadron headquarters I saw Buky, the mechanic. He was waiting for me, eyes were sparkling with joy. "You shouldn't have been so hard on the brakes," he said, "a lot of beginners do it."

"So why didn't you tell me?" I asked.

"I was going to, but you shut me off," Buky said. "Next time let me talk."

From that day on, I let Buky talk, and we became friendly. He told me a lot about his desire to be a pilot, and his abilities, and to my astonishment, many years later he became one. After a few more flights I felt good about the plane. Since we ate lunch and dinner with all the experienced fighter pilots, I started to feel like one of them.

Two weeks into the OTU (Operation Training Unit), we had a weekend leave. It was a beautiful spring day in 1959, and my friend Asher and I were sitting in a cafe in the famous Disingoff Square in Tel Aviv munching on a plate of hummus, sipping good coffee and looking at the girls walking by. Asher and I had been good friends since I was 16, and we'd long shared two forbidden hobbies—smoking cigarettes and watching girls.

The most prominent newspapers, magazines, and billboards had the slogan *The Best Go Flying* splashed all over them, so I wore my uniform at all times, the uniform of an Air Force Second Lieutenant with my pilot's wings prominent on my chest. Asher was trying to hitch a free ride on the aura of my uniform.

"Look Asher, what a beautiful girl," I said as two girls walked on the wide sidewalk of the circular square toward us. One of them carried an accordion, and there was no question as to which of the girls I was referring to. She was slim and had an angelic face, and she walked gracefully, like a model, and was dressed in a beautiful white men's shirt tucked into a sarafan.

"She looks like Natalie Wood," I said.

"Oh, that one?" he said, "I know her."

I was always surprised by how many people Asher knew. "You know everybody," I said.

"She's from Holon," he said. "Would you like to meet her?"

That she was from my home town sounded to me like an advantage. "Of course!"

"Dina, Dina, hi." Asher jumped to his feet and walked toward the girls. "What are you doing here?"

Dina, the beautiful one, explained she had just finished teaching her dance class for which her friend had played accordion. I was still sitting, processing the beauty.

"Eitan, come meet Dina," Asher said. "She's an old friend of mine."

I stood up and walked up to them. Dina and I shook hands. She had a small, delicate hand with a nice grip. She introduced her accordionist friend.

"Eitan is a fighter pilot," Asher said.

I felt slightly embarrassed, the way I had been when my mother used to brag about me in my presence.

"I can see," Dina said.

"He's from Holon too," Asher said.

We talked for a while, and Dina told me she had been a member of the United Movement, a competing one to mine. I had a strange feeling that I had seen her before, but I quickly dismissed the notion, and after we had talked for a few minutes, she said, "Nice to meet you," and she turned to walk away.

I summoned all my social courage. "I would like to see you again," I said. She blushed, "Okay," and my courage rising, I asked where she lived.

"I live on Mendelson Street, number 8 in Holon," she said, and then she was gone.

Back in our seats at the café table, Asher said, "What do you think?" I didn't answer.

"Eitan, what did you think?" Asher looked like an anxious broker.

"I think she's the most beautiful girl I've ever met," I said.

* * *

We were a small group at Squadron #113 in Hatzor. Four of us had just received our wings, and two other pilots joined us in the training on this Uragan. Fuxy, from course #24, had been grounded for a while, and Paul Keydar had just come back from serving as the military attache in the Israeli Embassy in Turkey. He was 30, and we called him the old man.

About midway through our training program we finally were briefed about air to air combat, dog fighting.

For my first dog fight, more formally called an air battle exercise, I went up with Rafi Harlev, the squadron commander. We took off, and a few seconds after he had, I started to roll. I could see the flame coming out of the engine at his tail, and I made a note that it was the view I should have if I were to win the battle.

I joined the leader in a battle formation, and when we reached 20,000 feet, we turned out, flying away from each other, as in an ancient duel. Then we turned 180 degrees back in so we were flying head on. Once we passed each other head on, we both pulled up and turned left, trying to get behind the tail of the other. That's the position you try to be in when you shoot your enemy out of the sky, using the cannons. In training, we used gun cameras, shooting pictures instead of bullets.

In the first battle, the moment after we saw each other head on, we both pulled up and turned, and I slowly gained on him. After a few more steep turns, I was sitting solidly on his tail; I pulled the trigger.

"Terminate contact," he radioed. "Rejoin me in formation."

We disengaged and organized for a new fight. The entry to the second dog fight was the same, and I repeated what I had done in the first. Before long I was sitting on his tail again, breathing heavily, my head pounding, in part because the dog fight was the most exciting maneuver I had ever flown, in part because the controls were heavy, and mostly because I had just defeated my squadron leader in air battle, twice, on my very first dog fight.

That Friday I went home for the weekend. In late afternoon, I rode my bike to Mendelson Street #8. It was a narrow street in a somewhat better area of town from ours with small, single story homes. As I pedaled, I saw the street blocked by a wide American car, a Chevy, a rich man's car parked in the middle of the street, leaving barely any room between the car and the houses. The car, sparkling new, was parked in front of house #8. I leaned my bike against the front block fence and saw Dina on the front porch, sitting beside a young man. She ran toward me and told me this boy who was visiting had come in his father's big, new car, but she would soon be rid of him. "Come on up," she said.

Soon he was gone, and Dina and I sat on the porch and talked for a long time under the watchful eye of Rivka, her mother. After a while, Dina walked me back to the gate, and there we agreed we would see each other again. "But not this Saturday night," she said. She already had a date. I touched her arm and said goodbye, and for hours afterwards my hand buzzed, as if electrified.

On Saturday night at 10 p.m., a truck was picking us up in town to take us back to base. The truck parked on the wide sidewalk across from the Mugraby movie hall, and just before I climbed on, I looked up and saw Dina. She had come, with her date, to say goodbye, and she stayed for a few minutes. I saw my fellow pilots eyeing her, and when we climbed into the truck, I turned and waved goodbye.

Dina stood there on Alenby Street watching after us until we had disappeared, and my friends crowded around. "She's impressive," they said. "She looks like Natalie Wood."

I barely slept that night.

At the squadron, for my second dog fight, I was paired with Amos Lapidot, the Deputy Commander. He was a stocky blond who spoke in a slow, deliberate manner.

"Rafi tells me you beat him in your first dog fight," he said in his briefing.

I did not react.

"That's good," he said, "so rather than a lengthy briefing, let's go up and see what you can do. We'll do the same exercise and talk about it after we return."

Confident, I took off and entered the first battle, but before I knew what was going on, he was sitting on my tail. We disengaged and entered one more battle, with the same results. I realized this wasn't as simple as I'd thought it would be, but I didn't mind losing. I was mostly thinking of Dina.

A month after I met Dina, the *Kibbutzim* Teacher's Seminar sent her for a teaching practice run in *Heftziba*, a kibbutz in the Jezrael valley, at the foot of Mount Gilboa. We planned for me to visit her on the weekend, a drive that would take, from my base at Hatzor, about four hours. I arranged to have a light aircraft, a two-seater Piper Cub, to fly to Ramat David. Then the drive to kibbutz Heftziba would be just 30 minutes. My plan for the weekend included taking Dina up for a ride in the Piper. I thought that would impress her.

That Friday morning, I flew two flights on the Uragan, but I noticed the weather was deteriorating. At noon one of these rare storms moved in from the southwest, the type of summer sand storm that occurs once or twice a year. The African wind disturbs the topsoil of North Africa, in particular the dusty soil of the Sinai Peninsula, and lifts the fine grains up to tens of thousands of feet, making the air unstable and visibility low. In the afternoon, after I finished my flights and was ready to fly the Piper Cub north, the controller told me that no light aircraft would be allowed in the air that day.

All week I had thought about my weekend visit—what I would say and do. Even during flights on the Uragan I'd thought about that. Raffi, the squadron commander, empathized with me and lent me the squadron's Ford pick-up truck. I drove for close to four hours to Heftziba, and as tired as I was on arrival, with the first kiss I was re-energized.

We talked late into the night.

In the morning, after a brief sleep, we went with a couple, Dina's friends, to the famous nearby Sachne Pond, created by a natural spring that was always cold. Tired, but still trying to impress, I jumped into the icy waters, swam for a few seconds, and climbed out to chat with Dina and friends. Next thing I saw were people standing all around me; I was on my back on the rocky ground. I had fainted and fallen straight backwards, hitting my head on a rock.

I survived—it's good to be young—but I was deeply worried. This was a lousy way to impress a beautiful young girl on one of our first dates, especially since I hadn't brought the Piper up to impress her in the sky.

Late Saturday night I arrived back at the base; I had to fly early Sunday morning. When I entered the room I shared with Yuval, he was already in bed, reading. I got quickly in bed and we turned off the lights. In the darkness he asked, "How did it go with your new girlfriend?"

"Not exactly as I planned," I said. I told him about the cancelation of my flight north, the long drive and the fall at Sachne.

"That's not bad," he said. "It'll bring you closer to each other. Was she OK?"

"Yes sure, but it's not so easy."

"Why?" he insisted, "You spent the night together, didn't you?"

Yuval was beginning to annoy me; I didn't want to talk about my girlfriend with him. We were friends, but I thought talking about emotions was not macho enough, and here we were in the dark, the question hanging in the air. "She didn't let me move past first base," I said.

Yuval was quiet, and I thought he had fallen asleep.

Minutes passed. "She seems to be a wonderful girl, Eitan," he said at last.

"I know," I said.

"Be patient," he said.

I knew I would. I had fallen in love with Dina, but I didn't tell him that I would stay with her even if she only let me hold her hand.

We continued to train in combat flying, including using live ammunition. We shot on targets in the air and on the ground with the cannons, rockets, bombs and napalm, and the period ended with days of simulated war in which we took part with the whole Air Force. We flew four, five or more missions a day and ate and slept in the field, near our jets. From the moment I had received the letter from General Dan Tulkovsky inviting me to join the elite of the country's men, the Air Force trained me, tested me, built my character, cradled me, invested hundreds of flying hours in me and bolstered my ego, all to bring me to this moment.

I became a certified fighter pilot.

My elite new status helped me to lure Dina and solidify our relationship, and before long we were not only deeply in love but also the closest of friends. I woke up mornings wondering how I could have been so lucky.

From the moment we met, my thoughts were about her, about us, about our future together.

Flying had taken second place.

Fighter Squadron 113.
Standing: Fooxy, Kishon, Harlev, Lapidot, Keydar.
Kneeling: Ashkenazy, Makogon(Gonen), Hochman, Efrat, Ronen.

CHAPTER TWENTY-SIX

That fall I was transferred to flight Squadron #109 and flew on the more advanced French jet, the Mystere 4A. I moved north again, this time to the Ramat David air base built by the British and they named it after David Lloyd George, the Prime Minister of Britain whose government had issued the 1917 Balfour Declaration promising to establish a homeland for the Jews in Palestine. It was a beautiful air base in the Jezrael Valley, unusually green and surrounded by trees. It was built beside a kibbutz of the same name and a farming village (a moshav) called Nahalal, and to the west was Mount Carmel and the port city of Haifa, to the east Mount Gilboa and the Jezrael Valley.

My new jet, the Mystere 4-A, was a single engine, single seat, sleek airplane whose wings swept back at an angle. As with the Uragan, because there was no two-seater version, we had no training with an instructor. We learned on the ground about the Mystere's systems and flight characteristics, and then we flew on our own. The advanced controls operated by the same stick in the cockpit but were assisted by a hydraulic servo system, which made it sensitive and easy to maneuver, sometimes almost too easy. The Mystere also had better cannons for air to air and ground strafing and carried more rockets, heavier bombs, and napalm.

The more experienced veterans treated us rookies as full-fledged pilots and comrades in arms. Only one veteran pilot did not like me; Captain Egozy who was liked by many and was recognized as a daring pilot gave me bad vibes, and everyone knew he was nuts. We'd heard many tales of Captain Egozy's escapades. He'd been known to fly on the Mystere jet at 400 miles per hour, or faster, under high voltage grid wires. One story we heard was about how much he liked, when flying in close formation, to tap with his plane's wing the plane beside him. In fact a good friend of Egozy's, General Ran Ronen, a brave and distinguished pilot, had this to say about him in his memoir, "*Hawk In The Sky*". He tells about a flight with Egozy at the controls of a Harvard that he flew down in a canyon, "…those minutes were the most frightening of my life." And " …I closed my eyes and waited to hear the metal sound of crashing on the rocky canyon."

I had met Egozy months earlier when I was flying on the Meteor at this base. One evening in the dining hall he was telling jokes about us rookies. He said, "They don't know how to drink, how to fuck or how to fly," and the pilots sitting around him began to laugh.

"Hey Egozy," one of the pilots said, "show them your shaving blade trick."

His eyes glowed, and he stopped eating and pulled out of his pocket a couple of those old fashion, paper thin, double sided, stainless shaving blades wrapped in tiny wax paper envelopes. He slowly unwrapped two blades. While I was trying to guess what he might do with them, he put the blades in his mouth and began to chew, opening his mouth to show everybody the broken pieces; his teeth broke the blades into a dust of metal which he swallowed.

Everyone laughed, including me, and when the excitement had died down a little, I said, "You must be crazy in some other ways too."

Egozy just looked at me with disdain and later told everyone I was arrogant. By the time I joined the 109 squadron, he was already a senior flight leader, and although I thought he was a fun guy, he ignored me. When I said "hi," or "good morning," he didn't answer. One morning in the briefing room, Captain Egozy explained to me and another pilot the battle formation maneuvers we were going to fly that day. Our call sign would be Formation Red; he would be called Red One, the leader, I was Red Two, and my fellow pilot was Red Three. There was nothing unusual about this set-up. Each of us was going to carry two bombs, one on each wing, and 30 ammunition rounds in our cannons. We would enter our bombing runs, in numerical order, drop one bomb at a time on the target, and shoot the cannons at another target. Each of us had bullets of a different color so we could check the results afterwards. The bullet holes in the cloth target would reveal the colors of the bullet heads, and the officer in charge of the bombing range would report the results.

I donned the G-suit, took my helmet and was driven to the pen. I checked the aircraft, got in my seat, connected my mask into the oxygen source and G-suit to the pressure hose, my helmet cord to the radio, adjusted the instruments on the panel, turned on the radio and waited.

"Formation red, ready to taxi," Egozy called over the radio.

"Clear to taxi, runway 27," the controller said.

I taxied onto the runway. The three jets were beside each other, with

Red One, the leader, in the center. I was Red Two to the right, and Red Three was on the left. The leader raised his hand, his finger up, and in a circular motion instructed us to open throttles to full power. The rumble of our three jet engines on the runway gave me an adrenalin rush. Number one rolled. I started the stopper, and ten seconds later released my brakes and rolled down the runway.

Even as I was taking off, I was wondering what trick he was going to play on me. During the briefing I had seen a twinkle in his eyes.

Runway 27 was long, but the day was hot, which reduced the power generated by the jet engine, and the heavy ammunition load caused the plane to gain speed more slowly than usual. In front of me I saw Egozy's plane cling to the ground, finally taking off, raising a cloud of dust from the decomposed ground surface at the end of the runway. I glanced at my speed-- 100 knots and rising. I had disengaged the ground in time, and although my plane was sluggish in takeoff, I kept it close to the ground to gain speed. Red One was to make a shallow climbing turn to the right, thus helping Red Two (me) and Red Three join him by turning inside his radius.

My speed was rising; I was careful with the stick because the controls were so sensitive. If a pilot pulled on the stick too hard, it had to be pushed back and that could be easily overdone and in need of a counter correction which would cause the nose to pump up and down in a motion the French called *pompage*. The only, or best, way to stop the movement was to let go of the controls and allow the plane to stabilize, but right after takeoff and close to the ground, such a maneuver was risky.

My plane was comfortably steady. I looked at Red One. He had not started the climbing turn. Contrary to his briefing, he was flying straight and low, staying on the 270 west direction, close to the ground, with Mount Carmel in front of him.

Mount Carmel, where the Biblical prophet Elijah made his home, was 1,300 feet high, and we were flying at 200 feet. In a formation, pilots must follow the leader, so I pushed to remain at his level; my high speed soon brought me abreast, on the right, of Red One. He maintained direction and altitude, and just when I thought it might be too late to turn, he said over the radio, "Red formation, turn 90 degrees to the right."

He started to turn right and so did I, but he kept close to the ground which caused all of us to fly at high speeds. From my position I had to turn right and slowly slide past him, below his plane and in front of it while keeping his plane in sight at all times. I started the turn and immediately lost sight of the mountain. As my plane flew belly towards the mountain, I was watching Red One above, and out of the corner of my eye I saw the beautiful trees of Mount Carmel, too close for comfort. I pulled lightly on the stick which, at this high speed, caused the nose to move too much, and when I tried to correct it, the *pompage* motion began, the movement more violent with each vibration cycle.

Suddenly I heard and felt a big bang and had difficulty looking outside the cockpit. I thought I had touched ground. I did not want to let go of the stick so near to the ground, but I realized if I didn't, I might hit the mountain, and so I let go. The plane made one last big move and stopped, its nose pointing to the sky. In seconds I saw on the altimeter that I was at 10,000 feet, but I still could hardly see out.

I soon realized the bang had been caused by the high G force; because of a malfunction in the seat mechanism, my seat had lost its position and had dropped, with a bang, to the floor. I raised the seat and at once had a wonderful view of the green mountains of northern Israel, the Galilee to one side and the port city of Haifa on the blue Mediterranean to the other. I took in the view along with a sigh of relief that included a curse of the fucking bastard.

Down below I saw the two Reds gleaming as they climbed, their bare aluminum reflected in the rising sun.

"Red Two from Red One," the radio sounded.

I did not answer, still cursing, still in a rage.

"Red Two from Red One," he repeated more urgently. I detected some anxiety in his voice, and I realized he had no idea of what had happened to me or where I was. I kept quiet, eager to let him sweat this out.

"Red Two, what's your position?" he called.

"Red Two at ten thousand feet, and I have you in sight," I said in the coolest voice I could muster. A moment of silence passed, and the radio came alive again.

"Okay, okay. Take it easy and join the formation again," he said, his cool fighter pilot voice taking over again.

I joined the formation and we flew to the bombing range in a dune area by the Mediterranean shore. Red One entered first, released his bomb and pulled up. The bombing range officer called over the radio: "Red one, two o'clock, fifty yards."

"Red Two entering," I called into the radio and entered a steep dive, looked at the target through my bombing sight and peeked at my altimeter so that I would release from the proper altitude. I released my bomb, pulled up and said, "Red Two exits." After a long moment, the range officer reported, "Red Two, bullseye." Inside the cockpit I shouted, but I didn't shout into the radio. After landing I joined the Red Three pilot in the briefing room to discuss our bombing and strafing experiences and waiting to be debriefed by Egozy.

Thirty minutes later he came in and looked at us for a long moment. "It wasn't that bad," he said. "After takeoff we were at least 100 feet away from the mountain."

That's all he said.

A few years later, Major Egozy flew the same Mystere, and on the final leg, approaching land, he ran into the ground and was killed a few feet short of that same runway, Two Seven. The cause of this fatal incident remains a mystery, but I wouldn't be surprised if he was trying another one of his daring tricks—perhaps trying to land with his eyes closed, or without hands.

* * *

On the wall in the squadron office the bombing and shooting results for all pilots were posted on a board by the female soldiers who worked in squadron operations. I was no sharpshooter; my results were average at best, but my performance in dog fights was superior.

"If you can't get behind your enemy - you have nothing to shoot at," I would say to my fellow pilots when they brought up my results. On the day I was scheduled to go up for a dogfight with Captain Badman, nicknamed Baban, one of the best pilots and one of the friendliest, I was determined to win.

We started out flying head-on toward each other, passing to the left. We broke up and turned steeply to the left, and the struggle to get behind each others' tails started. I turned as steeply and tightly as I could, but so did Captain Baban, and for long minutes we were locked in a left turn, both trying to get behind the other's tail; they don't call it a dog fight for nothing.

After a while I delicately pulled up while keeping the turn; I came back down and slowly gained only a few degrees at a time, but I was closer behind him. Realizing I was gaining on him, Baban changed direction, and suddenly we were flying in the same direction, next to each other, slowing down in an effort to slide back. In a moment we started to cross each other in a scissor-like maneuver, moving slowly, close to each other, and gradually losing altitude. In one of these crossovers I passed a few feet above him, but before crossing, I saw him clearly give me the finger, Middle Eastern style.

211

I thought we could cross each other like this forever, but I noticed I was gaining an inch or two, so I decided to do a maneuver I had heard about that would bring me below him and then above him in an upside-down position but with little control. I moved my head up and saw him looking at me, his plane against the background of the beautiful earth below, the Galilee. After slowly crossing and rolling back to upright position, I saw his tail in front, up close.

Shouting for joy, I almost forgot to pull the trigger to take the evidence pictures, but I did not need those pictures. Back in the squadron, Baban told everyone about our dog fight and thus sealed my enhanced reputation as a fighter pilot.

In G-Suits with the Mystere Jet.

CHAPTER TWENTY-SEVEN

The Air Force was expanding and needed more pilots. The stringent requirements made the crop of graduating pilots small, and to train new generations of pilots, many more flight instructors were needed. Most fighter pilots were assigned at flight school for a two-year tour of duty. I was sent in early 1960. Twenty-two of us started a four month course for flight instructors, trained in the techniques and methodologies of flight instruction. Daily we flew the AT-6 Harvard with veteran instructors who played the part of cadets and watched us teach, identify faults, and correct them. On Fridays I went back to my fighter squadrons to keep up my expertise in flying the Mystere.

I did not mind the hard work the course required because it was back in Tel Noff base, closer to Tel Aviv, and that meant I could spend more time with Dina. By now we spent every free minute together, and often I visited her from the air, flying low, buzzing her house with the Harvard, making so much noise the whole neighborhood knew Dina had a new pilot boyfriend.

Since there was no phone at her home, I would just go to her house hoping to find her there. One evening I arrived, and we walked out to the nearby park where we sat hugging and kissing on a bench, when suddenly she asked, "Where are we going to live?"

We had never discussed such specifics; I had never gotten down on my knees and asked her to marry me—I thought people did that only in American movies. But we both knew this relationship was it, that we were going to live together for the rest of our lives. "I can get a place in the Tel Noff air base," I said, "temporarily."

Dina was quiet. We held each other. "Why temporarily?" she asked.

She looked more beautiful than ever, those blue eyes and her pointed nose, small ears and that little mole on her chin, all projected love, good nature and innocence. Even her taste in clothes was lovely. "I still have about a year until the end of my obligation to serve in the Air Force," I said.

We sat quietly for a while surrounded by new spring growth; in a corner the almond tree was in full bloom, and the last of the evening light was slowly dying. "What do you plan to do?" Dina asked.

"You mean after leaving the Air Force?"

"Yes."

"We'll go to America," I said. "I'm going to study engineering."

Dina said nothing. She liked the aura and importance of the Air Force, but I could tell she also liked the idea for the future I had in mind. "Why America?"

I told her this had been my plan for years, that I had joined the Air Force on a whim and for many years had wanted to see the world. I explained that going to school in the US would be more interesting, and easier, but while I talked, Dina looked straight ahead. In the light from the streetlamp, I could see her eyes growing moist. At last she said, "I still have to serve in the army."

The evening that had begun light and easy was growing heavy. "You won't go to the Army," I said. "We'll get married." Married women did not have to serve.

Dina now teared up and wiped her eyes with the back of her hand.

"Did you want to serve?" I asked.

She shook her head. "I don't mind either way."

"So why are you crying?"

Because I had asked, she cried still harder. "I'm just thinking about leaving my mother. And my brother and sister," she said.

Dina's mother, Rivka, was a war widow. Her father, Shevach Bloch, had been killed in the War of Independence in the city of Tsfat in the Galilee when he was just 34, leaving Rivka with eight-year-old Dina and pregnant with Benny. Later she married a Polish newcomer named Israel, and they had a daughter named Irit, but Dina felt little love for her stepfather.

"It's going to be a year before we can leave the Air Force," I assured her. "We have plenty of time to plan." I wanted to make this easy for her, but from that night on, we always referred to our lives in the singular, "our life, together."

* * *

I received excellent reviews in the flight instructor's course, and the end of the Period was in sight; in a week we would be certified instructors, but first would be the Aerobatics Competition among the fighter pilots from the various squadrons. Each one of us was allotted five minutes in which to demonstrate his aerobatics skills. I took off in my Harvard and climbed to 5,000 feet to wait for my turn to perform. Fifteen competing pilots had completed their shows, and the sixteenth was looping and rolling under me; I knew my performance was going to be better than his.

"Number seventeen, get ready," the controller said over the radio.

I silently re-ran my series of aerobatic maneuvers through my mind.

"Seventeen, your turn," the controller said.

"Roger, seventeen enters," I said, and I moved into the space above the runway where the judges stood looking up. To insure impartiality, they knew no names, only our numbers.

I performed the Loop, Himelman, Slow Roll in stages, Barrel Roll, and Stall Turn in which I climbed straight up until my plane came close to a complete halt, pushed full radar and turned down, falling on one wing into a vertical dive. I made sure every movement was sharp, and I made sure not to drift from the spot directly above the judges.

The last required exercise was to idle the engine and come in for a forced, powerless landing. This required judgment of speeds and altitude--too high or too fast, the plane would touch down far from the start of the runway; too low and slow, the plane would never reach the runway. Opening the engine for power would result in disqualification. The ultimate goal was to touch precisely the white line at the start of the runway.

I watched the wind. Most of my competitors were overshooting, but I carefully planned my turn, lowered the flaps and the gear and came in low and slow, with just enough speed to enable me to touch the white line.

That day I took first place as the best aerobatic pilot of the 21 competing pilots. At the party that evening, Captain Yossi Chankin, an excellent pilot and experienced flight instructor who was one of the judges, said to a bunch of the pilots, "When I saw that one Harvard, the only one in the competition touching the white line--the wheels actually touched the line--I knew it had to be Eitan Makogon."

I was elated, not so much for taking first place as for hearing that my fellow pilots had expected me to win.

My friend Haggai Ronen, the pilot from Kibbutz Afikim who had graduated with me in course 27, could not participate in the competition that day, but two days later he convinced someone to give him a chance to perform his aerobatics, and he scored one point higher than I had, bumping me to second place. He took away my trophy.

But I didn't mind. At the graduation ceremony I was declared flight instructor of excellence and received another trophy with my name engraved on it along with names of all those who had received it before me. I cherished the recognition, and even better, Dina was there to witness my receiving it.

I loved the Fridays we flew solo in the Mystere. It was a relief from the tedious job of flying every day with three cadets. On one of those Fridays I was scheduled to stay at Ramat David base for the weekend as the standby pilot on duty. The Israeli skies were defended against potential attack by neighboring air forces—Egyptian, Jordanian, Syrian, Iraqi, Saudi and others. On the Sabbath, those skies were defended in the north by two standby Mysteres in Ramat David; two others from Hatzor guarded the south. That weekend, my squadron commander, Amnon, and I were the two defenders of the north of Israel, and on Friday morning I flew north on a transport aircraft. Dina and I had planned that she would travel north on her own, and we would spend that weekend together.

Friday morning I flew twice, target shooting and bombing training missions, and by early afternoon most of the pilots and other soldiers had left for the Sabbath. The squadron was deserted and eerily quiet. Amnon and I stayed in, wearing our G suits, ready to scramble if the alarm sounded; outside, the two Mysteres stood at the ready 100 feet from the squadron structure. We were on standby during daylight only. At night another squadron, a night and all weather one, would take over, and I was looking forward to spending that evening with Dina.

Israel was relatively calm in those days; there had been no real wars, just skirmishes on the Syrian border over water source disputes, so we expected no problems. At around 4 that afternoon, the MP at the gate called to tell me a girl was there looking for me. I told the controller to sound the base siren if there was a scramble, climbed into the Ford pickup and drove out to fetch Dina.

As Sabbath approached, Major Amnon came to let me know he was going to leave the two of us alone. He wanted to have dinner with his family who lived in the air crew residential area of the base. I was surprised, and my face probably showed it, but I said, "No problem."

"If the alarm goes off get in your cockpit and wait for me," he said.

"Should I start the engine?" I asked.

"No, turn the radio on and wait. I've practiced it. It takes me a minute and a half to get here from my house."

I saw Dina's eyes growing wide. She had known she was coming to a fighter squadron, but she hadn't realized how close to the jets she would be spending the night. I explained to her that in the event I had to scramble into the air, she would be alone. She understood.

216

"Don't worry," I told Amnon. "I'll wait in the cockpit."

"Don't take off by yourself," he joked. "It ain't going to happen. There've been no scrambles for months."

Dina and I spent a nice evening alone in the squadron, and when it was late, we went to sleep on the folding cot barely wide enough for one.

In my dream I heard the school bell ringing loudly, but when I tried to run into the classroom, I could not move. I dreaded the punishment for being tardy and woke, but I could still hear the ringing. It took me a few seconds to realize the sound I was hearing was the scramble alarm. I jumped into my G suit, ran out, got in the cockpit and switched on the radio. The base siren sounded the up and down cycles, and as I waited for my leader, I could see the first light of dawn.

It felt like an eternity, but two and a half minutes later, Amnon was getting into his cockpit. "Formation Black, ready," he transmitted. His engine was just starting.

"Black, two Migs crossed the border flying south, take off as soon as possible. Control will direct you after take off," the tower instructed us.

"Roger Black," Amnon said. Seconds later he looked in my direction, and I gave him the thumbs up. I could hear my heart thumping in spite of the engine noise, but I was excited at my big chance to shoot down an enemy Mig.

Black One taxied to the runway at wildly high speed, and I followed closely. I tried to remember all the items on the checklist, but I worried I hadn't done everything.

When we reached the runway, we didn't stop. "Black, taking off," he said and started to run. Soon we were in the air, and I was busy joining Black One in battle formation.

"Black, I have you in sight," the controller said, "turn right to zero seven zero."

We turned in a north easterly direction and climbed as fast as possible.

"The Migs are still north of you, Black," the controller said. "They're flying south at twenty two thousand."

"Roger Black," said number one. I detected a shade of nerves in Amnon's voice. This was his big chance too; he had spent many more years than I hoping to have the opportunity to hunt and shoot down an enemy plane. "Where are they now?" he asked.

"Distance is ten miles," the controller said. "Keep climbing."

"Fifteen thousand feet."

"I know, I can see you," the controller said calmly. "I'll get you in position behind them."

"Roger, Black."

I detected Black One's doubt about the controller's ability to get us into the right position. We needed to be behind the Migs and at most 300 yards away if we hoped to shoot them down. We had no missiles, only 30 mm. cannons with a few hundred rounds. "Migs now at two miles, ten o'clock."

"Roger."

"Black, turn right one six zero."

"Turning, Black."

We turned, and I ended up to Black One's right side. As we turned to the south, I was searching so hard for the Migs, I felt as if my eyes might pop out of my head. Morning sun was rising over the mountains of Jordan directly into my eyes. I slipped back a bit so I could see Black One's tail and still look forward as I tried to locate the Migs.

"Black Two, where are you?"

"At your four o'clock," I said.

"Move back to three o'clock!" he said impatiently. "And stay there."

Reluctantly I moved abreast. From that position seeing the enemy in front of us was more difficult. "They're twelve o'clock, two miles," the controller said.

"Why so far?" Amnon complained. "I can't see 'em."

"Black, increase your speed. They're at twelve, two miles, a bit higher."

"I don't see 'em," he said.

He sounded angry, and rightfully so, I thought. The controller had incorrectly managed intercept, and now we were too far behind the Migs.

"They just started a left turn," the controller said.

I kept abreast of Black One and at the same time searched the sky, and suddenly I saw them, quite far away, two gleaming dots in front of us, with the sun rising like a fireball in the east, the Migs reflecting sunlight off their aluminum skin.

"Black Two, I see them, eleven o'clock high," I said, trying to stay calm.

"I don't see 'em," Black One said.

"Eleven o'clock, they're turning back, higher," I said.

There was no answer. I waited for Amnon to see them, but a few seconds that felt like hours passed in silence. Finally I said, "We're closing in, ten o'clock now."

Quiet on the airwaves.

"Where are they?" He sounded desperate, and I was petrified we would lose them if we didn't act now.

"Ten o'clock!" I shouted. "Turn left now!"

Black One started a turn, but it was a hesitant one since he still could not see them.

"Nine thirty now," I said. "I'm turning left, steep."

"Still don't see them," he said, his voice so low, it seemed he was begging someone to point them out.

"Follow me Black One," I said, and I turned to try to catch them.

"Roger," he said.

I turned hard. They were passing us to the north, trying to escape back to Syria. For a moment, I was elated—here was my chance to get at least one Mig. I knew Black One was behind me, but I couldn't see him. I pushed the throttle fully forward. Still, the descending Migs in front opened some distance between us. We had turned too late; while preparing my trigger, I realized that unless they made a mistake, we would not get close enough to shoot.

"They're crossing the border to Syria," the controller said. "Black, you have to disengage now!"

"Roger," he said. "Black Two, turn left and join me." He sounded mad, disappointed.

"Roger, Black Two," I answered. My stomach felt sick, and I was shaking. We'd been so close, but there would be no fame, no honor, no victory buzz over the runway. It was only when I remembered that Dina was down there in the squadron waiting for me that I cheered up a little.

We landed and walked back to the squadron. For the next hour Major Amnon was on the phone talking to the controller, complaining to him, letting him know he should have used his radar to better position us in a shooting spot behind the Migs. I sat with Dina who was slightly shaken after having listened to the radio transmissions over the office radio. My G-suit was wet from sweat, and we sat quietly, holding hands.

The squadron commander walked in. "She can't stay," he said. "She has to leave now, I'm sorry."

I arranged a driver to take Dina to the adjacent moshav, *Nahalal*, where her family friend Ziva and her husband, Yacov, an elite army unit captain, lived. That evening I joined them, and all evening long they asked questions as if I had just returned from war.

CHAPTER TWENTY-EIGHT

Dina's mother, watched our friendship with growing concern. It was clear to us that we would marry, but she did not know our plans and still hoped Dina would marry a boy from a wealthy family, someone with a more stable profession. Dina had a number of suitors who fit that bill. One afternoon I went to visit, she had not yet returned from the dance class she was teaching. I sat on the patio reading the paper and sipping coffee, both of which her mother, Rivka, had served me, when she came to sit next to me.

"Do you plan to keep flying?" Rivka asked.

Her face looked tortured. She was considered a good looking woman, and I agreed she certainly looked better than her women friends, but at that moment her lipstick was smudged, and she looked older, and deeply worried.

"Yes," I said, "at least for another year or so."

"Why?"

"Because I signed for five years and I still have over a year to serve."

She was quiet for a moment, looking at me and my uniform, focused on my wings. Then she turned away and looked at the air in front of her, day dreaming. "So many boys want to date Dina," she murmured as if talking to herself.

"I'm not surprised," I said.

"From good families," she said just as quietly.

I felt insulted, but I said nothing.

"One is a doctor's son, another's father is very rich," she said. "He is the exclusive distributor of cigarettes."

I kept quiet.

"They have cars!" she said. "What are you going to do after the year?"

"I'm not sure."

"This flying," she said with some disdain, "it's not a real profession."

As much as I didn't want to discuss my future, I decided to tell her what I had discussed with Dina. "I may go to study engineering."

"It takes a long time, no?" she asked.

"Yes, four years."

"How will you live? Have you saved money?"

"Some," I said, "but I'm exploring the possibility of going to America to study."

I thought this might alleviate her worries and stop the interrogation, but from the look on her face, I could tell I had only deepened her concern. I was glad when Dina appeared, and Rivka left us alone.

* * *

In the spring of 1960 I flew daily with my three cadets on three flight lessons. I liked instructing, but it was repetitive and tiring, so when I got the note summoning me to go to headquarters for an interview with Major General Eyzer Weitzman, the chief commander of the Air Force, I looked forward to a possible change of pace.

The morning I entered the Air Force headquarters was beautiful, though scores of officers coming and going still wore their blue winter uniforms; I noticed their insignia medals shining—Majors, Colonels, Generals. The assistant, the clerk who kept Eyzer's appointments, was a good looking woman, and I noticed even she was a Captain. Suddenly, my Lieutenant's rank on my shoulders felt lighter, almost insignificant.

"I'm Lieutenant Makogon," I told her. She looked down at her calendar.

"Yes, I'll let the commander know you're here," she said. "Have a seat."

As I sat I watched the commotion around me. I was surprised by the number of high ranking officers, but even more surprised at the unassuming, bare look of the office and the building. A few black and white photos of airplanes hung on the walls, but otherwise the place looked plain and worn.

"How long do you have?" the Captain at the desk suddenly asked.

"Excuse me?"

"How long do you have left on your contract?"

"Oh, a year and three months to go," I said.

"Really," she said. "It's sort of an early interview."

She wrote something on the paper attached to the file in front of her, read something in the file that made her glance at me for a second, and then she said, "I'll let him know now."

As I waited I reviewed the few personal contacts I'd had with Major General Weitzman over the years—the first being the day he congratulated me for my one sentence speech as the newly appointed leading cadet; the

221

second, when he came to my Meteor squadron number 117 with Danny Kay; the third, at the graduation and wing ceremony when he told me he expected a lot from me. The official reason for that day's meeting was a "personal review," but I knew his purpose was to request that I extend my service contract for a few more years.

Holding my file, the Captain stood and walked to the closed door of the commander's office. I thought her skirt was too short for those long legs. She walked into his office, closed the door behind her, and a minute later came out without the file. She took her seat again, and a minute later, the intercom buzzed, and I heard Eyzer's familiar voice, "Send in Lieutenant Makogon."

She smiled at me, embarrassed at having left the speaker phone on high. "He'll see you now," she said, and I walked in.

"*Ahalan,* Makogon," he said, smiling. "Come in, come in, have a seat."

I was struck again by the simplicity of the room. It was big for an office, but small for a conference room, with no windows. Two tables were arranged in a T-shape, one the commander's desk with a telephone and a long speaker on one side. It was there Eyzer sat. The other table stood perpendicular to the desk's center and was surrounded by ten chairs of the same light wood as the desks. The white walls were covered by black curtains, and as in the squadrons, those curtains hid the data posted on charts behind them.

I sat in the chair closest to the commander.

"Relax," Eyzer said, trying to be friendly. He was tall and slender, his blue uniform perfectly pressed, the rank of Major General—two crossed swords and an olive branch—shone brightly under the white fluorescents. "I see here that your commanders are quite happy with your performance," he said. "So there's no real reason for me to review it."

"Thanks, sir," I said.

"You know how important it is for us to defend our skies. The Greens will not be able to do much without us." By Greens he was referring to the Army, whose uniform was khaki or green. We in the Air Force were dubbed The Blues.

"Yes, sir."

"We have the best pilots," he continued, "and the whole world recognizes that."

I was not sure why he would waste his time preaching to a member of the choir, but I patiently waited for him to get to the point. "How long do you have?" he asked.

This time I knew what he meant. "A year and three months, sir."

"Good. I assume you're going to extend and sign for five more years."

I was ready for this, but with his friendliness and piercing eyes directed at me, I lost my confidence. "Sir, I wasn't planning to sign on for more."

His smile faded. "Makogan, you've just started your flying career."

"Yes, sir."

"You have a great future with us. You could go far, as high as you want."

"Yes, sir."

"Don't 'yes sir' me, I want you to commit!" I admired his style—his sharp tongue and his great one liners. He never minced words, and as I sat before him, I thought about our history—about the Holocaust; he had volunteered for the British Air Force. I thought about how close we had been in 1948 to losing our independence.

"The best go flying," he said, offering up our mantra, but he said it not as a slogan but as a manifestation of his beliefs—we were necessary to the survival of the Jewish people. Suddenly under his onslaught, my plan to tell him I would not extend my service because I had other plans looked naïve and insufficient. "What do you want to do?" he asked.

"I plan to study engineering."

I saw some light return to his eyes.

"No problem. You sign up for five more years and then you can study. I'll send you to the Technion in Haifa, and we'll pay for your studies."

When I said nothing, his face grew darker, and he began to turn pages in my file. "We're going to get the most advanced fighter jet," he said quietly. "The Mirage. When we get it, I'll move you into that squadron." He looked up at me again, and our eyes locked for a few long seconds. I had no words to break this log jam, but I was determined not to sign up. "Why did you come to flying?" he asked. Now he was angry.

"Because General Dan Tulkovsky invited me." I told him that I had never thought about joining the Air Force until his predecessor sent me that letter, and I'd decided to try it. But, I explained, I had never intended to make flying a career. The intercom beeped. He looked at his watch. "Our time is up, but I want you to think about it. Remember, we need people like you."

I was relieved he had found a gentler way to end this interview. "Yes, sir," I stood.

"We'll talk again in a few months," he said.

I saluted and walked out, exhausted.

A month after that interview, Dina and I started to plan our wedding more seriously and we discussed renting an apartment, her gown and searching for a date and a place for our wedding. One Friday, as I did every Friday, I boarded a transport plane to go north to fly the Mystere. The transport was a Nord, the French transport used for dropping paratroopers and their equipment from the sky, and the cabin was noisy. Ten pilots talking; one of these was Aaron Markman, a nice guy from kibbutz Kfar Giladi. Aaron was older than I, but we had become friendly, and he had frequently sought me out to chat when we were together in the evenings on the base. That morning, he sat next to me in the noisy Nord and all the way to Ramat David he shouted his thoughts to me. He had heard I was going to marry Dina and was giving me advice based on his married life.

At the squadron I looked at the flights planned for that day and saw that I was going to fly some target shooting. Markman was scheduled for the same exercise in another formation, but in spite of his long time in the squadron, he was still flying in a junior position, as number two. At noon that day I took off and joined my leader, climbing to 20,000 feet where we started our quarter attack runs, trying to sharp shoot cannon rounds into a white cloth flag dragged from the end of a long cable behind another plane. We took our turns, shooting short bursts of rounds, then turning out to get organized for the next run. I had to turn my head sharply to make sure I could see the flag, the leader and that the space was clear. I made sure my oxygen mask was securely connected since it was prone to disconnect without warning, leaving the pilot with no oxygen which at first made him feel happy but later caused a loss of consciousness.

When we were almost done, we heard over the radio, "Yellow Two, pull up now."

This was unusual, and I knew immediately someone was in some sort of trouble.

"Number two, pull up."

No answer.

"Yellow Two, what's the problem? Pull up." The speaker dropped the call sign and said, "Aaron, pull up, Aaron pull up, Aaron..." My friend Aaron Markman was in trouble, and his leader was trying to pull him out of a dive.

"Mayday, Control from Yellow One, number two is in a steep dive, no radio contact."

"Roger, are you north of Haifa?" the controller sounded technical, matter of fact.

"Yes, north of Haifa Yellow One," he said. "Yellow Two pull up, can you hear me, Aaron?" He sounded desperate. Then there was a long silence.

"Yellow One from control, what's happening?"

"Oh shit."

"Yellow One?"

"Yellow Two hit the ground. His plane exploded."

"Roger, a helicopter is on the way. Have you seen a parachute?"

"Negative. No parachute."

Back at the squadron at first we all were quiet and depressed, but after a while someone cracked a joke, and we all laughed nervously. Aaron Markman had not been the best pilot, but he was a nice guy, a friend, and he was certainly the most handsome of us. He was not the first friend fatality I experienced, and his death drew the same reaction as many others had. No one cried. Some jokes were cracked. Someone checked his locker to see if his flying jacket was newer and worth switching. All our defense mechanisms were at work.

Everyone thought: That will never happen to me.

In the afternoon, I was about to board the Nord transport to go back to Tel Noff; I would hitch a ride home from there for the Sabbath, and the journey would take me three hours. I noticed a pilot I knew checking a helicopter next to us, and I learned he was flying directly to Tel Aviv. When I asked he told me he would gladly take me along, and I was thrilled to be able to reach home and Dina two hours earlier.

Then he said, "That is, if you don't mind flying with Aaron for the last time." He grinned. Aaron Markman's remains were in that helicopter, on their way to the morgue in Tel Aviv. For the next half hour flight, I sat beside his body, remembering our times together, thinking of his wife and of Dina. I decided not to tell her about Aaron for a while.

At that time, Golda Meir, the Minister for Foreign Affairs in Ben Gurion's government, had invested great effort on her initiative to befriend the newly independent African nations. Little Israel provided assistance to those countries in areas where we had some experience—particularly in major construction projects and military training. A group of experienced Israeli Air Force pilots and mechanics were sent to Ghana to establish a flight school and an Air Force for the young independent nation.

At the end of April 1960, my squadron commander assigned me to be a pallbearer for a pilot who had been killed in a plane accident while instructing his student in Ghana. Captain Alex Safra's body was flown back to be buried at the farm village of Kfar Vitkin. Six pilots of his rank or higher would carry his coffin to its final resting place. Many members of his *moshav*, pilots who had known him, were at his funeral as was the chief rabbi of the Air Force and Major General Eyzer Weitzman. The honor squad shot three rifle shots into the air, and he was laid to rest. Afterwards we stayed to hang out around the chief commander who told everyone some stories. After a while, as I turned to leave, Eyzer said to me, "Nu, Makogan, how's it going?"

"Very well, sir," I said.

"Have you thought about our discussion?"

"Of course, sir."

"Are you going to sign your extension?"

I was busy with the wedding plans at the time, and I was thinking a lot about my discharge day; I was eager to see the world. But I suddenly had an idea. Even in the face of the funeral, the rumors were that the pilots on assignment in Ghana love their experience.

"Sir, I would like you to consider me when you look for a pilot to go to Ghana to fill Safra's position," I said.

Eyzer was surprised by the idea, but I could see it interested him. "This is a two year tour," he said. I said nothing; I hadn't been ready. "You'd have to sign up to cover the two years."

"Yes sir, I understand," I said.

"I'll let you know."

I thanked him, and he walked away to his shining official American car where the driver opened the rear door to let him inside.

* * *

Dina and I had picked our wedding day—August 3rd, 1960. In June we had our invitations printed, and I continued to work hard in flight school, teaching three times a day. This meant I did many take-offs, landings, and hundreds of aerobatic maneuvers, and although I was tired, I also was happy.

Dina and I wanted to live on base, but we got a small home, part of a group of homes for pilots the Air Force had purchased in Gedera, a village just south of the base. The house was a wood structure with the floor made of sidewalk concrete pavers and reminded me of the shack. On weekends Dina and I visited to clean, and we met the neighbors, families of long-time pilots. Zorick, a 30-year-old legendary pilot, was our next door neighbor, and he and his wife helped us prepare the house. Dina was not yet 20; I was 22. But felt accepted by the veteran pilots.

That same month my squadron commander called me to his office and told me I was to leave immediately for Ghana. This was the first I had heard I was selected to go there. "But I'm getting married in August," I said.

"Re-schedule the wedding for next week," he said bluntly.

"My invitations are printed and ready and so is everything else," I said.

He picked up the phone and called headquarters, and I listened as he explained my predicament. When he hung up he said, "You have until July 15 or they'll send someone else. What should I tell them?"

"I'll go," I said.

"Okay, go prepare. "I'll assign your cadets to another instructor. Good luck."

That evening I sat with Dina at her mother's home, the pile of our printed invitations on the table, and we scratched out the date on each and wrote in the new date, July 9, 1960. We had selected that night because it was the only night the military wedding hall was available, and we had many friends and family, a large group of pilots and Eyzer Weitzman to invite.

At the wedding when Ezyer said to Dina, "You're taking away one of our best pilots," I blushed with pleasure at the compliment.

The Air Force rabbi sat with my father, Dina's stepfather and me to fill in the *Ketuba*, the wedding contract. My mother sat close by. When we reached the item that set the amount of money I would pay Dina in the case of divorce, God forbid, the Rabbi suggested two hundred Liras, about $100.00. I didn't care – I was in love, and I knew I would never divorce this woman.

But when my mother overheard the Rabbi's suggestion, she cried, "So much?"

I signed the *Ketuba* and we married, and then we ate and danced late into the night. We arrived exhausted at the cheap hotel on Hayarkon Street I had booked for our first night as a married couple. When we entered the lobby, I realized the street stewardesses used this place for their trade, an odd choice for a wedding night, but we were in love, so it mattered little.

At the wedding with our parents.

CHAPTER TWENTY-NINE

Two days after the wedding, I went to the Defense Ministry in Tel Aviv to arrange our trip to Ghana. I entered the office of Colonel Moka Limon who was in charge of all officers serving abroad, and he asked me to remind him of my mission.

"I'm going to Ghana to teach flying," I said.

"Oh yes, you're replacing the pilot who was killed, Safra."

"That's me," I said, "Safra's replacement."

"Okay, you'll fly next Wednesday to Rome and catch the weekly flight to Accra on Thursday."

We would have only one evening in Rome. I knew they wanted me to arrive in Ghana quickly, they were missing a flight instructor, but I wanted to spend a few days in the Italian capital. So I searched for a good official reason to stay longer; I found none, and finally I decided just to tell him. "Sir, I want to spend a week in Rome with my wife. It's our first trip abroad, and our honeymoon."

The tack proved to be wise, as Limon was generous with the allowance. "This is the Air Force wedding gift," he said when he signed the order to give us a week's per diem abroad. "You'll have to get passports," he explained. "Let me check to see if you get diplomatic ones." He picked up the intercom and conveyed his question, to which the woman on the other end explained we would need Service passports.

"But still you'll have to change your last name," he said.

I had heard that ambassadors of Israel abroad had to have a Hebrew name but didn't think it applied to pilots. "Why?"

"This is Ben Gurion's order," he said. "Anyone who represents Israel abroad must have a Hebrew last name."

I explained that Dina had just changed her name from Bloch to Makogon, but rules were rules. She would have to change hers again, and so a few days later Dina and I went to the Department of Interior and changed our last names. We used the last three letters of our last name, adding en. *Gonen* is a Hebrew word (to defend), and was at least in part tied to my original last name. And so in three short weeks, Dina had had three different last names.

When I told my parents about my new last name my father was upset and asked how we could do this. I tried to explain we had no choice, but he was distraught that I hadn't consulted with him. "Just like that?" he said.

"This was ordered by Ben Gurion," I told him. My father admired our prime minister, so this softened the fact that his son would no longer carry the name he had carried from the Ukraine, the name his family had used for generations.

"It's a nice and strong Hebrew name," my mother said, and in an explanation well ahead of *women's lib*, she added, "It's not such a big deal. Women change their last names when they get married."

We flew on the Greek airline, Olympic, so we could stop over in Athens. As we were landing, I saw the remains of Olympus and began to feel the excitement of our adventure. When we landed, we walked down the steps to the tarmac and for the first time stood on foreign soil. I was elated by the feeling; I felt free for the first time in my life. Although I knew I had to report in a week, my mind whirled back to the days in Jerusalem, under siege, to high school, to the Kibbutz, to the Air Force. Although I had freely made many choices in my life, my time had always been structured, and now, for just this moment, I felt as if I were at the start of a long, delicious holiday. I would finally see the world, and better still, Dina would be at my side. Ever since childhood I had to leave people I knew and loved behind, and with each move I had made my way in a brand new place, with a new group of people. I was accustomed to moving on, and now, after the years in the Air Force, I was restless and ready for a new challenge.

"Sir, this way to passport control," a Greek policeman stirred me from my reverie, and we moved with the crowd.

In Athens on our way to Africa 1960.

Afterwards, for two wonderful days, we toured Athens, the birthplace of free democracy, and then we flew to Rome. There we spent a week, visiting all the sites--the Coliseum, the Spanish Steps, the Trevi fountain, Tivoli Gardens. The Israeli Embassy had given us an allowance, and those Italian *Liretas* were so large, we dubbed them bedspreads. We ate Italian food and for the first time drank Coca Cola. By the end of the week, we were sorry to leave the good life but also excited for the unknown that awaited us in Africa. Sitting aboard the British Overseas Airlines Boeing 707 in economy class, we felt like royalty.

The plane was filled with people dressed up as if they were about to attend an important business meeting. The tall British stewardesses served us meals on china. When we asked if we could purchase the glassware embossed with the airline's insignia, the stewardess said no, but we took it with us anyway, a souvenir of our joy. Dina had been apprehensive about going to Africa, but on that flight she began to think this was a good move, and after 6-1/2 delightful hours, we touched down in Kano, Nigeria.

When the door opened and the sub-Saharan heat invaded the interior, all the European pleasure dissipated. After an hour on the ground the heat was brutal, and Dina, near fainting, changed her mind about Africa. I assured her Ghana had better weather, and after take-off, with the air conditioning running full steam and the cabin crew serving us dinner, she once again began to like Africa.

As we began our descent to Accra, I looked out the window and saw only green. The jungle stretched as far as the eye could see, and in the distance I saw smoke rising from between the trees and wondered if there were people living there. We saw no villages, no structures, only the tops of trees for miles. The Captain began to speak, and I tried hard to understand what he was saying through his thick British accent.

"What did he say?" Dina asked.

"I didn't understand."

"Are you going to instruct in English?" she asked me.

It was the first time I had thought about this. I had learned English at school; I'd even read *MacBeth*. But I had never used the language in any practical way after my teenage job at the movies. "Yes, I think so," I said.

"Where are we going to live?" Dina asked.

"I don't know."

"But is it a home or an apartment?"

"I don't know."

"Do we have enough money?"

"I have some Italian *Liretas* left," I said.

Dina's practical questions quickly made me realize I knew little about what awaited us. I'd been so eager just to get out and see the world, I had paid little attention to the conditions under which we would live—I had no idea what sort of home we would have or what my salary would be or whether or not we would have a car. I had no address or phone number to call. After years in the Air Force, I had become accustomed to having details arranged by others.

Once we landed in Accra, as we started climbing down the stairs to the tarmac, I saw a line of officers in the light blue uniforms, the Dress Uniform of the Israeli Air Force; Colonel Adam Shatkay, Major Yoel Dan, Captains Reuven Hirsh, Isaac Hirsh and Zev Sharon were waiting for us. We saluted and shook hands. "Welcome to Africa," Colonel Shatkay said.

The Israeli Air Force was small, so naturally I knew all the pilots, and Dina, more beautiful than ever in her civilian clothes, was especially relieved that we would not be left on our own, abandoned in vast Africa.

"You look so young!" Captain Sharon couldn't contain himself. Later I learned the men thought I had married a teenager, and it took some time to convince them Dina was nearly 20.

Major Dan looked at our two pieces of luggage and asked, "Is that all you have?" He loaded our bags into his Fiat and drove out of the airport. I heard the British drove on the left side of the road, but this was my first experience of the act, and as we drove, I felt as if we might collide with another vehicle at any moment. To my amazement, it all worked fine along the paved road. "It will take you a day or two to get used to it," Dan said.

Traffic was light until we approached a more populated area and were suddenly surrounded by small trucks overloaded with passengers. "These lorries," Dan Yoel explained, "are the only public transportation available." I watched as people climbed up the lorries and climbed back down even as the truck continued to move. There were no white people on the lorries, and the few I saw on the road drove private cars.

The buildings in Accra were low and gave the feeling of being in a colonial city, like those I had seen in movies. Women in colorful dresses sat on the side of the road, piles of merchandise in front of them. They sold fruit, vegetables, firewood, and mostly yams. The side streets were unpaved, the dirt reddish and adding to the bountiful colors—the cars, the homes, the women, the clothing, the lorries. I could not stop staring, and then, as we turned onto a dirt road, Dan said, "Here we are."

Like most of the houses we had passed those in this area were one story, small, with corrugated metal roofs. Smoke rose from many of the back yards.

Dan pointed to the only three-story house on the street and said, "this is it," as he pulled around back and parked the car.

We walked up exterior stairs to our second floor apartment. The entryway led into a large living room with rooms on both sides, three bedrooms on the left, and a large master bedroom and dining room to the right.

"Where's the kitchen?" Dina asked.

"Oh, the kitchen and the bathroom are outside," Dan explained.

The families who lived below and above came to meet us. The men were Israeli Air Force mechanics. Dina and I checked the apartment, and we quickly decided to lock the three extra bedrooms; we would never use those. That evening after we had unpacked, we went for dinner at the home of Dan and IlanaYoel. Ilana served a lavish dinner and the men spoke rapidly in Hungarian to each other. That was the first I realized they were all born in Europe.

During dinner Ilana would occasionally clap her hands and call, "Ali, more bread!" and from the kitchen a young black man would appear carrying slices of English style white bread that were, to me, like slices of white cotton wool. I watched Dina's eyes widen in amazement.

"Dina, we'll have to find a servant for you," Ilana said.

Dina quickly glanced at me, and I saw her face pale as a faint smile broke out on her face. Dina came from a working class family, and we both had spent years in socialist youth movements. We associated ourselves with the working class and the kibbutzim, and the idea of having a servant in our home was alien.

"I don't think we'll need one," Dina said, arousing a heated discussion about the necessity and appropriateness of having a servant. In the end Dina was persuaded to accept a servant for two weeks only, until we settled in.

We hired a young man named Abu who came with a booklet that gave an account of his work history for the British masters. His last job had paid him 4.50 pounds per month, but we started him at 6 pounds; this was one day after we were told that my salary would be 200 pounds a month, six times my last salary in Israel. We felt suddenly rich, and we bought a VW from a Flight Commodore who had gone back home to India. The Ghanaians, only recently independent, were making hasty decisions and changing them often, so they had abruptly terminated the pilot from India's contract.

On my first day at the flight school in the Accra Airport, I had a checkout on the Hindustan HT2, a two-seat propeller trainer that Ghana had purchased from India. In a meeting with Dan I learned the details of my contract. The pay was the equivalent of $600 a month, but even better, we were entitled to accumulate a one-week vacation each month. I was assigned three flight cadets. When we met, I noticed most of all how very black their skin was, and how young they looked. Years later when I looked at the photos, I saw that I looked just as young.

Our cadets' lack of mechanical background or experience made flight instruction more complex than it had been at home. It required much patience, but our students were eager and determined, and slowly we advanced. Slowly we also grew closer.

Dina wanted to get her driver's license, so we signed up with an instructor who came daily to give her driving lessons. Each day when I came home, she told me about her driving experience. She was eager for me to come watch her, and so one day I agreed I would. A small blue Peugeot stopped at the house and a big burly black man stepped out. He spoke the local version of English--Pidgin English--that was hard for us to understand.

"Meet my driving instructor," Dina said.

I shook hands but I couldn't for the life of me understand how he fit into the little car. The car's blue paint was flat and worn, with patches of corrosion everywhere. It was a convertible, and the roof mechanism was visible through the torn, dirty cover. The big instructor was barefoot, and two boys sat in the backseat, half-naked and barefoot. They had scars on their faces, three parallel diagonal scars on each cheek arranged equidistant from each other. These, I learned, were their tribal markings; I wanted very much to learn about their tribe, about the meaning of the design, and more, but they spoke no English.

"I would like to join you today," I said.

"Yes, Massa," he said. "Please Massa sit in the back."

He shouted some instructions to the boys who moved to make room for me in the center. I climbed in the back and Dina sat on the driver's seat, the instructor beside her. "Ready?" he asked. He turned and shouted to the boys, who jumped out of the car and began to push. The instructor, from the passenger seat, reached over Dina for the steering wheel, and with his bare foot he handled the clutch. As the boys pushed and we gained speed, he released the clutch, and the car jerked back and forth, the motor started, and the boys jumped back in.

"Is this how you always start?" I asked Dina.

"Of course," she said. "There's no starter."

The instructor let Dina drive for a while, but when we reached an uphill road, the engine died. The two boys jumped out and pushed again, this time uphill. The engine started, but when Dina tried to drive, it stalled again. Once again the boys pushed, and the driver placed his bare foot on top of Dina's to show her how to release the clutch gradually. Dina later told me the bottom of his foot was as hard as a shoe. After a few more starts, the boys began to talk nonstop in their tribal language, and I saw that they were furious until finally Dina learned to engage the clutch smoothly, and we drove back home. A few weeks later, she passed her test and got her first driver's license from the government of Ghana.

Dina and I loved our first home. We spent all our free time together which helped Dina overcome missing her family, and which was a pleasure for both of us since we were so deeply in love. Still, this was the first time Dina had ever spent any extended time away from home, and the adjustment was more difficult for her than it was for me. But we both loved being in Africa, and we accumulated vacation time to travel, enjoying our VW and traveling extensively through Ghana as well as Togo and Dahomey, now called Benin, both ex-French colonies which retained some of the French flair. We traveled as far east as the city of Cotunu, at the border of Nigeria.

In November 1960, Dina and I decided to take a journey together with all the pilots in our group. Two of the pilots were bachelors, and the wives of the two others wanted to stay home. We traveled in three cars, an Italian Fiat, a French Renault and our German Volkswagen, into the jungle on dirt roads, until we'd arrived at Komassi, the second largest city in Ghana and situated in the middle of an endless jungle. There we participated in a colorful celebration installing a new tribal chief. Then we continued north, on the way meeting people of many different tribes.

We stopped to take pictures with the locals, naked women and half-naked men, some with deep facial scars, others with extended lips and earlobes, all very friendly. When we arrived at the northern border and crossed over to Upper Volta, the country now called Burkina Faso, we stayed for a night at the town of Po at the edge of the Sahara desert. The Harmattan, a trade wind blowing from the Sahara Desert accompanied with fine dust, made the place extremely dry, a sharp contrast to the weather we had thus far experienced in Africa—it had been steadily hot and humid and rainy up until that night. When we asked about a hotel, we were directed to a mud hut in the middle of the village. The walls of our room were dried mud, our door a hanging cloth. At night, our noses and throats dried out, and we woke every half hour to wet a towel with dirty water to breathe through until it dried and we woke again.

We left this sub Saharan village and drove southeast, back through the jungles, heading to the country of Ivory Coast, west of Ghana. A few times we stopped to deal with mechanical problems with the Fiat and Renault, while our VW Beatle never had a problem. We drove through the jungle, stared at by hundreds of gazelles, and then, suddenly, we began to see road signs written in French, and we knew we had crossed the border.

On the road in Africa with locals.

That evening we arrived at a big city with wide roads and boulevards and impressively modern buildings. We entered Abidjan, the capital of Ivory Coast. The French touch was obvious, and we checked into the best hotel in town. Dina and I both basked in the tropical luxury of the place, the kind of luxury we had never experienced. We had a huge room with a sitting area where we could have a drink we chose from the refrigerator. A waiter waited just outside the door to fulfill any of our wishes. In the evening we all gathered in the lobby and Yoel Dan, the "the elder"--he was 26 and spoke some French--ordered for us. He motioned to the waiter. "Une bouteille de vin blanc, s'il vous plait," he said. "Liebe Frau Milch."

I looked at him, admiring his lingual prowess. I had understood the last three words—"milk of a loving lady" in German, and I thought he was ordering milk, so when the waiter returned with a bottle of white wine and poured a glass for each of us, I was surprised. It was the first wine either Dina or I had ever had besides the sweet wine we drank at Passover.

"This is the best German wine," Dan Yoel said.

I looked at Dina and felt the wine and the pleasure of this life deep inside. Here we were, a bunch of Israeli pilots sitting in an ex-French colony in Africa drinking German wine, eating French food, and my beautiful wife was beside me. How lucky could I be? I wanted this night to never end, and I was glad I had signed up for two years in Africa.

As our cadets accrued more flying time, their level improved and they began to fly solo. The Ghanaians appreciated our team's efforts and treated us accordingly. President Nkrumah invited us for cocktails at his mansion and thanked each of us personally. Whenever an important visitor came to Ghana, the President brought them to the new Ghana Air Force Flight School to show his country's progress. Among the heads of state we met on these visits were Haile Selassie, fondly called the "Caesar of Ethiopia" or the "Lion Cub of Judea."

One day in January 1961 we were called to a meeting with the Israeli ambassador to Ghana. Under influence of the Russians and the Brits, Nkrumah had decided to, abruptly, terminate our contract. We would be leaving at the end of February. When the ambassador left, we pilots sat in the meeting room saying nothing for several minutes. Finally, Dan Yoel broke the silence, "Time to move on."

Dan was handsome and tall, and he projected decisiveness and optimism while the rest of us remained quiet and gloomy. I looked around at the others and asked Dan what he would do.

"I'm going to take my family straight back to Israel," he said.

"But what about your career?"

We all knew that just being in Africa meant we were out of the mainstream, out of the race that might take us up the ranks in the Air Force. Our path was a diversion from the main career path; pilots with ambitions to be squadron commanders or higher would never have taken these positions. "How far you think you could go?" Zev Sharon asked, a question he was likely asking of himself, but for now he wanted to hear Dan's opinion.

"You never know," Reuven Hirsh said. "I'm going to study in the Technion."

"What about El Al?" I asked.

Pilots who flew for the Israeli Airlines were paid handsomely and were highly respected, a dream job except for one drawback--long periods away from the family. I'd heard some flights required the pilot to stay away for up to two weeks.

"My wife wants me to fly for El Al," Sharon said. "She wants me to make money and doesn't mind getting rid of me for a week at a time, but I'd prefer to fly in the Air Force."

For quite a while we quietly pondered our future. Dan turned to me. "Eitan, what about you?" I noticed he had not answered the question about his own career, but I told him I planned to study engineering.

"In the Technion?"

"No, I'm going to take Dina to America," I said.

"Why?" He seemed surprised, and I had to think before answering. It was a tough question, but although I had never precisely made plans or figured out where my desire to go to America stemmed from, I had always thought I would never break out of the working class if I stayed in Israel. That's not what I said that night. I told him I wanted to see the world. "I want to encounter new challenges, new opportunities."

"It's not going to be easy to be a starving student in a foreign country," Dan said.

That didn't register with me. Going to America simply felt like an exciting adventure, though I was unhappy at having to leave Africa; and I didn't relish telling Dina the bad news.

Back home I opened the door and saw half the living room covered with a white cloth on top of which were arranged, in random order, wood carved African figurines, dolls, head sculptures and various sculpted ivory pieces. Two African men dressed in long white dresses and caps—African art merchants from the Houssa tribe—had come from Nigeria to sell their art door to door, and now Dina was inspecting it and selecting some pieces. "How do you like this head?" she asked as I walked in. It was a wood carving of an African woman's head, the largest we had seen in the many months of these salesmen's visits.

"Take it," I said.

"Ask him how much it is," she said.

"It doesn't matter," I said. "I like it."

Dina looked at me, puzzled. I always bargained with any and every salesman. "Don't you want to negotiate?"

"We don't have much time," I said.

"Why?"

"We're going home," I said, and I told her about the termination. We agreed we would buy the big wooden head as well as some other pieces including a fertility doll the Ghanians believed Dina should wear on her belly if she wanted to have children.

That evening, I heard Abu, the housekeeper, calling Dina. "Missie…"

Abu, who had come to work for us for two weeks only had stayed for the duration as Dina became accustomed to the idea. We did, however, refuse to call him our "servant" as the others did. "What is it, Abu?" Dina asked.

"Tse, tse, tse." Whenever Abu was stressed, he made this sound between his lips and teeth. "Missie uses too many utensils." He had gained self-confidence over the months. "Too much to wash after dinner," he added, but Dina simply said, "That's life." She didn't like to give orders, but Abu and I were both learning, she liked even less to take them.

Over the next few weeks we bought many things we did not exactly need, but we wanted memories. We shipped our belongings back to Israel. One day, during our last week in Ghana, we noticed Abu talking and laughing through the window with our neighbors. He was leaning out, touching the neighbor's tree, the branches of which reached our second floor windows. For months he had been picking the fruit from this tree and trying to convince us to eat it, and now he insisted we try it. The fruit turned out to be Cherimoya, an aromatic and delicious tropical fruit. When we tasted it, Dina and I were upset with ourselves for not having tried it before. From that time on, whenever we traveled, we always made a point of searching for and trying both cherimoya and any other exotic foods.

We felt we had not completed our discovery of Africa and the enjoyment of it, and I also felt I had not fulfilled my mission with my cadets, who threw a party for me. In addition to flying, I had taught them meteorology lessons and when I had explained how fog forms I used a glass of beer (which they all liked) as a prop to show the moisture forming on the cold glass in a similar process. For a going away present they bought me a beer glass with double walls that prevented the moisture forming and claimed I was wrong.

Our small group of pilots and technicians grew close in the months we spent in Ghana. Sorry it had come to an end, we said our goodbyes in small gatherings and vowed to keep in touch, and at the end of February 1961, Dina and I sold our beloved Beatle and departed Africa and the tropics on our way to Europe.

In Ghana with my cadets.

Air crew with Israeli Ambassador to Ghana.

CHAPTER THIRTY

The stone floors were clean, yet women dressed in dark dresses were constantly scrubbing them. It was morning when we landed in Barcelona, and we were surprised by the vast difference between this world and the one we had just left behind. Accra was noisy and dense with people dressed in bright, colorful clothes, a young nation, the people outgoing and lively. In contrast Barcelona felt dark and dreary, its people clad in dark clothes and rarely smiling or congregating. Generalissimo Franco had ruthlessly depressed the country.

This is where we began our trip around Europe. Dina and I joined two pilots, Reuven Hirsh and Itsik Hirsh, for the journey, and from Barcelona the four of us flew to Italy, picked up a new Fiat 1100 that Itsik bought at the factory in Torino and spent the next two months driving around a dozen European countries. We separated only for one week in Germany where Dina and I wanted to visit my Uncle Moshe who was living in Berlin. This required crossing the territory of East Germany, something the Hirsches were loathe to do. In Munich we agreed to meet in a week, and Dina and I boarded a luxurious train to Berlin.

In the restaurant car we were enjoying the service when the train stopped at a border station. Through the windows we could see the rundown terminal, at the end of which stood a freight train with open cars; female workers were shoveling asphalt from the cars onto the ground. We could tell we had arrived in East Germany; neglect was evident everywhere. As the train moved forward, I remembered how hard my leaders in the youth movement *Hashomer Hatsair* had tried to convince me only a few years back of the supremacy of the "Dictatorship of the Proletariat." They had spent many hours explaining why the tyranny of the workers was good for all, but the reality outside the train proved them wrong.

We were pleased to arrive in Berlin, a flourishing city with brightly lit cafes serving excellent coffees and cakes to well-dressed people. Stores overflowed with food, and I loved the choices of hundreds of different kinds of salami hanging from a wall at the gigantic KDV. My Uncle Moshe lived in a nice apartment in the center of the city. Just 15 years had passed since the end of World War II; that my uncle chose to live in this city struck me as odd. This, after all, had been the heart of Nazi Germany.

But Moshe was one of these guys haunted by bad luck. From his days as an orphan after the Cossacks killed his parents and burned their home, to his entry to Palestine in the early '30s, he had had little luck. In the orphanage they trained Moshe to be a jeweler, but Palestine had little need for jewelers, and he worked instead as a policeman, a construction worker, and numerous other odd jobs he never liked. He had never stopped dreaming of becoming a jeweler.

Friedle, his wife, was born in Germany and had been living there with her husband and children when Hitler came to power. Friedle lost everyone in the Holocaust but escaped to the east, spent years in Shanghai, and in 1948, when Israel was established, Friedle made *aliya* to Jerusalem where she met my Uncle Moshe. She was ten years older than he and five inches taller, but they married and moved to Berlin in the early '50s.

"Here is where I sit in the morning," my uncle said. "They keep this table for me." He and I were in a nice little café in the center of Berlin eating excellent cakes and drinking hot tea. Men in expensive suits and overdressed women surrounded us.

"Moshe, how do you make a living?" I asked.

He stopped looking around, turned and looked at me, surprised. "I'm a jeweler," he said.

I had known he dealt in jewelry, but I never saw him actually making it. When Dina and I got married he sent us a letter, directing us to his friend, a jeweler with a store on Alenby Street in Tel Aviv, where we purchased two gold rings for $10.00. I never had found out if this was a good price or not. "Don't you want to have a store?" I asked.

"I work at home," he said, "and I have this table in the café. What about you? Dina is a nice girl, no?"

"Yes, she is nice."

"You see, everyone knows me," he said, nodding to people at the adjacent tables.

I nodded approvingly.

"Why did you become a pilot? Did they make you go to the Air Force?" he asked. It became clear to me he had been gone from Israel for a long time, so I told him the story of my invitation, my volunteering, and how hard becoming a fighter pilot for the Israeli Air Force was. I described the prestige that came with the position.

"Do you fly these jets?" he asked.

"Yes, I fly the Mystere," I said. "A French fighter."

"Aren't you afraid?" His question brought to mind some of the good scares I had had—the day I almost flew into the drone trying to get closer for a better shot and the time I nearly collided with Baban during our dog fight, and the time I was nearly pushed into Mount Carmel. "Sometimes, but I get over it," I said.

"You always wanted to be an engineer, no?"

I felt close to Moshe, and not just because he remembered my long-held desires; I remembered fondly his coming to our house after falling from the Ben Yehuda Street apartment when it was destroyed by a car bomb. I remembered visiting him in the Christian Hospital after his brain surgery to remove a tumor. We had experienced some important times together. "Yes, I still want to study," I said.

"You will go to the Technion?"

"I want to study in America," I said.

"And you'll take Dina with you?"

I couldn't tell if he was joking or not. "Of course," I said.

"How will you support yourself? If you go to Technion, I'll send you money."

"We'll be all right," I said, touched at his offer but certain of my dreams.

"But why America?"

I began to talk about how *Ima*, my mother and his sister, had told me stories she had heard of America, of her long-held dream to see it, and how that desire had given me the yearning to see the world and to study in America. A woman approached and my uncle stood, doffed his hat and kissed her hand. For a while they conversed in German, and she left.

"Everyone knows I have the best jewelry," he said, and for a few more minutes we ate in silence until he broke that silence, saying, "I always wanted to go to America."

At the end of that week I went to the train station to purchase our tickets to Munich, but there I learned we would need a special visa to leave Berlin and cross East Germany. Our Israeli service passports in hand, we walked to East Berlin, crossing at the Brandenburg Gate which loomed over a large, open and deserted area—no people, no cars, only East German border guards. There Dina and I explained in English what we needed, and the guards directed us to an office in a vast building on the other side of the gate. The East German officials we encountered were serious and suspicious, their faces and eyes revealing both authority and fear. When we finally reached the small office where our passports could be stamped, we saw a small man watched over by two mean, Russian-looking police officers who carefully followed his every move.

The man smiled and studied our passports. *"Israelische* Diplomat?" he said.

"Yes," I said, and I turned to look at Dina's anguished face. He was staring at her.

"Yoong!" he said. *"Sehr shoen."* And he stamped our passports.

We joined our friends in Munich and continued to travel Europe in the little Fiat, driving from town to town, from one tourist attraction to another. In restaurants Dina ordered full meals while I ordered little since after she was finished, there would be enough left to fill me. After two months I had gained a few pounds and Dina was thinner than she had been when we married. We ended our journey in the Italian port city of Genoa, and the Fiat owner shipped the car to Israel. We boarded the train for Rome. From Rome we flew back to Israel, landing at Lod Airport where Yudke and Dina's mother awaited us.

"Happy Birthday," they said. It was my 23rd.

Back from Africa.

Dina and I moved in with her parents, brother Benny and sister Irit, in their one bedroom house. We had the 6 x 10 foot addition at the back of the house, the room which only a few months earlier, when we dated, Dina's mother had not wanted us to use; now she didn't want us to leave. We rested from our European vacation and the trauma of leaving Africa prematurely. We couldn't stop telling stories of Africa, accompanying our tales of animals, jungles, deserts, people and art with slides of our pilot friends, our planes, my cadets, with Kwame Nkrumah, Haile Selassie and naked women in the jungle. People told us it sounded as if we'd had a year-long honeymoon, and we couldn't argue. But after two weeks we came back to earth and decided we needed our own place and a car. But we had spent our small savings in Europe.

Still, I was set on my dream of going to America. After all those structured years, in school, in the kibbutz, in the Air Force, I detested authority and yearned to be free. I had tasted freedom in Africa and Europe, but it only whetted my appetite. I decided to talk to Eyzer Weitzman again.

The chief of the Air Force received me in his office with warmth and camaraderie. He stood and offered me his hand with the greeting, "Welcome back, Makogon." For a year now I had been using my new name Gonen, but I did not correct him. "Rumor is you enjoyed your mission in the black continent," he said.

"Yes Sir, I did."

"What do you want to do now?" he asked abruptly. Weitzman had no time to waste. People often complained that I talked slowly, and in that moment I realized it was true—I talked slowly because I seldom had planned what I would say; I never rehearsed conversations. I would listen to what people said and react to it, so I needed time to process. But it seemed to me that Weitzman wanted to hear me say that I wanted to go to the most advanced squadron, the squadron with the Super Mystere, a newer, more powerful fighter than the Mystere I had flown. I was sure he thought I would ask to be assigned to fly this plane, and I saw that he had my personnel file in front of him. He was well known for memorizing details about his personnel, and especially his air crews.

In truth I knew what I wanted to do and hesitated only because I didn't know how to tell him. "Don't be bashful, Makogon," he said. "I read your file. You can go anywhere."

I had already told him I wanted to study engineering, and knowing that his friendly attitude would vanish if I said it again, I kept my mouth shut. I dreaded his wrath.

"So, what do you want to do?" he asked again, letting me understand I was beginning to waste his time.

"I want to be discharged," I said.

He looked at me, puzzled, opened my file and shuffled some pages. "You have signed up until when?" he asked.

"My five years will end in three months," I said.

When I started my flight training, like all pilots at the time I had signed up for five years, but through no fault of my own, by the time I got my wings, the time left on my original commitment was relatively short. My contract with the Air Force would end in July.

"But you extended for two more years."

"Yes, sir, but that was only because you sent me for a two year stay in Ghana."

"But you signed," he insisted.

I continued to argue. "You know I didn't want to extend my contract. I signed only to serve as a flight instructor in Ghana for two years." I had been there just eight months.

His face reddened, and his eyes were so fiery, they seemed they might shoot flames. He leaned his large torso across his desk towards me and pushed his face close to mine. I thought he might slap me with his enormous hands. "But you signed," he raised his voice and suddenly stood so that he towered over me. On his pressed uniforms, the rank of General gleamed.

I stared at the war medals lined up across one side of his chest, his pilot wings on the other. "Do you think you're in kindergarten? You signed on and you'll keep your commitment. This is the Air Force!"

He sat and for a while we both were quiet. The truth sank in. He was right. I had signed on for two years, with no conditions, and legally I was locked in. Still, he knew this was unjust. After a few moments, he leaned back and said, in a more conciliatory tone, "Look Makogon, I started my service in 1942. I joined the damned British Army and was a truck driver in Africa. Do you know why?" I understood he was about to take the patriotic angle, but he gave me no time to respond. "Because we all had to defend the Jewish people and Eretz Israel. A truck driver!" He paused. "Then we went to Rhodesia to learn to fly for the same reason. I even spent time in a stinking base in India!"

I sat there pondering his sacrifices, but the more he talked about the places he'd traveled, the more I wanted to get out of the Air Force to travel.

I wondered if I ought to tell him that I came from poverty, that I had suffered the war and the siege in Jerusalem as a young refugee. Still, he was right. I was not prepared to devote my career to the country, but I had given my share. I had served more than many others, more than any of my youth movement friends. Many pilots I knew, including some of my best instructors, left the Air Force as soon as they could to fly for El Al. I resented his dictating to me. I wanted my freedom.

"You can have a great future in the Air Force," he said. "If you try, you could sit in my chair one day."

I looked at him. I had no aspirations of leadership, had never dreamed of climbing the ranks or becoming a great commander. But I said nothing. I wouldn't win this argument. Seeing the frustration in his face, I couldn't understand why he wouldn't end our interview and throw me out of his office. But there was something in his eyes that told me he was not yet finished.

"I don't understand," he said. "Are you afraid to fly?"

I was stunned by the question. Talking about fear was taboo among pilots, the white elephant in the realm of the Air Force. His faked question angered me. Why was he trying so hard to keep an undistinguished Lieutenant? Did he actually believe his punches below the belt would change my mind?

"Sir, I'm sure you've read my file," I said slowly, trying to tamp down my rising anger. "Have you found anything at all, any clue in it that led you to such a question?"

"That's exactly the point!" He pounded his fist on the desk. "I don't understand why you would give up such a promising career."

Like a salesman unable to close a sale, his expression turned from fury to disappointment. "If you plan on going to fly for El Al, forget it. I won't let you."

I had no doubt he could make good on this threat. El Al had always been an option, the quickest way for an Israeli pilot to earn money and quasi celebrity. But that had never been my plan, and I knew Dina did not want me to go there. "For now you'll go back to flight school. And you'd better do a good job." He stood.

Feeling dizzy, I said "yes, sir," turned and walked out of the room, but as I opened the door I heard him calling behind me.

"Makogon!"

I turned.

"You are still in the Air Force," he said. "We salute when we leave."

I straightened my body, saluted properly and left. Outside a pilot I knew was waiting his turn, and he looked at me, puzzled. "That bad?" he asked. "What happened in there?"

I realized I must look exactly as I felt—dejected. Later this man told me I had ruined his interview because Eyzer spent most of the time talking about me, my selfishness, lack of courage and patriotism. I decided that in this public relations fight with Eyzer, I could never win.

At Dina's mother's home, I told Dina about the interview, and although she felt bad for me, she didn't think it so terrible. "You'll still fly. He could have forced you to stay *and* grounded you altogether," she said, trying to lift my spirits. "And the two years will pass quickly."

I looked at my beautiful girl and wondered at my good fortune. She had a rare combination of a nature that was highly sensitive and emotional but also strong and practical. "We need to look for our own place," she said.

CHAPTER THIRTY-ONE

When we moved into our new pad in the air-crew community of the Tel
Noff air base, Dina decorated the one bedroom duplex, choosing to paint
one wall of the living room pitch black. This caused a bit of sensation
among our fellow pilots and their wives. Later, when our things arrived
from Africa—things that included a carpet and a modern semi-automatic
washer, which required Dina to move the wet wash by hand from one side
to the other to be rinsed and in the process, messed up the whole house—it
began to feel like a home. We had also shipped a Kenwood mixer that we
never used, but we couldn't return to Israel without one. Still, our most
prized possessions were the African art pieces, and these decorated our
walls.

Dina got a job teaching first grade in the school in Gedera - a few miles
south of the base - where the children of the base went to school. She liked
teaching and the kids loved her. But the parents loved her even more. She
was a serious, pleasant, devoted teacher, and the most beautiful teacher most
had ever met. Uri Yarom, the commander of the first helicopter squadron
in the Israeli Air Force, known for his sense of humor, told everyone that
he couldn't wait for his son's teacher's conference because he loved to just sit
and watch Dina for an hour. Four decades later, at the beach in Hertzelia
one day, we met again with Sarah and Raffi Harlev who told us it had been
a consensus among the families that Dina was the most beautiful woman
in Tel Noff.

We settled into our new neighborhood and made friends with our
neighbors who also flew jets, helicopters, transports and trainers. Among
our friends were Etti and Nissim Ashkenazy, who had graduated flight
school with me and later ejected over Egypt, was injured and became a
POW. He eventually reached the rank of Brigadier General. Other friends
included Arie Oz, Solly Amiran, and Uri Margalit most of whom went on
to be El Al Airlines captains.

I returned to teach flying and flew the Harvard and later the twin

French jet, Fuga Magister. In time, I became a course commander and a senior flight examiner. I commanded, examined, and flew with numerous cadets, a whole slew of whom became the future generations of Israeli Air Force pilots, some of whom gained considerable fame. Among them, was Ron Goren, a future Deputy Chief of Staff of the Israel Defense Force and Hertzel Budinger, who rose to become a General-Chief of the Air Force. My deputy in this effort was a young handsome pilot who was efficient, dedicated, ambitious, and helped me a lot. He came from a well-to-do family, evidenced by his brand new VW. "Imagine, brand new!" people exclaimed when they saw it. He, Avihoo Ben Noon, later became a General and chief of the Air Force.

Still, despite our pleasant life, I was counting the days and months until I could leave. In the meantime, I worked hard and collected hundreds of flying hours on the Fuga and was assigned to help start an emergency squadron that would utilize this plane in a future war. The Fuga had machine guns and could carry air to ground rockets and small bombs. Our mission was to attack enemy ground forces, convoys of vehicles and armor.

During the second half of 1962, I was the deputy commander of the squadron that trained future flight instructors, and at the time I had more flying hours on the twin jet Fuga than anyone else in the Air Force. On a wintry December day, when I still had ten months left in the service,

I flew to the Negev, to a spot near Beer Sheba on a mission to simulate landings and take off next to Kibbutz Hatserim. The Air Force had planned to build a new air base there, and I was to fly the takeoff and landing patterns without touching ground; I was to try to convince the kibbutz members that the noise wasn't so bad in order to stop their lobbying against the new base, that years later housed the Flight Academy and a number of fighter squadrons. When I landed back at Tel Noff, the flight academy administrative officer, a young, energetic Lieutenant, called me and told me I had to sign some forms. I was used to signing forms for the squadron, so I walked to his office, but when I arrived he said, "Eyzer's letting you go. All you have to do is sign this."

He handed me a form requesting early discharge.

With no questions, I signed it and Dina and I started to arrange our move.

I was not ready, but I could not wait to go to the U.S, so I sent a few letters to universities. I wanted to go to UCLA. I received a response to my letter along with a catalog, half of which was promotional material. I studied the pictures of students on the beach, playing volleyball and basketball and drinking at a party. Those pictures threw me; I suspected UCLA could not be a serious learning institution. In the letter they told me I needed to go to the American Embassy and take the SAT test which was to be given in a few months.

"We're going," I said to Dina, and I slapped the big UCLA envelope on the table.

"Did you get accepted?" Dina asked, excited.

"No, they want me to take a test in a few months."

Her face fell. "So why do you say we're going?"

"I can't wait," I said. I had begun to feel more and more like a prisoner, longing to depart. But my wife looked at me with tears in her eyes, her lips quivering.

"Don't worry," I told her. "I'll get tourist visas."

I went to the American Embassy and applied for visas. Dina and I agreed that we had flown enough over the last few years, so we decided this time we would travel by ship, a chance to rest for the two-week trip from Haifa to New York. Arranging visas, travel and exit permits from Israel took over two months.

When we visited my parents to say goodbye, my father asked what last name I used on my new travel documents, and when I told him Gonen, he asked, "Not Makogon?"

"What's the difference? They're going to America!" my mother said it as if we had won the lottery.

"I can't believe you discarded our name," my father said, "just like that." He was forever disappointed at my name change.

On March 3, 1962, Dina, her mother, and I took a taxi to Haifa. A taxi to Haifa! It was extravagant, sixty miles in a taxi, but we wanted to leave the neighborhood in style. Dina's neighbors gathered around the cab, looking on as we left. When we arrived at the port, Yudke and his wife, Ziva, were already on the platform. It was time for us to board.

"Oy vey, when will I see you again?" Rivka wept.

"It won't be long," Dina said, crying just as hard.

"I always lose my family," Rivka wailed, referring to the loss of Dina's father and to her parents and siblings. I felt guilty.

"Rivka, it's only four years," I said.

"Oy vey," she wept.

"We'll visit often," I lied.

Many other families taking leave of their loved ones surrounded us on the platform and officials were working hard to herd everyone on board, with little success. But when the ship blared its horn, we hurried to say our last farewells, boarded, put our luggage in our room and walked back to the upper deck as the "Jerusalem" slowly pulled away from the dock.

Rivka, Yudke and Ziva stood at the edge, Rivka waving her handkerchief, wiping her eyes with it, then waving again. I wished the ship would move more quickly, but for a long time we could still see them; they continued to wave. Behind them, the dark clouds above Mount Carmel could not diminish the magnificent view of Haifa built on its slopes.

We stood silently at the railing as it began to rain, but we kept watching that sight until Haifa and its port and people were no longer in view. I looked at Dina. She had stopped crying, but I could see her concern about leaving our homeland for the unknown, in her eyes.

"It's going to be all right," I said, hugging her.

"Promise?" she asked. And she smiled.

CHAPTER THIRTY-TWO

We walked across the damp deck toward the steps leading to the dining room, looking forward to our first lunch on board. Half an hour had passed since we had left the pier, and the wind had picked up. The sea was rough as we walked the re-varnished stairs with their worn carpet; some of the lights were burnt out, and we discovered the ship was old, only partially renovated. Suddenly we didn't feel we were on the luxury liner depicted in the promotion brochure of Zim Israeli ship lines. We could smell soup, chicken and roasted beef as we approached the dining hall, but the ship was pitching side to side, and I felt my stomach lurch and saw Dina's face grow pale. We looked at each other and without a word turned and walked back to our room.

We had booked one of the best rooms, just below the top deck, with a little glass window, barely bigger than a passenger airplane window. With no private bathroom, the ticket agent had arranged for us to have the room closest to the public bathroom, "Just across the hall," he had said.

The hull was creaking more loudly as the storm gathered strength and heavy rain pounded on our window. Outside our room, we heard a persistent banging sound every time the boat pitched side to side. My nausea was bad, and I didn't want to get up, but the banging grew worse, so I stood up and realized it was the bathroom door slamming against the wall. I secured the door and returned to our bedroom. That evening we skipped dinner, and for the next three days, as the storm continued, we skipped all meals. The boat was bobbing as if it were a paper boat until the fourth day as we approached our first port of call, Napoli. There the sea grew calm, and we went ashore and ate a bowl of real Neapolitan spaghetti and meatballs.

After a few hours in Napoli, our "cruise" continued and the sea, though not calm, was not as rough as in prior days until we passed the Straits of Gibraltar. Once we were out on the Atlantic again, the storm turned violent, and we realized there was nothing to do on this ship where we would spend two weeks--no music, no movies, no sports, no swimming pool.

Most of the passengers were emigrating to the States, and many had spent a short time in Israel waiting for their visas to the States to be approved. They spoke in a number of languages and we did not connect. Like most Israelis, we despised them. They were *Yordim*; when an individual immigrates to Isael, he makes *"Aliah"* – he comes up. When he immigrates out of Isreal, he goes down – *"Yored"*. After the troubled history of the Jews in the Diaspora, we believed they should not return there. We, on the other hand, were going to America for a temporary stay only, to study for just a few years.

Dina had not eaten for ten days, but having become accustomed to the nausea, occasionally I went to the dining room. On the eleventh day, I insisted Dina join me on the deck. When the passengers saw her, they were astonished by how thin she had become, and I got an apple for her, which she began to nibble—to our neighbors' relief. On deck, just a few chairs away from us sat an American family, a couple and their two children. For a while the eleven-year-old boy stared at us, and finally he walked over and asked, "Are you newlyweds?"

I chuckled. Dina and I had already experienced so many and varied experiences, I felt as if we'd always been together. "We've been married over two years," I said.

"You look so young," he said.

An Israeli boy never would have spoken this way, so at ease and chatty, and I realized I had met a different breed. He was handsome, well dressed, and his blue eyes projected youthful intelligence. I was glad he had come by to chat, glad not to be hearing the Poles and Rumanians and Russians and Iraqis chattering about their unhappiness with Israel's taxes, unions, discrimination, leftist government, their jubilation at going to America. This was a refreshing conversation, so I asked, "What brought you to Israel?"

"My father is a diplomat," he said, "in the American Embassy in Tel Aviv. We're going back home. Why are you leaving Israel?"

Listening to those words, I felt as if a thin dagger had pierced my chest, although I understood the question was natural and one I would hear many times in the coming years. "We're not leaving," I said.

"So why are you going to America?"

"To study in college," I said, "Engineering."

Dina smiled at me as if she had suddenly remembered why we were enduring this suffering, and could for one moment, focus on our bright future. "My husband is very smart," she said, and I was relieved that after all these days without food she could still speak.

The boy was curious now. "What did you do in Israel?" he asked.

When I said I'd been an Air Force pilot, he looked stunned. "You're not shitting me, are you?"

But I didn't understand his question. "What?"

"Are you telling the truth?" he asked and without waiting for an answer he called to his father. "Daddy, this guy's an Israeli pilot!" His father looked over with a smile and waved. "And you left *that* to go to college?" he asked, incredulous.

After he walked away I looked out at the rocky sea—a cloud had descended, and we couldn't see more than 200 feet beyond the ship; it was only the monotonous whirr of the motors and the splash of the waves that kept me thinking we were heading to New York. But now I wondered. Had I done the right thing? The boy's question—you left *that* for college?—whirled through my mind in an endless tape as the hours passed slowly. Dina was watching me. "You'll do well," she assured me, "We'll be happy."

Late that afternoon, as a little light penetrated the clouds, the young boy came to visit us again. "Where are you going?" he asked.

When I told him Los Angeles, he wrinkled his nose in disgust. "It's the worst place you could have chosen."

"Why?" I asked.

He pointed out to sea where I saw only a hint of the ocean and a larger sea of thick clouds and said, "It looks like this all the time."

"We heard the weather is good," Dina said.

"But the smog is terrible," he answered.

Dina looked at me to see if I knew what he was talking about, but I didn't, and when the boy saw this, he explained. "The air is dirty. You can't see anything, and you cough all the time."

"How do you know?" I asked.

"I live in San Diego, not far from L.A."

I looked at Dina and said in Hebrew, "Don't worry, it's only a boy's imagination."

"What school are you going to?" he asked.

"I don't know yet," I said. His difficult questions were beginning to annoy me, and I was hoping he would leave us alone, but he went on.

"At least if you're going to LA. You should go to Cal Tech. My uncle went there."

"Is it a good school?"

"The best!" the eleven year old expert said. At last darkness chased us back to our room.

At midnight I woke to hear the bathroom door across the hall slamming against the wall. Fourteen nights of these bangs, and I still got angry every time I heard that sound. I climbed out of bed, walked across the hall and secured the door. The banging stopped but the violent movement continued as I staggered back to bed where Dina was fast asleep. Just as I began to fall asleep, the door began to bang again—someone had used the bathroom and left the door ajar.

I gave up on the possibility of sleep, dressed and walked up to the top deck. There the ship's lights reflected on the fog and giant raindrops slapped the deck. Within moments I was soaked as the ship plowed into waves. I walked to the bow, careful to hold tightly to the railing.

The bow was rising as high as 40 feet with each wave, splashing down again with such tremendous force, the deck seemed to dive under water. At that moment, a great wave carried the bow and me up into the air; water on deck flowed to the back, and a moment later we slammed down again. I wasn't sure we would make it. As I walked back along the edge, holding on for life, I noticed a few people standing on the side deck. Coming closer I saw they were crew members vomiting over the side railing. It wasn't a reassuring sight.

On our fourteenth day at sea, Dina and I began to count the hours and to search the horizon for New York. We were scheduled to arrive that day, but we saw nothing ahead. The captain at last announced we would be delayed by a day or so. As consolation, he threw us a party in the dining room. About ten minutes into it, a woman and her chair slid across the hall with one of the waves, hit a post and broke her leg. The party was over.

On the morning of the seventeenth day we woke to a strange silence. We walked on deck and saw the New York skyline--just like in the pictures, tall, and grand. "Why are they so damn slow?" I asked no one in particular.

"When you're on a boat you got to have patience," said the old man standing next to us. I recognized his accent as Romanian.

"We just had seventeen days of learning about it," Dina said.

The boat was slowly towed into port. As we moored at the pier, we could no longer see the big picture of New York, only the dirty, dilapidated pier and the structures around it. We had come to the land of unlimited possibilities, the richest land in the world, but it looked worse than anything we had seen anywhere. Even Napoli had looked better than this.

Still, we longed to stand on solid ground.

We were standing on deck, our two suitcases beside us. One was heavier than Dina, and I laughed when she offered to help me carry it to shore.

Finally when we did reach land, we felt as if the ground were still moving; seventeen days at the mercy of the sea had changed us, and we needed some time to get used to the stillness of the earth. We hugged each other. "Welcome to America," I said.

"Never again on a boat," Dina said.

I had paid double the price of airline tickets for our "pleasure cruise," and now I was looking to save. We had landed in America with $500.00 and an address from Flochick who was in school in New York and had told me we could stay with him. The only problem was, the storm had delayed us, and I didn't know exactly how to find him. At the gate a line of yellow cabs awaited us, but I thought taking the underground train might be better.

"Kumst foon Israel?" an elderly taxi driver asked in Yiddish, assuming we understood no English. "Where are you going?"

I showed him the piece of paper with Flochick's address.

"Oy vey, I can't take you there," he said.

Dina had heard stories of how dangerous, big and unfriendly New York was, and this comment caused her another wave of despair.

"Don't worry," I squeezed her hand and spoke in Hebrew, "I'll take care of it."

"Oh, you speak Hebrew? Shalom," the driver said, and he went on to explain that the place we were seeking was on Staten Island; he would take us to the ferry that would carry us there. "My luck," he said. "I stand here and wait all day and what do I get? The shortest fare in the city." He lifted the suitcase into his trunk and began to speak in English. "What have you stuffed in your suitcase, your mother-in-law?" With his thick New York accent, Dina could not understand him.

"What did he say?" she asked.

"Nothing," I said.

"This your wife?" the driver went on. "You need to feed her."

I looked at Dina and saw that every bone in her body was visible; still, to me she was more beautiful than ever. "Don't worry," I assured him as he drove, "I will."

He drove us to the ferry and I read the meter: 70 cents. "A dollar," the driver said.

I decided not to argue and paid a dollar. "And tip?" he asked.

I had never paid a tip anywhere—not in Africa or Europe where service was always included in the bill. In Israeli restaurants tips were not required and in fact were frowned upon, and even when we wanted to reward excellent service, we both felt awkward, fearing the recipient might be insulted.

But now we were in America, so I added a dime to the fare and listened to him cursing after us as we walked onto the ferry.

Flochick lived in a third floor walk-up and was happy to see us, but when I looked around I realized he lived in a studio apartment with just one bed.

"You'll sleep here," Flochick said. "I'll go next door. My neighbor is away."

Two years had passed since I had seen him, and I was surprised to see how small he looked, particularly among his tall American neighbors. He explained that he had chosen to live on Staten Island because Manhattan was too expensive, and he told us the story of his difficult entry to the States. He had spent a few months working as a telegram delivery boy for Western Union, riding his bike on freezing cold, snowy nights and earning just one dollar per hour.

"But now it's much better. I sell Encyclopedias, and the pay is better. I'm a door-to-door salesman."

I could see he was embarrassed—he had grown up, like us, admiring physical, productive work on a kibbutz; a sales job did not seem honorable.

"How do you know where to sell?" I asked, and he explained the company gave him addresses.

"I just started," he said, "so now I sell in Harlem."

I had heard about Harlem, the place the basketball team the Globe Trotters came from, the place where many black people lived. As a teenager in the youth organization, we had sung the blues and heard stories about black American culture. I told Flochick I would like to join him one night, to see how he sold.

"Are you sure?" he asked, laughing nervously. "You know I sell to Negroes," he half-whispered.

"So what?" I asked.

He pointed to a spot on his neck. "See this scar? It's from a knife." One night as he was leaving a tenement in Harlem, a black guy had held a knife to his neck. When he started to cut him, Flochick gave him his money.

I knew Flochick did not tell fables, but I thought this could happen anywhere. But Dina worried, "We're here for a short visit. Don't take him there, Flochick."

"Where should we visit tomorrow?" I changed the subject.

On our second day in America, I took Dina to Manhattan. We toured Fifth Avenue, climbed to the top of the Empire State Building, and that evening, back at the apartment, as Flochick and I got ready to go out, Dina said, "Don't go. Why do you need this?"

"She's right," Flochick said.

But by then I was curious and up for the challenge and didn't want to back out. We took along only two dollars in case we were robbed. On the subway Flochick took out the list of leads the company had provided him, people who had responded to advertisements and expressed an interest in purchasing the Encyclopedia. "We'll go to the best prospect," he said, but as soon as we exited the station and saw the towering tenements surrounded by trash, overturned garbage cans and graffiti everywhere, I realized how bad this area was. Shadowy figures stood near a wall, and every person we saw was black.

"You see this entry," Flochick said in his military briefing voice. "We're going to rush through it and run up the stairs to the sixth floor. Follow me." We ran in, past two figures leaning against a wall, smoking. I had to use all my strength to keep up, and by the time we reached the door, we were breathing hard. Flochick knocked. "What is it?" a man's voice called.

"I have an appointment with you," Flochick said. "*Encyclopedia Britanica.*"

We heard the man talking to a woman. "We don't have no appointment with nobody," he said.

"*Britannica.* You called for a presentation," Flochick told the man who opened the door a crack. "It'll take only ten minutes," Flochick said.

The man let us inside. In seconds Flochick had opened his bag, unfolded a large colored presentation flat on the floor. I looked around and saw traces of an old fire on the walls of the small open kitchen and a sink overflowing with dirty dishes. Gushing holes perforated the living room walls. The couple—the woman held a child—eyed us suspiciously. I was amazed by Flochick's professional-sounding pitch. "For only a few cents a day you may get your children to college," he said, pushing them hard to sign the purchase papers.

After ten minutes, they actually did, and we left the apartment for another.

In the hallway Flochick smiled. "Okay, I made some money," he said. "Remember those two guys we saw smoking at the entry? They're waiting for us with knives. They want our money."

"How do you know?" I asked.

"We're going to run down and run all the way to the station. Keep up with me," he said skipping three, four and five steps at a time. I ran behind him, keeping up, and we stormed past the guys in the entry hall. They tried to grab us, but they couldn't, and they began to chase after us, but we were too fast for them. Flochick even had the time to show them the finger before we dashed into the half-empty train.

For a while we sat in silence.

"A few more sales and I'll get a better area," Flochick said.

"You were very good," I told him, but I was wondering what the hell I was doing here. It had been only a few months since I was flying for the best Air Force in the world, instructing and commanding the elite of Israeli youth, and here I was in a dirty, noisy train, happy to be traveling out of Harlem. I felt as if I'd just been in an interesting but depressing movie, and I watched Flochick inspecting his list, planning and choosing his prospects for the next evening. Perhaps it would be another black family fumbling in the swamp of life, but willing, "for only a few cents a day," to buy hope. He wasn't sure *Encyclopedia Britannica* would help their kids get into college, but he knew it would sustain him to graduate from one.

Back at Flochick's home, I called the offices of TWA. I needed to get out of here before my American dream crumbled.

On the boat to America.

CHAPTER THIRTY-THREE

Boarding the plane at La Guardia gave us great pleasure. Dina and I both felt as if we had been re-crowned royalty. True, it was late in the evening and we were embarking on a TWA Redeye to Los Angeles—one of the last flights of the Constellation, with its recognizable triple tails and four propellers—and I had chosen the flight because it was least expensive. But we didn't care that it stopped over in Washington D.C., St. Louis, Missouri and Dallas before landing twelve hours later. As we approached LAX in the last minutes of darkness, we stared at the carpet of lights on the ground and wondered if and where we would fit in to this megalopolis.

As we touched down, we saw the first rays of sun over the horizon.

In the terminal, Dina's Aunt Shulamit awaited us. Her mother's sister, Shulamit was a survivor of the Holocaust and spoke Lithuanian, Yiddish, German, Hebrew and English—each with a heavy accent. Beside her stood a tall man, and she introduced us. "My cousin, Manny Cohen."

"Nice to meet you," he said in a rolling American accent. He looked at us a little perplexed, but I detected a smile.

"He didn't want to come," Shulamit said in Hebrew.

Our natural reaction was to look at him. I noticed he was well dressed. "What did Sylvia say?" he asked as he pulled a pack of Winston cigarettes from a pocket.

"My American name," Shulamit explained.

"She said that it wasn't easy for you to come so early," I said.

"Yeah," he said. "My mother made me come."

"*Hoo meod asheer,*" Shulamit told us in Hebrew that Manny was very rich as he lit a cigarette and offered it to me. I smoked with pleasure. They were much better than Israeli cigarettes.

He kept looking at Dina, his cousin. "Would you like to have breakfast?" he asked.

"Sure," I said.

"He never invited *me* to a restaurant," Shulamit lamented in Hebrew.

Dina looked at me with a worried expression; the tension between them reminded me of the tension we'd felt in Israel right after the war between Holocaust survivors and *sabras*. I hadn't realized this same feeling existed in America, but Shulamit was from the old country, with a heavy accent, and American-born Jews kept away from the Greeners, those who had emigrated from Europe.

"Would you like eggs with bacon?" Manny chuckled.

"Sure," Dina said.

He couldn't believe his ears; he'd been joking, and he was shocked to learn that a couple of kids from Israel did not keep Kosher. While we were eating, he called his family on a public phone and talked for a while, laughing frequently. I could catch just one sentence. "They're just like a couple from Chicago." Later he told us he had been sure we would come dressed in long robes, like the pictures he'd seen in the Bible and in movies about Moses, but as we stepped into his car—a brand new Lincoln Continental—I thought about those American cars passing me on the road to Jerusalem in my days as a shepherd.

Manny's car was the epitome of luxury, metallic blue with soft blue leather seats, and when he opened the door, I could see it was at least 10 inches thick. He drove us out of LAX as the sun rose higher into the bright blue sky. Sitting in our air conditioned, soundproof car, we drove quietly into L.A.

Exhaustion from the flight did not diminish our excitement as we sat in the soft leather seats and looked out at the view of the city we were going to live in for the next few years. Manny drove the Continental in slow deliberate movements, steering with two fingers. "Power steering!" he crooned, as he drove up a ramp onto the San Diego Freeway. Traffic flowed in all four lanes at great speeds, and still Manny complained about the LA traffic getting too congested in recent years. "Do you drive on the freeways in Israel?" he asked.

With each question, I was amazed by how little he knew about our country. His parents were Jewish immigrants from Lithuania, and I expected him to know a bit more about Israel where his cousins lived and died.

"No freeways in Israel yet," I said. Construction of the Ayalon freeway had started but wouldn't be completed for a few more years.

A few minutes later we drove off the freeway onto Pico Boulevard. The wide street and low structures, with only a few cars and even fewer pedestrians and palm trees in some spots gave me the sense that I was in a sleepy colonial town.

Manny pointed to a large vacant area with a windowless structure and told us it was the studio of 20 Century Fox. "Is this Hollywood?' I asked.

"No," Manny laughed and lit a cigarette. "They make movies all over town now." He pulled a pack out of a carton and tossed it to me. "Winstons, best cigarettes," he said, as he pulled into a gas station. Two men rushed toward us. One began filling the tank, and the other washed the windshield. I noticed the price of gas: 25 cents a gallon.

Two more minutes later we stopped at the apartment building near Robertson Boulevard where Manny's parents greeted us. "Ve vere vaiting for you," his 80-year-old mother said in her Lithuanian Accent, "you vill stay vid us, yes?"

Along with her aunt, Dina had other relatives—Shulamit's husband, Yankle who had also come from Lithuania and survived Dachau concentration camp and Dina's second cousins. After the war Shulamit and Yankle came to America, first to Cleveland, Ohio and then to L.A. where they owned a liquor store. From the day we arrived, they never stopped complaining to us about their American-born cousins who did not socialize with them and had not helped them enough.

A few days after we arrived, we rented a one bedroom furnished apartment on Sepulveda Boulevard in West Los Angeles. The ease of getting it and the low rent ($125 a month) gave us the feeling of having made a good start. Before long the Cohen family, the cousins who had rejected Dina's aunt, adopted us as their long-lost family. Manny, with his giant metallic blue Continental, drove us to a supermarket where we discovered the abundance and variety and cleanliness of the American supermarket—the sight amazed us. I was trying to limit how much we spent, but as we shopped, Manny noticed a sliver of tension between Dina and me.

"Did you bring any money with you?" he asked.

"Sure," I said.

"How much?"

"Five hundred dollars," I said.

He laughed nervously, looking at Dina to see her reaction. She wasn't worried. I was the one who would take care of all our finances. "That's all?" he asked. "Are you planning to get anymore?"

I wasn't sure where this line of questioning was headed, but apparently my responses were causing Manny concern. "That's all we have," I said. As Dina added a box of biscuits to our cart, Manny followed it with his eyes. "You said you came for college," he said.

"Yes."

"How long are you going to survive on five hundred dollars?" He looked at me as if I had made a risky move and surrendered Dina's survival to a life of poverty in America, but I couldn't alleviate his fears. I had no detailed plan for long term income, no calculated list of expenses. "We're both going to work. Don't worry," I said.

But just two weeks later, leaving the campus of Los Angeles State College, I felt desperate. I had visited most of the public universities and colleges in town, all of which were willing to accept me as a student but none would provide me with the I-20, a form needed for the immigration office to issue a student visa and work permit. They told me I ought to have waited in Israel for this form before coming over.

I was taking a break from my hunt for a college when Dina's uncle Harry invited me to visit his business in Culver City. I arrived at a cul-de-sac and saw the large sign "Harco Aircraft Supply, Inc." on a big industrial building. Trucks were hauling materials, which I assumed were aircraft parts, out of the warehouse. As I entered the office I noticed how well lit and clean it was. Young men and women worked in open booths. Harry led me to his large office, furnished with a black desk and sofa. On the wall were pictures of horses.

"This is mine," he pointed with pride to a picture and awaited my reaction. "Look at his muscles; he won an important race at Hollywood Park." We sat down at his desk. Behind him were trophies in various sizes.

"So what do you want to do, Eitan," he asked. I was surprised at his sincere interest in helping me, which he expressed calmly.

"I came here to study Engineering," I said, and told him about my search for a college.

He asked whether I wanted to go into some business. I looked at his office and the thought of changing my plan crossed my mind, but I wasn't *that* flexible. "I think I'd better get my education first," I said.

Still, Harry gave me a part time job. I worked in the warehouse where I learned that all the company had were self-locking nuts for aircraft. He had millions of nuts he bought from the US Air Force and Navy as surplus after the Korean War. Before I left that day Harry said to me, "If you change your mind let me know, I can set you up in business." Soon after Dina began to work as Manny's secretary; he had a similar business located across from the main entrance to MGM. Meanwhile, I kept looking for a school to provide me the legal papers.

One morning Harco Aircraft Supplies called to tell me not to come to work because a man from INS had paid a visit to their offices looking for me; someone had called to report an illegal worker, and the INS representative said if he found me he'd deport me. In the meantime, I had seen an ad about the Berlitz School of Languages and signed up for English lessons at the Beverly Hills campus that consisted of two private rooms, they provided the form I needed. Through all these years later, the only thing I remember from those lessons was learning the idiom "full of hot air."

One weekend, Dina and I went to explore our neighborhood. We walked from our apartment on Sepulveda across National Boulevard and into a big Save-On drugstore. As we marveled at the variety of products and how inexpensive they were, Dina said, "I think I heard people speaking Hebrew." We looked up and down the aisle and found an Israeli couple. We introduced ourselves. They were as happy as we were—we felt as if we had found a long lost relative. They offered a slew of advice, the kind of suggestions veterans give to newcomers ; they had arrived three months before we did. We stayed and talked for some time, and I told them about my school predicament. The man said, "I know what you should do."

I was skeptical. Israelis tend to tell others what to do. But Dina asked, "What?"

"A friend of ours goes to Northrop Institute of Technology," he said, "tuition is higher than UCLA but it's a good school."

In the fall of 1963 I started my engineering studies at that school near LAX. Most of the students were just out of high school, and at the ripe old age of 25, I felt ancient. Two weeks into the semester, we took a test on the algebra and calculus I had studied in high school in Israel, stuff I was good at, so I hadn't studied hard for the test. Halfway in, I realized I remembered few of the formulas and that was all. I flunked the exam. A week later, the aging, silver-haired math teacher called me in for a conference.

"Mr. Gonen," he said, "I'm not sure that this school is for you."

I was stunned. His rejection had caught me unprepared, and despair choking me, I promised to try harder. He looked at the paper in front of him and shook his head, then looked at me and said, "In that case, you'll need to get some help."

Back home I didn't tell Dina about this conference, but she sensed I was upset and at dinner she asked what was wrong.

"I made a mistake," I said and at once I was sorry I said it.

"What?" she asked.

"I should have waited."

She did not know what I was talking about, and I realized I would have to spell out my feelings. But I held back, trying to delay the pain I knew she would feel. Her eyes were already filling with tears.

"I should have waited for an opening. I should have taken a job with El Al."

Dina had always hated this idea, fearful that the time apart such a job would have required would ruin our marriage. "After all the trouble?" she said. She stood up from the table and walked into the bedroom where she climbed into bed and cried herself to sleep.

In the morning I went to school. I knew I would have to finish what I had started, not only because of Dina's feelings but because of mine; I would not finish this venture in defeat. I would show the old professor he was wrong.

I started to study in earnest. Dina hated her jobs, but at the end the day when she came home and saw me with my books, she was happy. And a few weeks later, On November 22 I took another test in math; I had studied hard for days. We planned that night to celebrate Dina's 23rd birthday at Bob's Big Boy restaurant with a good hamburger.

In mid-morning, during the last few minutes of the test hour, most of the students were still working, but I had finished and was checking my work when the classroom door opened abruptly. A young student stood there, pale, his eyes rimmed in red.

"They shot the President!" he shouted.

"Shush!" the class said. Stunned by the reaction, he closed the door. The engineering students cared about the President, but they cared even more about finishing their test, and it was only later in the corridor that we learned that President Kennedy had been killed.

We celebrated Dina's 23rd birthday at home, watching Walter Cronkite reporting, running tapes of the scene in Dallas, Texas for the hundredth time. For three days the country shut down while the solemn television reporting continued non-stop until the procession at Arlington ended with three-year-old John F. Kennedy, Jr. saluting his father's casket.

That day I got an A on my test, just as I would get on all my future tests in engineering school.

* * *

We were excited to drive our first American car, our silver Ford Falcon. But I was even more excited when I saw a car parked near our home with a "For Sale" sign. That car reminded me of the ones I had seen on the road to Jerusalem in my shepherding days. I bought the 1952 Plymouth for $80 and worked many evenings overhauling it.

By the following spring, one year after our arrival, we were settled in Los Angeles. Dina was now working two jobs as a Hebrew teacher and attending an undergraduate program at the University of Judaism. I was taking a full load of engineering courses and working a few hours a day in the warehouse. One evening, almost four years after we got married, we decided it was time for us to have children.

Before long Dina was pregnant. She gained some weight and became still more beautiful, and as we awaited the arrival of our first child, we moved to a new two-bedroom apartment on Palms Avenue. Since the rent was more than we could afford, we agreed to be the managers of the building - a considerable addition to our workload.

On December 14, 1964 Dina woke me at midnight to say it was time, and I drove our car at full speed through all the red traffic lights on Olympic Boulevard, past Westwood, La Cienega, Fairfax, and at La Brea Dina's complaints about her pains got louder, but we still had to drive to Western Avenue. At the entry to the Cedars of Lebanon Hospital I was surprised at how old the building looked, like other buildings in this area close to downtown Los Angeles.

Dina's doctor arrived at 2:00 a.m. while I awaited news in the waiting room. Because we had planned to return to live in Israel, we did not bother with American sounding names and had decided on Ron if we had a boy or Ronit for a girl. I sat there for ten hours, and at last the doctor walked in to tell me we had a daughter; Ronit – "a little song" in Hebrew.

I wanted to bring my ladies home in style so I drove the big old Plymouth. As we drove, we were surrounded by Christmas lights and decorations. Our workload tripled, adding washing and changing diapers, sterilization of bottles, giving Ronit baths and calming her to sleep. Between the holidays and our work at home, we felt like strangers in paradise, a repetition of the feeling our parents had had when they came to *Eretz Israel* without friends or family to help. But as time passed, we became friendly with many of our fellow students, and we created bonds that continued for years. In the evening Dina attended classes at the university a few times a week, and those nights I stayed at home to care for Ronit who cried a long time before falling asleep. Her crying saddened me, especially when I was trying to solve an engineering problem, but Dina knew how to comfort her, and I was glad when at long last she outgrew her colic and became a beautiful and happy little girl.

A year into my engineering studies, I enrolled in a computer programming course and immediately fell in love with programming. The school had an IBM 1130 computer where I spent many hours writing programs which we punched into IBM cards and then ran them through the card reader. The computer stood in its special air conditioned room, its floor elevated to provide space for the cables. The computer's memory was only 8K, like the simplest cell phones of today, but I was enamored with it and spent time assisting the teacher—a young guy from Norway—with his work. When he left his job, he asked if I would want to take over teaching the course and I jumped at the opportunity. For the next year and a half I was known as the school's computer expert.

Teaching computer programming was a fascinating psychological experience. Programming required students to be open-minded and flexible, to think logically and out of the box. Every time I started a new class, I could guess who of the students would get hooked and enjoy it, who would hate it and who would do just the minimum required to pass.

I felt good being a teacher and a student at the same time. Two of my students were officers in the Jordanian Army who had been sent to get degrees in engineering. They were too stiff for computers, and because they knew I had been an Israeli pilot, they never looked me in the eye. During tests I gave, I saw them struggling, and a few times I heard them cursing my mother under their breath.

Another student in the computer class was an Israeli who approached me after a lesson. "Hi, I'm Dan Polani," he said. He looked like a hippie with long hair, a messy moustache and unkempt clothing. I already knew he was active in the Israeli student organization of LA and known to pull practical jokes. "Say, where did you learn this computer shit?" he asked.

"Right here," I said, "and it ain't shit."

"And they made you a teacher?"

I heard in his voice both pride in the fact that a newcomer Israeli could do this and some contempt for the subject. I watched him quietly thinking for a few minutes, before he said, "Look, I'm about to graduate and I need a good grade." He twirled his moustache uneasily.

"Not a problem," I said. "I'll help you if you want."

He wiped his eyes. "These damn contact lenses. Are you a *kibbutznick?*"

"Not really," I said, "but I lived in Kibbutz Harel for a while."

He chuckled uncomfortably. "You look like a kibbutznik," he said. "Too serious."

I chuckled. It was a good observation. "How about you?" I asked.

"I'm from Tel Aviv, and I really need you to bump my grade up a little."

Finally I understood. I explained I would tutor him for free, but I wouldn't give him a free ride. He agreed, and for a few hours I tutored him so he could earn a decent grade. I laughed at a lot of his dark jokes about Jews, some of which were about the Holocaust and concentration camps; the subject obsessed him. Later, I also helped him with a difficult thermodynamics course, and when he graduated, he came to thank me.

We said goodbye, and it was a long time before I saw him again, but he was destined to enter a later chapter of my life.

CHAPTER THIRTY-FOUR

Back in high school I'd had to write an essay on the subject "Out of sight-out of heart," and after two years in LA, I experienced it. Dina and I wrote and received some letters from family, but in those days phone calls to Israel were ten dollars a minute, and even when it was her mother, Dina considered this excessive. Our circle of Israeli friends in LA was expanding, and friends from Israel—many pilots—visited. Two cadets I knew from the flight academy—Ran Avshalom and Yehuda Koren—were now pilots and stopped in to see us on their cross-country vacation.

These visits were always a surprise and enjoyable. One day Haggai Ronen and Nissim Ashkenazy, my Air Force classmates, and Ohad Shadmi, my beloved instructor who had sent me on my first solo flight, showed up. They were in the U.S. training with the Navy on Skyhawk fighter planes, and as we sat and talked, they told me tales of the US Navy, particularly how favorably our Air Force compared. Another friend, Asher Hashiloni, the man who had introduced me to Dina, showed up too, and I helped him get into Northrop Institute of Technology.

One day I got a letter from my sister Shifra's husband, Yoseph Peri, who was contemplating continuing trying for a Ph.D. at UCLA. He asked if we thought it made sense for him to move to L.A. with my sister and their three children, and I wrote to encourage him. I told him we would help. A few months later they moved to L.A. and for a while all five stayed with us in our two bedroom apartment—eight people in a tiny place, but we were happy, and happiest of all was Ronit who suddenly had a big family and wonderful cousins, Bossmat, Nerit and three-year- old Haggai.

In the spring of 1966, Ben Gurion, the ex-prime minister and founder of Israel, visited Los Angeles and agreed to spend time with the Israeli community that filled an enormous theater to hear him speak. In his lecture he told us we all should return to Israel; the country was in a deep recession. Our desire to return to Israel was unconditional. Still, during a question and answer session after his lecture I asked him how he expected Israelis to

271

return with no jobs available. In his answer he talked about Zionism ideals and reminded us that our parents came to the country driven by vision, not by practicality.

In June, three years after I had started college I graduated with "high honors," first in my class. I was eager to go to work and make some money, but I had already taken the national graduate school entrance test, and as I was interviewing companies for a job, I received the results. I was in the 95th percentile nationwide, and Dina urged me to go to grad school. I had already applied to Cal Tech, one of the two best schools in America for engineering, and when they received my test scores, they sent me an acceptance letter. I gave in to Dina's pleas and accepted my position in graduate school; Cal Tech was, at the time, at the forefront in the race to the moon.

We decided to visit Israel before school began; it had been three years since we were there, and we missed family and friends and the ambiance of our country. We wanted Ronit to see the country, and we wanted to show her off to our family. We used our meager savings to buy tickets on a student charter flight and flew in a Britannia turbo prop airplane full of students and their little children. The flight stopped to refuel in Toronto and London before arriving in Tel Aviv. Throughout the twenty hours on the plane, babies cried continuously, and Ronit, not yet two, was puzzled by the commotion. Her calm, mature behavior alleviated all our anxiety.

I planned to cash some of the bonds I had left in a bank account back home to serve as our living expenses while in Israel. I had left a couple of thousand dollars in an account and given my brother power-of-attorney to handle it. It was Yudke who threw a reception for the whole family in his home the night we returned. The three years away had left their mark on everyone, but especially on my parents.

"So, did you finish the university?" my mother asked.

"Yes, I graduated with a B.S. degree in engineering," I told her.

"That's great," Yudke said, truly happy for his little brother, but without enthusiasm in his voice. He was just 38, but he looked older.

"So, what are you now?" my mother continued her practical inquiry.

"I'm a mechanical engineer," I said.

"Things are bad here right now," Yudke said.

My father, who talked only when he felt he must absolutely do so, said, "Yudke, why do you tell him the bad stuff? I'm sure if Eitan stays here he can find a job as an engineer." Like a true and dedicated pioneer he had always been on the same page with Ben Gurion, whom he admired. He wanted us back in Israel.

"I just tell him the truth," Yudke said. The brother I adored, my brother the *Palmachnic,* a guy who could arrange for anything I needed seemed to have disappeared; in his place was a worn out man; he had always wanted to be in business, had started a few, but nothing had worked out. I asked, "How are things with you?"

"So so," he said, facing away from me.

"What do you do now?"

"Espressos," my mother said with a chuckle of disdain. Everyone laughed except my brother.

"I'm in business. I build and maintain espresso machines," he said.

Like everyone else, I had expected grander things for him, and I felt a pinch in my stomach, but my father wasn't finished. "I'm sure Eitan could get an engineering job with the government."

"We service Italian machines," Yudke said.

"Eitan, how long are you staying?" My mother, disturbed by the fact that her elder son had a job she did not consider honorable, wanted to change the subject.

"Three weeks," I told her, which reminded me; I needed some money, and I took Yudke aside to tell him I wanted to go to the bank to get my cash. "I closed the account," he said.

And when I asked why, he said, "High fees. Didn't make sense."

"So where did you move the money?" I asked.

He looked down. "You know the situation is bad," he said. "Really bad."

I looked at him with disbelief.

"I had to pay some loans…"

"But I trusted you," I said.

"I know, I'll make it up to you."

Suddenly, scenes of my life with my big brother rolled through my mind as if I were watching a documentary—the time he first gave me a ride on his bike, how we missed him when he fought in the Galilee during the war, how he taught me to drive his jeep when I was only 14 and we barely avoided the traffic cop. I smiled at him. "Don't worry, these things happen," I said, hugging him, and he wiped his eyes with my shirt so no one would see his tears.

"I'm going to make it up to you," he said.

One thing I understood fully that night. If nothing else is permanent, change is, and even in three short years, much about my country had changed. But one thing defied even the deep recession, and that was the gathering of people on the streets on weekends and evenings.

During our visit we spent many evenings going out with friends, particularly one couple who invited us out a lot, Yehuda Fuchs and his wife, Leah. He was the pilot who, after he had finished flying school, had been grounded for a while and had joined us when we started to fly the French fighter plane. That summer, 1966, we connected with Yehuda and Leah and enjoyed his special sense of humor, generosity and culinary hobby. We laughed heartily together and enjoyed many white steaks in pita on his account.

When we visited their home, I saw maps and flight plans all over the floor of his room. He flew the Boeing 707 for El Al and was studying and preparing for his Captaincy tests. He made good money, had a high standing in society, bought delicacies from Europe and New York, and I envied him. El Al had openings for new pilots, and I couldn't stop thinking about it. Still, I said nothing because I had decided first I must go for my Master's degree in engineering, and after three weeks, Dina, Ronit and I boarded the British charter plane full of students and families and returned to Los Angeles.

* * *

Two weeks into the school year, our professor walked into the classroom , chalked two problems on the board and told us we had two hours to solve them and turn in the test. He left the room. I had no idea how to solve these problems. I looked at the blackboard and tried to concentrate on the solutions. My classmates, 15 graduate students, were writing feverishly.

I had befriended a few of my fellow students. One came from Japan, sent by Sony Corporation. One came from Nigeria, sent and supported by his government. One came from India, sent by his rich family, and although he had the smallest head of all of us, he was able to look at ten numbers of twelve digits each for two seconds and give us the sum. One was a Russian Jew who somehow escaped his country, and he was a chemistry genius. All were years younger than I, and everyone was single.

I had come to Cal Tech because I was first in my graduating class, but I quickly realized that all my new classmates had been first in their class. Competition was fierce. When the professor left us alone, I thought I could hear the wheels turning inside my fellow classmates' heads, and I realized if I wanted to graduate from Cal Tech, I was going to have to take on a more professional attitude. That winter, 1967, I put extra effort into my studies, but I still needed to work many hours a week. Dina worked full time to provide for our little family. Every day, on my way back from Cal Tech, I would stop to pick up Ronit from her day care, and many times I took her to get the doughnuts we both liked. These excursions were wonderful and a break from the tension of graduate school.

One day one of my professors, a starchy, waspy man who was teaching us vibration analysis called me for an interview. "Hi Ethan, or Mr. Gonen," he said. "Is that how you pronounce your name?"

"No, my name is Eitan," I said.

"I have so many foreign students, but I never can pronounce their names correctly. Eethan, is it, then?"

I looked at his office. He was the top authority on earthquakes in California, using his expertise in vibration analysis to find the proper design for high rise buildings to withstand strong quakes. His office was small and the walls were covered with books.

"Six ton, seven ton," I said, "I am eight ton."

He laughed violently, his voice reverberating in the empty corridor outside.

"Well, eight ton," he said, "have you decided what your subject of interest for your Ph.D. work will be?"

I felt as if those book-laden walls were closing in on me. I could not see myself spending my life in a small office, trying to learn everything about one subject. I wanted to work outdoors, in a job with no fixed hours, or place or subject. I wanted to have a flexible schedule.

"No," I said.

"You know you could choose to work in my department," he said.

"I actually decided to end my studies with a Masters degree only," I said.

I could see the shock and disappointment in his face. He could not understand anyone giving up such an opportunity. He tried to argue me out of what he clearly thought was my foolishness. "We do very important work. You could become the top expert on earthquakes."

I tried to explain that it wasn't that I disliked his subject, but I was already 29, a husband and a father, and I had to get back to earning a living.

"Think about it," he said. "I can help you."

"Go back to flying," I heard a voice in my head saying to me.

* * *

In the spring of 1967, Dina was pregnant with our second child, and we both looked forward to my graduation and getting a job. We thought we'd work for a while and after we had saved some money, we would return to Israel. But news from our country was bad. Israel was in the deepest of its recessions, and the unemployed were demonstrating in the streets. The neighbors, Egypt and Syria, had increased the tension in the Middle East in an attempt to take advantage of what they perceived as Israel's vulnerability.

In May the President of Egypt, Gamal Abdel Nasser, moved his army into the Sinai Peninsula, threatening Israel whose Prime Minister, Levi Eshkol, was reluctant to take any military action. On May 23, 1967, Nasser declared the Straits of Tiran leading to the Red Sea closed; he would allow no Israeli ships to go either to Eilat or the Suez. It was clear that such an action would lead to war, and in the States the Jewish Organizations called for President Johnson to help Israel and declare American support for the war. Johnson was reluctant, especially because of his involvement in Vietnam and the country's deep division about that war. In spite of meetings with influential Jews and prodding by members of his government, including the U.S. Ambassador to the U.N., Arthur Goldberg, Lyndon Johnson pushed back. In response to the Israeli supporters, he said, "Y'all are foolish Zionists."

The newspapers, both in Israel and the U.S., predicted dire consequences, and Jews all over the States assembled in stadiums to demonstrate their support for Israel.

Although I had been out of the Air Force for four long years, I remembered some of the briefings we had received about the balance of power. I remembered the superiority of Israel's Air Force over any of the Arab Air Forces, separately or combined. I was certain that in a conflict, Israel would win. I began to think about volunteering to go back in case of war, but moments later, it was clear I wouldn't leave Dina with two-year-old Ronit and pregnant. She had lost her father in the War of Independence, and I was more committed to my family than to patriotism.

In the beginning of June, I took my last test at Cal Tech. Pasadena, a quaint little town at the northeast corner of Los Angeles, had been an island of tranquility in the world of tumult we watched daily on TV. The noise coming from the Middle East as war approached and the matching noise from American Jewry in its protest and lobbying, reached a crescendo, and even in the scholastic sphere of Cal Tech, people hotly debated Middle East politics.

After the last test, a group of my classmates sat in the cafeteria for lunch, the Russian chemist said, in his deep accent, "The Arabs are celebrating already." Like all Jews, he felt connected to Israel although he had never been there.

"You can tell them," I said, "they shouldn't start their Kozachok dance yet, their celebration is premature."

"Maybe a third world war is coming," the guy from Sony said.

"I don't think so," said the Nigerian. "It's just the Arabs and Jews who are going to kill each other."

I sat there and remembered our training exercises at the end of each period in the Air Force. "Battle Day," as we called it, always started with take-offs at dawn to attack the enemy air bases precisely at morning's first light, preferably approaching the enemy base with the blinding rising sun behind us to enhance the surprise of the attack. "Don't worry," I said to them as well as to myself. "We're going to beat the hell out of them."

"I don't understand your belligerence," the Nigerian said, "In Africa we look to build our new free countries in peace, in science and prosperity."

The little guy from India was moving his head side to side, the sign I had learned over the course of the year, of his approval.

"This time," he said slowly, "the Arabs are going to kill you. Finish you off." His face seemed to me to express satisfaction at this outcome he predicted.

"You need a tune-up for your little computer head," I said. "We'll meet after the war."

Despite my bravado in the face of my colleagues' conversation, like all Israelis, we were worried. Shifra, her husband, Yoseph, and their kids spent the weekend with us watching endless dispatches from Israel on TV, listening closely to the many analyses and predictions.

Sunday evening, after Ronit fell asleep and Shifra and her family left for home, I told Dina to make plans to attend my Masters of Science graduation ceremonies in the coming week, but before that graduation, war broke out.

The war was all over the TV, no matter which channel we turned to. On the morning of June 5, 1967 we kept hearing conflicting reports coming in; some reported Israel's success, others reporting Egypt's declarations of their success. At mid-morning when I left for work at Harco Aircraft Supplies in Culver City, I was surprised to see the streets looking normal; Israel was fighting for its life, but no one in Los Angeles was paying attention.

At work I couldn't concentrate and finally decided to call the Israeli embassy in Washington. I dialed again and again, but for an hour I heard only a busy signal. Just as I was about to give up, a woman answered. "Israel Embassy, Shalom."

"The Air Force attaché, please," I said.

She told me to hold on, and I did for long minutes until I finally heard another young woman's voice on the line. "Air Force."

"Can I speak to the attaché?"

"And you are?" she asked, the Israeli way.

"Captain Gonen, a reserve pilot."

"What do you need?"

I heard voices in the background that sounded like a noisy crowd in a party.

"I want to ask if I can help," I said.

"Captain Gonen," she said, "you're late - we already won the war. Thanks for the offer anyway." She hung up.

I knew she was right. We had planned to attack the enemy on the ground and finish it.

In fact the war continued for six days, and when I called home I learned my brother served at the ripe old age of 40. In the midst of it, I did not attend my graduation ceremonies that now seemed trivial, and I received my Master of Science diploma in the mail. This was not just one more war. In this war Israel conquered vast enemy territories, and the course of life in the Middle East and around the world was affected for years.

Dina and I invited our group of student friends for a victory party—our Los Angeles veterans, we called them, a close-knit group that included Shifra and Yoseph. Our friends piled into our small apartment, and I raised a glass for a toast: "We are celebrating a great victory tonight, but I am sure that we soon will find out that it required the sacrifice of many lives. I am sure that some of the casualties are pilots, paratroopers and soldiers who are our friends, people we know. Let's drink to their memory."

In the following weeks we did indeed learn the terrible news: 983 Israeli soldiers were killed and 4500 were wounded, among them many of our friends.

CHAPTER THIRTY-FIVE

During the second half of 1967, General Westmoreland informed President Johnson, "We are about to start winning the war," but the bodies kept coming home from Vietnam—hundreds of bodies in plastic body bags. As I watched it all on TV, I remembered my friends killed in action or air accidents. In Israel the dead were never so anonymous as they seemed to be here in America; in Israel the entire nation wept at the demise of each soldier, mourning each loss. I remembered a day when I was ten, sitting down for dinner with my mother and listening to a description of a recent battle in the War of Independence. The announcer finished his story by stating that the enemy had lost 30, and our forces had suffered only two casualties.

"Only two dead," my mother said. "For their mothers it means the whole world shattered. Their mothers' souls are dead."

I was reminded of that each time I saw those body bags.

* * *

The aerospace industry dominated the market for graduate engineers in Los Angeles, but the most interesting jobs in aerospace required citizenship, which I didn't have. In addition, I wanted to gain engineering experience in a field I could use in Israel, and I wanted eventually, as soon as possible, to have a business of my own. So I accepted a job with White Motors in their advanced product division. They were building trucks in the Midwest, but they designed new prototypes in L.A., new and improved diesel engines they had previously bought from their competitor, Cummins.

From the first day on the job, I was treated like an oddball and a celebrity. Most, if not all of the engineers and technicians came from the company's Midwest plants, and I was the first foreigner in their midst as well as the first who had come from a big name school with a Master of Science degree. That I preferred to work with them on diesel engines to going to work on airplanes or spacecraft made them appreciative and respectful.

The president, impressed with my credentials and background, asked me to spend time finding ways to improve their diesel design, and they paid me a good salary. I was glad I had invested the nine months to earn an advance degree since this meant I would earn more than $1000, much more than any previous offers.

"But I don't know much about diesel engines," I told the president.

I worried he might regret hiring me, but to my relief, he only smiled. "I know," he said. "Your assignment is just to sit and think about it."

"I certainly can do that," I told him.

Over the next few months I spent my time learning about engines and decided to combine my knowledge of computer programming and the theories of friction, heat transfer and thermodynamics. We had a small IBM 1130 computer, and I wrote a program for it that simulated a diesel engine. The program provided the ability to change the characteristics of any engine feature and find what the torque or power output would be. Previously, in order to change the size of a valve, for example, they had had to make a new steel valve and a new engine and afterwards run it in the test chamber. Then, of course, they had to make another engine with a different size valve and test it again. With my creation, we could run the program with new engine sizes and get immediate answers, and this saved the company millions of dollars. Once they were satisfied with the results, they built a real engine and tested it to confirm the results. The efficiency of the new engine was significantly improved, at low cost. The management treated me like one of them, and some of the engineers didn't like it.

Dina was late in her pregnancy with our second child, and once again she had not gained much weight; her belly bulged only in front, ending in a point; women kept telling her she was going to have a boy. On December 10, 1967, I called Shifra to ask her to watch three-year-old Ronit and drove Dina once again to Cedars of Lebanon Hospital. I waited for hours in the corridor until the doctor announced we had another daughter. "All is well," he said.

When I walked into the room, Dina was half asleep from the anaesthetics, and our new daughter was wide awake and beautiful. We called her Hadar, and that weekend, while Dina and Hadar were still in the hospital, I spent time with Ronit, telling her about her new sister. Together we shopped for a present for Dina; Ronit helped me choose a little diamond ring we took to her in the hospital.

The year 1968 began beautifully for us. We were enjoying our expanding family, and Ronit was developing into a beautiful, expressive little girl.

Hadar was a good baby - she rarely cried. And at work I enjoyed the respect and approval and the relatively high salary.

Soon, however, we realized we could not save any money on my salary, and saving was crucial for my plans. I wanted a business of my own, and we wanted to save enough to go back to Israel. I was already in advance preparation for a partnership with a smart stockbroker I had met. We were going to open a school for computer programming since at the time programmers were in short supply, and computers were becoming more popular. My partner was rounding up the funds. I would manage the business.

One evening Dina was at her class at the university when the phone rang. I jumped up to grab it so the ring would not wake Ronit. "Yello," the caller said.

"Yes?"

"Is this Mr. Go-Wan?"

He had a southern accent, and I didn't understand him well. "Who?"

"I heard y'all is an engine expert," he said. "My name is John."

I thought someone was trying to pull my leg. "Who told you?" I asked.

"Not much important, is it? You can make millions."

One of those free offers advertised on TV, I thought. A friend of ours had signed up to get a free sewing machine and when she went to pick it up, she realized they indeed would give her the machine free, but she had to pay a high price for the box. "Okay, how?" I asked.

"I manufacture race cars," he said.

"Yes?"

"Help me soup up my engines, using them computers of yours, and I'll make you millions." If true, this would be a fantastic opportunity, but when I did not answer, he said, "You won't waste no time for a pittance. Them White Motors don't pay you no real money."

In that regard, I thought, he was right so I agreed to meet him.

On Friday afternoon during the first week of February, John visited me at home. I already had the simulation computer program I would write going round in my head, and I explained to him that I would need his input. He told me to give him a list of questions, and as we walked outside to discuss our next meeting, I led Ronit by the hand to join me outside. We stood on the sidewalk where he continued to ask questions. Suddenly Ronit stepped off the curb into the road. I grabbed her and pulled her back. I slapped her bottom. "How many times have I told you not to step off the sidewalk?" The slap was because I wanted her to remember, but she began to cry.

"Y'all is too strict," John said. "See you next week. We're gonna make tons of money."

I felt sorry I had slapped Ronit, and later that night I woke up and went into her bedroom to check on her covers. When I pulled the blanket up, I felt her body—she was burning hot. Dina gave her some medicine, but by morning, she still had a temperature, and we called her pediatrician. We learned he was out of town for the weekend, in Palm Springs, but the operator gave us the name of the doctor covering for him. She told us he would call, and that afternoon when he did, we asked him to come to the house to see her.

"Don't worry," he said, "it's nothing unusual." And he told us what medicine to give her.

In the evening, Ronit's temperature climbed, and we called him again and once again asked him to come.

He would not. He told us there was a virus going around; he had seen a few cases. He advised us just to give her the medicine and wash her with cold water to lower her temperature.

For hours we washed her with a cold damp cloth, and sometime after midnight, we fell asleep.

On Sunday morning, I called the doctor again and told him he had to come immediately. Ronit was burning up; the thermometer kept climbing. At long last he came, and when he tried to bend her head forward, she moaned in pain.

"Your daughter is very sick. I'm calling an ambulance," he said.

I had a strong urge to strangle him. Rage coursed through my body as he called for the ambulance. We called Shifra and Yoseph to come babysit Hadar.

As soon I heard the ambulance arrive, I put Ronit on my shoulder and carried her downstairs. She was unconscious now, and she felt as she always had when I carried her from the car to her bed after she'd fallen asleep. She moaned, and I felt sick to my stomach, wanting to cry, but I focused on getting her to the hospital.

"Why don't you put the siren on?" I asked the driver. It was mid-morning and the streets were nearly empty, but he was stopping at red lights and it was driving me crazy.

"Don't worry, we'll get there shortly," he said.

I was appalled by the paramedics' indifference as my daughter lay there unconscious. When they stopped for a red light on La Brea Avenue, they began to gossip, and I screamed at them, and, at long last we arrived at the Children's Hospital on Sunset Boulevard. Ronit, who lay on a gurney, was immediately rolled in by a nurse, through the emergency entrance.

"Wait over there," she pointed at the hospital corridor, and we sat on a bench waiting for the doctor to appear. I tried to find where Ronit was, but the chief nurse told us we should just wait. An eternity passed, and pessimism crept over me, taking a bite of my heart.

At long last an Asian doctor appeared. "I'm Dr. Chen," he said, his voice so serious, my heart sank.

"Your daughter is now very comfortable," he said. "We gave her some medicine to make her comfortable."

"What does she have?"

"She has contracted spinal meningitis," he said, "a bacterial infection affecting the envelope of the brain and spine."

We began to weep.

"Many children recover from it," he said, and although we wept still, I felt a little optimism push some of the sickness in my stomach away.

"How long?" I asked.

"We'll know in a couple of days," he said. "But I must tell you, it's very serious and even in recovery, some children do not recover one hundred percent. In many cases, it leaves some scars on the brain that may cause serious handicaps."

Dina was wailing. The doctor whispered to the nurse to give her something to relax her.

"The good news," he said, "it's not a virus. Viral meningitis is hard, but this one is bacterial and we can fight it with antibiotics. She is especially lucky because her doctor didn't administer any antibiotics. This will allow us to test and find the exact bacteria and give her the appropriate medicine."

"When will you know which bacteria?" I asked.

"In a few hours," and when I shouted, he said, "she's comfortable. I'll come to inform you when we know more."

We waited a few hours. Shifra and Yoseph joined us, and we waited together.

Growing up in the early '50s, some people and children got very sick. One day they were running around, but the next they would have polio, unable to move. But that had been years ago, I thought. I was sure by now no such thing could happen. As a kid I had heard about meningitis - people called it "inflammation of the envelope of the brain," but I was sure it had been eradicated from the world, like polio.

In the late afternoon, Dr. Chen came out and told us they had started Ronit on the proper antibiotics. He told us to go home and return in the morning.

"I want to see Ronit," Dina said.

"She's in intensive care," he said. "It's better for her not to be disturbed right now."

We went home to take care of Hadar.

The next morning the nurse led us in to see Ronit. "She has her own room," she said.

Ronit was asleep on a big bed, connected to numerous thin plastic tubes, and Dina lightly touched them and asked, "What are all these?"

The nurse patiently described the purpose of each tube.

We stayed until visiting hours were over and we had to leave. The nurse assured us the antibiotics needed a day or two more to take effect.

The next day, Tuesday, we came again, but as we neared Ronit's room, we heard a strange psshh, psshh, psshh-- a cyclical, monotonous noise, and when we entered the room and saw our daughter connected to more tubing, a small plastic mask on her face, we were terrified.

"She needed some help breathing," the doctor said as he walked in. "We put her on this new machine." And I felt another bite torn from my heart.

Every day we came to visit in the morning, and each day as we neared her room and heard the pssh-pssh of the breathing machine, we became more terrified. When visiting hours ended, we remained in the hospital, sitting in the entry corridor.

On Friday afternoon, Dina left to go home to take care of Hadar, and I sat on the bench in the corridor and cried quietly. I could hear the breathing machine in the distance, and I sat there and prayed to God to save Ronit, to give her life.

"I will do anything you want," I prayed to the God in whom I did not believe and knew did not exist. "Please, at least make her breathe on her own."

On the bench in the hospital corridor it became clear to me why most people believe in God. It is impossible to live with the idea there is nothing you can do and no help anywhere. No help for your child. You have to ask for help from somewhere, so we create our gods and ask for help.

I did, desperately.

Minutes later, Harry Cohen, my boss and Dina's cousin, walked into the hospital. I was surprised and glad he had found the time to leave his multimillion dollar business to come. He was a tall, handsome 50-year-old self-made man with a great heart, and he sat on the bench next to me without saying anything. He hugged my quivering shoulders. "God acts in mysterious ways," he said.

I was already full of rage against this God I knew did not exist. Still, I felt, I would have choked him if He did exist. "But what does He want from an innocent three year old angel?" I wailed.

We sat quietly for several minutes.

"I'll go see the doctor," Harry said. He walked to the back of the hospital, came back and sat next to me again. Long quiet minutes passed.

"You know, Eitan," Harry said, "sometimes it's better to pray for death rather than life."

He hugged me and patted my back while I wept.

The phone woke us up at 2:00 a.m. on Sunday morning, the eighth day of Ronit's stay in the hospital. Yoseph was on the line.

"We are coming to pick you up," he said. "The doctor called."

"What happened?"

"He says there was a sudden change in Ronit's condition and we should come over."

We made arrangements for Hadar and drove from our apartment on Vinton Avenue in West L.A. to the hospital on Sunset Boulevard. There was no traffic, and for the entire drive no one uttered a word. As we entered the hospital, the lights were dim, the hallways silent, and I realized as we neared Ronit's room, the breathing machine noise had stopped.

In the room we saw Ronit lying in bed, clean and combed, looking like the little angel we knew. All the tubing was gone. Stupid hope sprang again into my heart.

Dr. Plockte, her pediatrician, stood behind her bed. At first, the words stuck in his throat, but at last he said, "Your daughter passed away an hour ago. I'm so sorry."

In that moment my world, my life, crumbled. In the back of my mind I knew I would continue to live for Dina, for Hadar, but I didn't want to. We stood at Ronit's bed for a long time until the doctor said, "I think it's best if you go home now and rest." But how could we leave her alone? What would happen to her? Irrational thoughts flooded me, and as Shifra led Dina out of the room, Yoseph gently touched my shoulder and led me after them.

In the hall, I felt the urge to see Ronit one last time. I turned and walked back. I looked at my beautiful daughter. She looked not only beautiful but calm and free of pain. I fell onto the bed and hugged her for a long time until at last Yoseph gently pulled me away.

I could hear Dina's wails.

* * *

"El Malle Rahamim," the Rabbi chanted about God being full of mercy.

The skies were a brilliant blue as only a windy, mid-February day in California can be. We were standing in the West Side Cemetery in a courtyard named "Court of Love," surrounded by a wall of vaults fifteen feet high. I could hear the sound of the 405 Freeway muffled by the walls. In front, on a cart, lay a small closed coffin. Many of the vault plaques displayed the deceased's names. Some had the names of husbands and wives with their birth and death dates. Until then I had not known people were buried in stacked graves, vaulted in the wall like a stack of drawers in a desk, six high.

"Our dear Father in the heavens," the Rabbi raised his pleading voice.

Behind the coffin in front of us, one drawer, one vault, a grave, was open. It was the top one, 15 feet high. I hadn't been involved in the arrangements, and I wondered why they were placing Ronit so high we could not touch her.

Behind Dina and me stood our friends and relatives, most of our "Los Angeles Veterans" group.

"Read this," the Rabbi told me, pointing to a portion in his little prayer book. The yard was now shadowed by a dark cloud swept inland by the wind. All morning I had told myself to be strong, to behave like a man in front of all these people who had come to accompany Ronit in her last moments on earth. I didn't want to arouse her distress at hearing her father cry.

"Ytgadal Ve Ytkadash…." I began to read but immediately broke down and my words were accompanied by my thick, low voice wailing, the sound reverberating between the walled graves. Many of our friends joined us in crying. We had thought we could plan the story of our life, but Ronit's death made clear to us the story line was not in our control.

"You're young, you'll have more children," people tried to console us. "Time heals," or "with the years you'll get over your grief." Their words only angered me.

Some bereaved parents create a little worship corner with mementos and pictures in their home as a memorial for a dead child. Dina and I decided early on not to burden our children with our tragedy. Besides, we needed no reminder; we've never gotten over our loss of Ronit, and over the years, we have continued to cry, even now, sometimes, mostly at night.

Some years ago I read the words of a psychologist, Dennis Klass, who conducted a 10-year study of bereaved parents and published a book called *Parental Grief*. In that book published in 1988 by Springer Publishing, Klass concluded:

The bereaved parent, after a time, will cease showing the medical symptoms of grief, but the parent does not 'get over' the death of a child. Parental bereavement is a permanent condition.

Dina's mother traveled from Israel to offer moral support and to watch Hadar. The *Shiva*, the Jewish seven days of mourning when friends and family visit to console, day or night, unannounced, ended; the fountain of tears dried up a little. And somehow, though it made no sense, I was able to get up and go through the motions of dressing and driving to work where colleagues expressed their shock and grief at our tragedy.

One day an engineer, George, offered to buy me lunch at a nearby coffee shop. In the coffee shop, over sandwiches, he said, "I'm awfully sorry. How are you feeling?" His face and nose were red, and I suspected as I always had that he drank too much.

"Lousy," I said.

He was eating his sandwich with nervous energy. "You know Eitan," he said, "maybe you and your wife should come to church with us on Sunday."

I stared at him. How stupid could he be? He envied me because he did not understand computers and thus did not understand my work; but I thought he was a smart engineer.

When I said nothing, he went on. "My wife thinks that what happened to you was because you and your wife do not believe in Jesus."

That day I decided to take my family back to Israel.

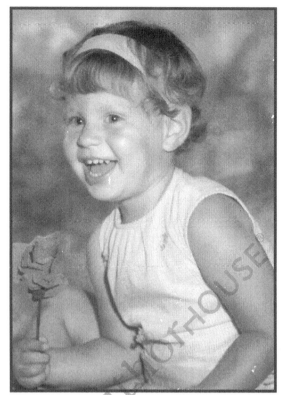

Ronit.

CHAPTER THIRTY-SIX

On my 30th birthday, in April 1968, Dina, her mother, three-month-old Hadar and I landed in Israel. It was ten months since the phenomenal victory of the Six Day War over Egypt, Syria and Jordan, and the country was still euphoric, full of energy and brimming with somewhat justified arrogance. The story had played out like a Hollywood movie—some bad guys held a gun to the country's head and the future looked bleak, but in a fantastic maneuver, Israel wrestled the guns from the bad guys and shot them dead. The world—the spectators—were applauding. At the last minute, Moshe Dayan, with his one eye, had grabbed the leadership and become the hero. He was now waiting for "a phone call from the Arabs."

The jubilant ambiance contrasted sharply with my deep sorrow, and for a few weeks I was aimless and unfocused. Dina proved to be more resilient, and it was she who started to look for a place to live. We rented a house in a neighborhood of Ramat Gan, built for paratrooper officers, one street of red roof single homes; the back of ours faced Gehah Road, a main thoroughfare.

After we settled in, we spent weekends with friends touring the new territories, the "liberated areas" or the "west bank" — they had not settled on the name. We visited the old city of Jerusalem and the Wailing Wall which I had last visited 25 years earlier. We went to the city of Ramallah, where Israelis flooded Arab markets. The Arab merchants had quickly learned some Hebrew words: *Metsias* (bargains); *Bezol* (cheap or reduced); *Tov-tov* (good).

We drove to Nebi Samuel, an Arab village on top of a mountain in Judea. From there we could see all of Jerusalem, and it was from there that, for many days in 1948, the Arab Legion had bombarded Jerusalem with heavy artillery. That was the barrage I had survived. Everywhere we went, I tried to guess at the age of Arabs we passed, hoping I might find Achmed, my childhood friend from the Bucharim Market.

Before I left Los Angeles, Harry Cohen had helped me to meet with a number of manufacturers and suppliers of aircraft parts who agreed to let me represent them in Israel. I was slow to start my business, but Dan Yoel, one of the pilots I had worked with in Ghana, went with me to Israel Aircraft Industries and introduced me to a friend of his. Before long they were requesting parts, mostly aircraft fasteners, and I found a tiny office space for my new company, "Gonen International, Ltd."

The demand for aircraft fasteners and fittings was not great, nor was my salesmanship or enthusiasm, so the business grew slowly, as did our income. After a while I decided to interview for jobs, and at IBM I took a test and was quickly offered work as an analyst at a salary double what I was making. The job offered a bright future, but tempting as it was, I decided to stay independent and grow my business.

To supplement our meager income I took part-time jobs, some of which I hated. One of these detestable jobs was designing and drawing a section of a processing plant for the Potash Company to be built in Sodom at the Dead Sea. I also spent many evening hours at the kitchen table translating a "Who Done It" from English to Hebrew, and I assisted a mathematics professor at the Holon Institute of Engineering. All these jobs kept me both busy and frustrated.

Palestinian terrorists infiltrated across the Jordan River into the Jordan Valley, and a special brigade began to hunt the infiltrators, both by helicopter and by foot. The pursuit (*Mirdafim*) ended only after the terrorists were killed, but not without tragedy. Jordan Valley is full of uncharted caves in which the terrorists took refuge, and during one of the pursuits, eight terrorists were cornered in a cave by a unit commanded by our next-door neighbor, Lt. Colonel Arik Regev. Regev led the assault into the cave and was killed by a burst of AK-47 fire. That evening we sat with his wife and little kids, and along with the whole country, we mourned the loss of our highest ranking officer of the campaign

That was the beginning of the end of the intoxication of victory for Israel.

As we got closer to the end of our lease, we realized we could no longer afford it, and I began to look for a less expensive place. In Israel there were no apartment buildings for rent; units were houses or condominiums owned by private individuals who rented them by advertising in the classified section of the paper, and I scoured those ads. One Friday I called on a small ad describing a nice apartment with reasonable rent in Tel Aviv. The woman who answered repeated the sales pitch, and before I had a chance to ask a thing, she asked "How many children do you have?"

This question was the hardest we confronted whenever we met new people. Do I mention Ronit? Do I tell my life story? The question always caused a surge of emotion, and I answered, with a deep ache in my heart, "We have one daughter."

"And what do you do?" she continued the interview.

"Look," I interrupted; she was asking too much. "I just want to know where exactly the apartment is located."

"What's your name?" she asked.

Only in Israel, I thought, still more frustrated. But we needed a place to live. "Eitan."

"What's your wife's name?" she prodded further.

"Why the hell do you need all this information?" I demanded.

"Is your wife's name's Dina?"

Only in Israel. I tell some stranger my first name and she already knows everything about me, my wife, where I come from, who my friends are. As it turned out, Sara, the woman on the phone, was one of the Los Angeles veterans who had returned to Israel just before we had. When I understood, we laughed and talked about the coincidence.

"No, Eitan," she said. "This apartment is not for you." It was too small and in a bad building. But she continued. "We bought a new home in a suburb being built now called Ramat Efal. You should try to buy one too."

"That'll be nice," I said, "but we have no money."

"Not a problem," she said and explained that the government was giving returning Israelis like us big mortgages. She instructed me to go to Shikun Ovdim, the residential company owned by the unions, to inquire, but since I was on reserve duty, I said I would go in a few days.

"Go there in your pilot's uniform," she said. "The main man there likes officers."

I wore my uniform and took Dina along, but Calev, the sales manager, told us he was sorry. All the houses had been sold. "Too bad, we were looking for good young people like you." Then he was quiet a moment, and suddenly he said, "There is one home...the buyer may cancel."

A few days later we had the papers for a new home which was to be an 800 square foot building on one tenth of an acre for $18,000. We got a $14,000 mortgage and borrowed $4,000 from my parents. We were ecstatic. The future had begun to look better, but we still had the problem of finding somewhere to live while our house was being built.

We left the semi-prestigious paratrooper housing and moved in with the working class at the Ramat Yosef housing area in the beach city of Bat

Yam. The two bedroom ground level apartment was tiny, but rent was low, the stay temporary, and two-year-old Hadar had plenty of friends. Row upon row of four story buildings with hundreds of small apartments surrounded us, and our neighbors had come to Israel from everywhere— Bulgaria, Romania, France, Morocco, Tunis, and more. Most of us knew each other, and Moshe at the grocery store knew everyone. We had little privacy but felt embraced by the warmth of the community. And in that tiny home, Dina got pregnant for the third time.

Soon after we returned to Israel, I had received my reserve duty assignment as a flight instructor in the Air Force Flight Academy. Because I had more flight hours on the French twin jet trainer, I instructed cadets in their advanced training squadron in Hatzerim, near Beer Sheba in the south. A transport plane picked us up at Sde Dov Airfield in Tel Aviv in the morning and flew us back in the evenings for two to three weeks each semester.

My air academy classmates of course number 27 were still active in the Air Force working as professional pilots. Yuval had been injured in the Six Day War—shot flying over the Sinai Peninsula and the Twenty Millimeter anti-aircraft bullet shattered his heel and grounded him. Now he was flying helicopters. My two other classmates, Nissim and Hagai, flew the A-4 Skyhawk Israel had gotten from America. Both also flew at the Hatzerim base.

In 1969 Gamal Abdel Nasser, Egypt's president, raised the heat of a little war he had instigated at the Suez Canal, and Russia cooperated by sending Egypt Migs, pilots and SAM anti-aircraft missile systems. Israel's Air Force pounced on the Egyptian forces on the west side of the canal at a cost of many casualties. In July of that year, while I was flying as instructor at Hatzerim, my friend Nissim, on a mission over Egypt, was hit by a SAM missile, ejected from his Skyhawk and became a prisoner of war. The good news that he was alive was overshadowed by knowing the torture he would suffer. His family lived on base and I stayed that night to visit his wife, Etti and the kids. We had been close neighbors when we lived in the Tel Nof base.

I entered their house to find chairs lining the living room walls and people sitting everywhere. Young fighter pilots and their wives had come to keep Etti company and were discussing everything but Nissim's situation or the outlook for his release. Etti and I hugged, and I sat quietly trying to imagine what it would be like for Nissim in a jail in Cairo. I was the only civilian in the room, and though I was on reserve duty, flying at the same base, I felt guilty.

The next day, on the transport plane that took us back to Tel Aviv, my colleagues were discussing the intricacies of their collective contract with El Al; they were all pilots for the airline, and some were earning ten times what fighter pilots earned—and in American dollars. The country, it was clear, revered our fighter pilots but envied our El Al captains.

As the war in the Suez Canal escalated, Israel called it the "War of Attrition," because the intensity and number of casualties did not cease. That October my friend Hagai's A-4 Skyhawk was hit by a ground to air missile over Egypt. His plane burst into flames, and he bailed out, parachuting into the shark-infested Red Sea; his body was never found.

We scrapped our eleventh annual February reunion. Hagai was dead. Nissim was struggling to recuperate—the Egyptian doctors having treated his injured knee by fixing it so he could never bend it again. Yuval was recuperating from an injury that caused a permanent limp. And though my body was intact, I was licking my wounds from the loss of Ronit. Dina, in her ninth month of pregnancy, was eager to give birth.

The year brought still more tragedy. My mother suffered a stroke. On Saturday morning May 30, 1970 I drove to Tsrifin to visit my mother in the hospital. The grounds were crowded with patients in gowns printed with "Government of Israel", and visitors—old people, poor people, speaking in many languages and Hebrew in many different accents. I was surprised to find my mother with a private room in this government hospital.

When I sat beside her, if she was glad to see me, I could not tell. "Why did you have to come?" she asked. The stroke had made talking difficult, but she was alert and relaxed. Looking for something I could do for her, I asked her if she wanted me to raise the bed. She shook her head no, but asked about Dina and Hadar and said, "I still can't believe you lost your daughter."

Her eyes filled with tears. As we sat quietly, I remembered running home under fire in Jerusalem when we both were 20 years younger, I remembered the way she had tried to cover me with her body to shield me from bullets. "I thought in my hard life I had paid the dues for my children," she said, "and now you…" She held her hand to her chest and fought for breath.

"Don't talk about it, *Ima*," I said. "Think of yourself only and how to get better."

"Eitan," she said, and stopped. She toiled, breathing for a while with her eyes closed. She opened them and looked at me a long minute. "Don't make the same mistake I did," she said. "Why did you come back? This place was not good to us. I should have waited and gone to America."

Almost half a century after she had come to Israel, she still could not suppress her long-lost desire. If she had gone to America, I would not exist, but I did not say that.

"Go, Eitan," she said, breathing hard. "Dina needs you."

The next day my mother died at the age of 62. Her death was not a shock—in the last years of her life she suffered a few strokes which she bravely overcame. In some way, I thought, it was a relief for her, a relief from what she had perceived as a tortured life. Still I felt deep sadness about her missing the joy and calm of the latter part of life. She would not be here to enjoy her new grandchildren – Hadar and our yet-to-be-born third child.

We buried my mother on Sunday. At her funeral the Rabbi said she had returned to the creator—the one that disillusioned her. We sat the *Shiva* at Shifra's home in Tel Aviv, the one they bought when they also returned from the US. Family, friends and acquaintances filled the apartment in the evening, using all the rooms. Sitting with Yudke in the living room I heard a commotion in one of the bedrooms. Dina's water had broken, and we drove through the congested streets of Tel Aviv to the Assuta Hospital where I waited all night. Dina asked her doctor for a shot but he swayed her to give a natural birth.

On the morning of Monday June 1st, 1970 we had a son who we called Ron. We had no problems choosing a name for him.

* * *

Dina and I moved to our new home in the suburb of Ramat Efal and were ecstatic to bring three-year-old Hadar and six-month-old Ron to a place where each of them would have a room of their own. Thinking we had skipped one step of the ladder leading to the upper middle class, we felt we had cheated destiny. But we had no money left.

During the spring of 1971 our front and backyards were bare, and on Friday night Dina placed a big pot of cholent in the oven. On Saturday morning, all our friends from the Los Angeles Veterans group came to help with our landscaping. Under the direction of our landscape architect friend Uri Miller, we all shoveled and dug and wheeled soil. We worked until noon when we broke to eat the cholent for lunch. Everyone had brought along their children, so Hadar and Ron enjoyed the day, and for the next few Saturdays we did the same thing until the yard was filled with trees and plants. In those days we also spent time with friends from the Air Force, including Fooxy and Leah who invited us for dinners of shrimp, caviar and other delicacies he and his brother Isaac, another El Al captain, brought from Europe and America.

Frequently, every three or four months, my work was disrupted by reserve duty lasting three weeks. On one occasion we flew as usual from Tel Aviv to Hatzerim, and the noise of the engines of the C-30 transport did not stop the pilots of El Al from discussing their work, their income and their demands of airline management. With the end of the War of Attrition, the mood in the country was joyful and fraught with some arrogance. Army officers mingled with celebrities and daily saw their pictures in the newspaper. For one whole week that year David Elazar, the chief of the armed forces, toured Jerusalem, Tel Aviv and the Galilee with Elizabeth Taylor in his American car and American helicopter.

"This month," one of El Al captains said, "my paycheck was $15,000. I flew five extra hours and my overtime alone was $5,000."

At that time engineers were earning less than $1,000 a month.

"Yes, but you must have worked like a horse," his friend said.

"Yeah," the captain said, "three flights to Kennedy."

I never got used to this gap between my income and theirs, but on that particular day I was relaxed since my business was beginning to expand; the Ministry of Defense was close to issuing a contract for aircraft fasteners from VSC, a company I represented. The Air Force needed the fasteners for the redesign of the F-4 Phantom tail. For months I had worked with a buyer named Rivlin, providing him with specs, engineering papers and prices, and soon I would earn at least $50,000.

One day Dan Polani, the guy from my school in L.A. who had struggled through my computer programming class, appeared at my warehouse. He and his new wife, Talma, had returned to Israel; he joined me in a partnership to build pneumatic and hydraulic systems— ground support and test equipment for military aircraft. By 1971 we had won a few bids and delivered some units.

I returned from reserve flying duty, and for two weeks I daily called Mr. Rivlin to inquire about the pending order. He did not take or return the calls, and I became troubled since the last time we met I had given him all the information; his office told me the Air Force had doubled the quantity required. The day after my return I received a letter from VSC in Culver City, California with one sentence: "As of this date, you no longer represent our company. Your exclusive agency is thus terminated."

I couldn't yet be sure, but I suspected they would not pay the commission I had earned for the pending sale. For an hour I studied the letter, certain that the tens of thousands of dollars I had envisioned finally earning would evaporate. Finally I called John, the tech guy I had worked with at the company. It was late night in Culver City, and I called him at home. When I told him who it was, he said, "Hi, what are you doing up so late?"

John could never figure out the time difference, and he'd obviously been asleep when the phone rang. "I'm calling because I received a letter," I said.

For a moment the line was quiet until I asked, "John?"

"Yes, I'm here," he said. "You know, Eitan, two Israelis are here to visit with the corporate higher ups." I felt my stomach contracting.

"And?" I asked.

"You know I'm not involved in the sales side, Eitan."

"But what do you know?" I asked.

"Oh boy," he exhaled, "I shouldn't say it, but these guys, Jacobs and Rivlin, are pretty shrewd, it seems to me."

Jacobs was a supplier of metals and Rivlin was the buyer in the Ministry of Defense.

"They came together?" I asked.

"Yes, together," he said. "Sorry, Eitan."

"What are you sorry about?" I pretended I didn't understand.

"They said if we made Jacobs our rep, we would get the order on the spot."

I felt sick. Months of effort and one corrupt official and a corrupt supplier, an ex-colonel in the Army and from a rich family, had taken away my opportunity. Then and there I decided I would explore my legal rights in this matter. In the meantime, I would double my efforts on growing the manufacturing side of our business.

* * *

Trying to save and preserve foreign currency and lessen the country's dependence on foreign suppliers, the Israeli government was campaigning with the mantra "Make it Here," encouraging local manufacturers to replace imports. The Minister of Defense adapted the same mantra, and our company had the know-how and the agreements with American companies to build systems under a license. When the Air Force required nitrogen purifying systems for the Shafrir air-to-air missiles used by our fighters and planned to purchase them, we offered to build them in our place in Tel Aviv. We built one to prove that it worked and waited for a contract to build a number of them.

One day Danny walked into the office and said, "They decided to purchase the purifiers in the US."

"Who told you?" I asked. I was astonished by the news.

Danny's face was white. "You have to ask who? Ben Aaharon, of course!"

Major Ben Aaharon was the head of the ground equipment section of the Air Force. His office in the Kirya area of Tel Aviv was in charge of purchasing equipment, and he behaved as if it all belonged to him. "We won't give up," I told Danny.

"It's all because you wouldn't cooperate with him," Danny said. I sensed Danny blamed me, and I could read on his face regret at not going to work for our competitor when he had the chance.

"Let's have a meeting," I said, "with Meir Ben Aaharon."

Danny told me he would arrange the meeting but that I should be there. "And plan to make the Major happy," he said.

One month earlier Major Ben Aaharon had wanted to visit our facility and asked me to pick him up at his office. On our way back to his place, in my little red Fiat sports car I had bought used, he said, "You have a cute little car."

"I like it," I said, feeling slightly uneasy. I was not good at small talk, and the silent moments between us felt awkward. Usually Danny was along and he did the talking and joking.

"Let me ask you," he said, "are you profitable? Do you make a lot of money?"

I stammered a non-answer, and he interrupted. "I'm asking to know if you and Danny are making money, if you are reliable and stable."

"Yes, our company is still small, and we don't make that much, but we have enough and plan to grow," I assured him.

"Do you share some of your profits?" he asked.

"Sure," I said, "We're partners."

"That's not what I mean," he said.

I kept driving, but I sensed he was upset because I didn't know what he was driving at. "Let me try to explain," he said. "You know Amnon Avni?"

Avni was our competitor with a manufacturing facility out of town, but he did not have the engineering ability and was building mainly simple welded carts to carry bombs. "Yes," I said.

"I give him big contracts. Many orders," he said.

"I know," I said, staring straight ahead.

"And he shares," he said. "He is a very generous and smart man."

"He is?" I asked. I was pretending not to understand his meaning, but there was only one way to interpret his words.

"Yes, and he's given us good times. We even spent time together at the last International air show in Paris. You should learn to share."

"You went to France together?" I could not hide my incredulity.

"Yes, yes," he said. "Me and Amnon and Haim Yaron."

I knew Haim Yaron from flight school. When I was a course commander, he was a squadron technical officer with the rank of Captain. Each morning he allocated to our group the airplanes we used, and now he was chief tech officer of the entire Israeli Air Force, a Brigadier General. I couldn't be certain, but I thought Ben Aaharon was asking us to share our profits with him, something I absolutely would not do. Rage began to engulf me as I searched for some way to say something without antagonizing the Major.

"We can't do it," I said. "Amnon is very rich, you know."

"Yes, he is rich," he said. "When you are generous, others are more generous to you." We had arrived at the gate of Air Force Headquarters.

"Think about it," he said, "You're smart too." He got out of the car and walked through the gate where the *Shin Gimal* (MP) saluted him.

A few weeks later, Danny returned from the Major's office where he served his reserve duty and told me Ben Aaharon had told him to join our competitor. "He said I would be vice president of his AGI Corporation."

I felt my blood pressure rising. How dare this guy interfere in our partnership? I asked Danny why.

Danny hesitated a moment, "He said you're inflexible and tight and I would get more orders and make more money if I joined Avni's company."

"And what did *you* say?" I asked.

"Nothing," Danny said.

I was furious—angry at the corrupt bureaucrat and angry at Danny. "You can go anytime you want," I said.

"I'm just telling you," he said.

It was getting dark when I drove home. Our new neighborhood of red roofed homes had begun to show some greenery I noticed as I turned onto our street. All the streets were named after new settlements, ours after a young settlement on the Golan Heights called El Al. I saw Hadar and Ron playing with the neighborhood kids on the street, and when I climbed out of the car, they leapt on me, disappointed to see I was in a bad mood.

That night Dina served dinner, but we all were quiet, and after she put the kids to bed, she joined me in the dining area where I sat reading the paper, and asked, "What's the long face?"

"It's nothing."

"I know you," she said. "It's not nothing."

"I don't want to talk about it."

By then I knew her too; I knew she would not let it go, and so I told her about my conversation with Danny and his stories of Major Ben Aaharon.

"Can you do something?" she asked.

"I don't think so," I said. "I have to find a way to circumvent him."

"You have so many friends in the Air Force," she said.

I did not want to continue the conversation, but Dina pressed on until I was irritated. "I've told you a million times I can't bother my friends in the Air Force for the business. They put their lives on the line every day and I can't come to talk money."

The water was boiling in the pot on the stove and Dina stood to make us tea. She looked at me, worried. "So what will you do?" she was searching for a definitive answer; she was accustomed to my ability to come up with logical solutions.

"El Al is hiring pilots now," I said.

She placed the glass of tea in front of me with such force I thought it would crack, then ran to the bedroom to cry. Each time I had brought up working for El Al, she reacted emotionally, so we had never had an actual conversation about the pros and cons of the job.

"How can you even think about it?" she shouted from the bedroom.

"You'll wake the kids. Come here and talk."

She returned to the dining table, her face wet with tears, her eyes red. After drinking some tea, she regained her composure and said, "If you do that, you'll ruin our family."

"It's not like I'd disappear," I said. "It's only for a few days at a time."

Some El Al pilots flew to Europe for one or two days; others, those who flew to New York, spent a week away from home, and sometimes their absence stretched to ten days.

"A family cannot exist like that," she said.

"But I'll use my experience to make money. We could have a very comfortable life."

"I don't need the money," she said. "I won't stay home alone with the kids while you're having fun in New York with your friends." Dina and I had never left each other for any length of time, had never even gone to a movie or out for an evening with friends without each other.

"Look at Fooxy, Gideon and Ran," I said. "They spend more quality time with their families than I do." All their families were intact.

But Dina was adamant. "For years I worked hard so you could go to

299

school. For what? So you would go have fun flying? Do you want to throw away your education to be a glorified driver?"

"I can still use my engineering," I said.

"I can't believe that after what happened to us, you're willing to leave me and the children alone for days and weeks at a time."

"I'll make a great living for us, it's not for fun." It wasn't that having fun in Paris, London and New York wasn't part of the attraction, but making a good living was my main interest.

"I will not stay home alone. I can't do it. I know myself. If you go have fun in New York with all these…," she paused, "I'll find someone here." She said this last sentence with a strange expression, threatening infidelity but not convincingly. What most affected me was: "After what happened to us…" I knew then I could not leave her or the kids for any length of time.

I did not sleep well that night, but I woke the next morning with renewed energy and determination. I drove to 10 Charutz Street in Yad Eliahu, Tel Aviv, right next to the main basketball stadium, to the office and warehouse of Eidan Engineering, Ltd., my company.

On the way inside I stopped in at our neighboring welders and told them to start welding the frames for the purifiers, the units the bastard was going to deprive us from building. I told Danny about my plan to circumvent the corrupt Major, and as I spoke, I watched his morale and energy rising. He removed his contact lenses and wiped his eyes, and I felt like a basketball player who had just scored a three-pointer.

A few months later, I made a deal with Danny. I would work part-time in our business without a salary, and I would match his pay with what I received working for an airline. The next day I went to the offices of Arkia Airlines at the Sde Dov field in Tel Aviv. The itch to fly again would not leave me, and working for a local, regional airline would allow me to come home every day. It was a compromise, flying the smaller, older airplanes like the 70-passenger Herald and 120-passenger Viscount, neither of which were first class. Still, it meant flying again and not spending all day long in an office.

After training, my flying schedule took me from Tel Aviv to Eilat, Sharem-el-sheikh, Santa Katerina and other places in the Sinai, carrying tourists, workers and soldier passengers. I enjoyed the work, happy to be back in the air, back handling those flying machines. I tried to arrange my schedule so that I would fly in the early morning or late evening, leaving me ample time to work at my business. Danny returned to trying to sell systems to the Air Force. He had developed a relationship with Major Ben

Aaharon so much so that the Major arranged for Danny to serve his reserve duty in his office.

As a returning Israeli citizen, after five years of living in America, Danny was entitled to import duty free appliances. Since he was not interested in purchasing American washers and dryers, he agreed to transfer his rights for a duty free washer/dryer set for the Major. This was a common practice, to not let the duty free right go to waste.

And over the next three years Eidan Engineering became the foremost expert in sophisticated pneumatic and hydraulic ground support equipment for aircraft. The Ministry of Defense had to include us in any bid for that type of equipment, and one day I was once again summoned to their office in the Kirya.

The MP at the gate of the compound of the Ministry of Defense saluted as I entered. He had known me since my early days in the military, and that salute always made me feel good for a short time—until I had to deal with the bureaucrats inside. I was coming to see the buyer of ground equipment-- a young man whose overweight made him look far older than his 31 years. "Hi Eitan," he said. "This one's a biggie."

"Great, what is it?" I asked.

"A whole laboratory, and it's only the first one. We'll probably need a few more." He was in a good mood and seemed supportive, but we had rarely seen a big order from him. He handed me a packet of forms. "This time it's all our decision, a closed bid. If you want to make sure the right guys get it - you better sharpen your pencil."

"We always do," I said. "Who else competes for this?"

He laughed uncomfortably. "Your usual nemesis," he said, "Amnon Avni – AGI."

Back at the office, I opened the packet, and Danny and I looked at the bid with excitement. It included all the Air Force requirements for a major test laboratory to be installed in Tel Nof, but we noticed that the bid papers stated the tests for which it was required but included no diagrams—we would have to design the laboratory test systems and build them. We knew no one else in Israel, certainly none of our competitors, had the expertise to design it or to understand what it would cost to do so.

We spent many hours on this bid. Eventually it could be worth millions in additional orders. When we were finished, I delivered the bid to Michael at the Ministry of Defense, ten minutes before deadline—just enough time that our competition would have no time for shenanigans—a sneak peek at our bid or time to copy our design.

A week later they called to tell me we had lost the bid to Avni again.

"You were very close," the government buyer said. "His bid was 2% lower."

I felt the blood draining from my head as if I were flying a high G maneuver. I could not speak. Finally I asked, "Did he submit a design?"

"No," he answered.

"How the hell is Avni going to build it?" I asked. "He has no clue."

"That's his problem," he said. "I shouldn't really discuss it with you." He hung up.

Danny, with his long hair and sloppy dress, walked into my office, but when I didn't speak, he said, "Uh-oh, what happened? You're always quiet when you're angry." When I told him he burst out laughing but couldn't hide the bitterness in his eyes.

"You're distraught," I said. "You always laugh when you're stressed."

For as long as I'd known how to read, I'd read stories in the newspapers about corruption in the government, but never in the defense establishment. The security of the newly born state of Israel was sacred to the population, especially to the pioneers, the old timers and their children. When I first suspected corruption in our playing field, I tried to erase all thoughts of such a thing and concentrate on the task at hand. I was determined to compete by being better at the engineering and pricing than any of my competitors. But now I knew. Now I was looking ugly corruption in the face. I had no proof, but in my bones I knew.

At first I retreated. I flew more and took Dina and the kids on more trips abroad.

When Ron was a year old and Hadar was three, Dina and I traveled to America. Hadar stayed with Dina's mother and Ron with one of her neighbors, and to make the separation easy for Ron, we brought him to his babysitter's home after he fell asleep so he would not know we were leaving. When he woke and found himself in a strange home without his parents, he adjusted quickly. After a month abroad we returned home but didn't recognize Hadar. Her grandparents had stuffed her with buttery sandwiches, and her face was round, cheeks puffy. Ron, on the other hand, did not recognize us, and to this day we feel guilt about that trip. And so, from that time on, we always took the kids with us on trips. One of the reasons I'd taken the job with Arkia was the deeply discounted tickets we were able to get on many airlines.

As we watched corruption taking hold in the Air Force and Defense Department, the growth of our company slowed. Danny was in charge of systems assembly and testing, and I handled the business and financial side. We both did the engineering work. Danny turned cynical and began to complain that I was neglecting the business. At last we decided to put more effort into our work and set goals for the coming year. We visited other companies and made inroads with sales to Israel Aircraft Industries and began to represent more American companies in our field.

CHAPTER THIRTY-SEVEN

On the morning of Yom Kippur in 1973 I stayed home. Everybody did. Businesses were closed, and there were no cars, no busses, no trains, and no flights. The holiday had started years before as a religious holiday but had turned into a national obsession. The whole country was at a standstill. Often this holiest day was hot, the last hot day of summer, but that year the day was actually one of those nice, clear days with a bright blue sky, the kind of day that exists only in Israel. Through the window I saw our next door neighbor, Arie, a journalist, his head covered with a yarmulke and the prayer book bag under his arm. He was walking to the synagogue.

"Arie is going to pray for better critics," I said to Dina. "One said he's written more books than he's read." Our children were playing with the neighborhood kids in the middle of the street in front of the house. "Are you going to take the kids to temple?" Dina asked.

I hesitated. I wanted the kids to experience the tradition. My father had taken me to temple on this day every year of my childhood. But I was behind on so many chores, and this was like a bonus day. "I think I'm going to paint the living room," I said.

Dina offered no argument.

I had been painting for three hours when the ringing phone killed the silence. I climbed down the ladder to answer, and a young woman's voice told me to report immediately to my reserve base. She told me all the pilots were being called. "That's all I know," she said.

When I hung up, the neighborhood emergency siren started wailing its urgent up and down cycle, and I knew this was bad. Everyone knew.

Starting the car was a major event. All the kids in the street gathered, and neighbors looked through the windows thinking I must be important to receive a call so soon after the siren.

I drove through my neighborhood with exhilaration subdued by anxiety, a feeling I recognized from my earliest days as a fighter pilot scrambling to take off to intercept an intruding enemy. Except back then I was 20-something and now, at 35, though I'd been flying transport missions, leaving my family at home raised the anxiety to a higher level.

As I was driving, more and more cars appeared, some military tank carriers with their loads covered with camouflage netting. Still, the streets looked deserted. I turned on the news radio station but it was blurred with the code names of the reserve units being called to serve: Blue Shield, Strong Arm, White Elephant. What would usually have been a half hour drive took 15 minutes, and at the airport, in the operation room, I saw those who had arrived before me wearing long faces. "What's going on?" I asked.

"A surprise attack, the Egyptians are trying to cross the canal into Sinai, and the Syrians are attacking the Golan Heights."

That's all anybody knew, and for a while we waited until at last the administrative officer showed us to the rooms we would stay in.

The ringing startled me. It was the old phone ring and reminded me of the school bell calling for the next class. Five days had passed, and I had not yet become accustomed to this eight-by-ten room with two metal beds, one of which I was lying on. The beds' grey paint was peeling, the thin mattresses recorded the weight of many bodies that had lain on them before; the beige walls offered only a hint of their past whiteness, and one lonely electric bulb hung on a wire from the ceiling. These barracks were gifts from the old British Air Force.

I knew what the phone call was about. For days now we had been flying fresh troops to the battle zone and bringing back the wounded. Sure enough, Operations was calling to tell me my next take-off time. I called Dina and said, "Hi honey, I'm going up again."

"When are you coming home?"

"Not tonight."

"The kids are going crazy. We worry," she said, almost crying.

"I know, I'll try, maybe tomorrow night."

I wanted to say 'I love you and kiss the kids for me' but I was always stingy with expressions of emotion and I was trying to reduce the drama. "Say hi to Hadar and Ron," I said instead, and I put on my grey flying suit, grabbed the earphone set, struggled with the warped door that refused to lock and headed to the operations room. The small airport terminal was even more chaotic than it had been with civilians and soldiers of all ages talking frantically, receiving instructions, arguing with dispatchers and contesting their assigned destinations. Olive green, the color of battle uniforms, trumped any other color in the room as kitbags and gear sprawled across the floor and sweat humidified the air.

I made my way through to Operations where I met Shaya Gazit. He was to be the captain of this flight. After a short briefing, I walked out to the parked Herald, a twin engine British made turboprop aircraft that had the blue and white colors of Arkia Airlines but now was being used for military service. A line had formed in front of the plane, 50 soldiers in combat gear, each with a bulging mountain of a backpack, rifles, and front gear with big pouches for ammo and other supplies. They were mostly in their 20s and 30s, but a few grey hairs glowed under the bright afternoon sun. Citizen soldiers. The Mediterranean breeze was cooling the air.

I climbed in and took my seat in the cockpit, going down the check list. Gazit struggled into his seat, surprising me with his agility. He already was over 50. I remembered how energetic he had been 20 years earlier, when I was a cadet and he the commander of the Air Force flying academy, already a Lieutenant Colonel. I heard the cabin door closing and the mechanic in front gave his thumbs up signal. The left engine started, then the right.

"Arkia one five six clear to taxi runway 03, you are number one for takeoff."

We took off and leveled out at 11,000 feet. My sunglasses were no match for the afternoon sun. To the west the Mediterranean glowed as if on fire, ignited by the sun that was about to dip beneath those endless waters. To the east I could see the land rolling on as if forever, crisp and clear. Tel-Nof, one of the biggest military airports, lay in front of us. "Look at the Mirages," Gazit said, pointing to the airport now almost beneath us.

Two Mirage fighter planes were taking off along the long runway, immediately climbing like two shiny arrows shooting into the blue skies above us. They quickly disappeared. "You know they carry at least two Shafrirs each," I said, trying to make conversation.

The Shafrirs were the Israeli version of the American Sidewinder air-to-air missiles.

"Aren't you involved with that project?" he asked. A year earlier when we were flying together, I'd told him about my work and that in addition to flying for the airline, I continued to manage my engineering firm. He'd remembered.

"Yes, we build the units that service the cooling system of the missiles."

Our short conversation stopped abruptly, and I was sorry I had started it. We were at war and for a few days now I had not thought about the business; not thinking about it felt good. I tried to focus on the mission, but my mind wandered to review the previous month's events at the Department of Defense. Our suspicion had become a painful certainty, and Danny and I now knew who some of the bad guys were. For weeks I had been unable to shake it from my mind.

"Arkia one five six, descend to seven thousand," the controller jolted me from my thoughts. We started our descent and soon an old oasis in the middle of the Sinai desert with the Arabic name of Bir-gafgafa, now with a long runway built beside it, came into view in front of us. Ten minutes later we landed, and as we waited for the propellers to stop, cabin crew opened the door and the troops, heavy with gear, stepped down the five steps to the ground and into the darkening desert, into the war.

After a short jeep ride, some coffee and crackers for a meal, and an hour of rest, we returned to our aircraft. Helicopters were landing in the dark, unloading and taking off less than 30 feet away. The rotors' downwash steered the fine white desert dust so that it landed on everything, making everyone look like a baker. The cabin door was wide open revealing what looked like a hospital ER, and stretchers with wounded soldiers upon them were being loaded inside. For a moment I thought I recognized one of the wounded as someone who had flown on my flight two days earlier, but I did not inquire any further.

I finished the exterior checks of the plane and stepped in. The cabin was full, with two tiers of occupied stretchers. Medics leaned over a number of them. I wondered if they were medics or real doctors, and I listened to the cabin filled with the sounds of suffering—sighs and groans and doctors' shouted instructions. The smell of medicine and disinfectant trumped the usual smell of burnt fuel. On one stretcher, the third in from the cockpit, lay a soldier, blond, handsome, tall and muscular, wearing only his undershirt. Plastic tubing was attached to many parts of his body, and his olive green shirt with the rank of lieutenant on it was tucked beneath his long legs. The guy hovering over him held his hand with one hand and his face with the other. He was moving the wounded soldier's face side to side, as if trying to wake him.

"Yaron, what is your last name, tell me your last name," his mouth was barely two inches away, but his voice was almost shouting.

"I am Dr. Uri, tell me your name, what is your name? Your name? Wake up and squeeze my hand," the doctor tried repeatedly, but Yaron did not answer, and I could not tell if he squeezed the doctor's hand.

With my heart and stomach feeling like one big, heavy bundle in my belly, I pushed both throttles forward and took off into a wall of darkness. The air was black but calm, not a single bump, and in the distance, far to the

307

west, I could see faint red flare ups where the war on the ground was raging. We cruised comfortably, the engines sounding in perfect sync. There was no conversation in the cockpit, and of course we could not hear the sounds in the back cabin. Still, in my mind I could hear the moans, and the doctor's voice. My thoughts raced between what was happening in our cabin and the corruption in the Department of Defense, and it suddenly dawned on me.

I knew what I had to do when the war ended. Calm came over me, calm as thick and soothing as the calm skies outside.

"One five six clear to land," we heard from the tower.

It was after midnight when we came in to land. I saw the line of ambulances waiting for us on the ground, and touching down we heard the tires squeak as they kissed the runway. I had aced many landings, but this one was smoothest of all, like butter.

At the terminal I wanted to call Dina, but it was late, and I decided not to wake her and the kids. Instead I called Danny, and to his answering machine, I said, "Danny, we're going to blow the whistle on those bastards."

I hoped I could keep my resolve until the war ended.

* * *

The Yom Kippur war lingered on into 1974, but after two months I was released from active duty. In my absence, Danny had taken care of production, and my father, who now worked in the office, had done the bookkeeping. On the day I returned, Danny and I had our first meeting. "Are we going to do what you said?" he asked.

"What's that?" I said. I knew very well what he was referring to, but I was surprised this was the first thing he wanted to discuss even before talking about our business.

"Blow the whistle!" he said.

"Well, let's not rush. We have to do it the smart way."

"Have you thought about it?" he asked.

Throughout the war I had thought about it, ever since the moment I had called him that night. I told him as much. I told him we needed an attorney to help us. "It'll cost some money."

His eyes lit up. "Let's talk to Yehuda Ressler."

Ressler, his neighbor, was a young attorney who had gained fame when he sued the Government of Israel. In 1968, the government had caved to the demands of the orthodox religious party, a member of the coalition, to have no television broadcasts on the Sabbath. Ressler sued successfully and single-handedly forced the government to return to broadcasting on Saturdays. At the time Ressler was 27, and most of the population applauded him.

The next day Danny and I went to Ressler's office on King Saul Boulevard, in a good part of town, not far from the Tel Aviv Municipal Building. His office was in the basement of an apartment building, and when we stepped inside, we saw it was newly remodeled with wall to wall carpeting and expensive furniture. The door to his private office was closed, an opaque glass door, but we could hear him inside, talking on the phone.

After we had waited a few minutes, Ressler opened the door. I was surprised to see how small he was, not more than five foot five. "Come in and sit down," he said.

He sat behind a gigantic desk that exaggerated his diminutive figure, but despite his size, he projected unlimited energy. "What can I do for you?" he asked.

I told him about the "closed bid" we had lost just before the war, about Amnon Avni and his company AGI, about the corrupt bureaucracy and suspected "kick-backs" both in the Air Force and the Ministry of Defense. I explained we did not know exactly who all the players were, and we had no proof. He asked a few questions and then he sat quietly thinking for a few moments.

At last he asked, "What's your goal? Do you want to eliminate and punish corruption? Or do you want to get the purchase contracts you deserve?"

"Both," I said.

"You know, sometimes when you try to poke out your enemies' eyes, you get your own eye poked," he answered.

"Meaning?" I asked.

"I have excellent contact with Sergeant Zigel," he said, "the head of the white collar crime police department that investigates all fraud and corruption."

"That's the guy we want to talk to," Danny said.

"I can arrange it in a minute," he told Danny, and he turned to me. "But, to answer your question, the meaning is that you may be right and even succeed in eliminating those corrupt people, but you may lose a lot of business. People are fearful. They don't like to work with whistle blowers."

"We're losing business as it is," I said.

"Let's see," he said leaning back and looking at the low ceiling, again deep in thought. At last he said, "I think we first should exhaust all efforts to get the defense bid decision reversed and only then go to the police. I can help you guys." He was suggesting a long process, and I wondered how much this would cost.

"I understand you're a pilot," he said. "Don't you have friends in the Air Force you can talk to?"

"I can't do it," I said.

"Can't or don't want to?" he asked.

"Both," I said.

"Okay. To begin with, you have to go back to the clerks at Defense and demand to know all the details, the reasons and the procedure which led to your losing the bid. If nothing else, it'll scare them before the next bid."

"We'll go tomorrow," Danny said.

Ressler looked at Danny, then at me for a long moment. "I'll help you for free, no charge. We'll get the bastards."

I came home recharged with optimism and told Dina about the day. "We always get in trouble," she said. She was worried.

The Defense Dept. buyer's face paled when we asked him for all the details about how they had decided on the closed bid. He said he could tell us nothing and walked us into the office of his boss, who was an Air Force officer working for the Ministry of Defense in charge of the purchasing and bids committee; his walls were covered with pictures of aircraft. "Look guys, we just make sure the bid is good and the price is right," he said.

"But you know Avni isn't capable of performing. They don't have the know-how," I said.

"This is not for us to determine," he said.

"Then who?"

"Major Ben Aaharon."

"Did he tell you to give the order to Avni?" I asked.

"He certified that his company was qualified. If you wish to dispute this, talk to his boss Brigadier General Haim Yaron. Talk to *him.*"

Over the next few days, I managed to schedule a meeting with the Brigadier General, the chief technical officer of the Israeli Air Force. When we entered his office, I saluted him and said, "Sir, I'm Reserve Captain Eitan Gonen. We worked together when you were the technical officer and I was Deputy Squadron Commander at the Advanced Squadron in flight school."

He looked at me and Danny but offered no acknowledgement, no smile. "What are we discussing here?" he asked coldly.

I told him I thought the results of the bid for the lab would jeopardize the readiness of the Air Force because I knew Avni was not capable of producing the goods. He listened but asked no questions, and it was clear to me he had reviewed the situation before our meeting. "My officers determined that Avni was qualified," he said. "I trust Major Ben Aaharon in this matter. This discussion is over."

I had not forgotten that Major Ben Aaharon had told me that he and the Brigadier General and Avni had shared a good time in Paris together, so his response was not entirely a surprise.

Our office was small, partly open to the warehouse, and from my desk I could see Danny working on an assembly of systems. He repeatedly took out his contact lenses and put them back in, and I knew he was stressed. We all were. I walked over and asked, "What's up?"

"Nothing," he laughed nervously and continued, "I had coffee with Ben Aaharon."

"And?"

"He says I should not make waves. He says I should work for Amnon Avni who will pay me a high salary and give me a percentage, make me a junior partner. This way we could get a lot of orders."

"And?"

"He says you're not flexible. He said you're 'stuck up.'"

"And?"

"That's it," Danny said and began to remove his contact lenses.

"But what did *you* say?" I asked.

"I said I'd think about it," Danny said.

"Think about it?" I shouted.

I saw my father at his desk, looking worriedly in our direction. He had never heard us raising our voices at each other.

"Look Eitan," Danny said, "I have to make a living. I have a family to feed. You can fall back on your flying, but this is my only income."

Looking at him I thought the corrupt bunch was going to suck him in, and the bastards would escape. "You're right. I won't hold you down. Just let me know what you decide."

That evening Danny called me. "I spoke with Talma and we decided that if I couldn't make an honest living in our business, we would return to live in Los Angeles," he said.

"Great, let's see Yehuda Ressler tomorrow."

* * *

Two weeks later I asked Danny, "Is your harness tied?"

"Yes," he said.

We were sitting in a two-seater Piper Cub, and I pushed the throttle to full position and took off from Sde Dov airfield. After a short run, we were airborne, and I turned east, away from the shores of the Mediterranean, in the direction of Jerusalem. As part of our attorney's strategy, we were continuing to explore and exhaust all legal avenues to reverse the results of the closed bid for the laboratory we lost.

Our next move was to apply to the court of law, and our hearing was scheduled for that day. Since I had to be on Air Force reserve duty, my squadron commander let me take the Piper to fly north for the night, so I could fly to Jerusalem in the morning to be in court and fly back to the base immediately after the hearing.

The Supreme Court of Israel sat one day a month as the High Court of Justice. There, urgent matters of justice were heard and instant decisions rendered. The High Court of Justice sat in Jerusalem, and it was there that we requested the court to enjoin the government from giving the order to AGI, Ltd. Rather, we argued, the order should go to Eidan Engineering, Ltd.

"Where are we?" Danny asked when we were in the air.

I dropped the right wing in a swift move and said, "Look straight down. You can see Ramla."

"Are you crazy?" Danny shouted, surprised and frightened by my maneuver. He felt as if we were going to fall.

We landed in Atarot, Jerusalem's airport, took a taxi to the compound of the Supreme Court. The entire way we did not say a word, we were nervous. The courthouse was in the compound the British had used for their headquarters in Palestine. We walked into the stone structure and found our way to the courtroom, and as we entered we saw the room crowded with people seated on benches facing the elevated bench of the judges. Yehuda Ressler had saved seats for us. There were many cases on the docket that day, and the room was thick with attorneys in their black gowns and many clients, Jews and Arabs, seeking justice.

The court officer shouted, "Honorable Court of Justice!" and three middle-aged judges walked in and took their seats before us.

"Eidan Engineering vs. the Ministry of Defense," the judge in the center said.

Ressler stood, and with all the proper "Your Honors" tried to explain that the government had followed unfair and faulty procedures, that AGI was not qualified, and that we at Eidan Engineering should be the recipients of the contract.

The attorney for the Defense Ministry stood.

"Your Honor, without going into the merits of the case, AGI, Ltd. has

312

almost finished the work. As per precedent, because the work is substantially done, this case should be dismissed."

We were stunned. A week earlier we had talked with a junior officer who visited the AGI plant and told us the work had not begun. We knew they couldn't begin because they had neither the know-how nor the components to do so. Ressler jumped to his feet. "My clients say AGI has not yet even started."

The judge turned to the government attorney. "Do you have proof that most of the work is almost complete?"

Our hopes rose. He certainly could have no such proof.

"Well, I have here an Air Force officer who can attest to it," the attorney motioned to the officer to rise.

"State your name," the judge said.

"Major Meir Ben Aaharon," the officer said.

I looked at Ressler and Danny. They were pale.

"Do you know with certainty that the work of this subject contract is close to completion?" the judge asked.

There was silence in the room. Everyone looked at the Major who just nodded, yes. The judge in the center exchanged words with the others and said, "Case dismissed."

I wanted to go home and be alone, but I went to the airfield, took off in my Piper, flew to the Hatserim Air Force base, flew with three cadets and then flew back home, arriving in the dark, exhausted.

At home Dina asked "What happened?"

"The bastards lied all the way to the High Court of Justice," I said. "And they won."

* * *

In stark contrast to the newly remodeled office of our attorney, the office we were sitting in, a few days later, was old and unkempt, the bare walls once white now wore a gray patina, like an old man's skin. An old table with no drawers stood in the center. Ressler, Danny and I talked quietly. We had strategized in attorney Ressler's office where he repeatedly asked, "Are you sure you want to do it?"

"Yes," I said insistently. "We told you already."

A middle aged, heavyset man, his hair thinning, dressed in khaki pants that revealed his thin brown socks, walked into the room. His short sleeves revealed chubby, hairy hands. Two men in their 20s walked in with him. He said, "I'm Staff Sergeant Ziegel," and he sat across from us.

Ziegel was already a national folk hero, well known as the hunter of corrupt people in government. The newspapers called him and his staff " Ziegel and his Bulldogs." But I hadn't expected him to look like this; I had imagined the head of the department of police for fraud and corruption as tall and well-dressed, in a uniform with shiny medals.

"What can I do for you?" he asked, like a man in a hurry.

Ressler said, "Let me introduce you…" and Ziegel said, "Okay quick."

"This is Danny, a highly qualified engineer who came back from America to live here."

"Welcome," Ziegel said. He meant "Next."

"And Eitan here is an engineer, a businessman and an Air Force reserve pilot."

Ziegel curled his mouth and moved his head to indicate he was impressed. "Okay, guys, what are we talking about?" he asked.

Before I could open my mouth, Ressler began to describe our history of work for the Air Force, the faulty closed bids by the Ministry, our meetings with Michael Eatman and his boss, at Defense, with Brigadier General Haim Yaron. He talked about Major Meir Ben Aharon and about Amnon Avni. He told him about the government's lies in the high Court of Justice.

"So," Ziegel said, "what do you think is going on?"

"Tell him," Ressler looked at me.

"To tell the truth," I said, "we don't know exactly."

"So why are you here?" Ziegel asked impatiently.

"We think there is the taking and giving of 'gifts,'" Danny said.

"We're not sure," I said, "but it seems almost certain that Avni is gifting Major Ben Aharon and others." Ziegel's eyes ran from me to Danny and back, examining our faces.

"Are you here to try to get back the contracts you lost to your competition?" he asked.

"Sergeant Ziegel," I said, "yes, we would love to get back the contracts that we duly deserve, but…"

"I can't help you then," Ziegel cut me short.

"With all due respect, we did not think you could. Danny was a mechanic in the Air Force, and I was a fighter pilot, but we're not here as ex-Air Force soldiers. We come to you as concerned citizens. We can't stand by and let corruption, bribery and other shenanigans hit us in the face without trying to fight it. It would be easy for both of us to go back to America and have a good life over there, where the US Air Force issues much larger contracts than we may ever get here. I read about corruption in the papers. But it's different when we know exactly how bad it could be for the Air Force to not have the equipment it needs. Our concern is about the Air Force and its lack of readiness and the future of our country, especially after the Yom Kippur war. That's why we're here and why Attorney Ressler is here, helping us free of charge."

There was a long moment of silence.

"As for the contracts," I continued, "we are fully aware that once it's known that we were the whistle blowers, we might get none at all."

"Okay, got it," Ziegel said. "Now tell us all you know. Don't save any detail."

For long hours we told them all we knew.

* * *

In the aftermath of the Yom Kippur war, Israel won still more territory than it had before the surprise attack, and I flew to more and more destinations. The country realized that despite its great victory, in the first few days of the war there had been great risk of defeat and annihilation, defeat that was averted by the sheer heroism of our citizen soldiers, not by great leadership. The victory was painful. Over 2,500 were killed and 7,000 were injured. Our Air Force lost 100 of its aircraft. The country's arrogance, born of past victories and grown especially strong after the Six Day War, was injured, too. Golda Meir, Moshe Dayan and the Chief of the Armed Forces, David Elazar, had been ousted and Yitzhak Rabin became Prime Minister, with Shimon Peres serving as the Defense Minister.

One summer day, my father who helped us dailey with our office work, came to work complaining about pain. I was flying that day to Eilat, so Danny drove him home, and there he died of a heart attack. He was 72. We buried him the next day with a simple ceremony. No big speeches or fanfare; he was buried quietly, the same way as he spent his life.

In April 1975 we had the Passover Seder dinner in our home, inviting the extended family including Dina's uncle and his family who had just emigrated from Soviet Russia. When they arrived a few months earlier, I helped them learn the system, teaching them how to write and pay with checks among other capitalist customs. During the Seder, when we read of Moses telling Pharaoh, "Let my people go!" some of the adults cried.

At that moment, the phone rang. It was Yehuda Ressler. "They're going to arrest him."

Usually Ressler relayed news to Danny, his close friend and neighbor, but Danny had traveled to Los Angeles. I thought he had gone to prepare his return to live in America. On the phone Ressler didn't mention who was going to be arrested, but I was certain it was the main culprit. Still I asked.

"The Major," he said.

I went back to the dinner table with my heart racing, and it continued to race as we read about the punishing plagues God had brought upon Pharaoh.

From as far back as I could remember *Yediot* had been a popular newspaper. We had read it during the war in Jerusalem. Unlike most other papers, it was not aligned with any one political party and had none of the pretentious intellectual aura of some other newspapers. It had the highest readership and was always quick to pursue juicy scandals. After we gave police Staff Sergeant Ziegel the information about the suspected corruption we had encountered, we heard nothing for a long time. Our first indication that anything was happening was that phone call from Ressler.

I had been reading *Yediot* from beginning to end, but I'd found nothing.

On Friday, April 11, two days after my 37th birthday, I finally read an interesting news item on the front page. The main headline was about President Gerald Ford's speech before a joint session of Congress, but a small news item beside it read:

> A number of clerks in the Ministry of Defense will be
> brought in for interrogation at the police. It appears the suspects
> gave preference to suppliers in return for payments.

The news item mentioned no names, which was a little disappointing, but I was glad our names had stayed out of the paper. I had never talked with my friends about my business, especially not my fellow pilots, and although I was proud that we had broken the corruption to the police, I knew that I would have to explain a lot if our names appeared in the paper as having been involved with a corruption scandal. Over the next two weeks, news about corruption in the defense establishment and in the Air Force shocked the Israeli population. The size of the news items grew, and daily more names of arrested officers appeared.

The paper of April 22 had a big front page item with the headline: "An Air Force Major - State Witness." The story told of the arrest of Major Ben Aaharon and included information about the arrest of Brigadier General Haim Yaron, and others from Defense.

Another item was headlined:

"Who is Who - In the Ministry of Defense Scandal". Even though

Danny and I thought we knew who was involved, we were daily discovering more and more details about who bribed whom and how much money had changed hands for how long. I was astonished by the depth of the swamp into which we had unknowingly fallen. The stories had become more and more complex, and this news report was an attempt to sort out the details for readers.

I began to eagerly await each day's paper with more news of the scandal. Exciting as it was, I had no one but Dina to share it with. Danny had taken refuge in the States, and I would not talk about it. People were frustrated after reading the papers, and some of my co-pilots read the articles and made comments which I ignored.

On Thursday, April 24, the newspaper quoted the Prime Minister, "Rabin: Corruption is Out of Control." The same paper offered the Minister of Defense, Shimon Peres's view: "Everything discovered was discovered internally, by our own security officers."

Of course this was a lie.

The Justice Minister was quoted: "The suspects will be prosecuted regardless of their ranks."

Uri Avneri, the editor of the rebellious and famous magazine *Ha'olam Hazeh* (*This World*), called for Shimon Peres to resign. The magazine also blamed the Commander of the Air Force, General Benjamin Peled, for interfering with the judicial process by calling the editors to support his Chief Technical Officer Haim Yaron and proclaim his innocence. Ironically, shortly after the commander called, Yaron was arrested on suspicion of receiving bribes.

On the editorial page, the editor called upon Shimon Peres to show leadership and appear before the nation to promise to root out corruption. The courts continued to extend Amnon Avni's internment. Reportedly he had given tens of thousands of dollars and other gifts to Ben Aaharon, to the buyers in the Defense Dept., Haim Yaron and many others. The Air Force Major, who turned state's witness, was most vilified in the papers.

One Thursday Sergeant Ziegel called and said, "Eitan, I think you should be happy."

"Happy is not the exact word. But I am very satisfied," I told him.

"Well, I think we've got them all."

"It seems so," I said. Actually, I was ecstatic about all that had happened, satisfied that our suspicions had turned out to be true and that the players we suspected had all been rounded up and arrested. But happy I was not.

"Look Eitan," Ziegel said, "Could you come to my office tomorrow for a few minutes?"

"Sure, what for?" I asked.

He hesitated. "I think we have it all cleared up, but there is something I want to clarify with you to close the matter."

"Okay," I said.

"Be here before noon," he said.

That Friday the receptionist told me to wait in the same room where we had broken the scandal a few months earlier. A young man I recognized as one of Ziegel's Bulldogs walked in and said, 'The boss wants me to ask you a few questions."

"Shoot," I said.

"You know, Eitan," he began, "we made Major Ben Aaharon a state witness."

"That's the only thing that gets me mad about your good work," I said. "He's one of the main culprits and the most corrupt one, and he's going home free."

"He's not free," he said. "He'll just get a more lenient sentence. He helped us to get all the bastards."

I understood. "But I'm still upset about it."

The young investigator looked at the ceiling for a while, and slowly turned his gaze on me. "So, Ben Aahron said something about you guys."

"Like what?" I asked. I felt blood flowing to my head. In those days I was quick to anger. "Like a Moroccan," Dina liked to say.

"Don't get so excited," he said. "It's a minor claim. He said that Danny and you gave him a present. A washer/dryer from America."

"That's a lie," I said.

"It could be," he said, "but why would he lie?"

"Are you kidding?" I raised my voice. "He tried to hurt us even before the scandal. Now he knows as well as you do that we broke the scandal and caused all his troubles. He certainly would enjoy punishing us."

"Relax, relax. Tell me about the washer/dryer."

At the time I had warned Danny not to get too friendly with the Major, but under pressure, he would veer from our strategy, unable to take the heat. "I don't know the details," I said, "but I know Danny let the Major use his right to a duty free washer/dryer, that's all."

"Did you pay for it?" he asked.

"No, we didn't."

"Look, Eitan," he said, "it's not a big deal. If you paid for it, you'll just get a small fine and we close the case."

"I'm telling you, we didn't pay for it. He's lying."

"Believe me," he said, "I know you are the good guys in all this. However, he says Danny gave it to him, and I understand the pressure you were under."

"Please, save your sympathy," I said.

"Tell me off the record, and we'll find a way around it."

"Record?" I asked. "Is this an interrogation?"

"Let's call it an official conversation," he said.

"I'm flabbergasted," I said. "Do you think we would have come to you with the scandal if we were involved? It's ridiculous. You take the word of a corrupt Major who we brought to you, against our word? I will tell you again, it's a lie. This is the last time I am saying it."

He leaned back in his chair and wrote something I could not see on his pad. "Why isn't Ziegel here in this conversation?" I asked.

"He said it's too painful for him. Please wait here." He left the room for a long time, and I listened as people began to leave for the weekend. Finally he returned. "Again, Eitan," he said. "you can end it in a minute and we all go home."

"If you have any evidence, charge me," I said.

He exhaled as if he were desperate. "If that's the way you want to play it, I have no choice but to arrest you."

Damn it, I thought, "No good deed ever goes unpunished." Still, I didn't believe he would. "Do it then," I said.

* * *

I called Ressler to tell him the news.

"Stop kidding," he said.

I told him it was true and asked him to call Dina and tell her.

I climbed into the young Bulldog's car, and as we drove to Abu Kabir, he turned around and said, "Sorry, Eitan."

Abu Kabir was an old Arab neighborhood that straddled the cities of Tel Aviv, Jaffa and Holon. Until it was conquered by Israel in the War of Independence, it had been a source of vicious Arab attacks. The British had built a small police station there which eventually was built up and fortified and now served as the main jail for the central area of Israel. It was mentioned frequently in the papers as the jail where the players in the Defense scandal were detained with other criminals until the police had completed their investigation.

At the gate to Abu Kabir jail, the guard looked into our unmarked police car. The young Ziegel Bulldog showed him his police ID, and we pulled into a small parking area, fenced by a concrete wall, on top of which a concertina of barbed wire stretched to a height of fifteen feet. We got out of the car and waited in line. In front of us stood a man with his hands cuffed behind his back. Two policemen held his arms on either side. It took a few minutes to check him in, and then it was my turn. At least, I thought, they hadn't handcuffed me.

In the jail reception area, the "Bulldog" said to the policeman, "This guy is one of the good guys. Treat him nicely."

"Don't worry," the police sergeant said, "we always give good service here." He sat behind a counter, as if this were a hotel reception area; but instead of asking for my reservation, he placed a plastic bag on the counter. "Put everything in this bag. Empty your pockets."

I did.

"I said everything," the sergeant said.

The policeman next to me explained in a sympathetic tone, "Your belt, your watch, your ring, your shoelaces."

The policeman held my arm and walked me to my cell. Just walking with my pants hanging loose and my unlaced shoes made me feel like a prisoner. We walked up to the second floor and onto a balcony built around the courtyard. "This is your cell," he said, closing the steel door behind him. He locked the door and I heard his steps walking away. It was still day, but the room was dark.

"Welcome home," a guy said. "Ha, ha, ha."

Startled I turned. I could not see his face clearly. I had worried briefly about the possibility of being in the same cell with Amnon Avni who had been there for over 40 days; the newspaper reports had said the police intended to ask the court for yet another extension. "Home?" I said. As my eyes became accustomed to the low lighting, I saw six beds, with only one guy lying on one.

"Well, for fifteen days I'm here. I sleep here, I eat here, I..."

"Okay, okay," I said. "I get it."

"So, this makes it home," he continued. "Take that bed, it gets good moonlight. You could even read at night."

I unfolded the blanket and looked at the bare mattress, filthy with urine spots I could see even in this light.

"My name is Shlomo," my new roommate said.

My old friend Flochick's first name was Shlomo. I wondered what a laugh he would get if he knew where I was now. I wondered where he was. "What have you done?" I asked.

"Nothing, I'm innocent," he said. "They say I embezzled money." He told me he was a driver in the Army and then worked for the government. He was proud to end up as the driver for the President of Israel. They'd become good friends, he said. He had a budget for supplies and maintenance and someone squealed that he used some of the money for his own expenses.

"What about you?" he asked.

I was about to tell him when I remembered reading that jails are full of people who are innocent - if you don't believe it - ask them! Here I was about to tell my cellmate I was innocent. Instead I said, "I'm involved with the Defense bribery scandal."

"I follow it in the paper every day," he said. Of course the whole country and its leaders were. "So are you a taker or a giver?" he asked.

"Neither," I said.

"But why are you here?"

"I don't want to talk about it right now," I said.

Surprisingly the stench in the cell and Shlomo's snoring kept my mind off the outrage at what had happened to me. I had no doubt that I would eventually get out of this, but I was full of rage about the government, the police, and about my partner. At Ziegel's office they had shown me Danny's testimony. He signed it the bottom of the page that said, among other things, "I was in production, I knew nothing about the business side. Only Eitan knows about money and such."

I could not fall asleep.

I heard voices from the walkway outside the cell. As they came closer, I noticed one man speaking in Arabic, giving instructions. A key was inserted into my cell door and it opened. A guard pushed a man into the cell. The new prisoner was of medium height with long, unkempt hair, and was dressed in a short-sleeved filthy undershirt which was torn in places. That was all he wore. He would not step in, in spite of the guard's shouts in Arabic. The guard pushed him hard so that he just cleared the door which was locked behind him. My cell mate woke up.

"Hey guys, you better keep an eye on this Arab," the jailer said behind the door.

The Arab prisoner did not take another step. He stood at the door naked, his body shaking violently. Even in the scant moonlight, we could see how filthy he was. His eyes were wide open - expressionless, as if in a daze. His feet were planted on the floor, but he kept shaking, and his penis jumped up and down and sideways so hard, I thought it might fall off. "That's all we need," Shlomo said, "an Arab drug addict in our home."

With this guy shaking, we were afraid to sleep, so we decided to keep watch. Shlomo took first watch since he had slept a while, and finally I dozed. When I woke up about an hour later, the Arab was still shaking at the door, and I heard Shlomo snoring. In the morning, we found the Arab asleep on the floor.

At 10 a.m. a guard opened the cell door and shouted, "Everybody out!" We walked to the center courtyard for breakfast and to get some fresh air. In the dining hall they offered dry bread, margarine, jam, black tea and watery semolina cereal. I ate nothing and walked out to the yard which was surrounded by a three storied concrete structure and covered with barbed wire mesh.

Prisoners huddled in groups. Shlomo pointed out the different groups, explaining who were the pimps, the addicts, the murderers before their trials, the thieves and white collar criminals. A group of men walked the length of the courtyard, back and forth, exercising, talking and smoking. I recognized Amnon Avni in the group, and as they passed by me, he stopped.

"That's the bastard!" He pointed at me. His friends, dark skinned and muscled, looked at me and back at him, as if awaiting their leader's instructions to attack. "This is the guy who spilled my blood," he said.

I was sure they were about to spill some of mine.

"You couldn't let us all live," he said, his voice now one octave higher and louder, "we could all make good money, but you had to spoil everything. You had to see us all as prisoners." His face was red, his eyes bulged, and his considerable belly shook up and down as he spoke.

Two guards slowly approached us, and his buddies held him by the arms as he tried to move closer to me and shouted in my face. "You thought you were squeaky clean, ha? Now you're here, a prisoner like the rest of us. Happy now?"

The group moved closer, but I didn't back away. If they were going to fight me I wanted to get it over with.

"Come now, Amnon," the guard said in a friendly voice, "You don't want to lose your special privileges, do you?" The guard and Avni's muscular buddies laughed. Shlomo later told me he suspected Avni had already bribed the guards for food and hashish from outside and that he shared them with his buddies for protection. As Avni and his group moved away, he spit on the ground and cursed my mother. They never bothered me again.

All day I expected to be released any minute. I thought Ressler would call Ziegel and the sergeant would issue an immediate order to release me and apologize for the mistake. By late afternoon when nothing had happened, my morale dipped, and I thought of Dina and the kids and wondered how she would explain my sudden disappearance.

"It's like that on the first day," my new friend said. "I was totally depressed for the first few days. It could be worse. Look at him!" He motioned at our cell mate, the drug addict who slept on the bed next to me. He was resting from his night's convulsions.

Lying in my bed, I heard a woman shout. "What's that?" I asked.

Shlomo laughed. "It's the Saturday night show."

"You're pulling my leg," I said. "A show comes to Abu Kabir?"

"Listen," he said, and we heard more than one woman's voice. They were standing outside, close to the jail, under our windows.

"F-e-l-i-x!" a woman shouted, "This is Rachel, how are you my love?"

I waited for Felix to answer but we heard only men laughing from the floor above us.

"Abutbull," another was crying, "when are you coming out? I can't live without you."

"I love you, Moshe!" shouted another.

The chorus of women shouting to their lovers, mates and husbands continued all evening and died only at midnight. My cellmate explained mostly they were whores visiting their jailed pimps. I could not believe how low I had fallen.

In the morning I had a visitor.

I sat across the table from Ressler who looked at me for a long moment. I suddenly realized how bad I must look. I was outraged and humiliated and had been wearing the same clothes for three days. "What do they do to you in there?" he asked. "Is it that bad?"

He looked clean and free. In just three days in jail, I had lost some of my spirit. "It's just the bad company," I said.

"I called Ziegel and they'll let you go this afternoon," Ressler said. I should be greatly relieved, I thought, but I only felt rage.

I returned to the family. Dina and the kids looked at me as if I had come back from Mars, and as we hugged, Dina cried uncontrollably, and the kids ran to their rooms.

I went back to work and flew more hours than ever, always fearing my detention would be revealed and that there would be repercussions both professionally and socially. I decided I would not try to explain my innocence to everyone. "Where there's smoke there's fire," most people would say.

A week after my release, there it was on the front page of Ma'ariv, the story of my arrest, my name and the company's name. I was expecting calls and requests for explanation from my friends, copilots, and business people but only one pilot paid any attention.

"I read about you in the paper," he said in a soft, discrete voice. And he winked.

Danny moved with his family back to America while I continued to fly and manage our company. I worked on the contracts we had yet to finish and represented American companies, but I didn't want to work with the government, and the sentiment was mutual. Even the honest bureaucrats considered me their nemesis.

Corruption scandal headlines 1975

CHAPTER THIRTY-EIGHT

Arkia Airlines was in transition. Long flights to the far edges of the Sinai were cancelled, replaced by tourists who came by the millions. I often started flying in the wee hours of the morning-- Tel Aviv to Haifa to Jerusalem to Eilat to Sharem-el-Sheikh to Eilat to Jerusalem to Haifa to Tel Aviv, and after these tiring nine takeoffs and landings, I had to spend the day solving problems at the business. Dina watched me becoming increasingly tired, impatient and frustrated. One day she asked me what was going on.

"They're hiring," I said.

Tears appeared in her eyes. "Who?" she asked as if she didn't know.

"El Al," I said.

"Aren't you too old for them?" I didn't answer because I didn't know. "You don't know if you can get in," she said.

"I can only know if I try."

We were, by then, equally unsure. I was not sure I wanted to start a new flying job at the bottom of the pecking order, and Dina wasn't sure she could stop me. "Apply if you want," she said. "Let's see what happens."

I went to the offices at Ben Gurion Airport and was interviewed by El Al's "Hiring Committee." As I entered, I saw some familiar faces. The Chair of the committee was Captain Solly Amiran, who had started at El Al when we both were discharged from the Air Force, sixteen years earlier. I had flown with him, and we both worked on converting the flight school Advanced Squadron to become a standby attack and support squadron in war.

He asked me to tell the Committee my history, and I talked about flying for the Air Force, flying in Africa and for Arkia as well as about my studies at Cal Tech and my engineering work. When I finished, he told the members of the committee he knew me personally, that I was smart and an excellent pilot. "But I want you to know that you're going to start at the bottom," he said. "At your age you'd better think about it."

I was 39 by then, and after I received the letter accepting me to join the new course at El Al, I began to have second thoughts. I was reluctant to start all over in addition to my reluctance to change our family's lifestyle. Dina and I had long discussions about the situation and about our next step, and after weeks of conversation, I presented her a choice. I told her I could not just trudge along. I had to either fly for El Al or go to America to try doing business there.

"Why do you throw that decision to me?" she asked.

"It's your choice," I said.

"How will we make a living in America? How can you take such a risk with two kids?"

I told her we had enough resources to start and that we would find work in Los Angeles. After all, I had a Masters from Cal Tech. "So what is your choice?" I asked her the next day at dinner.

"Let's go to LA and try," Dina said. "But I will not go back to teach Hebrew."

The knot in my stomach instantly disappeared as I began to plan our move back to L.A. I had always felt that our abrupt departure had left many of my plans unfulfilled. I had liked the ease of doing business in the States, the civility, the freedom, the opportunity. I wanted to spend more time living and working in L.A., if only for a short time. There were still some obstacles to overcome.

I did not want to quit my job with Arkia, so I convinced management it would be mutually beneficial for them to approve my request for a two year "leave of absence." This would allow me to return to my flying position if I needed to, and it also gave me the right to free and discounted airline tickets around the world during my leave.

Our Green Cards— permits to permanently stay in the States— had expired, but we could enter the U.S. on the business visa we had.

Then came the question of a job. I had helped Danny establish a branch of our company in Los Angeles, and over the years I had frequently visited. Early in 1978 we had discussed starting a real estate development business as there was a boomlet going on in LA. When I visited, I saw a few new houses and the business attracted me, so we planned to begin the business when I arrived in L.A. at year's end. We told friends and family we were going away for two years, and the kids were excited to leave school in mid-year. Hadar, 11, was in fifth grade and Ron, 8, was in third. Ron came home and told us his best friend's mother said we were leaving for good, never to return. Many did not believe we would return.

On the eve of our departure, we were invited to our friends Ron and

Etti's house and there we met Yehudit and Avi for the first time. It was the beginning of a friendship that would last for decades. At year end, as we were busy with preparations for leaving our home in Ramat Efal, I received a call from Danny. "Are you still planning to come?" he asked.

"Of course," I said.

"Well, don't," he said. "The real estate business here is finished."

I thought this was one of his bad practical jokes.

"Interest rates went up," he said, "from 7 to 7-3/4, and real estate is finished. You'd better not come. I have to take a full time engineering job."

At that point I did not care about real estate boom or bust, and there was no way I would change my plans. "I'm coming anyway," I said.

And so in March 1979, eleven years after we lost Ronit and left Los Angeles, we locked our home in Israel and left for the States.

* * *

Renting an apartment and arranging schooling for the kids took some time. I watched TV and saw the Shah of Iran as a refugee in Egypt and PM Begin of Israel visiting Anwar Sadat in Cairo as he started to return the Sinai. One day Ron came back from Hebrew school complaining the teacher had not let him eat his lunch; we learned not to send him to that school with Pork & Beans for lunch. Though I enjoyed my time off, after a month I became concerned about generating some income.

One night we went to Danny's house for dinner, and when we arrived Danny asked me into another room for a private meeting. There he asked if I'd brought any money to the States.

"Some, but I'll need to get more," I said. "It's enough for a short time only."

He looked away, worried, and asked, "So, what's your plan?"

"We'll develop our business," I said.

"Right now business here is bad," he said. "Interest rates and gas prices are up."

"Well, I'll use some of our profits from Scientific," I said.

Danny and I had started a business in the States selling military equipment to foreign countries, mainly equipment for aircraft servicing, and over the years since he'd been back in the States we had accumulated some profit in the company we called "Scientific Airomotive, Inc."

Danny's face paled. "At the moment there's no cash in the account."

"Where is it?" I asked, thinking he might have spent it on inventory.

"I used it for the down payment," he said, and he went on to explain

327

the money in the company's account had just been sitting idle as real estate prices rose. "If I didn't buy something I'd never be able to buy a house. So I used the money for a down payment. I'll pay you back."

I was furious, but I said nothing more.

"I'll introduce you to my boss. You'll get a job for a while," he said.

At the dinner table Dina told Talma and Danny she liked the house.

"You helped us buy it," Danny said. "Thanks."

Later Dina asked me what he meant by that statement, but I told her I didn't know.

* * *

The company Danny worked for ran a test laboratory that was located in a remote canyon north of Los Angeles, near a small town called Saugus. When I interviewed, the boss asked me to join the company; they had a contract to test the fuel systems of the Space Shuttle Columbia, and Danny had told me they had a hard time hiring engineers.

The on-board fuel system of the Space Shuttle consisted of two chemicals called MMH and Hydrazin. When these materials came together they ignited to propel the spacecraft. They were unstable and vaporized easily, producing poisonous vapors, and few engineers were willing to handle them. When Danny asked me about the interview, I told him what I had suggested.

"I told him you wouldn't continue to work for eight dollars an hour, but we would sign a consulting contract for our services at four times that rate."

The color returned to Danny's face for he was convinced I was playing a practical joke; he had a mortgage to pay and was averse to risks. "Okay, what really went on?" he asked.

"Really," I said.

"What did he say?"

"He said he'll get back to me," I told him.

He did get back to me, agreeing to our offer, and so it was that Danny and I planned and built the system and tested the components of the fuel system for the Space Shuttle Columbia. We did all this in a desolate California canyon where we spent many hours of every day. Most of the time we were exhausted, but we still had energy and earned a great deal of money.

Tired one afternoon, I sent Hadar and Ron to the Ralph's market on Ventura Boulevard to buy a six-pack of European beer for me. They came back disappointed – the market would not sell beer to minors. Together we learned the new rules of life in LA.

CHAPTER THIRTY-NINE

A year after we arrived in LA, we bought our first home in America, a townhome in a complex of 100 units in Encino. We celebrated Hadar's Bat Mitzva in the pool area of our new place. In the spring of 1980, while I was working with Danny, I received a letter from the Tel Aviv court ordering me to attend my trial. Six years had passed since I'd broken the scandal, and I was sure everything had died down. To my surprise, the letter informed me I had been charged with bribing the Major. After I received this summons, Danny avoided looking at my eyes, he felt guilty for my troubles, I thought.

I left Dina and the kids and flew to Israel. Just before I left, our friend, an Israeli attorney in LA was kind enough to let us know that I could be sentenced to spend years in prison. "Are you sure you want to go back?" she asked.

"I'm going to prove I'm clean," I told her.

She warned me I was taking a risk, but I was determined.

In Tel Aviv I met my family and friends, but I told no one about the real purpose of my visit. I told my brother I had come to keep my pilot's license current, which was also true. I flew to Eilat and back to practice and to meet the licensing requirements.

The day before the trial date, I met with Ressler who assured me that the lawyer he had recommended was the best in the business. I went to see Moshe Shvaig in his office on the second floor of an apartment building not far from the courthouse.

I climbed up the stairs and knocked on the locked door, and a small man with a moustache opened the door. The apartment was bear with only a few old pieces of office furniture. I hesitated when I saw he was there all alone, I thought this was the wrong place.

"Come in, Come in," he said. "I'm Moshe Shvaig."

He asked me to tell him everything in detail, and I quickly skimmed over all the details of the case. Dissatisfied with my rendition of the story, he rehearsed with me questions I might be asked in court. I answered. He studied the file Ressler had given him. "You're not a good witness," he said.

"But I'm not guilty of the charge," I said.

"How come you're so cool?" he asked. "I would expect more emotions. More anger."

"Many years have passed," I explained. "My anger has dissipated. I'm tired of the whole thing."

For a moment he was quiet. I sensed for the first time I might be in trouble, but Shvaig said, "Don't worry, I'll get you out of this."

The next day we went to the courthouse together. The courtroom was small, in a new courthouse with modern furniture. When we entered I saw the prosecutor was already there; Moshe Shvaig shook his hand, and he laughed at some comment the prosecutor made. I sat next to Shvaig at one desk; the prosecutor sat at the other, both of us facing the elevated, elongated dais where the judge would sit. Behind us were three or four benches for the audience, arranged in rising levels as in a stadium. But no one was in attendance.

Both attorneys were looking through their files when a court officer walked in from a back door and shouted, "Honor the Court!"

We stood and the judge, in his black tunic, entered, took his seat and opened a file.

"State of Israel vs. Eitan Gonen," he declared, and went on to read the charge against me. "You are accused of giving a set of GE washer and dryer to Major Ben Aaharon thus committing the crime of bribing an agent of the Government of Israel." He continued to recite the relevant items of the law. "Do you admit your guilt?'

"No, your honor," I said.

"Sit down," the judge said. "Prosecution, what have you got?"

The prosecutor rose slowly with his head down, looking at the open file on the desk in front of him. The judge looked tired and bored in the near empty courtroom. There were no spectators on the benches and I missed the low murmur of the crowd we always saw in the movies.

"Your Honor, we have a state witness who will testify in detail and prove the guilt of the accused."

"Call him in!" the judge ordered. I thought: "Let the games begin!"

The prosecution motioned to the court officer who walked out the back door and walked back in with the witness. He looked much smaller, thinner, and older; his hair was gone. Without his uniform and the Major insignia on his shoulders, he looked mousy, his brown eyes dancing nervously from the judge to me, to the attorney and back to the judge.

"State your name and occupation," the judge said.

"Meir Ben Aaharon. I'm a salesman."

That was somewhat satisfying. I hoped they had stripped him of his rank and that he had had to work hard to make a living.

He told the court that Danny and I had given him a washer/dryer, and he offered details as to dates and models in response to the prosecutor's questions.

"What did you do in return?" the judge asked.

"Nothing, your Honor."

"Did they give you any other things?"

"No, your Honor."

"Had other people given you stuff?"

A faint, sad smile appeared on his face, but the prosecutor leaped to his feet. "Your Honor, he was a state witness against many people and admitted to receiving many bribes."

The judge asked for any corroborating evidence against me, but the prosecutor had none. Instead, he recited the precedents that a statement by a state witness should be considered sufficient evidence. The judge wrote something in the file. The Israeli courts had no court reporters. "Defense, do you want to counter question?" the judge asked.

Shvaig rose slowly. "Did you know how this affair, the scandal of the corruption in the Air Force and the Ministry of Defense came to light?" he asked the witness who glanced in my direction.

"I told everything about it to the police," he answered.

"But did you know who told the police about you?" Shvaig insisted.

"No, I'm not sure. No one told me."

"Did you know that my client took the Ministry of Defense to the High Court of Justice?"

"Yes," he said. "I was there."

He glanced at my direction. I saw his eyes were dimmed. A victim look of a cornered animal replaced the arrogance and confidence of yester year. I saw no contrition but rather an expression of "Why did you have to do it to me?"

"And did you bear witness in that case?"

"Yes, I did."

"And was that false witness?"

Ben Aaharon lowered his head and looked at the floor. He said, "Yes."

"Louder," the judge said. "I can't hear you."

"Yes, it was false."

"No more questions," Moshe Shvaig said and sat down.

The state witness was taken out the back door, and the judge asked Shvaig if he had any witnesses for the defense.

"I would like to question the accused," he said.

I stood and walked to the witness stand. At that moment, the entry door opened and a group of young Air Force officers walked in and took their seats on the audience benches. The last to enter was a Colonel, a pilot I knew. Shvaig, the prosecutor, the judge and I were all surprised, and my first thought was that someone had sent them to intimidate me. The judge had a similar thought. "Are you all here to strengthen the State in its case?" he asked, laughing out loud.

"No, this is part of my officers' education," the Colonel said. "We came to see the court in action."

Suddenly a young female lieutenant stood and said, "Eitan, what are you doing here?"

I was incredulous. The young lady was my niece, Yael Makogon, my brother's daughter. I motioned her with my finger to keep quiet. The Colonel waved to me. The judge ordered the audience to be quiet as my emotions began to run wild. Of all the days and years, I thought, what kind of luck was it that my niece was visiting the courtroom on that day. Now I would have to apologize to my family for not telling them the whole truth about the purpose of my visit.

The judge motioned his hand to Attorney Shvaig to go ahead.

"Okay, Eitan, did you give a washer/dryer to Ben Aaharon?"

"I did not," I said, "and could not."

"Why couldn't you?"

I explained that I did not have the right to the duty free machines, that only Danny had, and that he had assigned his right to Ben Aaharon only days before the right was to expire.

"Is that legal?" the judge asked.

"It's done all the time, it's customary," Shvaig said, "but in any case, such an infraction of rules is not a subject of this case."

"And where is this Danny Polany?" the judge asked.

"He lives in America now," Shvaig said.

"Oh, I see," the judge said, looking at me. "He left for America and left you alone here."

"No, Your Honor," Shvaig said. "My client lives in America as well."

The judge leaned back, puzzled. He looked at me. "Are you telling me that you came from America?"

"Yes," I said.

"You mean you came especially for this trial?" He was flabbergasted. "To stand here and be accused? It's hard to believe." He motioned to Shvaig to continue.

"Please tell the court what happened with the contract for purifiers," Shvaig said to me.

"The air-to-air missiles used on the F-16 to shoot down enemy airplanes use nitrogen. They have an infrared sensitive electronic eye that needs to be kept cool by nitrogen that must be absolutely clean of any micro foreign objects. For that purpose, the Air Force needed on-the-ground systems to purify the nitrogen before it went into the missiles."

"Is all this relevant?" the judge said. "Please get to the point."

"Yes, your Honor," Moshe Shvaig said. "Eitan, tell us what happened. The Air Force wanted to buy these systems?"

"Yes, they needed a number of purifiers on each base."

"So did you bid to make them?"

"The units were made in the U.S., but we acquired the plans from Air Dry, the American company and offered to make them here in Israel for much less and to save the foreign currency for Israel."

"What did you do next?" Shvaig asked.

I continued to tell the story of the Major's enthusiasm for buying the units locally for less and that later he wanted us to share the profits with him. I described his hostility when I did not agree to go along with his plan. "What happened next?"

"The Major declared that we were not qualified to build these purifiers, and he ordered them from the US."

"So, you didn't build these purifiers?"

"Well, actually we did," I said. "When Air Dry Corporation got the contract from the Air Force and heard our story, they were outraged and gave us the order to build them."

"So, you built them and delivered them to the Air Force?"

"No, we built them here in Tel Aviv," I said, "and then we crated the units and shipped them to Air Dry in Los Angeles."

I could hear the Air Force officers gasp in surprise as my story unfolded. Glancing at them I saw my niece holding up a fist in support.

"Then what?" Shvaig asked.

"The Americans changed the labels and shipped them back to Haifa where the Ministry of Defense picked them up," I said.

From time to time the judge rolled his eyes in bewilderment and disbelief.

"Do you have any evidence to corroborate this fantastic story about the units taking a round trip around the world?"

My attorney took out a set of pictures that showed me beside the units being built in our warehouse; they were crated with the US address on them. The next picture was one we took of the same unit once it was back in an Israeli Air Force base. "I've heard enough," the judge said.

"But there is more evidence, Your Honor," Shvaig said, "that my client's action to discover and reveal the corruption and his unwillingness to participate in it brought the wrath of the Major on him. This is why he decided to implicate Mr. Gonen, in revenge."

"I said I've heard enough," the judge said. "I will give my verdict in the near future."

The judge kept writing in the file as the group of Air Force officers, including my niece and their commander, waved goodbye and gave me the thumbs-up sign as they were leaving.

"As for the accused," the judge said, "he will not have to come back for the verdict. He can get it in writing."

"Honor the Court!" The court officer shouted, and it was over. I shook hands with Shvaig, who smiled for the first time.

"You are leaving a free man," he laughed.

"I came here a free man," I said.

* * *

I flew back to Los Angeles to continue work on the fuel system of Space Shuttle Columbia and when we finished this contract, we opened an office and expanded our aircraft supply business, selling parts to Spain and Korea as well as negotiating big contracts for F-16 fuel drop tanks with Germany and Israel.

Danny had never again mentioned the money he had taken from our account to buy his house and never repaid my share of it either. As our business grew, I still expected him to pay it back, but overtime it became less significant to me.

Oddley, the more money we made, the darker Danny's mood became. He continued to be obsessed with Hitler and the holocaust and never stopped his habit of telling jokes about it. Eventually I offered him the opportunity to buy me out, but he refused. I told him I would buy him out, but he refused that offer too. Ultimaelty I could not tolerate the atmosphere anymore, so I simply gave him my share of the company and walked away.

I bought Danny's share in a property we had invested in together, and there I built 40 apartments and began my career in real estate development.

CHAPTER FORTY

In the mid-1990s, after I had already "made it" in real estate development and accumulated some wealth from my projects and other exciting investment programs, I flew to Tel Aviv on business. I spent about a week presenting my newest projects to some companies and visiting family.

I flew El Al on the way back to the States, leaving Ben Gurion airport at midnight. The flight had become popular because one could sleep through the night and arrive in New York City in the morning, leaving a whole day for work.

The business section of the plane was full of businessmen, attorneys and wealthy Israeli families traveling to New York. I felt relaxed and more than ever before, comfortable in my own skin, pleased with my business achievements and with my family.

Dina, who had shed tears about our move to America at least once a week for the first few years in Los Angeles, was now content. The worst case she had always feared had never materialized. In our first years in America, she saw many kids leave home to go to university where they could be as far away as possible from their parents. She told everyone that in Israel, the kids grow up and stay close to family. Now Hadar graduated from UCLA and earned her law degree locally at USC. Ron also graduated from UCLA and went back for his Masters in Business Administration and eventually joined my business.

We moved into a house on a ridge of the mountains that divide the city of Los Angeles to the south from the San FernandoValley to the north, on a famous road called Mulholland Drive, high above Beverly Hills. Our view of the vast valley below and the surrounding mountains reminded me of the view from our apartment in Jerusalem that we had to leave forty years earlier; the muffled sound of a thousand cars on the distant freeway replaced the sound from the Minarets of Mosques.

I loved my new, second homeland, appreciated the limited government, the opportunities, the conveniences, the freedoms and the anonymity. When people asked Dina about a possible return to Israel and why she liked being in America, she would say: "I have lived with a husband who was frustrated about his job and with one who's happy about his business. I like the latter better."

When the plane reached cruising altitude, the stewardess came by.

"Sir, what would you like to drink?"

The intercom came alive and the Captain said the usual, "This is your Captain," and gave us flight information. He closed with, "Now just sit back and relax."

As the Captain was talking, I thought I recognized the voice, and I listened intently. The final word he uttered gave him up. The L in *relax* was unusually soft, and I knew it was my friend, Fooxy - Captain Yehuda Fuchs.

I had planned on a quiet night flight and did not want to spend it socially. "Sir," the stewardess cut into my thoughts, "about your drink?"

I ordered a glass of Cabernet Sauvignon from a winery on the Golan Heights and sipped it slowly, but I could not relax completely. I sat in the upper level section of the Boeing 747 jumbo, a few rows behind the cockpit. If I went to visit my friend Fooxy, I thought, I might bother him, and I might have to spend a lot of time in the cockpit with him.

Fooxy and I had been close in the past, but after all these years we had lived in the States, we'd grown apart. The last time I had spoken with him was when his brother died. I had called from Los Angeles to express our condolences.

His brother, Isaac Fuchs, had also been a captain for El Al. In October 1992, on a cargo flight from Amsterdam, two engines fell off one wing of the jumbo he was flying. This happened just once in history; there was no checklist for a case of fallen engines. He ended up crashing into an apartment complex adjacent to the airport. The moment the engines fell off, I'd thought he was doomed, but Boeing and El Al who built and maintained the aircraft and allowed for something catastrophic to happen, succeeded in deflecting some of the blame onto the pilot.

"Here are your hors d'oevres," the stewardess said.

I was still debating whether or not to visit Fooxy. What if he came out of the cockpit and saw me? That would be embarrassing.

"Could you hold the food for now," I told the stewardess, "and could you also tell Captain Fuchs that his friend Eitan Makogon says hello."

"Eitan who?" she asked, Israeli style.

"Makogon," I said.

Before long she came back to say that the captain had invited me to visit the cockpit.

Entering the cockpit felt like entering a bank vault. After I walked through the first door, it closed behind me and the inner door opened, and I walked into the cockpit.

"Hey, Eitan," Fooxy said, "It's been a long time."

I stood at the door getting used to the semi darkness. The view was magnificent. The 747 cockpit was much larger than any I was accustomed to. In the center were the usual four throttles, but the array of the modern instruments on the wide panel, including what looked like computer screens, glowing in soft red, amber and green, were unfamiliar. Outside it was dark. On one side I could see the Mediterranean and on the other the dancing lights of Europe 40,000 feet below. The surprisingly dampened noise of the most powerful four engines was monotonous and added to the tranquility. The air was absolutely smooth.

"Yes, a long time," I said.

Fooxy, who sat comfortably on the left, introduced me to his young co-pilot. "The kid pilots don't know you anymore," he said. "That's what happens, Eitan. We're now the old guys."

He had been 21 years old when we flew together on the French fighter jets, married with a child. He had a great sense of humor that lifted the mood of the squadron. He still looked the same, still with a baby face, but his blond curly hair had thinned, and so had his spirit.

"This cockpit is magnificent," I said. I felt a slight pinch in my heart. I could be flying this magnificent airplane, I thought for a fleeting moment, if Dina had made a different choice.

"You were smart," Fooxy said quietly. "You did well by not coming to El Al."

"What?" I asked.

"I hate this company," he said. "Look what they did to my brother and his family."

"I know, that's terrible and sad, but don't forget the good times you had, flying around the world, spending time in Rome, Paris, London, New York, Bangkok..."

"Yes, yes, but..."

"No buts," I said. "Have you forgotten the mussels and shrimp you brought from Paris, delicacies from Frankfurt, steaks from New York? The delicious dinners you prepared?"

"Yes, but look at you, you made millions," he said.

"We went through tough times, and I worked hard," I said. "It wasn't as easy as you think."

Fooxy turned to look at me. The co-pilot didn't say a word. "I know,

Eitan. You had your share of tragedies and you worked hard but look at your achievements. You were a pilot, an engineer, a businessman, you lived in different countries, you built a business. You created something from scratch, homes that will stay here after we are all gone."

He looked straight ahead into the darkness outside. After a long moment, he said, "You had an interesting life. Look at me. I spent my life here. I wasted it in this cockpit."

I could see Fooxy was still mourning his brother.

Back in my seat, the lights dimmed, and most of the passengers in the business class were asleep.

"Would you like your dinner now, sir?" the stewardess asked.

"No thanks, just one more glass of wine," I said.

"Cabernet, was it?"

"Yes, please."

I could not fall asleep. Shocked at Fooxy's revelation, the Cabernet from the Golan Heights made my head light as I recalled the history of my life – from Jerusalem in war, the shack in Tel Aviv, Holon, Sodom, the kibbutz, the Air Force, Africa, America, my family— the hard times, the tragic times and the good times. I could write a book, I thought, about all that happened.

The more I sipped my wine, the better I felt, and the more I could not wait to get back home to hug Dina, Hadar and Ron, and tell them I loved them.

I wanted to tell Dina she had made a good choice.

Dina, Hadar and Ron.

Made in the USA
Middletown, DE
05 May 2022